Teaching Children 3 to 11

Teaching Children 3 to 11

A Student's Guide

Second Edition

Edited by
Anne D. Cockburn & Graham Handscomb

P·C·P
Paul Chapman
Publishing

First edition published 2001
Second edition published 2006

Paul Chapman Publishing
A SAGE Publications Company
1 Oliver's Yard
55 City Road
London EC1Y 1SP

SAGE Publications Inc
2455 Teller Road
Thousand Oaks, California 91320

SAGE Publications India Pvt Ltd
B-42, Panchsheel Enclave
Post Box 4109
New Delhi 110 017

Library of Congress Control Number: 2005929748

A catalogue record for this book is available from the British Library

ISBN-10 1-4129-2027–2   ISBN-13 978-1-4129-2027-8
ISBN-10 1-4129-2028–0   ISBN-13 978-1-4129-2028-5(pbk)

Typeset by Dorwyn Ltd, Wells, Somerset
Printed in Great Britain by Athenaeum Press, Gateshead, Tyne and Wear
Printed on paper from sustainable resources

Contents

Biographical details of contributors

Rob Barnes teaches art, design, and information and communications technology (ICT). He has researched formative assessment methods and ways of creating a positive classroom. His publications include four books about art, study skills and classroom psychology.

Ann Browne works with intending and practising teachers on primary language and literacy courses. She trained as an early years teacher and spent many years working with young children before entering higher education. She has written a number of articles and books about language and literacy.

Stephen Chynoweth is the headteacher of The Tyrrells School, a large primary school in Essex. He is committed to leading a child-centred learning school and embraces innovation and learning research, developing links with national and international colleagues, including Cuba and Sweden. Before headship, Stephen was an Advanced Skills Teacher and developed a wide range of experiences working with colleagues from a variety of different teaching backgrounds and school contexts.

Anne Cockburn has been a teacher and researcher for many years. She was Co-Director of the Primary PGCE Course at the University of East Anglia (UEA) before becoming Dean of the School of Education in 2001. Her books include *Teaching Mathematics with Insight* (Falmer Press, 1999) and *Recruiting and Retaining Teachers* (RoutledgeFalmer, 2004).

Sue Cox is an early years specialist who joined the UEA Primary Team in 1999 having come from Nottingham Trent University. She has a particular interest in art education. She is also a professional development tutor and is responsible for the general professional studies course.

Graham Handscomb is Principal Adviser in Essex Children's Services Authority and has held a number of local education authority (LEA) senior management roles. He works with many primary schools on the identification of successful practice and on promoting enquiry and research. He also heads initial teacher training development within Essex. Graham was originally primary/secondary trained, has taught for 18 years, and was a secondary deputy headteacher. His publications include *The Research Engaged School* with John Macbeath.

Derek Haylock is an education consultant and author, specialising in primary mathematics. He has worked in teacher education for 30 years, which included the position of Director of the Primary PGCE at the University of East Anglia, Norwich. His books include *Mathematics Explained for Primary Teachers* (third edition, 2006, published by Paul Chapman).

Alan Pagden joined the Primary Team at UEA in 1999. Prior to that he taught across the age range in a number of schools. He has a wide range of expertise including ICT and design technology.

Gillian Preece has worked in schools teaching throughout the 3–11 age range. She came to UEA in 1997. She currently directs the Primary PGCE course with Ann Oliver and lectures in advanced early years education, primary music and drama.

Ann Oliver was a primary school teacher for several years, working with children across Key Stages 1 and 2 before becoming a Primary PGCE tutor at UEA. She has written articles about interactive science centres, teaching science through stories and peer support. She is currently researching reasons behind some teachers' lack of enthusiasm for science.

Jenifer Smith spent many years as a teacher and as an adviser before joining the primary English team at UEA. She is particularly interested in helping pre- and in-service teachers devise strategies to continue their own professional development.

Acknowledgements

The authors would like to acknowledge the wisdom and support so generously given by PGCE students, teachers, colleagues and, last but by no means least, children. It has been greatly appreciated: thank you.

Preface to the Second Edition

We were delighted when Marianne Lagrange asked us to consider producing a second edition of *Teaching Children 3 to 11*. A surprising amount has happened in education since we completed the first edition only four years ago. Most notably the National Literacy and Numeracy Strategies are now well embedded in classroom practice and, more recently, the Primary Strategy has been introduced. Recent developments have also seen the advent of 'personalised learning' with its emphasis on aligning teaching and learning more closely to the needs of the individual pupil, and the rise of collaboration within and between schools. New recruits to teaching will increasingly join a profession where all schools are expected to become part of networked learning communities, and to seek out and share successful practice. The number entering the teaching profession via school-based routes has also risen considerably since 2001. This new edition offers readers a comprehensive introduction to the complexities and pleasures of teaching children in the 3–11 age range. All the chapters have been revised – some more extensively than others – to reflect the changes in primary education in the last five years. We have also added a new chapter – 'Working together and enquiring within' – as we felt it important to signal prominently major developments in the working environments of nursery and primary practitioners.

I was very pleased when all of the original authors were willing to contribute to this new edition. I am also greatly indebted to Graham Handscomb (Essex Local Education Authority), my co-editor for this new edition, and Stephen Chynoweth, primary headteacher, for sharing their expertise with us and bringing some new perspectives to our work.

Finally I would like to thank Helen Fairlie of Paul Chapman Publishing for her support and encouragement in the production of this work.

Anne Cockburn
June 2005

Chapter 1

Setting out

Graham Handscomb and Anne Cockburn

Teaching is a great paradox. On the one hand it can be one of the most rewarding and even life-enhancing experiences. On the other, teaching can be extremely demanding and challenging. In 'Setting out' Anne Cockburn and Graham Handscomb explain how reading this book will provide an overview of what a career in teaching might have to offer you. They stress, however, that it is essential to obtain practical primary classroom experience before embarking on any form of teacher training.

INTRODUCTION

Teaching can be unremittingly dull, repetitive and stressful. We know: we have been there. It can also be one of the most stimulating, enjoyable and rewarding jobs in the world. We know: we have been there too. This book is about how to make the difference. It does not claim to have all the answers but it will certainly present enough material and thought-provoking ideas for you to see the tremendous possibilities which lie ahead. You may think that this is slightly over the top but, as you may already have discovered, very few people feel neutral about teachers and teaching! In this chapter we will very briefly describe the intended readership, authors, origins and uses of this book. We will then outline some of the most important issues you would be wise to consider before embarking on a course, let alone a career, in teaching.

SO WHO ARE YOU?

We, the authors, envisage you, the readers, as:

- someone who might be contemplating primary teaching as a career

- someone who is about to embark on a 3–11 training course or one of the variations currently on offer (for example, 3–8, 7–11)

- a trainee already part way through a teacher education qualification

- a tutor receiving books with a view to recommending them – or not as the case may be – to any of the above audience.

We also see you as someone who, although generally enthusiastic about the idea of teaching, sometimes becomes depressed and demoralised by the struggle. There is no doubt about it – learning to teach is hard work. It is not easy being an experienced learner one minute and a relatively inexperienced teacher the next. You are, however, undoubtedly intelligent and our intention is to demonstrate how, by making the most of your experiences, skills and intellectual capacity, you can gain the most from your training and chosen career. Even so, you will, inevitably, sometimes feel like packing the whole lot in. Obviously, if this feeling becomes all-consuming you should look for a career elsewhere: teaching – just like dentistry, social work and plumbing – is not for everyone and there is no reason to suppose that it should be. If, however, you just occasionally feel depressed, overworked and under-appreciated, hang in there: it will be worth it!

SO WHO ARE WE?

This is not a profound philosophical question but rather a practical one about the nature of the contributors to this book. We feel it would be helpful for you to know something of the 'voices' that will be speaking to you through its pages.

When writing the first edition we were the nine members of the Primary PGCE Team at the University of East Anglia. Between us we had about 120 years' experience as school teachers and over 100 years in teacher education which, coupled with very high grades in HMI inspections, suggest that we had at least an idea of what we were talking about! Since then Alan Pagden has returned to the classroom but, we are pleased to report that he agreed to revise his original chapter. Further we are delighted to welcome Graham Handscomb – Principal Adviser in Essex Children's Services Authority – and Stephen Chynoweth – an experienced headteacher – to our team. Graham brings a range of experience from how local authorities support training and development, including School Centred Initial Teacher Training (SCITT). Stephen has led innovative work on teaching and learning in his past role as an advanced skills teacher and in his current headship.

Some of the Team have already produced several publications on primary education.

Indeed, it is quite possible that you might have books by Derek Haylock, Rob Barnes and Ann Browne on your recommended reading lists. Others, having recently left the classroom, are relatively new to writing for academic and professional audiences. So, in all we represent a range of experience, combining considerable insight and expertise in teacher education, as well as continuing engagement with the classroom practicalities of teaching and learning.

We might not always agree. It would be odd – and, indeed, rather disturbing – if we did. It is always healthy to have a good debate! Nevertheless, we all share the same underlying philosophy that reflection is a crucial aspect of professional develop-ment. Throughout the book therefore – and particularly at the end of every chapter – we will invite you to reflect on various issues in order to extend your own learning. We believe this to be an important feature of the book. The business of teaching is learning. Obviously, this particularly means promoting the learning of the children we teach. However, if we are to be effective teachers, and remain so throughout our careers, we also need to be accomplished learners, who continue to reflect upon prac-tice. So this book is designed to encourage you to connect with a range of issues and guidance within the body of each chapter, and then to actively reflect upon what this might mean for you in the context of your own particular outlook and experience.

WHY DID WE WRITE THE BOOK?

A simple serious answer would be because Marianne Lagrange of Sage Publications asked us to write such a volume. Flattered though we were, even that alone would have been insufficient to get our pencils and word processors going. Rather we wrote this book because – at the risk of sounding corny – we want to share our belief that education should be an enjoyable, challenging and valuable experience for teachers and learners alike. What also unites us is a conviction that you are the future of the teaching profession and our strong desire to make some contribution that you will find helpful at this early stage in your career. Given the media, some of your expe-riences and some of today's teaching materials, you might be forgiven for thinking that teaching is all about finding something to teach, teaching it and then testing your pupils to ensure that they have mastered the topic to a sufficiently high stan-dard. Teaching can be about that but education cannot. Education is about engaging the mind and helping learners realise their full potential. It is also about a sense of worthwhileness, where those involved – teachers, pupils and others – share a belief in the fundamental value of the enterprise: 'Education is for individuality. We all think, feel and learn in distinctive ways. Good education works with the unique grain of our personal capacities to help each of us become a better version of our-selves – and with luck and determination, to make a living at it too' (Robinson, 2005). The best educators are those who inspire their pupils and enable them to continue learning long after they have left the confines of the classroom.

It would be ridiculous – not to say arrogant – to claim that this book covered everything you needed to know to become a successful primary school teacher. We recognise, however, that you are likely to be short of reading time. We have therefore endeavoured to focus on the issues we consider to be particularly important in the hope that we will complement your course and prompt you into continuing your own professional development. Should you find yourself becoming particularly intrigued by specific topics, we have listed and commented on books for further reading at the end of each chapter.

HOW MIGHT YOU USE THIS BOOK?

This book does not need to be read in any particular order. Indeed, you may find that there are some chapters you wish to refer to immediately, others you will want to consult later and still others you would prefer to just dip into. The chapter titles are all pretty well self-explanatory with the possible exception of Chapter 3 – 'Continuity and progression from 3 to 11'. In this chapter Alan Pagden discusses the similarities and differences between the phases currently used to describe children between 3 and 11 years of age – the Foundation Stage (3–5); Key Stage 1 (5–7) and Key Stage 2 (7–11). Unless otherwise stated, the principles considered in the book refer to all three of these phases. The chapter emphasises that whatever you teach, it is important for teachers to be aware of each phase and to help ensure children's educational journey is a joined-up and meaningful experience.

Similarly, unless the author has specifically said otherwise, most of the principles discussed apply to all – or certainly almost all – subjects. Thus, for example, in Chapter 13 Derek Haylock stresses the importance of having specific objectives when teaching numeracy: the same is usually true of other subjects. We could, of course, have covered the full range of subjects taught in school emphasising the similarities and differences between each. Certainly this would have reduced any hint of our being elitist in our choice of subjects but, not only would it have made the book overlong, it would also have made it rather repetitive and boring. As it is we opted to focus on the subjects which currently seem to be taking up the most teaching time and attention. Having said that, it is important to stress that we see music, art, history, geography, physical and religious education and design technology as playing crucial roles in primary education and think it would be a disastrous day if any of them were removed from the curriculum. Similarly there has been a great deal of emphasis on the importance of 'creativity' within the curriculum and you will find throughout the chapters on specific subjects, such as science and ICT, a considerable emphasis on creative teaching and learning.

PREPARING FOR YOUR TRAINING

To make the most of this book and, more importantly your training, you would be wise to do some preparation.

School experience

Very occasionally we interview people with little school experience. Sometimes we accept them for training. Often all is well, but not always. Despite our detailed interviewing, two difficulties can arise. The first is when someone realises that they have opted for the wrong age group. Unfortunately this usually strikes them when they are several weeks into their training, when it is difficult to change from a primary to a secondary course, for example.

The second problem is that a few people embark on their training with an insufficient appreciation of the demands and challenges of the teaching profession. We do our best to warn everyone at interview but, unless you have had first-hand experience of working closely with a teacher, you may not realise what you are undertaking.

In brief it is *essential* that you gain experience working in a school with a range of children from different age groups *before* submitting your application form. If you can, try for half a day a week in a school for a term. Even better is to gain experience in two or three schools, but this is not always possible if you are working or in full-time study. The chapters on the three related processes of learning (Chapter 3), observation (Chapter 4), and reflection (Chapter 9) will be particularly useful in helping you make full use of this opportunity. There are a number of ways to arrange work experience in a local school. You can simply telephone them and ask to make an appointment to discuss the possibility with the headteacher. You can make contact through your local careers centre. You can speak to someone in your local education department or you can ask advice from the Teacher Development Agency (TDA) or the Department for Education and Skills (DfES). Schools will generally be positive about such requests, though occasionally – perhaps because of timing or particular school pressures – you may receive a negative response.

Pre-course reading

Some of you will be completing your degree when you read this. Others may not have done any studying for more years than you might care to remember. In both cases some pre-course – and, indeed, pre-interview – reading is strongly recommended. Not only will this prepare you for what is to come but it may also give you the opportunity to do some reading at a relatively leisurely pace: you'll soon discover that you'll have little time for it once you have started your PGCE course.

What you read is largely down to you, although it is likely that your intended teacher education institution will provide some suggestions. If you know you are weak in specific subjects, it is a good idea to do some work on them. At the end of this chapter are listed some books our students have found helpful in this respect. It is important to remember that you will be given up-to-date subject knowledge on your course but, with only 38 weeks, it is valuable to have a head start.

It is also useful to read some general books about schools and schooling and some suggestions are given at the end of this chapter. Reading such books can help develop your insight into your chosen profession. The more you know about it the better prepared you'll be for your interview and, with luck, your training. If you have not done any studying for a while or, if you are lacking in confidence in your ability to work effectively, you would be wise to read a book on study skills. There are likely to be several examples in any good bookshop. Choose one that appeals to you and see if it does the trick. If, however, you find yourself struggling several weeks into the course, speak to your tutor who may be able to help directly or who might advise you to contact a study skills centre at, for example, your institution. Declaring such a difficulty is not a problem. Training institutions will be aware that many people entering the profession may not have had recent experience of study. Rather than feeling at all awkward about such a need, you may find that this helps you empathise with difficulties that children have with their learning and study.

Being organised

There is no doubt whatsoever that teacher training is highly demanding both intellectually and organisationally. If you secure the opportunity to train – given that you already have a degree, are well prepared and have succeeded on interview – you are likely to take the intellectual challenge in your stride. You may not, however, be so well prepared to meet the organisational challenges your training presents. We suspect you will never have been so busy. For example, on most training courses you can expect sessions from 9 a.m. in the morning until 5 p.m. Getting from a lecture to a workshop to a seminar before lunch can be no mean feat, especially if they are at opposite ends of the campus, you have lecture notes to organise and follow-up work to do after each session.

Tiring though that might be, it is minor compared to what is required when you are on teaching practice. Here, for example, you will be expected in school by 8.30 a.m. – some schools say 8.00 a.m. – and questions will be asked if you leave before 4.30 p.m. There may well be staff meetings to attend and after-school clubs, not to mention putting up displays together, and the next day's marking and preparation. As will be discussed below, it *is* important that you have a life beyond teaching but, before embarking on a course, you must ensure that you are as well organised as you can possibly be. This might mean reducing your shopping from every two to three days to once a week, arranging for dependants to be cared for in your absence, ensuring that your car is in good working order, and so on.

Finally, before accepting an offer for a training place, talk it over with your family and friends. Ultimately it has to be your decision, but it is important that you have their confidence and support. You will find, for example, that your training will be a time of great personal discovery: this can be extremely exciting and liberating but it can also be a little daunting at times.

Your colleagues

Everything is in place and you are about to start your training. Who will your colleagues be? What will they be like?

In all probability there will be more females than males. This is particularly true if you have opted for early years or lower primary training. There will be a wide age range and we think you may well be surprised by the number of more mature people. Every year at the University of East Anglia we take students in their early twenties, some in their late forties and early fifties, and many in between. The average age is generally around 30 so you can be sure that many of your colleagues will have worked and had a range of life experiences prior to embarking on the course.

Attendance

Becoming a teacher is a full-time commitment. Before enlisting on a course or embarking on any training therefore it is *vital* that you recognise that you will be extremely busy and that you appreciate that – except in cases of illness or serious domestic need – missing sessions simply is not an option. Indeed, the Department for Education and Skills insists that everyone attends all timetabled sessions otherwise they will not issue you with a certificate.

Theory and practice

Sometimes when people come to interview for training they tend to think that this involves a programme of tips for teachers. Fortunately, teacher education is not like that. We are all individuals, we work in different situations with different people and we do not know what the curriculum of the future holds.

Accordingly, although we may suggest some handy hints and useful approaches from time to time, we strive to provide a dynamic mix of theory and practice. There are some in the profession – experienced as well as beginning teachers – who have a rather negative view of 'theory'. They tend to see it as an intellectual indulgence, at the expense of concentrating on the important matter of classroom practice. Theory has certainly got a bad name! However, this is rather a simplistic view and overlooks a crucial point – the important relationship between theory and practice: 'No action, unless it is the action of an irrational being, is devoid of theory, for theory involves beliefs, ideas, assumptions, values, and everything we do is influenced by theory' (Fish, 1995a, p. 57). Also, this is not just a 'one-way-street' relationship – that is, that you learn some theory and then apply it in practice. The relationship is much more fundamental than that. It is about how you use theory to make sense of your practice and, indeed, as Fish powerfully explains, how as an individual you develop your own theory from your practice. 'At best in teacher education programmes, there exists a constant interplay between the taught course and the school experience through which students are encouraged to draw out personal theories from practice' (Fish, 1995b, p. 55).

You will find Chapter 2 by Graham Handscomb, 'Working together and enquiring within', and Chapter 9 by Jenifer Smith, 'Reflective practice', explore the need for teachers to reflect upon and critique their work. In Chapter 6, 'Approaches to learning and teaching', Sue Cox demonstrates that the kind of teacher you become will depend on the personal qualities and values that you bring to your teaching. So, developing as an effective teacher entails emerging as a reflective practitioner where you ask searching questions of your teaching, and by striving to increase understanding of your practice are able to feed this into further improvement. In this way we produce flexible teachers fit for the demands of the twenty-first century curriculum and the adults of the future. In other words, people with a real understanding of teaching and learning, classrooms and schools, pupils and colleagues, and themselves as educators.

Maintaining perspective

As we mentioned earlier, teaching is not an easy option. It is important, however, that you do not let it consume your life. If you do, you will cease to be a first-rate practitioner. It is undoubtedly true that you must be prepared to work hard, but you must also be prepared to play hard. Too many teachers suffer from stress having succumbed to the pressures of the job. Added to which, your hobbies can provide an interesting and important dimension to your teaching: your musical or sporting talents, for example, will almost certainly enhance your own and your pupils' experience in the classroom. While you may find teaching satisfyingly challenging and enjoyable, make sure that there are other dimensions to your life which are equally fulfilling.

CONCLUDING REMARKS

Some might feel that we have painted a slightly negative picture of teaching in this chapter. This has not been our intention: far from it. We both find teaching – whether it be at school, college or university level – to be an immensely satisfying career. It is also important that you see the stresses as well as the triumphs, the challenge as well as the rewards. It is not, however, the job for everyone and you would be doing both your-self and numerous children a disservice if you entered the profession unknowingly.

In brief, primary teaching is hard work but, ultimately for many, worthwhile and per-sonally satisfying. We hope that this book will help you as you move towards your goal.

SUMMARY

Successful primary teaching is:

- a highly satisfying career
- hard work and demanding
- not for everyone.

It is, however, ultimately a vocation in which you can make a real difference for children and their lives.

The authors of this book are:

- successful teachers and teacher educators
- people who enjoy teaching
- educators who consider reflective practice to be of fundamental importance.

Make sure that you are well prepared for your training by:

- gaining experience in schools
- doing some pre-course reading
- addressing the need to develop organised behaviours
- remembering that commitment to training and 'follow-through' is important
- recognising the value of theory and practice, and their interrelationship
- ensuring you care for yourself and have a life beyond teaching.

ISSUES FOR REFLECTION

- What do you think a career in teaching has to offer you?
- What do you consider to be the main aims of primary education? Why?
- Think about the most inspiring teachers in your life: what made them such successful educators?

Further reading

Cockburn, A.D. (1996) *Teaching Under Pressure*. London: Falmer Press. We hope you will not be needing this book but, if life does become stressful, we are told it is a reassuring and helpful read.

Desforges, C. (ed.) (1995) *An Introduction to Teaching: Psychological Perspectives*. Oxford: Blackwell. This is a very comprehensive book which covers a wide range of important topics for intending and student teachers.

Haylock, D. (2001) *Mathematics Explained for Primary Teachers*. 2nd edition. London: Paul Chapman. If you are worried about teaching mathematics this may well be the book for you as it covers the subject in a very detailed and sympathetic manner.

Moyles, J. (ed.) (1995) *Beginning Teaching: Beginning Learning in Primary Education*. Buckingham: Open University Press. This is a series of chapters written in a very accessible manner by experts in primary education. They cover a wide range of important issues for the beginning teacher.

Waterland, L. (1994) *Not a Perfect Offering*. Stroud: Thimble Press. This is a very easy and enjoyable read describing what starting school feels like to 4-year-olds, their parents and teachers. It provides real insight into the process of early years education.

Wenham, M. (1995) *Understanding Primary Science*. London: Paul Chapman Publishing. Our students find this to be a 'brilliant' introduction to primary science.

Working together and enquiring within

Graham Handscomb

Gone are the days when teachers were left to sink or swim behind the closed doors of their classrooms. Graham Handscomb explains that it is *cool to collaborate* and how communities of practice within and beyond the school can provide extended opportunities to develop your teaching and enrich pupils' learning. He shows how enquiring and researching into your own practice is a key part of this new shared professionalism, and how genuine partnership, particularly with one key group – the children – is at the heart of successful teaching.

> No one had told her that teaching was difficult, and beginning as a teacher most difficult of all. (Stevenson, 1989, p. 116)

There are few professions like teaching, where one individual is called upon to give in such a personal way to, possibly, 30 other individuals on a day-to-day basis. This personal dimension of teaching is probably what you will find most rewarding, and why you went into teaching in the first place. At the same time you will also find the personal demands made on you as one of the most challenging features of the job. Teaching can be daunting and stressful, and there are occasions when you may feel rather isolated and alone in your endeavours. But it does not need to be like this, and indeed you will find that in order to grow into an effective teacher you will need to work collaboratively with others.

YOU ARE NOT ALONE

The quote at the beginning of this chapter comes from Anne Stevenson's biography of the poet Sylvia Plath. At one time Plath was a teacher and prior to this quote we are given extended extracts from Plath's diary at the time. In this she describes her feelings, which reflect the pendulum swing of emotions experienced by many beginning teachers, alternating between soaring confidence, when things appear to be going well, to abject despair when lesson planning seems to fall apart and her students are unresponsive. Plath's response to the low times is to feel inadequate and inferior compared to her more experienced colleagues. So she decides to keep the 'demon' of her doubts to herself: 'I shall show a calm front & fight it in the precincts of my own self, but never give it the social dignity of a public appearance, me running from it, & giving in to it' (ibid., p. 115). She makes the fundamental mistake that is still common among teachers starting out on their career – of feeling that difficulties encountered are an individual failing and must be struggled with on one's own. Consequently, as Stevenson notes, 'none of her colleagues, young or old, had the least inkling of her personal distress' (ibid., p. 116).

In today's schools and classrooms collaboration and teamwork are vital. On your teaching placements you will find that a great deal of emphasis is placed on teachers working together. This may involve joint planning (short, medium and long term – see Chapter 3) and development of schemes of work, but you may also have the opportunity to be involved in team teaching. In some schools there may be arrangements for trainee teachers to be allocated a personal mentor who will be available to give one-to-one support and critique. There may also be coaching opportunities, where you can work with experienced colleagues on specific teaching skills through observing each other's lessons, giving reciprocal feedback and thus honing and improving your teaching technique. In some cases this can effectively be done as a trio of teachers, where teacher A observes teacher B, teacher B observes teach C, and teacher C observes teacher A (see also Chapter 4). Schools that have established such mentoring or coaching arrangements find that it is not just beginning teachers that benefit. What happens is that a true sense of partnership and collaborative working is developed where the mentor and coach find they reflect on their own practice and learn as much as those they are assisting (Cordingley et al., 2005). If you have the good fortune to teach within a school that fosters such a culture of mentoring and coaching, be sure to grasp the opportunity with both hands.

COLLABORATION AND TEACHING IN THE PRIMARY CLASSROOM

So working as a team is to be seen not as a desirable extra on top of the main business of you coping on your own and 'cutting it' in your classroom. It has now become a fundamental part of teaching in the modern primary school. You will find the schools you work in are highly complex places where people have to deal continually with an array of changes, ranging from new developments in curriculum to revised approaches to behaviour management. Moving forward on all these things requires that school staff work effectively together. Indeed, it is not an overstatement to say that it would be difficult to survive and flourish in a school today without learning to work as part of a team.

Your common purpose is the learning and development of the children you teach. This is not a solitary exercise and can only be effectively achieved through a joint approach of a whole range of people within and beyond the school. The effective management of your classroom, and making sure you address the needs of all the individuals within it, will depend on how you work with a number of others – including teachers, teaching assistants and parents (see Chapter 16, 'Working with other adults'). These collaborations tend to work best when they are part of a genuine partnership in which there are no distinctions of status between yourself as the teacher and the parent or teaching assistant who works alongside you in the classroom. Rather you fulfil different roles operating within a complementary team. Being part of such an atmosphere can be one of the most rewarding aspects of your teaching experience. So be prepared to share, to open up your classroom to others, and to support and be supported. MacBeath and Stoll describe what this collaborative culture looks like when it dynamically takes off in a school – aim to be part of this:

> Collaboration and partnership are a way of life. People work together. People are not left to sink or swim. People are available to help each other. Team teaching, mentoring, peer coaching, joint planning and mutual observation and feedback are a normal part of the everyday life of the school. (MacBeath and Stoll, 2001, p. 154)

COLLABORATION BEYOND THE SCHOOL

In your teaching practice placements you will gain experience of working in a number of schools, often arranged by a higher education institution. If you are trained as part of a School Centred Initial Teacher Training (SCITT) partnership, your training will be organised and delivered by a group of schools working together. So, for example, in Essex there are a number of SCITTs where headteachers and teachers from a range of primary schools get together to plan how trainee teachers will have experience of teaching in at least two schools. Trainees' academic training, together with the development of curriculum and assessment knowledge and expertise, also takes place within this collaborative on-the-job setting.

This is just one example of how schools are increasingly working together in ways that would have been unheard of even a few years ago. Nowadays it is very likely that in whichever school you work you will also have a range of opportunities to link with colleagues in other schools. In the past this was less common. During the mid-1990s the government emphasised that schools were autonomous and self-managing, and the responsibility for school performance and improvement rested primarily with schools themselves. This meant that schools tended to be locked in competition to attract pupils. Nevertheless there were many people working in schools during this time, myself among them, who felt that this overemphasis on competition rather than co-operation between schools was not the way forward. I remember somewhat idealistically portraying this as:

> taking a stand against the view that a coherent education system can be built from the innumerable, self-interested decisions of individual parents and schools. It means holding proudly aloft the banner declaring that schools need to collaborate and share good practice to achieve the best for all our children. (Handscomb, 1995, p. 12)

Well, much has changed in the intervening years and it is now clearly 'cool to collaborate' (Handscomb, 2002, p. 3). The reason for this is not just a cosy view that it is nice for schools and their teachers to work together, but a growing realisation that further improvement and raising of standards will rely on such collaboration. So, for instance, Clarke argues that as schools continue to improve, 'they will eventually come to a point when they need to communicate and examine what other schools are doing' (Clarke, 2000, p. 16). Above all, the momentum towards greater joint working between clusters of schools was given new impetus by the government itself lending political weight to this development. Now schools were to be both self-managing and collegiate:

> They must plan for continuous improvement and need maximum freedom to make decisions and manage resources. But autonomy does not mean acting in isolation. Schools work best when they recognise the value of the family of schools to which they belong locally and nationally. The most effective schools are those which are open, both in sharing their own best practice, and looking for best practice elsewhere. Working in co-operation with each other, as well as Local Education Authorities and private and voluntary bodies, they can raise standards and improve pupil performance. (DfEE, 2000, para. 2)

COLLABORATIVE PROFESSIONAL DEVELOPMENT AND GROWTH

Initial teacher training is a pretty intensive period of professional training and development. During your placements in schools you will quickly discover that this emphasis on the importance of professional development is a continuing feature of what it means to be a teacher. There will be a range of continuing professional development (CPD) experiences provided by the school. Much of this will take place within the school itself whilst other activities will take place outside the school, facilitated in some cases by the local authority or, increasingly, by a local cluster or network of schools. Whilst you are on placement you are a member of the school, and it is obviously important that, if given the opportunity, you participate in these activities and, of course, make the most of the benefits that they provide. This experience will also help you appreciate that your initial teacher training is but the first part of a continuing process of professional learning throughout your teaching career.

It is useful to consider the nature of this ongoing development and its important connection with collaboration. There is now a growing and authoritative consensus that the most effective professional learning is focused on teachers' classroom practice and is collaborative. The government's professional development strategy has consistently stressed the importance of *learning together, learning from the best, and learning from what works* (DFES, 2001). Similarly, the General Teaching Council's *Teachers' Professional Learning Framework* states that teaching has often been experienced as an isolated activity and that teacher development has consequently suffered from this. It claims that there is increasing evidence which demonstrates 'the value of moving collegial learning from the margins of professional practice to the heart of it'. The GTC sees teachers as 'not only classroom experts in a single school but also as members of a broader education community' (GTC, 2003, p. 15).

So learning together is advocated because it tends to focus development on classroom practice. As Harris (2002) puts it, 'improvements in teaching are most likely to occur where there are opportunities to work together and to learn from each other' (p. 102). She also identifies gains in terms of teachers' professionalism and well-being, stating 'collaboration is important because it creates a collective professional confidence that allows teachers to interact more confidently and assertively' (ibid., pp. 102–3). There are particular benefits to be gained for beginning teachers from schools working together on professional development. I discovered this through a year-long research project undertaken by Essex Local Authority and the General Teaching Council. It involved 21 schools working in eight clusters and over 120 teachers at the beginning of their career (Essex County Council, 2003). The investigation clearly showed that clusters of schools were able to develop joint approaches to the identification of beginning teachers' needs, and were able to draw on a wider range of CPD opportunity and training expertise from across the variety of schools in each cluster. The teachers also greatly valued the facility to visit other schools and exchange experiences. These positive learning outcomes were clearly reflected in the comments of teachers involved (see Box 2.1).

Reflecting on your own practice is a key factor in developing as a learner and teacher (see Chapter 9). To able to do this with other colleagues in a collaborative setting across a number of schools can be particularly powerful, and it will be important to make the most of such an opportunity when it arises.

THE RISE OF SCHOOL NETWORKS

To a certain extent schools have always loosely liaised with each other, even in times of intense competition between them. During the early years of the new century there has been a considerably increased drive for schools to work in more structured

Box 2.1

Some beginning teachers' comments on the value of collaborative professional development
(Essex County Council, 2003, pp. 11 and 13)

I have found the activities I have undertaken very useful and I have a much better idea of how to develop professionally.

The area that was extremely beneficial to me was the opportunity to visit another school. This developed me as a teacher and I took many ideas back to school, some of which I could implement immediately, others that I will include in my next action plan.

Networking for Foundation Stage co-ordinators was valuable.

Talking to other beginning teachers about professional issues has made me realise that many of us have the same concerns and issues. This project has given me some time to reflect on professional knowledge and understanding. It has afforded me with opportunities to develop and consolidate transferable skills such as those connected to classroom management.

networks that make a significant contribution to learning and teaching. The National College for School Leadership (NCSL) led the *Networked Learning Communities* (NLC) initiative in which groups of schools could get together to bid for up to £50,000, which had to be matched by the group of schools itself. The funds were to be used to promote collaborative learning of teachers, school leaders and pupils within and between schools. Some of these NLCs are made up of primary schools and secondary schools respectively, whilst others are mixed phased.

With the development of such initiatives, schools have devoted more time and energies to collaborative activities. Some observers have questioned whether all this has been worthwhile (Reynolds, 2003). Even strong advocates of collaborative networks have warned of the need to guard against cosiness and instead be committed to 'quality, rigour and a focus on outcomes' (Hopkins, 2002). The government too are keen that all the efforts put into networking should pay tangible dividends. So, at the time of writing, it has launched the *Primary Strategy Learning Networks* development, with the aim of ensuring that over a number of years all primary schools will be an active and committed member of a network, and that these networks should have a discernable impact. The aim is for schools in these networks to work together to raise standards in literacy and mathematics, and to increase the capacity of schools to deliver a rich, broad curriculum. The way in which these networks would achieve this was by focusing on strengthening pupil learning and teacher development which concentrated on improving classroom practice, enriching curriculum provision and raising the attainment and achievement of all pupils with a particular emphasis on improving progress for our most vulnerable groups of pupils.

Hargreaves (2003) sees networks as one of the most significant educational developments in modern times. He portrays them as potential hotbeds of innovation in which good practice can be identified and spread more quickly than it has done between teachers and between schools in the past. Networking between primary schools has certainly arrived, and it is highly likely that the schools where you have your placements will be active members of one of these networks. Although many schools and networks will wish to involve trainee teachers in their activities, it is also fair to warn that there may be some cases where this practice is less developed. However, if these networks are effective then they will increasingly be an aspect of school life that you will experience and that will influence the way in which you plan and teach.

COMMUNITIES OF PRACTICE

One of the greatest benefits of networking between schools is that it provides teachers, including those at the beginning of their career, with opportunities to work in a wider community where practice can be shared and compared. You will find that this is an exciting time to be entering the teacher profession. Too often in the past teachers operated within the 'closed doors' of their classrooms and schools, and this meant that often valuable experience was not shared and the profession failed to learn and grow.

Nowadays this has changed and *communities of practice* have developed within and between schools. The really valuable feature of these communities is that they *can* foster a climate of dialogue, reflection and exchange between teachers. This is so important because research has indicated that the communication and transference of practice from one teacher to another is difficult to achieve. This is because good teaching is often intuitive, uses tacit experience and knowledge, and is focused on the particular and immediate context of the individual teacher (McIntyre, 2001). Hargreaves has given considerable thought to this problem of how to 'bottle' and share teacher practitioner knowledge:

> If one teacher tells another about a practice that he finds effective, the second teacher has merely acquired information, not personal knowledge. Transfer occurs only when the knowledge of the first becomes information for the second, who then works on that information in such a way that it becomes part of his or her context of meaning and purpose and pre-existing knowledge and then is applied in action … Transfer is the conversion of information about one person's practice into another's know-how. (Hargreaves, 1998, p. 46)

One of the problems in this area is the casual ease with which people sometimes talk of sharing *best practice* to be used as models for others to emulate, when actually what is being disseminated is untried, untested *interesting* practice. 'The sharing of *good practice* and the dissemination of *best practice* is widely advocated. Unfortunately our knowledge of how to do this is frighteningly slight' (Hargreaves, 2003, p. 44). David Woods makes the following helpful distinctions:

> In the literature on school improvement the terms 'best', 'good' and 'innovative' practice are used in a variety of ways. Good practice is generally used to mean practice which is professionally judged to be effective, but may require further evidence and validation; best practice is used to mean practice which is proven over time, backed by supporting evidence; innovative practice may highlight new and interesting ways of doing things, with early indications of success. (Woods, 2000, p. 2)

This is perhaps most helpfully illustrated as a continuum (see Box 2.2) ranging from creative practice, to good practice, to best practice. So, for example, if you develop a set of practices in your classroom that works well with your group of learners, this might be characterised as being at the left-hand side of the continuum. As this is shared with other school colleagues, who adapt and apply it in their different settings, it gets tested against a range of teacher perspectives and might then be termed 'good practice'. Eventually it might be developed into school-wide approaches, shared in other school settings, benchmarked and validated by supporting evidence and proven over time – and thus merit the accolade 'best practice'. Clearly calibration and judgements made about such distinctions should be part and parcel of the professional discussion, debate and collaborative agreement amongst teachers, schools and other parties like higher education institutions and local authorities. If you have the chance to be part of such a dynamic professional community then count it as good fortune, and be ready to contribute!

ENQUIRY AND RESEARCH

We have seen that there are likely to be opportunities to work collaboratively with a range of colleagues within your school and with others in the wider educational community. We have also reflected on how powerful these opportunities can be, but also that energies devoted to such collaborative activities can be wasted if they lack rigour and focus. This concern about 'soft' unproductive collaboration is resolved in Alma Harris's view if a strategic link is made with teacher enquiry and research: 'For teacher development … to occur commitment to certain kinds of collaboration is centrally important. However, collaboration without reflection and enquiry is little more than working collegially. For collaboration to influence personal growth and development it has to be premised upon mutual enquiry and sharing' (Harris, 2002, p. 103).

> **Box 2.2**
>
> ## A continuum of practice (Handscomb, 2002/03, p. 20)
>
> *Continuum of interesting, good and best practice*
>
> | *Interesting and innovative practice* | *Good practice* | *Best practice* |
> |---|---|---|
> | Encouraging creativity, innovation and a sense of dynamism. Generating a culture of dialogue and exchange. 'Letting a thousand flowers bloom.' | Effective practice. Ideas shared with others, adapted to new contexts and tried out. Learning communities which promote sharing and trialling and critique of practice. | Best practice validated by supporting evidence and proven over time. Structured systems: benchmarking; monitoring and evaluation; quality assurance; formal dissemination. |

I will argue in the next few pages the merits of research practice in schools and of you developing as a teacher enquirer. This may appear to you to be a rather strange proposal. The image of educational research for many teachers is something done by others in academic institutions – complex, difficult to access and of limited relevance. Unfortunately, some developments in educational research have suffered from these features. However, this is changing. Increasingly, classroom practitioners have discovered the merits of investigating an aspect of their work that directly contributes to improved practice and benefits the children they teach. I have worked with teachers at various stages of their career – during initial training, as newly qualified or as experienced teachers – where they have actively undertaken enquiry into their practice and all have found this experience manageable, relevant and often transforming.

Most teachers would not readily engage with the notion of being a 'teacher-researcher'. A more helpful term, which describes the skills that are part of good teaching, is the teacher as enquirer. This alludes to teachers who are keen to reflect

> **Box 2.3**
>
> ## Why engage in research?
>
> Teachers who have engaged in researching their own classrooms and schools have found that it:
>
> - encourages them to question, explore and develop their practice
> - to be a highly satisfying and energising professional activity
> - has become an integral part of their continuing professional development
> - has enhanced the quality of teaching and learning.

upon and critique their practices. They make good use of research and evidence to stimulate new ways of thinking and to try out new ideas, and then systematically to evaluate the impact of any subsequent change they have brought about (see also Chapter 9).

Teachers have long been involved in examining their practice in this way to make further improvements. But when does such activity 'count' as research? What is the relationship between large-scale research conducted by, for instance, a university department and a piece of evidence-informed practice carried out by a teacher within the classroom? And how is such evidence-informed practice any different from what good teachers do anyway in refining and honing their craft in day-to-day lesson preparation and evaluation?

One view is that evidence-informed practice typically involves individual teachers reflecting on their own classroom practice and sharing this with colleagues; in contrast, 'research' is seen as involving a larger-scale more systematic enquiry. Another view is that these two characterisations are not different in kind, but rather two ends of a continuum of practice in which 'evidence-informed practice' merges into 'research'. However, many have found this a difficult debate and would be uncomfortable about making too sharp a distinction between evidenced-informed practice and research. There are tensions between the world of academic research and teachers pursuing research as part of their professional learning and practice, but many have become convinced of the great potential of practitioner research to transform both the classroom and the teacher (Handscomb, 2004).

In fact it may be useful for you as a teacher approaching this area to adopt the definition of research as simply being 'systematic enquiry made public' (Stenhouse, 1981, p. 34). In other words, it is not different in kind to good classroom practice and reflection, but requires that you do this systematically and share both how you went about it and the outcomes (Essex County Council, 2002). I think this idea of incorporating rigorous enquiry into your everyday practice, is best explained by John Mason who sees it as a disciplined approach to 'noticing': 'The Discipline of Noticing is nothing more than an attempt to be systematic and methodical without being mechanical. It is a collection of practices which together can enhance sensitivity to notice opportunities to act freshly in the future' (Mason, 2002, p. 59).

It is a powerful argument that as teachers we are continually encouraging our pupils to engage in enquiry, systematically and with a concern for evidence. So why do we not apply these same principles of learning and development to ourselves as teachers? To get under way, just start by asking the everyday but critical questions that are live issues for you. Why do children behave the way they do? Why do some children find it difficult to stay on task? Why is my teaching sometimes effective and at other times not? How can I foster a more stimulating and productive classroom environment? Once having arrived at a focus for an area of your practice that interests you, embarking upon the investigation is not as forbidding as it may seem.

There tends to be a rather off-putting mystique about the steps involved in the research process but in fact it mainly involves those listed in Box 2.4. These are basic, but rigorous, stages and, perhaps with the help of a mentor within the school or possibly a colleague from the local authority or a partner university, are well within the scope of classroom teachers wanting to enquire into their practice.

Certainly there is now a view held by many that 'all teachers should have an entitlement to research thinking in order to develop their role as critical users of research. All schools and colleagues should have an entitlement and perhaps a responsibility, to

---

Box 2.4

Steps in the enquiry process

- What do you want to find out? (The research problem and research questions)
- What is already known on this issue? (A basic web-search)
- What information do you need?
- What information is already available in the school or elsewhere?
- How will you obtain the information?
- How will you check that the information gathered is sound and the methods for gathering it effective?
- How will you make sense of, and use, the information?
- How do you draw secure conclusions?
- Making judgements about recommendations for changed practice.

---

participate in a relevant research partnership for appropriate periods' (Dyson, 2001, p. 7). Such voices are arguing that teacher enquiry and school-based research are not just desirable extras once the core business of teaching and raising standards are done, but that such activity is becoming essential to school performance and success.

In some schools and local authorities in which you will work there may be a growing commitment to supporting teachers enquiring into their own practice. For instance Essex has established a Forum for Learning and Research Enquiry (FLARE) which is made up of teachers and headteachers dedicated to promoting teacher and school-based research. Building on what is known about teachers as researchers FLARE explored the features that might typically be found in a school that was 'research engaged'. FLARE's thinking is that in such a school, research and enquiry are integral to its approach to teaching and learning. It is built into the school culture, fostering research in collaborative groups and partnerships within and beyond the school. Above all, what distinguishes a research-engaged school is that such activity is at the very heart of the school, pervading its outlook, informing its systems and stimulating learning at every level (Handscomb and MacBeath, 2003, p. 4).

Of course, this is the ideal and the schools that you experience may not exhibit all these characteristics and to this degree. However, it is possible that in many schools there will be opportunities for you to investigate an aspect of your practice, and be given the support needed to do this.

COLLABORATION WITH PUPILS

It may seem self-evident and somewhat superfluous to advocate collaboration with pupils! Surely this is something you will do automatically. Gone are the days when teaching was seen in terms of simply filling empty vessels, but there remains concern that we insufficiently take account of the 'voice' of pupils. Yet, it is essential that as teachers, we work in a truly collaborative way with children in order for effective teaching and successful learning to take place.

The emphasis on collaboration, consultation and participation of pupils has gained momentum in recent times as the result of a number of important developments. Possibly one of the most important is the work done by Jean Rudduck and her colleagues on how giving pupils a voice and listening to what they say can make a significant difference to how they perform and achieve. So, for instance, from the early 1990s the Chief Inspector's Annual Reports showed that there was a sustained 'dip' in the progress of children at Year 3. The initial reaction was to blame the teaching but, by conducting extensive research into the pupils' view, the situation was shown to be far more complex and related to a whole range of issues such as different expectations, different ways of working, and features of curriculum and school organisation (Doddington and Flutter with Berne and Demetriou, 2001). So, for example, pupils had the following to say about how they felt the work to be more demanding and being disorientated: 'Well, last year I found it a bit easy but now we're up here it's a bit harder and I don't know what to do'; 'You have to like get [the work] done in 25 minutes or 45 minutes and it's really hard, hard work'; 'Well you have more writing than in Year 2'.

By listening to what children have to say, and attempting to gain an appreciation of their perspective, new light was shed on problems of this kind. The power of Rudduck's work is that it clearly shows how important it is for you and I as teachers to really engage with pupils, and the benefits of genuinely making them partners in the teaching and learning enterprise. On your teaching placement, and in your teaching career beyond, you can do no worse than to have the following exhortations always in mind:

> We should
>
> - take seriously what pupils can tell us about their experiences of being a learner in school – about what gets in the way of their learning and what helps them to learn
>
> - find ways of involving pupils more closely in decisions that affect their lives in school, whether at the level of the classroom or the institution. (Rudduck and Flutter, 2004, p. 2)

Other work about the value of teachers overtly consulting pupils about their teaching has been equally illuminating. Dave Pedder (2005) reflects that although some teachers may find this a rather vulnerable thing to do, children usually are very constructive. When consulted, rather than wanting the teacher to stop doing some things, they often select some aspects of the teacher's repertoire and ask for more of this! So, if you build in consultation with children as part of your teaching, this can be liberating rather than threatening:

> You know – that's what made me enthusiastic, because I suddenly saw all that untapped creativity really ... You can use pupils' ideas in a very valid, interesting way and it can make the pupil excited, the teacher excited and you know obviously the lessons will take off from there ... if you can actually collaborate with pupils it's equally – I didn't realise it – it's equally exciting, isn't it? (Pedder and McIntyre, 2004, p. 30)

The potential for consulting pupils and actively using pupil voice is therefore great. The important thing is that you genuinely let the pupil's voice count, and Michael Fielding (2004) warns against making this a passive token exercise. It is only by embracing real collaboration with pupils that dividends will be gained in the quality of teaching and learning in your classroom.

This very much fits with two government-led developments which are likely to have a considerable influence on your approach to teaching as you embark upon your career. The first is the focus on *personalised learning*. This is an approach to teaching and learning that concentrates on an individual's potential and learning skills. It also involves the organising of learning experiences that extend beyond the school context into the local community. The other initiative is the *Every Child Matters* development (DfES, 2004), which emphasises addressing the needs of the whole child in terms of five key outcomes:

- Be healthy.

- Stay safe.

- Enjoy and achieve.

- Make a positive contribution.

- Achieve economic well-being.

This stresses the importance of multi-agency collaboration, so that in helping to achieve these outcomes for your children you will need to be working with a range of professionals, including those from social services and health. Thus collaboration with a host of colleagues within and beyond the school, and particularly with children themselves, has come centre stage and will be a fundamental feature of your role as a teacher.

SUMMARY

- Beginning as a teacher can feel a daunting and isolating experience, but it is important to remember that you are not alone.

- Teachers, together with other colleagues, rely on one another and often bring the best out of each other when working together.

- Teamwork is now a fundamental feature of teaching in the modern primary school.

- There is a strong push for all primary schools to be active participants in school networks.

- Collaboration and networking between schools has considerable potential to promote innovation and help share successful practice more widely.

- Some of the most effective professional development experiences are when teachers undertake them together.

- It is valuable to share interesting practice, and to identify and disseminate proven best practice.

- Enquiring into your practice can be a very rewarding experience, and can help transform your teaching and improve pupil learning.

- Teacher research, through systematic enquiry which is shared with colleagues, is within the reach of all, including beginning teachers.

- Partnership and consultation with pupils can pay great dividends in your teaching.

- Paying attention to the 'voice' and perceptions of pupils is an important ingredient in promoting successful learning.

ISSUES FOR REFLECTION

- Make arrangements with a fellow trainee to talk about the difficulties you each encounter on your placements. When listening, try not to make evaluative comments or pass judgement but concentrate on letting each other tell the details of what happened and share how it felt. Talking about your experience in this way may help to put incidents in perspective and avoid blowing them up into major crises.

- During your placement explore whether it would be possible to jointly plan a number of lessons with an experienced school colleague, to observe each other teaching this programme of lessons and to have time together to reflect on the observations.

- Think of a time when you have been involved in a collaborative activity with another person or a team. What were the advantages in doing this? What difficulties and strains were encountered; how were these dealt with?

- Think of a network to which you belong (this can be a 'local' one involving meetings and activities, or a virtual online network). How would you describe the main features of this network to someone who knew little about it? What aspects of the network are key factors in keeping it going?

- 'To get under way, just start by asking the everyday but critical questions that are live issues for you' (page 20 in this chapter). Consider what classroom practice issues might be of interest to you as potential areas for investigation and enquiry.

- Consider in what ways children perceive school differently to adults. What do you think would be the main significant features of school and classroom experience from the child's perspective?

Further reading

General Teaching Council. *Teachers Professional Development Framework*. GTC (2004). This is a 16-page booklet in which the General Teaching Council sets out your entitlement for professional development throughout your career. It describes this in terms of a variety of formal and informal experiences, including the importance of collaborative learning with other colleagues. The publication can be downloaded from the GTC website: http//www.gtce.org.uk/TPLF.

Handscomb, G. and Macbeath, J. (2003) Th*e Research Engaged School*. Essex: Forum for Learning and Research Enquiry (FLARE), Essex County Council. This 15-page booklet describes the main features of a school that is *research-*

engaged and includes a basic health-check audit to help teachers and schools to check out their own practice.

Hargreaves, D. (2003) *Working Laterally: How to Make Innovation an Education Epidemic*. Publication in partnership with DEMOS, NCSL, and DfES. This concise 19-page publication will help inspire you to see how you can use networks to develop innovation, share practice and help pupils to learn better. It can be downloaded from www.standards.dfes.gov.uk/innovation-unit or www.demos.co.uk/workinglaterally.

MacBeath, J., Demetriou, H., Rudduck, J. and Myers, K. (2003) *Consulting Pupils: A Toolkit for Teachers*. Cambridge: Pearson. This is a practical pack for teachers and trainee teachers wanting to develop pupil engagement and achievement through opportunities for consultation and participation.

Mason, J. (2002) *The Discipline of Noticing*. London: RoutledgeFalmer. A very readable manual to help you develop practical approaches to incorporating 'noticing' and enquiry into your everyday practice and professional development.

Rudduck, J. and Flutter, J. (2004) *How to Improve Your School: Giving Pupils a Voice*. London: Continuum. This book gives a compelling account of schooling from the pupil's perspective. It brings together all the major work done on 'pupil voice' and conveys the important messages: not to underestimate pupils and to ensure you work in partnership with them.

Chapter 3

Continuity and progression from 3 to 11

Alan Pagden

Educating 3-11 year-olds is an intricate business. Should I be concerned with just the age of children I am going to teach? Should I be a generalist or a specialist? How do I get to grips with the WHAT and the HOW of planning, and will I be able to nurture a love of learning in children? These are all big questions which Alan Pagden guides you through in this chapter. He discusses the key differences in the curriculum and teaching styles throughout this age spectrum, and explains why understanding of this is important for you to become a successful primary practitioner.

INTRODUCTION

The aim of this chapter is to help you to develop an understanding of the big picture. You might well intend to spend most of your teaching career working with a particular age group – Year 3/4, for example. However, even with this narrow focus, in order for you to do your job well you will need to know about the characteristic experiences of teachers and children throughout the primary age range. Of course, the kinds of experiences that I have in mind are those which, by realising the potential of children as they progress through school, can be shown to meet clear educational aims. The National Curriculum *Handbook for Primary Teachers in England* (DfEE/QCA 1999a) now has a section where two key interdependent aims for the 'school curriculum' (one element of which is the National Curriculum) are spelt out. This is a welcome development and I shall look at these aims in the third section below.

The main themes running through this chapter are 'continuity' and 'progression'. For a child to succeed there are some things that should stay the same throughout their time at school: most obviously, the combination of physical and social factors which ensures the child's right to feel safe and cared for. Other things should change progressively in order to support the child's growing competence and maturity: for example, the complexity of texts designed and/or chosen to foster the development of literacy skills. As a teacher of Year 3 children, for example, you need to have a good understanding of how your colleagues in adjacent years work if you are going to offer your children an experience that incorporates relevant aspects of both continuity and progression.

More generally, all teachers in a school should have a good understanding of the child's whole experience. At one level this obviously refers to the experience of the children you teach directly, that is, in most cases, your class. A 'complete' knowledge of the learning experiences on offer to the year group in which you teach is essential if you are going to provide balance and coherence in your planning, and take full advantage of opportunities to build links between different experiences. At another level, however, it is also important for you and your colleagues to know about the experiences of the 'average' child as they progress through possibly eight continuous years in the same institution. In the following three sections I describe aspects of the situation you will find yourself in as a trainee teacher and newly qualified teacher (NQT), in terms of some of the constraints and possibilities that primary schooling currently presents in this country. The areas that I look at are: the curriculum and the organisation of schools; planning for progression; and nurturing the disposition to learn. I hope that this will help you to understand the broad context in which you will be working.

THE CURRICULUM AND THE ORGANISATION OF SCHOOLS

The curriculum

Typically you will be aiming to qualify as a teacher of 3–11-year-olds, specialising in either the 'lower' (3–8) or 'upper' end of the age range. There are clearly enormous changes that take place in a child's development through the seven or eight years they spend in primary school. Individuals, of course, will develop at different rates in different areas of learning, but schooling as a system, through the statutory curriculum, is organised into phases which structure provision in a way that is designed to meet the characteristic needs of different cohorts. The National Curriculum (DfEE/QCA, 1999b) together with the Early Learning Goals (QCA, 2000) set out the statutory entitlement to learning for 3–11-year-olds in England, defining for primary schooling three phases: the Foundation Stage, Key Stage 1 and Key Stage 2.

You will notice that, although they are officially called 'stages', I prefer to use the word 'phase' which is familiar in professional discourse. It is appropriate also because the idea of a 'stage' of development has played a key role in developmental theories (notably Piaget's) and it is important not to confuse the way a system of schooling is structured with ideas about how individual children develop and learn. As you are no doubt aware, in other countries the structure is different: most start their children on a 'formal' school programme later than we do. Whatever advantages different systems might have, it is invariably the case that a system designed to cater for the majority will not suit everyone. The Foundation Stage, for example, refers to the first two years of schooling (nursery and Reception classes), during which time children in the 3–5 age range encounter experiences which are intended to meet their learning needs. Some of the children who enter Year 1 classrooms at the age of 5 (that is, move into the next phase – Key Stage 1), will not be ready to take advantage of the learning experiences which are typically organised for children in this phase. For these children teachers will continue to draw on the ideas and resources intended primarily for children in the Foundation Stage.

The Key Stages of the National Curriculum were initially defined along with an assessment system which was deliberately designed to avoid the creation of a testing culture in schools (TGAT, 1987). This is why the levels of achievement (originally ten) are very broad and the average child is expected to progress through each of them in two years. The original idea was to keep testing to a minimum (that is, at the end of Key Stages) and to ensure that the curriculum was not assessment led. Unfortunately, high-stakes testing now dominates the curriculum in Year 6 and, perhaps to a lesser extent, in Year 2. With pressure to meet government-set targets and a general obsession with measurement, numerous children are now doing Qualifications and Curriculum Authority (QCA) and other tests every year, and the curriculum, to a great extent in many schools, is being led by this drive. This reality undermines some of the key principles that the National Curriculum embodies, for example, the importance of balance. It is therefore important for you to understand what your overall statutory responsibilities are, so that you will be able to make judgements in your planning and your teaching in the best interests of the child. I shall return to this issue in the final section.

Built into the statutory curriculum are ideas about the progress that the average child will make as they move through the three phases. On their third birthday children enter the Foundation Stage, where they remain until the end of their Reception year. During this time the curriculum is organised around six 'areas of learning' and expectations are described in terms of 'early learning goals'. There is a great deal of flexibility at this stage as regards the kinds of experiences that might be planned. In Key Stage 1, comprising Years 1 and 2, teachers must follow the much more tightly prescribed National Curriculum in three core and seven foundation subjects. They also have an obligation to teach RE, and will normally have a PSHE programme to follow. The emphasis in Key Stage 1 is on the core subjects, particularly English and maths, and there is little prescription in terms of content across the foundation subjects. In Key Stage 2, the same subject areas are followed and, in some schools, children begin to learn a modern foreign language.[1] The programmes of study are more prescriptive in terms of content than they are in Key Stage 1, although the latest version of the National Curriculum is much better (that is, thinner) in this respect than previous versions. The general pattern, then, is for the content of the curriculum to become increasingly prescribed as children move from 3 to 11.

Different kinds of school

So far, I have described our national system for primary schooling as comprising three phases defined in terms of the requirements of the school curriculum (including the National Curriculum). At the same time, however, across the country we have a range of different systems for staging children's progress through school; in other words, we have a plethora of different kinds of institution. Children might, for example, move from 3–9 primary schools to 9–13 middle schools (for example, Isle of Wight), or from 3–8 first schools to 8–12 middle (for example, parts of Norfolk). In the past, school transfer could occur at virtually any age, depending on where the individual lived. In recent years, however, many Local Education Authorities (LEAs) have reorganised in order to align their times of transfer with National Curriculum defined phases. On balance this is a good development, but it has put the existence of certain kinds of school under threat. In this respect, middle schools are the most obvious examples, and some would argue that there are sound educational reasons for keeping them. More interesting, I think, is the case of nursery schools which might, in the future, along with an overall expansion in provision, be replaced by nursery classes in primary schools.

Before the establishment of a Foundation Stage there was a lack of clarity in relation to the kinds of learning experiences that should be on offer during the Reception year. The advantage of a nursery class attached to a primary school lies in the possibility, under the framework of the new 'Foundation Stage', to develop a coherent programme for the 3–5 age group. This is very difficult at the moment because Reception classes are generally regarded as part of the main school, a presumption normally reinforced by a common basic timetable structure which is out of sync with their feeder nurseries. Even very recently, where nursery classes have been built onto established infant, first or primary schools, they have typically not been integrated with Reception classes, and are often built as completely separate units, sometimes a significant distance from the main school building. Nursery schools, which are separate institutions in their own right, often with two or three classes, are even less open to integration with the Reception classes that they feed, which are often in more than one school. They do, however, have the freedom to concentrate all their efforts on early years practice and some have become centres of excellence, providing a model, not only for nursery classes in primary schools, but also for the many other settings where young children find themselves (for example, playgroups). The Foundation Stage offers a framework for a coherent approach to learning and teaching in the 3–5 age range. However, there remain significant physical and temporal obstacles to nursery/Reception integration, and whether you work in a nursery school, a nursery class or a Reception class you will need to make a special effort to co-ordinate your efforts with colleagues across the nursery/Reception year divide.

The second phase that children enter into in their primary years is Key Stage 1 (Years 1 and 2) which covers the age range from 5 to 7 years. These are the children to whom the somewhat patronising title of 'infants' has traditionally been given. 'Infant' schools, which include Reception and sometimes nursery classes, typically feed 'junior' schools which cover the 7–11 age range – the third phase of primary schooling, which is Key Stage 2 (Years 3 to 6). Some Key Stage 2 children attend middle schools either from Year 4 (8–12 schools) or from Year 5 (9–13 schools), and you might well find a job in one of these. The experience that children have of their schools as institutions can be profoundly different. Some will move through two or three separate schools, even if they don't move home, while others will stay in the same school from nursery to Year 6. The main reasons behind the decisions that lead to different arrangements for schooling in different areas are economic and demographic. There are, however, educational reasons why some arrangements might be better than others, and it is a good idea to consider some of these.

Size matters

An advantage of schools that encompass all three phases is their potential to ensure a high degree of continuity and to plan for progression through the whole age range. By contrast it is arguable that every time a child changes school they are faced with challenges and potential discontinuities which could set them back. Most schools prepare children for their move to a new class at the end of the school year by introducing them to their new teacher, and by giving teachers time to talk about members of their new class with the previous teacher. This is obviously supported with transfer records of various kinds. Even more important is the need for liaison between teachers across the years of transfer from one school to the next, and for children to be made to feel welcome at their new school. Some schools put a great deal of effort into making the experience of transfer positive, but even when this happens there is often a markedly different culture that children have to get used to when they move, for example, from an infants to a junior school.

Another key factor determining the character of a school is its size. Possible educational advantages of large schools include increased opportunities for:

- specialist and/or team teaching

- the acquisition of specialist resources

- grouping children in different ways (including setting/streaming)

- dynamic management structures

- school-based staff development.

The success of a school in making good use of these opportunities will obviously depend on many things; chiefly, I believe, the quality of leadership and the degree of collaboration among staff. A major challenge in large schools encompassing all three phases is the need to ensure that the interests of certain age groups (typically the oldest) are not given special attention at the expense of others. This is an issue that often comes to the fore when attempts are made to plan for continuity and progression throughout the school.

For every advantage that a large school has there is a corresponding disadvantage. Very small schools which encompass all three phases are perhaps the best placed as regards their potential to provide continuity of experience for individual children. Teachers and other key adults can establish supportive relationships with all the children in the school and maintain them through a number of years – sometimes up to eight. This is the firmest foundation that a young learner could ask for but again it does depend on the quality of leadership and collaboration within the adult team. For most children in primary schools their class teacher quickly becomes the most important adult, and this is especially true when the individual concerned exhibits the qualities that, in the children's view, make a good teacher. Which is not to say that children shouldn't be taught by more than one person. Indeed, it can be very beneficial for children to have regular contact with a number of adults, as they typically do in an early years setting.

So what is the ideal primary school? As a rough guide I would say one that encompasses all three phases without being too big or too small. In my view, two-form entry, 3–11, schools are about as big as any school should get. With up to around 500 pupils they are, in some respects, too big: the headteacher cannot realistically get to know all of the children individually. On the other hand, they are big enough to ensure that no teacher works in isolation and this, for me, is crucial. The very best years of my teaching career have been spent working closely with like-minded colleagues in teams, the most supportive being the year team or partnership. I am not trying to argue that size and structure are the most important things that make up a school or determine what your experience in it will be like. The most important factor will invariably be your colleagues and how well you work with them. It is useful, however, to be aware of the dynamics which result, at least in part, as a consequence of the school's size and structure.

The generalist teacher

Running alongside the current drive to push up 'standards' there has been an emphasis on the importance of subject knowledge. Large schools are more likely to be able to appoint subject co-ordinators for each subject who have specialist knowledge and enthusiasm for their subject, whereas small schools have to rely on individuals to take on multiple subject responsibilities. Specialist subject teaching is also more likely to take place in large schools where, even within the year team, there is scope for varying degrees of specialisation.

However, the emphasis on subject expertise is not, in my view, necessarily a good thing. In most primary schools, even large ones, you will be a generalist class teacher and your responsibility will be to teach most, if not all, the National Curriculum subjects to your class. You will be supported in this by documentation of different kinds (for example, the programmes of study, school policies and schemes of work), by various other resources and by colleagues (for example, subject co-ordinators, teaching assistants), but what actually happens at the chalk face is your responsibility. Does this mean that you should be an expert in every subject? Or does it mean that as long as you have enough expertise to teach the 'basics' you'll get by, since all you need to do in relation to the other subjects is trust the plans that you are given, for example, the QCA Schemes of Work? I say no to both of these questions.

From their inception in the nineteenth century, primary schools have always had at their core the basic structural unit of class teacher and class; one teacher responsible for the delivery of the whole curriculum (however impoverished that might be) to a number of children (for example, 30), normally for the duration of a year. The main reasons for this form of organisation are probably economic. The case for the generalist teacher, however, can be made on a number of grounds. I have already stressed the need to achieve an acceptable degree of balance and coherence in the curriculum on offer to a particular class or year group. When you are intimately acquainted with the whole, through teaching every subject, you are obviously better placed to do this. I have also stressed the importance to children of supportive interpersonal relationships and the key role that the class teacher has to play in establishing these. Perhaps the greatest potential of generalist teaching, however, lies in what Edwards and Mercer (1987) refer to as the formation of 'common knowledge'. The classroom is a social interactive context in which the teacher can play a pivotal role by establishing routines, referring back and forward to key events, making conceptual links between diverse learning experiences, and so on. Through their interactions with the class as a whole over a period of time the teacher is able to establish and develop a shared culture (system of meaning) which provides a basis for much of the learning that takes place.

In my opinion, as a primary school teacher you should think of yourself, first and foremost, as a generalist. This might appear to be a rather old-fashioned claim. In the past primary teachers would say 'I don't teach subjects, I teach children'. While secondary colleagues identified themselves with their subject, and enjoyed a degree of status from their evident expertise, primary teachers would claim that their own expertise lay not in subject knowledge but in knowledge of child development. This, I believe, was a cop-out. Knowledge of how children grow and learn is very important and it is unfortunate that you are unlikely to cover it in depth during your training. However, you do need a certain amount of subject knowledge in order to teach effectively and this too should be seen as an essential part of your professional expertise. Problems arise, I think, when subject knowledge is reified (that is, separated from the context in which it is put to use) and you are led to believe that once you've acquired it, that's all you need to do.

This can lead in one of two unfortunate directions. In areas where you lack confidence, you become too reliant on other people's plans and fail to engage with the children at their level of interest and understanding. In areas where you are confident, you present yourself as a resident expert, the fount of all knowledge, a role that many young children readily cast you in, and the children come to rely on you for all the answers. Of course, both of these scenarios can be avoided. A good generalist teacher has the confidence and enthusiasm to research areas in which their knowledge is lacking before they are required to translate this new learning into ideas for the classroom. This is part of the planning process, but it often goes further and deeper than the children would be ready to go themselves. You will always be able to teach better if you have engaged with the subject material yourself at your own level, which in primary teaching is invariably at least two or three steps ahead of the children. The ability and willingness to learn when new knowledge is needed is, arguably, more important than subject knowledge per se. In this regard, the generalist teacher represents an ideal role model for today's children who will grow up in an ever-changing world where, we are told, they will need to learn new skills and adapt to new work practices on a continual basis.

PLANNING FOR PROGRESSION

As a student teacher one of your most daunting tasks is to get on top of 'planning and assessment', and indeed this process is at the heart of what makes teaching both challenging and enjoyable. In Chapters 10 and 11 you are given some advice on how to go about managing planning and assessment in the medium and short term. In this section I am going to give an overview of the planning process, including long-term planning, and I am going to highlight the differences of approach found between the typical early years setting and, at the other end of the age range, the typical Key Stage 2 classroom. By exploring these differences in relation to planning I will also throw some light on two other key components of curriculum organisation – assessment and resource management. As you will see there are relationships that can be discerned between all three of these components which are relevant to the central goal of achieving continuity and progression from 3 to 11.

Preparation and planning

Good teaching will seldom occur in the absence of sound preparation, and even when it does it cannot be sustained over a significant period. Which is not to say that thorough preparation (including planning) will guarantee success – it won't, but at least it makes success possible. Written plans are not the only aspect of 'sound preparation' that you need to develop, and they are not the most important. If you intend teaching a unit on electricity, for example, no amount of written planning will help if you haven't made practical arrangements to provide children with the necessary equipment, in the right place and at the right time. This might require purchasing new resources and/or liaising with colleagues, well in advance of the planned series of lessons. Written plans are nonetheless very important for at least three reasons:

- They help you to think through what you intend doing, freeing up your ability to think on your feet while you are engaged in teaching.

- They provide a documentary account of your teaching through which you can justify your decisions, and in terms of which other people (senior managers in the school, Ofsted inspectors, your tutor) can discuss your work.

- They can and should be used to support key assessment strategies, but in this regard you must be careful not to allow assessment requirements to drive your planning, or to think of assessment as an add-on for which specific activities need to be planned.

Of course, not all the decisions that determine what or how you teach are made by you: some, for example, are made at the highest level, by the Secretary of State for Education and Skills. Planning decisions can be arranged along a continuum from the most general (for example, all schools in England should teach design technology) to the most specific (for example, child A should be given worksheet 25A for homework tonight). I illustrate this in the first column of Figure 3.1 where I have confined the decisions to those that might be made within a particular school. The more general the decision the more people it affects and, consequently, in a democracy, the more people we can expect to be involved. Higher-level decisions (involving most people) tend also to be those which are made in the 'long term', whereas low-level decisions affecting small groups or individuals are made in the 'short term'. Hence, the familiar distinction between long, medium and short term can be seen to parallel the continuum as described above.

The points along this continuum, at which distinctions can be made between long-, medium- and short-term planning strategies, are to some extent arbitrary, and they will vary according to where they fit within an overall planning system (see third column in Figure 3.1). Weekly planning formats, for example, can be used in a number of different ways and often are, in the same school or even by the same teacher. They might be used in the medium term to outline a coherent unit of work (usually a number of weeks in length), or as short-term plans, progressively adapted on a weekly or daily basis. Medium-term planning formats are sometimes used as 'schemes of work' updated and improved on an annual basis through an evaluation process. As such they could be described as 'long term' even though they are brought into use in the medium term. It is important, therefore, always to be clear about the

Figure 3.1   Planning decisions, levels and formats

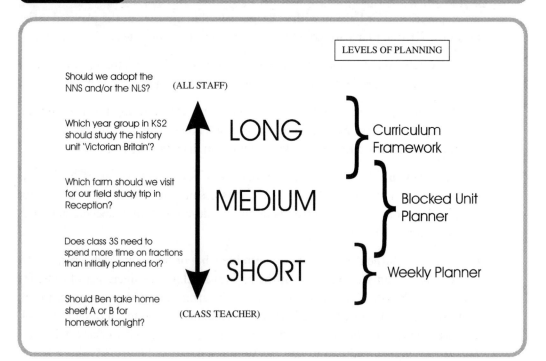

purpose(s) of a particular planning strategy and/or format, and to understand how it relates to others in the system.

Age-appropriate planning systems

My aim here is to illustrate, in general terms, how planning systems (incorporating long-, medium- and short-term plans) should, and do, differ to meet the needs of children in each of the three phases of primary schooling. I do this initially in Figure 3.2 which contrasts early years and Key Stage 2 practice. The purposes of planning at each level and in each phase are referred to with a question word that points to the overall purpose. This gives a very schematic overview, showing the main differences as occurring in the long and medium term, although there are differences in the short term as well. The differences should be thought of more in terms of a degree of emphasis rather than a sharp line of distinction. They reflect, I believe, more fundamental differences in practice which are based on ideas about how children of different ages should be taught, and they can be understood by looking at the way that the curriculum is resourced in developmentally appropriate ways. As I describe the different approaches at each level of planning, I will therefore look initially at how two qualitatively different kinds of resource are allocated – material resources and time. I will also describe differences which exist in the short term, even though they are not indicated in Figure 3.2, and in this context I will mention a third kind of resource – human beings. I spend more time looking at the Key Stage 2 classroom mainly because I believe that it is here that there is a greater need for the critical evaluation of current practice.

Providing material resources through long-term planning

There are some very practical reasons for planning in the long term. If you know that you will be teaching a local history unit, say in the spring term, then you will be able to prepare resources (for example, photograph packs) and make arrangements (for example, site visits, guest speakers) well in advance. This applies equally to teachers who work in the nursery as it does to those who work in Key Stage 2. At this level of planning, however, there remains an important difference of emphasis as regards the key planning questions which are indicated in Figure 3.2. In order to clarify the nature of this difference, and to understand the planning system as it operates in Key Stage 2, it is useful to think of the curriculum as comprising two different kinds of unit – blocked and continuous. This distinction, which you will find is used in the National Literacy Strategy (NLS), was initially deployed in an official document in 1995 which gave advice on how to plan the whole curriculum in Key Stage 2 (SCAA, 1995). While there are definitely areas of the English curriculum which can usefully

Figure 3.2   Systems of planning compared

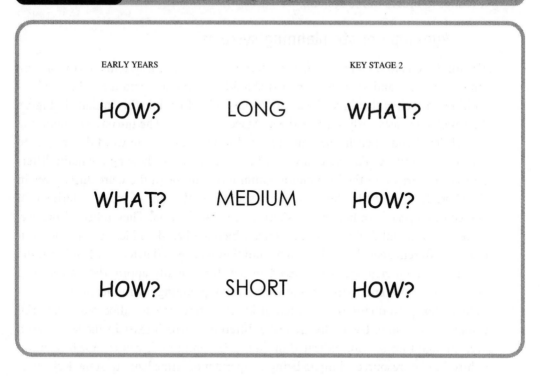

EARLY YEARS		KEY STAGE 2
HOW?	LONG	WHAT?
WHAT?	MEDIUM	HOW?
HOW?	SHORT	HOW?

be described as 'blocks', the distinction is at its most helpful when the aim is to get a clear picture of the whole curriculum, and in my view it is unfortunate that the terms 'blocked' and 'continuous' are now associated with the NLS, where they have a more narrow focus.

In Key Stage 2 a great deal of the curriculum (mainly within the foundation subjects and science) is most effectively taught through 'blocked units'. This is because they offer children (and teachers) a chance to become immersed in an area of interest, and an opportunity to work on extended tasks and self-initiated investigations. I expand on this below. On the other hand, the 'continuous' areas of the curriculum (including most of maths and English), are taught more or less on a daily basis throughout the year, requiring a range of resources which are always readily available. The typical Key Stage 2 classroom is equipped and organised with this in mind (that is, it has such things as dictionaries and number lines available all the time). Then, when blocked units are taught, additional resources are brought in and adjustments are usually made to the classroom environment. Hence the WHAT question in Figure 3.2 refers mainly to the blocked areas of the curriculum.

In all of this it is important to remember how children may – or may not – be coping with these changes in the classroom environment. You may find that this is particularly a problem at specific times such as when children move across Key Stages (see Chapter 2).

Long-term planning usually implies planning over at least one year. Schools normally have a document (a 'curriculum map' or 'curriculum framework') which sets out, in broad terms, the content of the curriculum for each year group. This is an effective way of answering the question WHAT? in relation to the areas of the National Curriculum which each year group in each subject should be expected to address. It is a way of ensuring adequate coverage of the different content areas and it provides an opportunity to look for interesting links that might be made between (mainly blocked) units in different subject areas. It is also normally at this point that notional timings are allocated to different units, with a view to achieving a balance across the year. It is very important in Key Stage 2 to establish an effective curriculum framework, most obviously because there is a great deal of National Curriculum content that needs to be covered.[2] These concerns, however, are far less pressing in an early years context where, with no prescribed content, there is usually a great deal of flexibility as regards the topics and themes on offer.

Even if the Key Stage 2 curriculum did not consist largely of prescribed National Curriculum content, the need would still remain to make decisions about the areas of content that are to be addressed in each year group as children progress through the Key Stage. Some of the reasons for this are obvious: for most 7–11-year-olds it is not very interesting to learn about dinosaurs two years in a row; it is also normally easier to learn about distant places *after* studying the geography of places closer to home. Decisions about content at this level of planning impact directly on issues of continuity and progression. If blocked units about electricity, for example, occur in Year 2 and then again in Year 4, it is essential that the experiences on offer are not only different, but that they incorporate opportunities for the children in Year 4 to build on what they learned in Year 2.

As I have explained, the WHAT question in Key Stage 2, which involves the allocation of content areas to year groups, refers mainly to the blocked areas of the curriculum which are not resourced on a permanent basis. The early years setting, by contrast, is typically resourced to provide opportunities in *all* the important areas of learning on a continuous daily basis. The important long-term planning question is about HOW children will be able to learn through an appropriate balance of teacher-directed and self-initiated activities, including play. The emphasis is on creating an appropriately equipped environment based on learning and teaching principles. Long-term plans spell out in detail the reasons behind the provision of particular learning areas (for example, outdoor climbing equipment) or classroom routines such as the Plan–Do–Review cycle. As indicated above, some significant areas of the curriculum in Key Stage 2, *are* continuous. Although there is an element of content to think about in these areas in the long term, the emphasis is more on HOW questions (for example, how children should be taught to spell) and in this respect the two approaches are similar. However, whereas the early years curriculum is 'resource based' in the sense that learners actively select the materials and equipment that support their interests, in Key Stage 2 the continuous part of the curriculum is supported by the provision of easily accessible resources which serve mainly to equip children with what is needed to fulfil prescribed objectives set by the teacher.

Managing time in the medium and short term

In the early years setting medium-term plans do not need to be *so* detailed since most of the key questions about HOW children learn will already have been set out in the long term. The approach at this level can afford to be much more open and responsive to the perceived needs and evolving interests of the children as a group. Typically medium-term plans will consist of general themes or topics, which loosely provide a framework around which to plan various activities. The emphasis at this level is on content (WHAT should we learn about this term – minibeasts, ourselves, babies?), but the activities planned will always incorporate sound learning principles, which have been established in the long term and will be used to inform more specific planning decisions in the short term. On the other hand, in Key Stage 2 after the long-term framework has been established the question that needs to be addressed, at least in relation to the blocked areas of the curriculum, is HOW – how will the key learning objectives (selected from the National Curriculum programmes of study) be addressed?

At this level of planning, that is, in the medium term, the Key Stage 2 teacher has an opportunity to contextualise and bring to life an area of learning by drawing on a range of different resources, many of which are specific to the locality of the individual school. Medium-term plans might incorporate opportunities for children to contribute to the direction in which the work goes, but the teacher does need to answer, in detail, a number of planning questions about how key learning objectives will be met. The success of a blocked unit will often depend to a great extent on the care that has gone into preparing appropriate and stimulating resources, and the quality of the related medium-term plans. These resources and plans will often be used repeatedly over the years, expanded and improved through a process of evaluation, becoming 'schemes of work'. There is a danger in allowing schemes of work to become too rigid, both in terms of the extent to which they are developed over the years and in terms of how open they are to input from children. As indicated above, blocked units can offer children a chance to become immersed in an area of interest, and an opportunity to work on extended tasks and self-initiated investigations addressing one or more subject areas.

The possibilities for teaching blocked units, however, were severely curtailed in primary schools with the introduction of the National Literacy Strategy and the National Numeracy Strategy, which were allocated prime chunks of time across the weekly timetable. Recently, schools have begun to be more creative with their use of time through blocking units of work and cross-curricular planning. This has occurred partly in response to the government's new 'Primary Strategy' (DfES, 2003) through which – despite its contradictions, its ambiguities and its 'spin'[3] – schools and individual teachers have been invited to take control of their planning and to be more creative. However, in order to achieve an appropriate curriculum balance and to make the most of available time, schools need a flexible system that accounts for everything that happens, including school performances and sports days. This cannot be achieved by relying solely on the weekly timetable. An effective way is to use what I refer to as a 'pacer' in tandem with the weekly timetable: a pacer is a medium/long-term planning tool. On this basis time is allocated through the timetable in balanced proportions of blocked and continuous units, and then through the pacer, blocked units are allocated chunks of time at appropriate points in the year. The size of these chunks will depend on the key aims of the unit rather than arbitrary cut-off points such as half-term holidays.

The fallacious assumption that numeracy and literacy can only be taught effectively by ensuring that all children receive their prescribed hourly dose should not be permitted to undermine their entitlement to breadth, balance and the opportunity to manage some time of their own. Time is perhaps the most valuable resource that we exploit through the planning process. As a trainee teacher you will be encouraged to 'pace' your lessons well. This is something that refers mainly to your own classroom performance, in relation to which thoughtful planning in the short term can help. The aspect of time management which receives less attention but deserves more, in my opinion, is our approach to the allocation of time in the medium and long term. Here a number of questions should be asked about how children spend their time, and the extent to which they are given opportunities to learn how to use it wisely.

Short-term planning and assessment

In Figure 3.2 the short-term planning emphasis for both early years and Key Stage 2 is the HOW question. This reflects a common set of concerns – chiefly the need to use assessment information to inform planning. There are, however, important differences between the two systems, which is not surprising to anyone who has spent a day in each of the two very different learning environments. To an uninformed observer short-term planning in the early years setting might appear to be based on fairly superficial decisions about which activities might be made available on a particular day (that is, an emphasis on WHAT rather than HOW). The emphasis, however, is very much focused on the needs of individuals as these become apparent through ongoing formative assessment strategies; chiefly through observation (see Chapter 4). Decisions are made on a weekly or even daily basis to provide opportunities which address the learning needs of individuals or small groups. Most obviously this can be seen in the teacher-focused tasks through which individual needs are most directly addressed, but it is often also evident in the range of other opportunities that are made available to the children.

In Key Stage 2 the medium-term HOW question shifts from a focus on the key learning objectives which have been defined for a typical group, of say Year 3 children, to a closer look, in the short term, at HOW the unit of work might be geared to the needs of a specific group of individuals, that is, your class. The extent to which you differentiate or extend the material will vary from year to year according to your judgements of the children's needs. Blocked units in subjects like art, history and design technology (DT) will, for the most part, be differentiated by outcome, and since the block runs for a limited period, the extent to which you might use assessment information to inform planning in the short term is also limited. It is probably fair to say that short-term planning in Key Stage 2 is more often informed by assessment information in the continuous elements of the curriculum which are typically taught on a daily basis, where planning decisions are made from one week or from one day to the next in response to ongoing assessments of children's achievement. In this respect the system resembles that of the early years setting. However, in Key Stage 2 there is less opportunity to adjust short-term plans in response to *individual* needs. Apart from a minority of SEN children who might be withdrawn during some lessons, children are normally taught as a class or as a group and there is always some pressure to cover the prescribed material. Adjustments to short-term plans are therefore normally made with the interests of the group rather than the individual in mind.

There are also marked differences in the way human resources are typically deployed under the two systems. In an early years setting, where there will usually be a minimum of two adults, the need to work collaboratively is inescapable. There are a number of reasons why a higher adult-to-child ratio is necessary, which I won't go into here. In relation to what I have said so far about planning and assessment, there is an important advantage worth mentioning, which comes with having 'extra' adults, and that is the opportunity to place an emphasis on observational assessment. By contrast, Key Stage 2 teachers have traditionally taught their class alone, opportunities for observational assessment have therefore been fewer, and reasons for using other assessment strategies such as marking have been more obvious. Recently, however, there has been an increase in the number of teaching assistants working in Key Stage 2, and the government has indicated its intention to fund this development further.[4] It will be interesting to see if innovative practices develop as teachers and their co-workers in Key Stage 2 begin to tackle challenges such as the need for more open-ended formative assessment.

NURTURING THE DISPOSITION TO LEARN

'Independent learning'

By describing these planning systems in a schematic way I have begun to present a picture of two contrasting learning environments. A further way of highlighting the difference is by looking at the balance between child-initiated and teacher-directed activities which is a key dimension of planning in an early years setting. For large parts of the day or half-day in a typical setting most, if not all, children will be engaged in self-initiated activities, many of which could be described in terms of some form of play. Play, in its various forms, is regarded as an essential vehicle for learning in young children. By contrast, in Key Stage 2 it is generally regarded as a leisure activity – something reserved for break time. In a typical Key Stage 2 class-room, children spend most of their time engaged in tasks which have been set by the teacher. Of course in the early years context the nature of the activity will be determined to a large extent by the quality of the environment which has been created by the adults. The children, nonetheless, exercise a far greater degree of autonomy over what they do than their counterparts in Key Stage 2. This raises some interesting questions about what we expect from children as they grow and develop during the 3 to 11 age range.

One of the aims of early years education is to encourage 'independence' in children, and this is implicit in the overall aims for the school curriculum which I will look at below. If independence in the early years setting were simply equated with freedom to choose, then we would have to conclude that children are given progressively less independence as they make their way through school. This would undermine, rather than support, the educational goal of achieving 'independence'. There are at least two things that most young children want: the first is to exercise control over their environment, including the other human beings in it, and the second is to participate in the social life that surrounds them. Giving children freedom to choose, and encouraging them to do so thoughtfully, is only part of the business of promoting independence. Children also need opportunities to act responsibly as participants in the social world, and there is no doubt that the classroom, at least potentially, provides a context for them to do just that. The child who is maturing as an 'independent learner' does not only show increasing awareness of their own learning needs or an ability to make sensible decisions in relation to those needs; they also show a growing understanding of their responsibility as a member of a learning community, and are able to assert themselves in relation to their own needs, and on behalf of others.

Young children exercise the highest degree of autonomy over their learning when they are learning through play. As they progress through school they quickly find out that the value of play as a vehicle for learning diminishes in the eyes of adults, and it is soon relegated to the lowly status of non-work. Play is not one thing and it is impossible here to give a comprehensive account of its different facets. Consider, however, the possibility that play in the early years provides, amongst other things, an essential foundation for certain ways of learning which we do value quite explicitly during the later years of primary schooling. What I have in mind here are such things as investigation, creativity, problem-solving, drama and the ability to work in teams. In relation to the central theme of this chapter the question arises: how does the planned curriculum support continuity and progression in these areas, whose roots lie in the spontaneous free play which is regarded so highly in the early years? My answer is, sadly, not very well. Opportunities for children in Key Stage 2 to participate in the kinds of experiences that genuinely build on the competencies that they developed earlier through play are very limited, and few schools have time to look closely at progression in these areas.

If we are serious about promoting such things as creativity, independence and the ability to work in teams, we must not be afraid to recognise the implications that this has for curriculum organisation. In Key Stage 2 the curriculum should be organised differently from how it is organised in the early years, and the change from one form of organisation to the next should be gradual – it should exhibit elements of both continuity and progression. Most children come to school with a desire to learn, and it is perhaps this, above all else, which we as educators have a responsibility to nurture. In practice our success rate is not very high, as demonstrated by the large numbers of demotivated 10- and 11-year-olds currently in our schools: children who do school work only because they have to. By implication I have already suggested that this is, at least partly, due to our failure to build progressively on good early years practice. I have also indicated, however, that there are things that can be done to free the curriculum from some of its most powerful constraints (for example, by managing time more creatively in the medium term). I will now explore further the idea that it is our responsibility as primary practitioners to lay down the foundations for 'lifelong learning'.

Getting the balance right

You can be forgiven for believing that there is one task above all else which you must succeed in: that is, you must teach your children how to read, write and do arithmetic. This is certainly the political climate that we appear to be working in. You will of course recognise that there is more to the curriculum than these so called 'basics', and if you are lucky during your training you will be given the opportunity to look at the curriculum as a whole. However, with the current emphasis on the 'core' subjects you are unlikely to get a solid grounding in all the important curriculum areas. There are, nonetheless, obligations that you have as a teacher which go beyond teaching the 'basics' or even the 'whole' broad-balanced curriculum. These obligations are evident in the two key interdependent aims which have been established for the school curriculum: to 'provide opportunities for all pupils to learn and to achieve'; and to 'promote pupils' spiritual, moral, social and cultural development and prepare all pupils for the opportunities, responsibilities and experiences of life'. The interdependence of these aims is emphatically stated in the official document (DfEE/QCA, 1999a, pp. 11, 12).

Hence our aim to push up standards, in terms of learning and achievement, must be supported by endeavours to promote and enhance self-esteem through the education of the whole person, that is, personal, social and moral. Having high expectations for the children you teach is a good thing, but if they are too narrow, failing to recognise the breadth of an individual's potential or too demanding, then they will serve only to crush self-esteem, and you will do more harm than good. Like a lot of things in teaching it is a matter of getting the balance right. The National Curriculum provides us with a guide to the levels of expectation that we should have for our children, as they make their way through primary school. For each individual child, however, the correct balance at any one time between levels of challenge and support will be decided by you their class teacher, and often you will find that it is more important to offer opportunities for success, in areas where an individual has demonstrated competence, than it is to concentrate on areas of weakness where the threat to self-esteem is ever present.

Working with parents

Parents, of course, have a crucial role to play in relation to their children's overall self-esteem and more specifically the image that children develop of themselves as learners. For the majority of children parental involvement in their education provides an important source of continuity and, depending on its quality, it can support progression from birth, throughout the pre-school and school years, and even into adulthood. Which is not to say that the contribution of parents is always positive. As a teacher, however, it is crucial that you recognise the significance of parents and try to work with them in the most constructive ways possible (see also Chapter 2).

Early years practitioners have long regarded parents as the child's 'first educator', and they invariably invest a lot of energy in forging as close links as possible between school and home. This usually begins well before the child's first day, with visits by teachers and other workers from the setting to the child's home. The majority of parents take advantage of the opportunity that the home visit offers, for them and their child to meet the staff in an environment where the child in particular feels confident. From the practitioner's point of view, seeing the child in context is an ideal way of gaining an insight into their young lives, and this enables them (the adults) to respond appropriately during the child's initial settling-in period.

Even when home visits don't occur there is normally more direct contact between parents and teachers in the early years than there is later on. As a teacher of younger children you will have face-to-face contact with parents on a regular basis. Mainly through informal discussion, you will establish and develop relationships with parents which have the potential to provide a foundation for future positive relations between home and school. As children get older and move through the system, direct parental contact becomes less frequent, although formal mechanisms for liaising with parents are maintained and developed, for example, reporting, conferencing, school events. This is appropriate since many children regard it as a mark of their growing independence that their parents no longer see them into school, and some increasingly view school as *their* space, keeping their parents in the dark as regards what they get up to.

However, the influence parents have on their children's ability to make the most of what school might offer can operate in some quite subtle ways. A home environment where books are valued and where adults are seen to enjoy reading, for example, can make a big difference to a child's approach to reading in school. Every parent has ideas about educational concepts such as 'learning', 'intelligence' and 'the curriculum', to a large extent formed through their own experience of the education system. In combination with the information about their child's achievements that they are provided with, this 'understanding' determines the ideas they develop about the child as a learner. Some parents, for example, form views about how 'academic' their child is, fairly early on in the child's school career, and this narrows their view of the child's full potential and preferred learning style(s). It would be naïve to imagine that children could negotiate their way through schooling without being influenced by their parents' conceptions of them as learners.

Through informal communication throughout the year, conferences and written reports you will feed and mediate information about how the children in your class are getting on at school. A school that sets or streams, and where great emphasis is placed on the importance of test results, will give very different messages to parents, as compared with one which is more concerned with the whole child, where difference is seen as a resource and something to celebrate, rather than a problem and/or justification for the 'inevitability' of competition. We live in a competitive world and in school there is no better example of this than the government-imposed high stakes testing which children have to participate in. As a teacher, however, in your discussions with parents, you are in a position to put things in perspective, and to support each parent in finding a way to value the unique achievements of their child.

Not all parents feel comfortable coming to school, essentially because school let them down, by failing them academically, by failing them socially, or both. Some schools are developing strategies to encourage these parents to participate more fully in their children's education; for example, adult literacy and other classes run during school hours. While programmes of this sort are laudable and are having some success, it is important to consider how better relationships with parents might be developed and sustained into the future. Parents who are now reluctant to come into school, even though they care about their children and want them to have the best education possible, were themselves once pupils in primary schools. The children we are teaching now are parents of the future, and if we nurture their disposition to learn, their self-esteem and their sense of well-being then we will be laying good foundations for the success of their, as yet unborn, children.

CONTINUITY AND CHANGE: YOUR CAREER

It is true that you cannot be a good teacher without being a good learner. Teachers who look at each new class in September, at the potential of a chance event (a snow storm or a local building initiative) and at each individual achievement of their pupils, with fresh eyes, will over the years acquire a store of immensely valuable experience. This is the kind of knowledge that will serve you well even when you move on to work with a different age group, in management or in an area of specialisation such as learning support. Some teachers follow very varied career paths in terms of the age groups they teach and the kinds of schools they work in, while others stay with the same age group in the same school for a much longer time. Whichever approach you take to your career, you will need to be able to adapt to changes that are beyond your immediate control. Since the late 1980s primary schools have been subjected to a continuous barrage of change initiated by central government, and it has been difficult for teachers to retain a sense of control over their work. Hopefully the balance of control will shift back to the profession, but this will not mean the end of change. If you enter the profession with a sense of moral purpose this will stand you in good stead; some things will always be worth fighting for. If you are starting your career as a young teacher you might well still be in the 'classroom' in 2030 or 2040. Then you will be able to look back on such things as overhead projectors and the NLS, and chuckle.

SUMMARY

In this chapter I have invited you to think about the three phases of primary schooling, covering the 3–11 age range, as a whole. I have highlighted issues of continuity and progression through a discussion of the curriculum, schools and approaches to planning in the long, medium and short term. Issues discussed include:

- the optimal size and structure of primary schools

- the advantages of generalist teaching

- the relationship between planning systems and strategies of resource allocation

- the need to find new, more flexible ways of managing our most valuable resource – time

- the responsibility of the teacher to find a balance for individual children, between high expectations and the need to nurture self-esteem

- the role of parents in relation to the child's developing image of themselves as a learner, and how teachers might mediate this process.

As I hope I have made clear, the system we currently work with is far from perfect. However, this will not necessarily stop you from having a positive impact on children's lives, or from playing your part in shaping the profession of the future.

ISSUES FOR REFLECTION

- Some subjects you will be teaching you will already know a lot about. Others you may well feel less confident about. How will you fill in the gaps in your knowledge?

- Take some time to observe one of the youngest and then one of the oldest pupils in one of the schools you are visiting (half a day for each child would be ideal). What similarities and differences do you see in the type of work they are given (for example, is it written or practical)? Why do you think this might be the case? Which child has more choice in what they do? Again, consider why this might be the case.

● Sometimes children have particular difficulty in moving from one Key Stage to another. Discuss this issue with one of the teachers in your school remembering to ask whether the school sees this transition as a problem and how they manage it.

● Try to see the journey through one of the schools you are working in from a child's point of view. In particular consider how the teachers manage pupil behaviour at the various stages of their educational journey. How do you think the differences and similarities might be perceived by the developing child?

Further reading

If you are interested in reading more about planning and assessment two books which give sound and practical suggestions are:

Clarke, S. (1998) *Targeting Assessment in the Primary Classroom*. London: Hodder and Stoughton. This correctly places an emphasis on formative assessment strategies most of which are suited to a Key Stage 2 environment.

Hutchins, V. (1999) *Right From the Start*. London: Hodder and Stoughton. This gives a very good overview of early years practice and a particularly clear explanation of the relationships between the different levels of planning.

In this chapter I referred to four official documents, one of which is statutory. As a general point, I recommend that you read the official documents yourself rather than trusting somebody else's interpretation of what is and what is not 'statutory'.

● NOTES

1. It is now a target of the government to introduce Modern Foreign Languages into all primary schools by 2010.

2. Some schools uncritically adopted the QCA schemes of work as a package and simply pasted them into a grid to form a curriculum framework. This practice results in lack of ownership, coherence and relevance to the local context, and is now discouraged.

3. For a critic of the 'strategy' see Alexander (2004).

4. With the new National Agreement on Workforce Reform, teaching assistants are being expected to take on more responsibility.

Chapter 4

Observation

Gillian Preece and Stephen Chynoweth

What is one of the most crucial ingredients to becoming a better and more effective teacher? Observation, particularly when it has a clear purpose and structure. Here Gillian Preece and Stephen Chynoweth give down-to-earth guidance on how this life-long skill can be learned, practised and refined.

INTRODUCTION

Stop for a minute and try to describe the face of your watch without looking at it. If you do not wear a watch try to describe in detail something which you use regularly. How did you get on? Despite the fact that you may have had your watch or treasured object for many years, we suspect that you did not describe it at all well. We were very surprised to find that we were not able to describe our watches accurately and yet we probably look at them several times a day. This activity demonstrates the difference between looking at something and noticing the information that you want, and observing what it is actually like. Even though looking at things is part of our everyday lives, detailed observation is not part of it.

This exercise also suggests that when we look at things in order to gain specific information – in this case telling the time – it is quite likely that we do not take in the context within which that information is situated; how often do we *look* but not really *see*?

WHY OBSERVE?

The point about observation for you – as a trainee teacher – is that observation will help you learn a tremendous amount about teaching styles and techniques. It will also help you to gain considerable insight into how children learn. Most importantly of all, it will allow you to observe the impact a teacher has upon a child's learning and the ways in which that impact can be measured. Effective teaching should be judged in relation to how it helps to promote learning, and helps pupils to make gains in their knowledge, understanding and skills. However, in observing detailed points about the way a classroom operates you must try not to lose sight of the context and the complex interactions which affect both teachers and pupils. Indeed, if you were to learn about the mechanics of a car, your learning would begin with how to change the oil or bleed the brakes, rather than how to undertake a complete service!

Trainee teachers are often asked to make observations from the beginning of their PGCE course. It is expected that, by looking closely enough at various forms of evidence, the trainee teacher will be able to focus on effective teaching and learning techniques.

Observation is not just something trainee teachers do. Experienced teachers also use observation to help them to understand how the children in their class are learning new concepts and consolidating existing ones. Teachers also use observation to develop their own classroom management and teaching skills. Teachers are used to working collaboratively, sharing ideas and strategies (see also Chapter 2). Indeed, through Learning Network clusters, the government encourages and financially supports the teaching profession to share approaches to learning and teaching so that it remains fresh, innovative and effective in maximising benefits to individual children's learning. This means that they understand the importance of observing how other teachers work as well as allowing colleagues to observe them. Established teachers will often set up formal observation times when they can make assessments about the learning that has been taking place in their classroom. They will also make ad hoc observations which will inform their assessments about both the learning taking place as well as the effectiveness of their teaching. This, in turn, allows teachers to alter their plans and activities to tailor them to the learning needs of their pupils.

However, for the trainee teacher class observation plays an additional role. Observation is a skill and, as with most skills, it requires practice and perseverance to become proficient in it. Classroom observation requires practice as there are so many things happening which require analysis both in terms of what is happening and in the observer's reaction to it. Each classroom or school setting will offer new experiences that will help an observer to build up a bank of knowledge and to develop a deeper understanding of what is occurring. When you are observing in the classroom remember that it has an end product – to make you a better and more effective teacher.

In this chapter we will look at the role of observation for trainee teachers in the primary classroom. We will consider some of the areas worth noting in both teaching style and techniques as well as the children's learning. Some advice will also be given on how to record observations in a practical and retrievable way.

TEACHING PRACTICE

Remember, teaching practice is exactly as it's termed – *practice*. There will never be an expectation upon you that you'll get everything right immediately. Teaching practice is an opportunity to begin to mould what you have learnt about effective learning and teaching with ideas of your own in different school contexts. Indeed, an effective teacher will always consider their teaching as 'practice' of sorts, as they look to develop, fine-tune and improve their teaching styles throughout their career.

Usually trainees are notified at an early stage of their course about their first school placement. Several days might be organised for you to visit your school to enable you to gather information which will help you have a successful teaching practice.

The information that you gather will arrive in several forms: school policy documents, the school prospectus, conversations with teaching staff and/or the headteacher and, almost certainly, by reading the most recent inspection evidence from Ofsted. Most importantly you will spend time observing the class within which you will be working.

Influencing practice

By observing the classroom setting in which you are placed you will begin to identify effective strategies which enhance the children's learning. The observations made can be both negative and positive – making judgements about why something appeared not to work can be as valuable a learning experience as noting positive things.

Children's learning

While much of the attention paid in the initial stages of the observation may appear to be towards the teacher, you will also need to make observations about how the children are learning; issues such as:

- How does the teacher motivate the children's learning?

- Which style of teaching appears to be most effective in a particular setting?

- Are different strategies adopted for different subjects?

You will also be gathering information about the children in the class to enable you to be able to plan your work with them effectively. For example:

- At what level are the children learning? Are there at least three clear levels of ability in the class?

This will help you to set appropriate tasks when your teaching practice starts. If the tasks set are too easy or too hard then this has a huge impact on how well the children learn. It can also start to affect the relationship you might have with a class if they perceive the tasks as being boring or unattainable.

- What strategies does the teacher employ to enable pupils' ownership of their own learning?

PREPARATION FOR OBSERVATION

Before the observation period begins there are many practical things the trainee teacher can do to get the most out of this experience.

Preparation

Try to find out in advance of your first visit as much information as you can about the school you will be visiting. Information such as:

- the name of the headteacher
- the size of the school
- whether it is a single/double/treble-form entry school
- the profile of the catchment area.

All this information will help you to build up a picture. Much of this information, and more, will be available through recent inspection evidence, known as the Ofsted report. Try where possible to read the most recent report available on the school. Information like this is usually available on the Internet (www.ofsted.gov.uk). Also, schools are now encouraged to be much more self-evaluative and the Ofsted inspection process deems that schools should have a good understanding of how well they are providing for their pupils and 'next-step'-improvement developments. All this information will be contained in the school's SEF (Self-Evaluation Form) Ofsted form, which you could possibly discuss with your school's headteacher or member of the Senior Leadership Team.

Once a class has been allocated to you ask for a class list, as learning the names of the children will help when making observations. It will also help when you take over responsibility for the class. A class list might also contain other information, such as the birthdays of the children, which will give you some idea as to whether the children's birthdays are fairly evenly spread out over the academic year or if there are many birthdays at one particular time. In Reception or Year 1 a lot of birthdays in the summer term usually means that the children have not been in school for very long.

Gaining agreement

Once you have been introduced to the class teacher with whom you will be working, try to come to an agreement as to how the observation period will occur.

- How will you record your observations? Your college may have provided you with a pro forma.

- Does the teacher mind you making notes during the teaching sessions or will you be expected to jot down your observations during break times or after school?

- Will the teacher want to see what observations you have made?

Although at first this might appear quite daunting, working with the class teacher and sharing your observations will provide a positive foundation to the start of your teaching practice. The teacher might be able to pick up on areas of confusion and be able to explain why something was organised in the way it was. The class teacher will also be able to give you their interpretation of something which in turn might help you to understand better the organisation of that classroom.

- Will the teacher be expecting you to be an observer who does not take part in the session, or will you be expected to take part in some way? If the teacher is expecting you to participate in the planned activities then this will have an impact on some of the issues covered earlier, such as how and when you will note down your observations.

- If you are given the opportunity to sit apart from the class, not taking part in activities, try to ensure that you are as unobtrusive as possible, particularly while making any notes. This is not to suggest that you should be hidden, but try to be discreet when observing, preferably behind the learners.

Should children approach you, then we feel you should be as honest as possible about what you are doing. We frequently find that children ask us what we are doing when we are observing trainee teachers on teaching practice. When asked the question 'Who are you and what are you doing?' we generally answer something like 'Ms/Mr X has told me about how hard this class learns and I've come along to look at all the good learning that is happening'.

Type of observations

Generally, the observations you will be making throughout any school experience will be qualitative rather than quantitative. You will not have the time, and indeed it will not be particularly productive, to quantify the practice you have observed. For example, you will not be counting up how many questions the teacher asks within a session, but rather considering the effectiveness and type of the questioning taking place with a view to gaining an understanding as to why the questions asked had a particular impact. However, this type of qualitative observation does carry some risks.

There is the issue of preconceptions – we all have opinions about the best way that things should happen. Our own experiences in school will have formed our opinions about education – a favourite teacher remembered, a mathematics concept struggled over, a detention from one particular teacher – and how we reacted to those situations will go with us into the classroom. It is therefore extremely important that observations where judgements are made are examined thoroughly for the value which has been placed upon them. As Wragg (1997) says in his book *An Introduction to Classroom Observation*: 'We often interpret events as we wish to see them, not as they are. There can be several filters along the route, as information about an event speeds towards the human brain. Good qualitative analysis of classroom behaviour involves rigorous scrutiny of these barriers to accurate perception' (p. 54).

To take this point further, it is possible to argue that it is the interpretation of the event which is critical, rather than the event itself. Therefore, it is important to attempt to look at events from as many different perspectives as possible. This can include the view of the teacher, classroom assistant and, most importantly, the pupil.

To participate or not to participate?

As mentioned previously, it will not always be possible to have a choice as to whether you take part in a session or are allowed to sit apart from the class. There are advantages and disadvantages to both approaches. If you are a participant:

- you have the opportunity to speak to individual children and to build up a relationship with them

- you get the opportunity to work at close hand with the activities planned by the teacher

- there is an opportunity to consider your own response, possibly reflecting on how you see your own teaching style, as well as adopting teaching methods adopted by the experienced class teacher.

However:

- you may be restricted in not being able to work with all the children

- it is easy to get caught up in the activity you have been given and to lose sight of the information which might be beneficial to you in the longer term.

You must also have thought carefully about any note-taking which you might wish to make while participating in an activity with children. The older the pupil the more inquisitive they are likely to be about what it is you are writing. Vicky Hutchin (1999) sums it up in her book *Right from the Start: Effective Planning and Assessment in the Early Years*: 'Usually the notes you make will be short and quickly done' (p. 44).

Obviously the opposite situation is possible in non-participant observation; you may not build up a rapport with individuals or an adequate understanding of the type of activities planned by the teacher. Pupils may also deduce that you are a trainee teacher and this can present difficulties when you come to lead the class. We've all witnessed how children can adapt their behaviour to the environment, often presenting more behavioural difficulties with some adults than others, often reliant upon the child's perception of authority figures within the community. By making it known too overtly to children that you are not yet a qualified teacher may give them opportunity to 'push the boundaries' with you rather than simply accept your authority as their class teacher. However, non-participant observation will probably enable you to closely observe more general areas like classroom management strategies, use of resources to illustrate key teaching points and use of learning support assistants.

The ideal situation for a trainee teacher would therefore seem to be a balance between the two approaches: time to sit back and observe the general running of the classroom as well as opportunities to become involved in working on activities planned by the teacher with groups or individuals.

MAKING OBSERVATIONS

Once you have agreed with the class teacher how the observation process will progress it will become evident that there is so much information to take on board it is difficult to know where to start. Returning to the analogy of car mechanics, it is much more effective to break down observations into 'bite size' pieces, the same way in which you would learn how to change a car's oil, rather than attempting to do everything at once, such as a complete MOT! One approach is to try to focus your attention on particular aspects of the classroom rather than looking at and noting down everything that will be happening. Below we have listed some possible aspects of the classroom that you may want to focus upon first; perhaps discuss these with the class teacher before your first observation. This way other aspects can be planned into future observations so that each area of classroom teaching can be covered in smaller, manageable pieces; you may want to break these aspects down into even smaller pieces, possibly as a chart or table, so that you can quickly make reference to your observations as you begin to plan lessons for the class at a later date.

Physical resources

Many aspects of this type of observation can occur without the children being in the room. Without providing an exhaustive list it is a good idea to note the following:

- How the room is laid out – are the tables in groups or pairs, for example? It is a good idea to draw a diagram of the classroom for you to look at later.

- Are the resources clearly accessible – are the pencils, rulers, and so on stored in one place where the children are expected to go to get them or do the children have responsibility for looking after their own resources? Are dictionaries, information books and resources for supporting curriculum subjects such as mathematics and English easily accessible or are they stored away with the teacher responsible for handing them out?

- Are there pupil whiteboards/digitcards/resources that enable interactive learning with the class teacher? If so, where are these stored and what is the system for providing the pupils with them?

- Are there areas for the children to learn quietly and areas designated for more practical activities?

- Is there an interactive whiteboard in the classroom? What make is it and what software is used? How does the teacher use it to enhance learning and teaching in their class?

- Is there a computer permanently in the room or is this a shared resource?

- What are the displays like? Do the displays show examples of a range of abilities in the class?

  Do the displays simply celebrate pupil achievement or are they learning opportunities for the class, asking questions of pupils or raising questions from pupils? Do the displays concentrate on one subject area for each display, for example, artwork, writing or mathematics? Or is a link made between the curriculum subjects which form the whole display; for example, some poetry about flight, some design technology drawings and models of aeroplanes and a write-up of an experiment in connection with flight? This might be part of a whole-school policy or it might be the preferred way of working of the class teacher, but either way there should be a whole-school policy on it.

● Is there a 'talking wall' or PSHE-type area to the classroom identifying pupils' concerns/comments with their school learning experiences?

● What is happening outside the classroom? Is there a practical area and, if so, how is that used?

● The organisation of the cloakroom: again, is this shared? What is the routine of this area?

In each setting there will be physical considerations which should additionally be noted. Each classroom will be organised differently. This will depend on practical issues such as the space available but it will also reflect the preferred way that the class teacher likes to work.

Organisational issues, such as do the children always sit in the same place or do they learn in different places depending on the activity they are doing, are important to notice. These cannot necessarily be noted without the children in the classroom, although the number of chairs to pupils in a class, or name places at each place may well give you a clue.

This is the time to put to one side your own experiences of how you remember learning when you were at school. This is the time to watch what happens in the forthcoming sessions, to try to understand why the teacher has organised things in the way they have and, most importantly, to consider how the learning environment is organised to best suit the learners in terms of effective learning.

● Rules, routines, procedures

Like all organisations, schools are to some extent governed by a set of routines. Furthermore, children find security in routine, therefore it is important that your teaching practice continues them. Individual teachers will not be able to change some things that happen within a school day although many things will have been agreed by teachers as a whole-school policy. Policy and practice should be strongly linked. A good example of this is with behaviour management. Schools will often have agreed policies which all members of staff are expected to follow. It is important to have read the school's behaviour management policy before your teaching practice begins so that you feel confident in applying it; it would tend to undermine your teaching authority with a child if it appeared you 'did not know what to do'. It is also important to see the policy in operation in the classroom and in other areas of the school, for example, in the playground and the school hall during PE and assembly. Other policies, which will have an immediate impact on the trainee teacher, include marking of work, display and the school's Quality of Learning and Teaching policy.

Fixed points

There are many fixed points in a school day and it is worth observing how the class teacher deals with these.

The start of the day

Schools vary in how the children start their day. Some schools allow the children to come into their classroom as they arrive, or only after a set time. The teacher may have tasks or activities for the children to do independently until the official start time of the day. Some schools have all the children coming into school at the same time usually after a bell or whistle has sounded and the children have been lined up and sent in class by class. Both of these approaches have organisational implications which you should observe as it will be important for you to fully understand and remember what happens when this becomes part of your responsibilities. Perhaps note down the different ways in which classes begin their day, commenting on possible advantages and disadvantages with both methods to help inform your own preference in the future,

Other fixed points

Try to observe the other fixed points of the day and how they are organised. Assembly times, playtimes, lunch times and the end of the day all bring their own organisational implications and it is important that you recognise the importance of continuing the practice of the class teacher. For example, being late for assembly upsets the routines of many other people, keeping the other classes waiting and possibly eating into valuable hall time at the end of the assembly time. In addition, many schools try to keep their morning sessions to a tight time frame to enable the literacy and numeracy sessions to be given their full time allocation, although the introduction of the Primary Strategy has resulted in many teachers looking to combine subjects through a multi-objective thematic approach.

Classroom management

Many areas of classroom management can be observed best when you are given the opportunity to sit back and observe without participating in a session. Observation times are an ideal way of learning from the class teacher how they achieve the working system that they do.

Style

It must be recognised that by the time the trainee arrives in the classroom the teacher is likely to have been teaching the pupils for some time and to have established many routines. A teacher who appears relaxed and calm with a class, making jokes with individuals, has inevitably worked hard to gain a shared understanding with the class of an acceptable way of learning. It is inappropriate for a trainee to start their learning relationship with the class in the same way. Wragg (1997) describes the observation of a trainee teacher during a secondary school science lesson. During the course of the session several classroom management problems were evident. At the end of the session the observer asked the trainee, 'Can you tell me a bit about what happened when you asked the children to get out the equipment?'

The student teacher then explained how he was simply imitating the casual way in which he had seen the class's regular science teacher start experiments. However, it became clear that he had visited the school to watch some lessons in December, after the school had been in session for three months. By then the class's regular teacher had forged a well-established friendly relationship and was able to be relaxed and jocular. The student assumed that he could imitate this manner, but was unaware of the considerable efforts made by the class's teacher in the previous September to ensure that pupils did not misbehave. Therefore, it is very important that you establish ground rules and enforce these in a consistent manner. (Wragg, 1997, p. 69)

Control and pace

Classroom management areas such as behaviour management, timing of activities and monitoring of children's learning are all important issues to consider when observing the teacher. These can be observed while participating in an activity, although a more accurate, holistic understanding of how these things work can be gained by watching the teacher as a non-participant. Observing the strategies that the teacher uses for behaviour management when they are effectively on their own in the classroom, for example, will help the trainee to understand what will be expected of them when they take over responsibility for the class. (See Chapter 8.)

Teaching

When training to be a teacher, a common approach is to be thinking 'What will I *do* with the pupils?' Too much anxiety can be caused by thinking about how you will open the lesson, introduce the learning objectives, what questions you will ask and so on. Whilst these are important facets of teaching, the teacher's mindset is best focused on 'How will these children learn best?' So why not try imagining planning the perfect lesson backwards, considering what you want the pupils to have learnt/be able to do by the end of the lesson and then 'rewind back' through the lesson to consider what you will need to do to teach and facilitate that end aim. To put it another way, in order to make a cup of tea, we boil a kettle, put a tea bag in a mug, perhaps add sugar and milk before finally adding water and stirring to our preference. We don't necessarily go through the actions to see if we *may* make a cup of tea; the actions we undertake have a clear purpose towards the end aim of producing a cup of tea.

Other areas to observe include teaching strategies such as, for example, the balance and choice of practical and written activities. When you are observing the class try to make a note of the type of activities organised by the class teachers. The teacher may have planned for their time to be spent working with one group. How then have the other groups been organised? Has the teacher been successful in planning activities that the remaining groups can maintain on their own with little input from the teacher? If it is a core subject, such as maths or English, is there a balance of activities across any given week? This is sometimes achieved by preparing a mix of practical and written activities. The balance and number of each will be dependent upon the previous experience of the children in learning in this way as well as the type of activities which have been planned. The independent activities planned may well be for reinforcement purposes, the teacher being confident that the children have previously been given a basis from which to learn. It is also worth noting how the teacher deals with hidden issues. For example, how does the teacher ensure an equal access for boys and girls to all areas of the curriculum? This is a large area to observe and one that you may feel you do not have time to look at in depth. However, observing how the teacher ensures that there is equal access to the computer when it is in use in the classroom will go some way to demonstrating possible strategies. (See Chapter 5.)

There are other routine points of the day which can be observed. Your observations should help you to come to a better understanding of how you might operate when the class is your responsibility.

Beginnings and endings of sessions

Most teachers have a set pattern for how they start and end sessions. To gain the children's attention and to indicate that a transition is about to take place teachers often have some sort of signal. This can be putting a hand up in the air and waiting for silence, or putting a hand up and saying something to gain attention. Some teachers have a musical instrument (bells, and so on) which the children have learnt to recognise as the signal to pay attention. The system that your class teacher adopts might not be the one which you would like to continue when you have qualified and have your own class but it is useful to know what the children are used to. Also note how the teacher gives out the instructions as to what the children are then expected to do. Does the teacher allow the children to all move at the same time or are the children moved group by group?

How are the groups selected? With younger children the selection might be by an attribute that the children might have – all those children wearing green, for example. With older children the selection might be based around those behaving appropriately. Similar routines can be observed at the end of sessions. Again, how does the teacher gain the children's attention? What instructions does the teacher give about what the children should do with their learning? Does the teacher share the learning objective with the class? Pupils should be partners in their learning and in order for them to be able to reflect upon how well they are learning, pupils need to know what the learning intentions of the lesson were in the first place. Do the children tidy away or are some resources left out for the next session? How does the teacher address misconceptions during the plenary session of the lesson? Do pupils reflect upon how successful they feel they've been with their learning? One useful tool to use here is the traffic light system. If a child has found their learning challenging, rewarding and successful then they are green, all systems go. If they have found their learning difficult and have had help along the way, then perhaps they are on amber, ready to go but require further assistance. If pupils have been 'stuck' and found their learning too difficult then they are at red, something is stopping them with their learning.

How does the teacher dismiss the children? Are the children expected to line up before they leave the room, do they stand behind their chairs or do they leave the room as soon as their name has been called? Alternatively, does the teacher simply say that the children may now all leave the room? If this is the case it might be worthwhile finding an opportunity to ask the teacher if that is how they have always dismissed the class. Remembering the example of Wragg, previously mentioned; it might be possible that the teacher has worked hard with the children at behaving sensibly when leaving the classroom. It is unwise to assume that you would be able to take over in the same way. The next set of observations are based around the teacher and again can be made whilst participating in an activity but would probably be better observed if you are able to sit and watch sessions without participating.

Movement around the classroom

Once the session is up and running, the teacher has delivered the key teaching points and the children are learning from the activities they have been assigned to, try to observe the movements of the teacher. Does the teacher sit in one place, working with one group of children? If so, there are several things to consider. Why do you think the teacher has selected that particular child or group of children to learn with? If the answer is not obvious to you it might be appropriate to ask at a later stage in the day or it may be outlined in the lesson's planning. Teachers make choices like this for all sorts of reasons. For example, the teacher knows this group will need more support than the other groups to sustain this activity. Or the teacher wants to assess how the children are doing on this activity. Or there is one child in the group who is causing concern and the teacher wants to be able to support that child appropriately. We are sure there are many more reasons. It is also important to notice how the teacher has managed the rest of the class in order to concentrate time with this one group. Are the rest of the class free to come and ask questions of their teacher, or are they limited to going to the teacher one at a time? Is there a learning support assistant in the class assisting with the learning of the pupils? If so, how are they used? Is it the same throughout a week or different for different subjects and pupils? Have the children been given strategies for doing their activity independently?

A very common situation is where the teacher is expecting children to write independently so that the teacher can support perhaps a guided reading group. A reel-to-reel tape recorder saying 'Right, how can you get on with your writing if you get stuck on the spelling of a word?' would be handy on these occasions! Fairly quickly, the suggestions come in from the children: 'Use the word bank, look in a dictionary, check in your own word book, ask a friend.' We would encourage all of these strategies. Ultimately, if we really did not want to be disturbed while working with another group, we might say to the children that it did not matter if they made the occasional mistake, that we wanted them to 'have a go'. This is linked to building up a relationship with a class as they will not always have the confidence to 'have a go'. The children have to understand that you will not be cross if the attempt was not successful. Even so, if a teacher is working in a classroom on their own with no extra support it is almost inevitable, especially with younger children, that interruptions will occur.

It might be that, from time to time throughout such a session, the teacher makes a point of commenting on the behaviour of some of the children in the remaining groups, 'I can see Jo learning very hard, I will be interested to see what he has done at lunch time'. This is positive reinforcement of good learning habits and is good professional practice. Developing the teacher's mystical 'third eye' of peripheral awareness can be a real asset of a skill to refine as a trainee teacher.

There are occasions when teachers do not stay in one position throughout the session but decide to move freely around the room. It is also important to observe how this is done. Does the teacher move around stopping for a few minutes with each group, making sure the groups are on task and learning effectively? Or is their role identified in a more disciplinarian manner? Does the teacher walk around insisting on quiet learning? It is important to observe how the children respond to these different approaches. Do you think that by moving around the class the teacher is able to support sufficiently those children who need it? Or are some children left unsupported because the teacher has been to them and has moved on to another group? Do you think that by the teacher staying with one group there are large numbers of children left unsupported? Or have the rest of the class been organised in such a way that they are confident about the activities they are doing? All of these issues should then raise more questions for you which you could address with the class teacher at a more appropriate time.

Asking questions, giving answers, pupils raising questions

The power of the question is one of the most important factors in effective learning and teaching. The question stimulates curiosity, a desire to know, understand and learn. A healthy classroom should reflect a broad use of questioning: teacher questions, questions raised by the pupils, prompt questions in response to pupils' tasks, questions in displays. Now that the literacy and numeracy sessions are established, the use of questions is planned in on a daily basis. The mental and oral starters in the numeracy session and the whole-class introduction of the literacy session mean that teachers have had to address the most effective ways of asking questions to better assess the children's understanding of what is being taught; how the teacher uses questioning to informally assess achievement and inform next steps in planning the pupils learning. Observing these parts of the sessions, as well as other times when questions are asked, will prove helpful to the trainee teacher.

When you are placed in the position of delivering your own numeracy session you will be able to bring to mind some of the questioning techniques you observed. You might try writing down the exact wording of the question asked and the answer that was given to it. If the correct answer was not given immediately but was perhaps given by the second child chosen, this might also be significant, so record both answers given. It can be useful to make a note of any groups of questions asked by the teacher, as there may be a progression or sequence which should be considered further. The same process is also useful for the explanations given by teachers to children's questions. For example, simply having large laminated cards with WHAT? WHY? HOW? WHO? WHERE? WHEN? written on the individual cards can help to prompt pupils to raise a variety of their own questions. It is also interesting to make a note of any situation where a teacher does not immediately know the answer to the question. How does the teacher respond? Does this response tell you anything about how you might respond in a similar situation?

IT'S ALL A MATTER OF PERSPECTIVE

All these different methods will give you an insight into the ethos and style of the teacher. Every teaching style has advantages as well as disadvantages. Moreover, it should be recognised that each observer will have their own interpretations as to what is actually occurring in the classroom and that one example or incident should not necessarily be used as the only evidence for something. Wragg (1997) gives an example of how two different supervisors were supervising the same trainee teacher but felt very differently about how that student teacher was performing. One felt that the student displayed an insensitive manner towards the pupils, the other supervisor that the student was being firm.

When pressed to explain what expression might replace an expression in contemporary language, the boy replied, 'That funky music from down the road'. The teacher went on to say, 'That's typical of the answer I'd expect from someone who gets as low marks as you do' (p. 63). Wragg comments that although both supervisors had recorded similar events in similar ways, their interpretations were completely different. Whereas the first supervisor deplored the student teacher's manner, the second supervisor wrote about the event described above, 'What I like about this is that he stands for no nonsense from any potential troublemakers'.

Vicky Hutchin (1999) shows how collecting evidence from as many sources as possible will help to build up the best base of information. Hutchin gives many examples throughout her book *Right from the Start* which show how important it is to gather evidence in many different ways so that a full appreciation of the child is gained. In the same way a trainee teacher should try to look at things from different perspectives before making judgements about how effective their class teacher's methods might be. There is a lot of information which can be collected before the trainee teacher comes into the school which might help the student to understand the context in which the teacher is operating. Several observations of that teacher might demonstrate that although some routines remain constant, the teacher changes other strategies depending upon the subject matter being taught. As mentioned, conversations with the teacher will also go some way to helping the student gain a clearer understanding of why things have been organised in the way they have. Another thing to consider is if the school has a policy on colleagues observing and working alongside each other to share approaches to learning and teaching. If so, perhaps you would be able to observe other teachers in different year groups so as to determine what is school policy and what are teachers' individual styles.

Within all these different approaches there are many other messages given out by the teacher which an attentive observer might be able to notice. These include those non-verbal methods of communication which are part of everybody's everyday life.

In the street as we see somebody walking towards us, even without talking to them, it is not unlikely that we have made some sort of judgement about them. This judgement might be made by the kind of facial expression they are pulling, for example.

In the same way, the perceptive observer can begin to gain a better picture about the classroom environment and the relationship the teacher has with pupils by trying to notice as many non-verbal messages as possible. For example, although formal and strict in the levels of discipline expected, does the teacher smile and nod approval a lot to encourage the pupils? When working with one group of pupils does the teacher take time to make eye contact with the pupils to demonstrate that they are aware of how well they are learning?

The other main methods of non-verbal communication employed to different effect include posture, gesture, facial expressions and different ways of moving around the room. All these things may be worth noting. It might well be inappropriate to expect you to mimic or imitate, for example, the class teacher's gestures, but observing the effect that the gestures have can help inform you as to how you would like to move and respond when working with children.

The same observations can also be made of the children in the class. Just because a child is sitting quietly, apparently with exercise book and textbook open, does not mean that they are on task in the way expected of them. Their body movements or facial expressions may well signal to the teacher that the opposite situation is the case. Again, the way a teacher deals with such a pupil can be the result of the teacher's understanding of how that child will respond to them. Sometimes the best thing to do is to go and stand near the child in question and that will be enough to get the child back on task. It might require more direct questioning to discover what the problem is. Again, a situation worth noting. For a trainee teacher, the danger of assuming that they have the same understanding as the teacher might lead to difficulties. The trainee teacher must realise that they will have to go through some process of establishing their own relationship with the pupils. Indeed, the crux of being an effective teacher is the attention and detail paid to relationships a teacher builds with their pupils and parents. Remember, you are not in the class to be a child's best friend or substitute parent; you are there to help them to learn as effectively as possible. Children need to know that you have their best interests at heart, that you care that they learn as well as they can as well as you wanting them to feel happy, secure and stimulated in the learning environment around them. Ultimately, you want your pupils to grow in self-esteem and confidence, to possess a broad and balanced perspective to their school experiences so that they can develop the skills and understanding needed to equip them for their lives ahead. In a nutshell, you will want to lead their learning rather than simply manage your own teaching.

Earlier in the chapter we mentioned that one way to be productive in what you are observing is to focus closely on a different aspect during different observation periods; for example, to look at the behaviour management strategies employed by the teacher and to all intents and purposes ignore other aspects of the lesson such as timings, beginnings and endings, and so on. It is then possible to focus even more closely within the generic term of behaviour management strategies to look at the use of praise by the class teacher and the effectiveness of the praise and reward strategies that are employed. Wragg (1997) describes this as a 'Critical Event' approach; the trainee teacher should attempt to look for significant examples of a specific thing occurring and then should attempt to document this event. Wragg suggests that a description should be given of the situation leading up to this event, the actual event itself (including why it was significant) and what the outcome was. It may also be helpful to talk to the teacher and/or the children concerned to gain a better understanding of its significance. However, as Wragg comments 'Talking to children either directly or indirectly about their teachers is not something that should be undertaken without permission, and even if agreement is secured, any interviews should be conducted in a sensitive manner' (p. 68). The term 'Critical Event' should not always imply something particularly important. Rather the events noted down should reflect something which is of interest to the observer. For a trainee teacher, the events should attempt to reflect something which will help them with their professional development in some way.

WHAT DO YOU DO WITH YOUR OBSERVATIONS?

Observations you make in the classroom will help you become a more effective practitioner. The type of observations you make can be split broadly into two categories – observations about teaching and observations about learning.

Observations about teaching

You will use the observations that you make about the way a teacher operates in the classroom as a personal bank of information to help you inform and guide your practice. You may be expected to bring your observations back to your PGCE course to discuss the implications and effectiveness of some of the things you have seen. However, the purpose of these observations as well as your discussions on your course is to help you to understand about effective teaching.

Observations about learning

The observations you make about the learning occurring in the class will help you to gain a better understanding of how children learn. You will also be able to use your observations to understand the role of the teacher in the learning which is taking place. For example, making judgements about how well the class has achieved an activity will help when you are responsible for planning the learning of that class on teaching practice. Additionally, you may be required to pass on the observations you have made to the class teacher who might wish to use your observations in the records of the class as well to help their planning of the curriculum.

Ethical issues

Observing in a school is about real people and real situations. Even if you feel you are looking at something other than the people in the school, the teacher or the child will be involved in some way. Looking at the organisation of the furniture in a class, for example, will demonstrate to some extent how the teacher has decided to organise it. The way a child is dealt with when misbehaving is not just involving the theory behind the behaviour management but directly involves the child and the teacher.

It is fundamental to your development as a professional teacher that observations are confidential. When discussing individual situations during your PGCE course, for example, names of children should be kept out of conversations; refer to specific pupils by a pseudonym or letter. Additionally, although you might see a teacher approaching some teaching in a way you feel to be ineffective, being overly critical of the teacher is counter-productive. Do not discuss your observations in a negative way; try to understand why the teacher has used the approach that they have. Then try to analyse what you feel would be the better way to approach that teaching point.

SUMMARY

Observation plays an important role in the routines and skills of the classroom practitioner. This is a lifelong skill which must be learned, practised and refined to build up a base of knowledge which will help to improve practice. At the beginning and end of your training you may well be given a chance to observe teachers and children in the classroom. This is only the beginning but these opportunities will provide a solid foundation that can be developed throughout your teaching career. Good teachers never stop observing and reflecting on how to translate their observations into better practice.

This chapter has dealt with how students can get the best out of the opportunities they are given to observe in schools. The key issues covered included:

- the purpose of observation
- how to prepare for observation
- types of observation
- what to observe
- how to interpret the observations
- what to do with the observations.

- Reflect on what it might be useful for you to observe on your next visit to school. Think about how you will discuss your ideas with the teacher and negotiate an appropriate focus. Consider how you might plan future observations in the light of what you see and hear.

- Observe teachers asking questions. What type of questions do they use? Do they encourage pupils to talk or give one word answers? Are certain types of questions more suited to one situation rather than another? Why do you think this might be the case?

- Take the opportunity to focus on one child for a session. Look closely at what the child says and does. How do these relate to the teacher's plans, words and actions?

- Listen to the summaries that teachers give at the end of sessions and consider how they relate to the session plans and the content of what has taken place.

Further reading

Hutchin, V. (1999) *Right from the Start: Effective Planning and Assessment in the Early Years*. London: Hodder and Stoughton. Includes some short case studies of children and how staff in various settings interpreted and acted upon their observations.

Sharman, C., Cross, W. and Vennis, D. (2000) *Observing Children, A Practical Guide*. London: Cassell. Contains information about various observational techniques and more information on how to use your observations.

Wragg, E.C. (1997) *An Introduction to Classroom Observation*. London: Routledge. Contains some suggestions for ways of recording observations as well as classroom situations observed.

Chapter 5

Motivation and learning within the classroom

Anne Cockburn

Reflecting on your own experiences you will quickly come to realise that you already know a considerable amount about motivation and learning. In this chapter Anne Cockburn encourages you to think about your own learning and use this awareness to gain a better appreciation of what motivates children. What becomes clear is that stimulating children is not about a 'one size fits all' approach.

INTRODUCTION

More than 40 years ago I took piano lessons. For the first few weeks I practised conscientiously: not because I enjoyed endlessly running up and down the scales but rather because I wanted to attain the dizzy heights of being able to play a tune with two hands without having to think about it. Unfortunately such enticement was insufficient and my practising gradually dwindled into non-existence. Ten years later I tried again. This time my aspirations were much humbler: all I wanted to do was pick out a tune with one or at most two finger(s). Here I met with far greater success for my teacher, realising my modest ambitions, found books of simple, popular tunes for me to play and made very little mention of scales and five-finger exercises. In a very short time I was able to play recognisable melodies and that was more than enough to keep me going until university – and its much broader range of opportunities – beckoned me.

In this chapter I want to talk about learning and, more specifically, the learning that goes on in primary schools. Why is it that some things are easy to learn and others are less so? How come I was able to learn the piano in my teens when I had failed ten years previously? Why do some teachers seem to encourage learning while others, who might be equally well meaning, are far less successful?

In the main I will use examples to illustrate the points I wish to make but this chapter is not about content. In part this is because it will be considered elsewhere in the book, in part because a discussion of content may obscure the main points I wish to make, and in part because I agree with Hurst and Joseph's (1998) view that we must strive for adaptability rather than a body of knowledge which has to be learnt. They argue that: 'Our fast-changing world requires ... openness about new learning and the precise kinds of qualities that characterise early childhood: clear vision, practicality, inventiveness, creativity and sensitivity' (p. 38).

AN INTRODUCTION TO LEARNING

By the time they start school, children have learnt a vast amount. From being crying babies squirming in their mothers' arms they have become articulate individuals who can run, jump and dance about. They can reason, make decisions, sing songs and so the list goes on. How did they learn so much in such a short space of time? The answer is multifaceted and complex but, briefly, comprises modelling others' behaviour, trial and error as they attempt to master a new skill and what some might consider innate programming.

Think about your own learning. What can you remember from ten, 20, 30 years ago? Can you remember first riding a bicycle, making a cake, learning to read? How did you acquire these skills? Did you learn to write using the same, or similar, techniques to learning to sing? I suspect not: different skills often require different learning strategies. Moreover I suspect you and I learn in slightly different ways: everyone does. Some people have very good visual memories while others learn far more effectively if they hear – rather than see – something. Nowadays more teachers recognise the importance of different learning styles than in the past. Thus, for example, one minute I saw a teacher using rhythm to teach counting in tens to 100, the next I saw her holding up ten fingers at each ten and the next I saw her pointing out the tens on a number line as the class counted.

Skills acquisition is one branch of learning but what about, for example, understanding and attitudes? How did you acquire your understanding of yourself or science or the English language? It would be an oversimplification to suggest that you learnt to talk through imitation alone for that would not explain why young children produce words such as 'goed' instead of 'went' or 'sheeps' instead of 'sheep'. Such mistakes signal a powerful understanding of how language works and how rules may be applied – albeit wrongly in these cases but, nonetheless, intelligently.

Humans are generally very quick and effective learners: your role as a teacher is to capitalise on this fact but, to do this, you need insight into schools, schooling and, of course, children as intelligent and thoughtful recipients of your teaching.

MOTIVATION AND CREATIVE APPROACHES TO TEACHING

Schools are rather odd places – they can be ranked with prisons and mental institutions as the only places people are compelled to attend. If you stop to think about it, it is hardly natural for 30 children to be cooped up in a small room, often with only one adult for hours on end day in, day out. As some of my Masters students commented: 'Children are expected to be together seven hours a day possibly with people they don't like: why should they learn?' (Eve); 'If you want someone to learn something, would you put 30 people in the same room?' (Sandy).

Good points and ones we should not ignore. As teachers at the start of the twenty-first century, however, we need to recognise that, to date, putting 30 people in a room day in, day out seems to be the most cost-effective and efficient way to educate them. Indeed, thousands of teachers all over the world do an excellent job but it is not through sheer luck or an abundance of good intentions. A multiplicity of skills and attitudes are required, many of which are described and discussed in this book. One approach you might not have encountered previously is the use of thinking skills. The aim is for teachers to encourage their pupils to think about and discuss a variety of situations and experiences. Fostering the use of thinking skills helps children to become better at the process of learning. They can then apply these *learning how to learn* skills to a variety of situations. This will help them to become increasingly critical, discerning learners and to carry the learning habit with them throughout their school careers and beyond into adult life. It is not an attempt to encourage children to think as adults but rather to nurture their ability to think for themselves and to make their own decisions based on sound principles and logic.

As a teacher you can promote this approach by asking open-ended questions, challenging pupils' reasoning, encouraging further insights and ideas. There has been a great deal of thought given to the development of thinking skills. In particular, Robert Fisher has provided a range of very accessible guides on development thinking skills in primary schools, including his work on philosophy for children (see Fisher 1995; 1998). Perhaps the best starting point for you to become inspired and committed to creative approaches to teaching which can powerfully involve and motivate children is Victor Quinn's (1997) *Critical Thinking in Young Minds*. It gives practical examples in which the voices and participation of children shine through.

THE CONDITIONS FOR LEARNING

Before I proceed, it is important to emphasise that all the examples in this chapter are genuine. I have, however, used the writers' equivalent of poetic licence and created the cases of Sam and Jo (below) from a collection of various observations of a range of children.

Imagine Sam and Jo. They are lively intelligent children who like to spend a lot of their time together. Both live in the same street. Both come from lower middle-class families. Both have spent the first four years of their lives with their mothers. Both their mothers are about to start full-time work and Sam and Jo are about to start school. They are going to the same school but will be in different classes: Sam will be with Mrs Jones and Jo with Mrs Green.

As the first day approaches they have very mixed views: one minute they are full of excitement – that they are more than happy to share – and the next minute they are quietly terrified. Fortunately they both thoroughly enjoy their first day and it looks as if all will be well. Over the next few weeks, however, Sam becomes increasingly enthusiastic while Jo's interest begins to wane: it is not so much that he dislikes school exactly, it is more that he is puzzled and bored by it.

A quick look at what the boys do at school shows that they have both made new friends and that they are covering much the same work. Both teachers are friendly, dedicated and well prepared. So where is the problem?

Let us look at three instances that Jo found particularly confusing. Early on in the term, Mrs Jones and Mrs Green agreed that they would both do sorting in mathematics. Mrs Jones asked Sam and his friends to sort out the farm animals that were all higgledy-piggledy in an old box. She explained that she was concerned about them being damaged or lost so it was important that they were sorted out and housed more appropriately. Sam and his colleagues duly put the pigs into pens and the horses into stables and so on. By the end of the session the animals were all newly housed and ready for use in the newly created farm corner. Sam was not particularly interested in farm animals but he had thoroughly enjoyed working with his friends and being praised by Mrs Jones.

Mrs Green started her session in much the same way: she had a bin bag full of junk that she said needed sorting as it was 'such a mess'. She duly tipped various cartons, yoghurt pots and pieces of material onto the floor and asked Jo and his friends to sort them out. This they did. Mrs Green had a look, praised them and then quickly gathered all the items up and bundled them back into the plastic bag: so much for sorting out the mess!

Several weeks later Sam and Jo were asked to 'build houses' in a corner of their classrooms. Sam and his friends were told that they could use any building materials they liked from those left out on the carpet, in the material box or in the wooden blocks area. Jo was given no such restrictions. All started well: both boys thoroughly enjoyed planning and 'laying the foundations'. Sam quickly finished his house and was delighted with the result. Jo, however, was abruptly stopped in his tracks when Mrs Green rather sharply told him off for 'moving furniture about when you should be building a house over there'. You can appreciate her concern: not only were Jo's actions a bit noisy but they were also somewhat dangerous given his relatively small stature and the weight of the tables he was trying to move. Jo, however, did not share the teacher's insight, and immediately felt deflated losing all interest in the task: what was the point in building a house, he thought, if he couldn't follow his brilliant design?

Towards the end of the term both boys were making good progress in mathematics. To check on their ability to put the numbers 1 to 20 in the correct order their teachers gave them dot-to-dot pictures to do. Both children were fairly enthusiastic about the task but both – having become a little bored from counting 1 to 20 – decided to join the dots in reverse starting from 20 and counting down. On spotting this, Mrs Jones watched Sam for a few seconds and was greatly impressed by his ability to count backwards. Seeing Jo start at 20, on the other hand, Mrs Green rushed over to him and said, 'No, no. You weren't listening were you? I told you to join the dots so you must start at 1.' So much for adding a bit of interest to a routine task.

Reading the above, one can appreciate why Jo began to be puzzled and bored by school: basically he could not see the point of it and, when he did try to introduce a little creativity and interest, he was reprimanded. Any motivation he had was slowly being eroded.

It would be wrong, however, to be too harsh about Mrs Green. If you think about it, the reasons she behaved in the way she did were not because she was unkind, ill prepared or a bad manager. Rather she lacked imagination and understanding of some of her pupils. Like many teachers (myself included I am afraid), she had a tendency to jump in when she thought she saw anything going contrary to her expectations. She did not fully appreciate that tasks are not only easier but more rewarding if they are done for a valid reason and if one is given scope to go about them in one's own way. Had she understood that Jo had a tendency to become deeply engrossed in his work and accord it purpose and meaning, she might not have gathered up the 'junk' so readily, assumed he was fooling about instead of building a house or thought he had not been listening to instructions. Doyle (1979) reminds us, 'A classroom is multidimensional in that many events occur over time, many purposes are served, and many people with different styles and desires participate ... Decisions must be made rapidly with little time for reflection' (p. 45).

As conscientious practitioners, therefore, we need to keep reminding ourselves that pupil motivation is an important key to successful learning. Fortunately for Jo, he was *intrinsically motivated* by the tasks he was asked to do. One day – when she had a student in her room – Mrs Green was able to observe him. On noting his absorption in his work she began to re-evaluate her opinion of Jo. As a result she was less hasty in assessing his behaviour and, in time, he began to flourish.

CHILDREN'S NEEDS, BEHAVIOUR AND ATTITUDES

Let us imagine that four years later we come across Sam and Jo again. They have grown slightly apart in the intervening years but they still both enjoy school: Sam because he likes being with his friends and he consistently gets good marks and Jo because he enjoys his work. A closer look is again revealing. The boys are in the parallel classes of Mr Grant and Mr Brown. The first session we observe is creative writing. Both teachers have begun the lesson in a very exciting manner by describing an earthquake and all the drama surrounding such an event. Appropriate key words are written on the board and the children are asked to write 'really exciting stories' on the topic. Sam starts work immediately and produces three beautifully written, well-punctuated – but rather dull – pages. In contrast Jo seems to work in fits and starts: first he looks out of the window for a few minutes and then he scribbles furiously. There follows more looking, punctuated with bursts of writing. The end result is a scrawl that, despite being difficult to read, is a very vivid and dramatic account of a village in the aftermath of an earthquake.

Some days later the boys can be found doing 'mental' maths. In Mr Grant's class Jo appears to be enjoying the experience and frequently has his hand up. He likes using his brain and finds such work exhilarating. In Mr Brown's class Sam also has his hand frequently up but, unbeknown to the teacher, he is busy consulting his calculator beneath his desk.

One day the headteacher observes the children at work. She is greatly impressed by Jo's enthusiasm and his very real interest in his work. In contrast, although Mr Brown praises him lavishly, the headteacher considers Sam's work to be rather pedestrian. Watching the teachers in action in English sessions she notes that they introduce their lessons in very similar ways; they are both lively and stimulating encouraging the children to take part and respond to their questions. In both classes the children then settle down to work with apparent enthusiasm. Here the differences begin to show. Mr Brown moves round the classroom in a very efficient manner reminding his pupils to write the date, remember their capital letters, and praising them for their neat writing. In contrast, at first sight, Mr Grant appears considerably less organised and he spends at least twice as long with each child: there is simply no way that he will be able to talk to everyone during the course of a session. Rather than reminding the children of the task, Mr Grant tends to read their work and then ask specific questions about each piece: 'Why were the people afraid?' 'How did they escape?' 'Whatever is going to happen next?'

In essence, Mr Grant was helping foster Jo's intrinsic motivation by demonstrating a real interest in his work. On hearing Mr Grant's questions Jo wanted to write more and become further involved in the fantasy world he was constructing. He was, in other words, becoming a creative writer. Similarly, in other subjects, Mr Grant used questions to promote Jo's interest in the topics providing him with a curiosity and enthusiasm that would stand him in good stead for the future.

For all his organisational skills, Mr Brown proved less adept at inspiring his pupils. They were, however, more than willing to work hard for him for they appreciated his praise. Indeed, they enjoyed being in his class because they knew exactly what was required of them and little effort was called for if they remembered the date, punctuated correctly and wrote neatly. Then praise was forthcoming. Unlike Mr Grant's pupils they were *extrinsically motivated*. They were given a task and they delivered what was likely to be praised but, because the nature of the praise was fairly superficial, they rarely became really involved and excited by their work.

A casual glance in both classrooms might suggest to the uninformed that Mr Brown works harder than Mr Grant and that he is the better teacher. In reality, however, Mr Grant's task is far harder as he responds to individual's needs, interests and understanding, and builds on them to develop his pupils into interested, informed and flexible learners. Mr Brown, in contrast, has a clearly stated set of standards that he requires his pupils to attain. Indeed, it is in many respects, probably easier to be a pupil in Mr Brown's class as you know exactly what is required of you and, if you deliver accordingly, you will be praised. The children in Mr Grant's class are required *to think* and that is far more demanding.

In essence, therefore, the implications of the above for you as a teacher are that you need to take into account your pupils' needs, behaviour and attitudes. Children *need* to know what is required of them and what will be rewarded. This in turn almost invariably determines their *behaviour* and their *attitudes* to working within a school environment. (You will note I used the phrase 'almost invariably': as you may already be aware, children are never entirely predictable and that is one of the many joys and challenges of teaching!)

MORE ON CHILDREN'S THINKING ABOUT TEACHERS' AIMS AND REWARDS

From the above, it is clear that teachers have considerable influence on their pupils. Indeed, children spend much of their time trying to interpret their teacher's behaviour so that they can do their utmost to please them. Paul – a Masters student of mine – recalled a conversation he had overheard. A small group of juniors were examining some work they had just received back from their teacher: they were convinced that those with a dot after their ticks (that is, ' . ') had performed better than those without. The challenge was then to see how many of them could achieve dotted ticks.

On hearing the above tale, two other Masters students immediately came up with examples of how some children will blindly follow their teacher's commands. Alison reported that, on being told to give themselves 'a mark out of ten' some of her pupils literally wrote, 'A mark out of 10'. Similarly two of Colin's pupils, having heard 'Just write Joe Bloggs' next to the space requiring 'Name' wrote 'Joe Bloggs'.

All the above examples came from experienced teachers with few discipline problems in their classes. The techniques for establishing appropriate classroom behaviour will be discussed more fully in Chapter 8.

That being said, it is important to recognise the importance of providing suitable work in the maintenance of good discipline. To return to Mr Brown and Mr Grant: although they had different styles, their pupils knew that there was a purpose to the tasks they were set. Mr Brown's purposes may have been more mundane than Mr Grant's but, nonetheless, his pupils knew what was required of them. Interestingly, a child's reason for doing a task might not be the same as a teacher's. When I explained this notion to a group of teachers, Shona immediately went off to ask her class of 5-year-olds why they thought they learnt about numbers. Their answers were as follows:

So when you're older you know about numbers.

So we know what adding up and taking away is.

To learn how to count to high numbers.

So we know everything when we're grown up.

So when we're older we know all the answers.

When we grow up we'll be really clever and gets lots of money.

So we will learn to count up to 100.

We come to school to learn numbers so when we grow up we'll be clever.

So we know how to count.

To do sums.

When we grow up and our teachers ask us we'll get it right.

'Cos when we come to school we have to learn things.

It did not appear to matter to the children that learning sums, to them, was a means to an end in accomplishing school work rather than something that would be more use to them in later life. They saw it as a job to be done and they did it. (Marshall, 1988, goes so far as to liken this approach to a production-line model where the product is of paramount importance.)

Interestingly, a few days after the above conversation, Shona asked her class to think of their hobbies and to describe how they used numbers as part of that activity. She described the following answers as 'very different and much more productive':

When you're sailing and you want the mast to go over you have to count 1, 2, 3.

Sometimes in the arcade when Dad doesn't know how much money he's got he has to count it to see.

To tell the time.

Sometimes when you go fishing to get the right number for tea.

To see if we have the right number of bridles and saddles.

If you had five horses and one had gone away you would have to count them and go and look for it.

To see how many tennis racquets you have got.

You have to count how many balls go over the net to see who wins.

So you know what to watch on television.

When my grandad watches the horses on the telly you have to see the number of the jockey to know if you have won!

Another teacher – Caroline – says that she has noticed that children often find it hard to say *what they are learning* but they can report *what they are doing* with little difficulty.

At the time of writing, 'key objectives' are very much in vogue and teachers are being encouraged to write on the board what is the main purpose(s) of each session. This may well reduce the likelihood of Caroline's pupils – and others like them – having difficulty in articulating what they are meant to be learning. A worry I have, however, is that it may confine pupils and teachers to the specified aims and constrain them from producing and rewarding a broader range of meaningful and valid work. This concern is shared by another student of mine – Sandy – who is worried that teachers – and perhaps children – 'may not value other learning' in the future. For example, a teacher's stated aim might be that pupils learn their tables by rote. Some might achieve this goal with little difficulty but some children might, instead, gain an understanding of how tables are constructed (for example, $5 \times 3 = 5 + 5 + 5$) which, in my view, should also be commended.

The provision of suitable work does not only mean pupils having a reason for undertaking it. In addition they have to have the ability to accomplish it. This, again, produces a challenge for teacher and pupil alike. The teacher's task is to set work that will be sufficiently interesting to the children and that will be within their range of intellectual capability. If it is too hard children will get bored and, possibly, dispirited. If it is too easy they may also become bored. In a classic study Bennett et al. (1984) observed that even experienced teachers find it hard to match tasks to their pupils' attainment levels: there being a tendency to underestimate high-attaining children and overestimate low attainers. It is not, however, always apparent to a teacher when a pupil has been mismatched to a task, as illustrated by Sam with his mini calculator under the desk (see above) and as discussed by Desforges and Cockburn (1987).

Reading the above, some might be tempted to criticise teachers and their ability to do their job effectively. Such a criticism, however, would demonstrate ignorance and be unduly harsh. Anyone who has tried to teach half a dozen children, let alone 20 or 30, will appreciate that it is a highly demanding task. Indeed, once in the classroom teachers rarely have pause for breath. Even routine sessions move at a 'fast and furious' pace which teachers described as 'relatively normal and containable' (Cockburn, 1986, p. 233). Tackle something new and the pace moves up a gear or two …

YOUR CHALLENGE AS A TEACHER

People learn best if they are well motivated. Our challenge in our quest to be effective educators is to ensure that we provide our pupils with tasks that they find interesting and meaningful. Moreover we, as teachers, should be clear about *why* we are providing these tasks and the *learning* we hope they will initiate. As will be discussed in more detail in the next chapter, the intended learning outcomes may be far broader than simply the acquisition of facts such as 'two plus two equals four'. As responsible educators we must also remember to respond positively to valid and appropriate learning whether it is anticipated or not, for we have tremendous influence over how children learn and their views of themselves as learners. If we discourage them from learning in the primary years we may discourage them for life.

SUMMARY

- Classrooms are very busy environments where teachers and pupils work together for long periods of time.

- Typically learners like to ascertain what their teacher requires of them and act accordingly.

- There is a tendency in some classrooms for teachers and pupils to focus on task completion rather than understanding.

- The development of thinking skills and philosophy in young children provides opportunities for creative teaching which can increase motivation.

- You are intrinsically motivated by a task when you are fascinated by the subject matter and driven to work because of that interest.

- In contrast, extrinsic motivation operates when you work on a task because you are likely to receive some sort of external reward – or punishment – for doing so.

- Teachers generally have a tremendous influence over their pupils and it is important that they provide interesting and meaningful tasks which will encourage specific learning outcomes but which will allow for the unexpected.

ISSUES FOR REFLECTION

- What kind of work motivates you intrinsically?

- When do you do things for extrinsic motivation only? Why?

- How do you learn most effectively?

- How can you more actively involve children in classroom dialogue to nurture their ability to think and problem solve?

- What kinds of activities are likely to incorporate a high degree of intrinsic motivation for pupils and why?

- How do adults fall into the trap of encouraging learning through offering extrinsic rewards? How might this be avoided?

- What are the purposes (from the pupils' perspective) of various kinds of writing tasks they are given in school? Can you give examples with genuine purpose?

Further reading

Desforges, C. (ed.) (1995) *An Introduction to Teaching: Psychological Perspectives*. Oxford: Blackwell. This is a very comprehensive book which includes several highly relevant chapters by experts in motivation and learning.

Fisher, R. (1995) *Teaching Children to Think*. Cheltenham: Stanley Thornes. A thought-provoking and accessible book which considers the nature of thinking and thinking skills.

Fisher, R. (1998) *Teaching Thinking: Philosophical Enquiry in the Classroom*. London: Cassell. An accessible guide to ways of using discussion in the classroom to develop children's thinking, learning and literacy skills.

Quinn, V. (1997) *Critical Thinking in Young Minds*. London: David Fulton. An inspirational book that will encourage creative approaches to your teaching.

Wood, D. (1998) *How Children Think and Learn*. 2nd edition. Oxford: Blackwell. This is a very interesting book which provides considerable insight into children's thinking and learning. It provides the most comprehensive guide to all the major thinkers on children's development.

Chapter 6

Approaches to learning and teaching

Sue Cox

Teaching is personal. Perhaps more than any other profession, it draws on the kind of person you are. The sort of teacher you become will not be about how well you apply a tool kit of techniques or approaches passed on by others, but rather dependent on how you use the personal qualities that are very much your own. In this chapter Sue Cox delves deep. She demonstrates the need for you to develop a broader understanding of the education process and appreciate how people's values influence their approach to teaching. You are asked to consider teaching and learning from a range of different perspectives, and to consider the values and outlook that will help shape the teacher you want to be.

INTRODUCTION

From your experience as a pupil and student you will already know that there is no single answer to the question of what makes a good teacher. If you think about why you have admired particular teachers you will probably come up with a variety of reasons. What they taught you and how they taught you, as well as their personal qualities and characteristics, will, no doubt, come to mind. In this chapter, I intend to focus on the question of 'how' teachers teach and how this is bound up with values. To help clarify this I will explain some of the influences on primary practice, in a historical sense. The chapter as a whole explores the way in which you might develop your own approach to teaching, in order to become a good teacher.

BECOMING A 'GOOD' TEACHER

To some extent, the way in which a teacher teaches is inextricably bound up with what sort of person they are and the kind of thing they are teaching. For instance, my 'best' teacher from my own primary school days was the caring and imaginative Miss T., who was my class teacher when I was 7. One thing I remember is that she taught us about all the interesting plant life in the vicinity of the school, by taking us out into the environment to investigate and observe it. It was because she was a caring kind of person, who had imagination, that she made sure what she taught us was always interesting in itself. But it wasn't only the subject matter which was engaging. It was also the way in which we learned about it, from first-hand experience and through working together with our friends. As well as setting things up in this way, Miss T. excited us by helping us to notice things. She encouraged us to be curious and to ask questions, and was always ready to listen to us.

What a contrast this was with the teacher I had had the year before, who provided us with endless little printed workbooks which we worked through, with hardly an opportunity to talk to the teacher. Likewise, I remember the teacher I had the following year as one who droned on at the front of the class and did not want to hear what her pupils had to say. As well as wanting to emulate the 'good' teachers you have known, you may also have a feeling that you could make a better job of it than some of the less memorable ones! Your own reflections will inevitably reveal that you value certain approaches to teaching more than others.

Making judgements

There is an understandable temptation, when you begin a teacher education course, to believe that you will be provided with a simple 'how to do it' kit that you can put into practice in the classroom. If teaching were as straightforward as this then it would lose much of what makes it infinitely interesting, challenging and worthwhile. Teaching is a complex business in which there are almost endless questions to be asked about what to do and how to do it. It is the fact that there are no simple, incontestable answers to these that makes your 'training' much more than merely acquiring a predetermined set of skills.

There is no straightforward solution because how one will act depends on what one *ought* to do. This takes us into the area of values, which, of course, are always open to debate. In other words, the questions of what and how will inevitably be linked to the larger issue of 'why': why do this rather than that? It is probable that, from your own point of view, some personal, deeply held beliefs or ideas connected to this question about 'aims' or 'ends' will have been part of your motivation for embarking on a career in education.

There are many issues that might be addressed here. There are those about what is worthwhile or important *educationally*. What should children be learning and what are educationally worthwhile ways of doing this? Then again, these kinds of questions are grounded in the larger moral issues of how we should treat other people – in the case of primary teaching, how we should treat children. The decisions that are required, then, are fundamentally ethical ones. It is this that makes teaching professional work. You are not training to be a technician. Considering the questions of how to go about the business of teaching, and deciding to do things one way rather than another, entails making judgements. Furthermore, it is not enough, as a professional, simply to assert that your way is the right way. If your way of doing things is to be professionally valid rather than just a matter of personal whim, then it must be justifiable.

Reflecting on practice

However, the need to address these kinds of issues should not prevent you from getting started on some teaching. After all, we wouldn't be able to *live* if our every action required us to think out beforehand what we should do and why. Since we are all initiated into ways of behaving, from the moment we are born, we are quite able to act appropriately in the course of our daily lives, without this level of reflection. Likewise, when starting out on your training, you will already have enough 'inside knowledge' of teaching to be able to take on the role of a teacher in a classroom. However, whatever we do, in whatever situation, reflects the values – even if we are not aware of them – that we implicitly hold as members of a social or cultural group that does things in particular ways, for particular reasons, in particular contexts. To bring those values into sharper focus we need to question what we do and why. This applies to what we do in the classroom in the same way as it applies to any other of our actions.

This suggests looking at things the other way round. Rather than working out what you ought to do and how to achieve those aims before you start teaching, you can begin to make sense of what you actually do and then develop and improve it. You will be able to participate as a teacher in a classroom when you first go into school, whether you are a student teacher on a Graduate Training Programme, a member of an undergraduate or postgraduate course, or a trainee on a SCITT programme, because you already know about the kinds of things that teachers do, both from your own experience as a learner in educational settings and, perhaps, from having had some kind of work experience in school before embarking on your teacher education programme. You will already have some role models to follow from your previous experience, or you could simply follow the examples of the teachers you are working with. You can also develop your teaching skills by practising what you already know how to do from your own experience. This is a valid and appropriate starting point. However, more will be needed if you are to develop your *professional* abilities.

Following a role model or honing your existing skills, in themselves, will not develop your understanding or your ability to make judgements. Following procedures with no concern for the reasons behind them may be appropriate for a technician, but being a professional demands more than merely doing what you have seen others do, doing what you have been told to do, or doing what you have done before. You need to make sense of what you are doing and to evaluate it.

The sort of questions you might ask yourself to help you to do this include:

- What am I doing? (Describing actions)

- What does it mean? (Interpreting actions)

- What values are implicit? (Analysing actions; identifying assumptions)

- What other interpretations are there? (Questioning interpretations; challenging assumptions)

- What other courses of action might there be? (Questioning actions)

- What alternative value positions might thus be brought into play? (Questioning values)

Learning from experience, then, requires reflecting on what you are doing, becoming aware of things that you do almost unconsciously when you are using your existing 'know-how'. It requires that you look critically and analytically at what might otherwise become a matter of habit or routine. (See also Chapter 9.)

As well as thinking about what you yourself do, you will look at what the children and the class teacher are doing. Do their actions tell you how they understand what is going on? Are there any differences between your own perspectives and those of the class teacher? Do the teacher's decisions differ from those you would make? If there are differences, does this tell you anything about the different kinds of values coming into play? Can you learn about your own practice from reflecting in this way on the practice of others?

CONCEPTIONS OF TEACHING AND LEARNING

As you consider your approach to teaching, and begin to assess the underlying values, it may be useful to ask yourself a fundamental question. Which, of the many and varied ways in which you might act in the classroom, would you *count as teaching*, and why. This might help you to work out whether your actions are educationally worthwhile.

To illustrate what I am saying, it can be helpful to reflect on 'learning' from the point of view of being a learner. This will help to throw light on the idea of teaching, for, if there is one general point that can be made about teaching, it is that it is conceptually connected with learning. We can hardly think of ourselves as teaching unless we at least intend that someone will learn from what we are doing. It can be taken as read that schools exist to help children to learn.

'What is your idea of learning?' When I have asked prospective teachers this question a common response is that learning is acquiring new knowledge – getting to know something that they didn't know before. The role of the teacher in this process is seen as in some way 'transmitting' that knowledge to the learner – 'passing on' knowledge, or 'telling' the learner what they need to know. However, I have then asked these same people to reflect on experiences they have had which have changed them in some important way. It is impossible to do justice here to the range of stories which they have told, but there is space to list some of the ways in which they have gone on to characterise the experience, and these may resonate with experiences of your own.

Some people have suggested that the personal changes occurred as a result of solving a problem, questioning their established ideas or being brought to see something from another point of view. Some had acquired a new skill. Others have recognised that they had been responding to a new challenge, had persevered in the face of difficulty or had collaborated with other people. Yet others had changed as a result of having experienced something first hand or through having time to think and experiment, or had seen new value in what they were doing. For others, the experience had been an emotional one, or one where they had been able to empathise with another person, or had needed to handle failure or insecurity. When I asked whether they would count these as *learning* experiences, they have always affirmed that they would. What is interesting to note is that none of these learning experiences involved 'the acquisition of new knowledge' in the way that they had anticipated. It was rarely the case that a teacher had directly 'transmitted' what the learner had learned. All the learning had occurred in a context that was personally meaningful to the learner.

Learning in classrooms

If we go back to your classroom, where you can observe children and teachers, you may well find them doing things which challenge your initial ideas about teaching and learning. To look at an example, you might go into a classroom where the children are examining a collection of toys from the Victorian era. They are working in a group, sharing their ideas on what these artefacts tell them about the lives of children at that time. As far as you can see the teacher's role is that of joining in the conversation to make observations that encourage the children to notice more features about the toys.

She responds to comments that the children make and she asks questions which encourage them to make deductions. At no time does she appear to tell them directly how children lived in Victorian times. She keeps them focused on the clues that are presented by the artefacts. For instance, she asks them questions about similarities and differences between these toys and their own toys, and they very quickly realise that none of the Victorian toys are made of plastic and none of them are electronic. She prompts them to put forward their own ideas about what this suggests.

Again, imagine going into a Reception classroom to find that the children are playing in an area that has been converted into a shoe shop, with pairs of shoes in boxes, seats for the customers and a till with coins in it. The teacher is joining in the children's play as a customer in the shop. The children are also in role as customers and shop assistants, and the teacher responds to what they say to him. He initiates conversations about which pair of shoes he wants to try and talks about the size he needs and the price he wants to pay. Then again, there might be some children in the outdoor play area of the nursery. The teacher had been throwing and catching balls with them, but now they are all on their own, using balls of different sizes and weight, which the teacher has provided.

In these situations, it might seem that the teachers are not doing their jobs as they do not seem to be 'teaching' in that apparently obvious sense of directly transmitting knowledge. But given that they are competent and professional teachers, who know what they are doing, perhaps there is a wider definition to be given to teaching that would include these actions. Starting by asking what the children are learning and what part the teachers are playing in that, it does appear that there is more to teaching than simply sitting the children down and giving them information.

In the first example here, the teacher is challenging the children to think about the toys as evidence of how people lived in the Victorian era. She could simply tell them – but she wants them to think about how we know about the past; to look at the kind of evidence that is available and to make inferences. These are the kinds of things that historians do to arrive at the facts. Clearly, this teacher thinks it is important for children to understand this *process*, as well as knowing the facts. And again, she doesn't only tell them about what historians do, she lets them experience this for themselves, so they gain first-hand insight into what the process involves. The teacher values children's autonomy and clearly believes that this is an effective way for children to learn, partly because her definition of learning is the kind of expanded one that I discussed above.

In the second example, the teacher, likewise, wants the children to understand what goes on in a shop and how we buy things. The children are not being formally taught that shoes come in different sizes and that coins have value and can be exchanged for other things – rather they are learning this in a context which is meaningful. The teacher lets the children take the lead in their play and participates in it on their terms.

In the third example, the teacher has let the children continue practising throwing and catching the balls on their own, knowing that they need time to master this. She has made it quite challenging by providing a range of different balls. Her actions, in both instances, suggest that she respects and values children's play and, furthermore, sees it as a vehicle for learning.

There are parallels to be drawn with the examples of learning processes I discussed earlier, provided by prospective teachers. The children, here, are facing challenges; solving problems; seeing things differently; finding new ways of thinking about things; experiencing things first hand and having an opportunity to work things out and try things for themselves.

So, while the 'transmission' view of teaching may seem obvious enough, it may well be the kind of commonly held conception that belies the complexity of teaching and learning.

What I hope is becoming clear from all the above examples is that if learning can involve a range of processes, that extend beyond being on the receiving end of knowledge that is 'transmitted' to the learner, this has implications for the way we might see teaching. As well as transmitting information through imparting, instructing, telling and explaining, which might be described as 'didactic' approaches to teaching, there are other ways of helping children to learn. In the above examples of teaching, some children are making deductions from primary sources of evidence; some are learning through playing; others are learning through practising a new skill. The teacher's role is partly one of providing the right kinds of situations and resources to allow this to happen. Children cannot learn to make inferences unless they are given some sources of evidence; nor can they master the skill of ball-throwing without the balls and the space in which to throw them being made available. Children cannot, of course, learn through playing, unless they are given the opportunity to play. Centrally, the teachers' role entails interacting with the children in productive ways within these situations, having conversations with the children, responding to them and asking them questions. The teachers can demonstrate or 'model' *how* to do things they want them to learn, especially when what they want them to learn is a process (such as 'making deductions from evidence' and 'giving change') or a skill (such as throwing a ball).

In contrast, the examples of trainee teachers' learning given earlier show how we can learn from our life experiences – and these are always a very important aspect of our education – which tend to happen randomly. Teachers, on the other hand, take responsibility for making sure that children are provided with specific and worthwhile learning experiences. Moreover, teachers can also ensure that children get the most out of the learning experiences which both life and school may offer, by making sure that they *learn how to learn*. They can ensure that the children encounter and learn from the many and varied processes involved in learning for oneself, some of which were identified in the examples of trainee teachers' learning. Collaborating, co-operating, communicating, responding, questioning, investigating, experimenting, enquiring, exploring, creating, inferring and solving problems are all such processes. Clearly, they all require the involvement of the learner in many more ways than as a receiver of the teacher's word! Again, they demand the involvement of the teacher, interacting with the children in ways that help them understand what these processes involve. Teachers may model these processes, as did the teachers who worked alongside the children interpreting evidence from the past, and playing shoe shops. What is more, if teachers value children's independence and autonomy then part of what they do may be to make provision for children to learn in these ways with their peers or, where it is appropriate, on their own. (There was discussion of 'Nurturing the disposition to learn' in Chapter 3.)

VALUES AND PRIMARY PRACTICE

At this point I want to explore further this relationship between approaches to teaching and the issue of values. The examples given above help to clarify ways of thinking about learning and teaching. They extend the ways in which you might identify what is educationally worthwhile, beyond the transmission model of teaching. If these more broadly based interpretations are given to learning and teaching, then you will be able to consider the value of a wider range of approaches than you might otherwise have done.

One way of understanding teaching approaches is to be aware of the way in which, historically, primary teaching methods have evolved. Changing values in the wider world of education shape what happens in schools and influence the way we see learning and teaching in the classroom. It is useful to see how different ways of approaching learning and teaching are aligned to distinctive ways of looking at children and thinking about education, and how these have influenced developments in primary practice. To make sense of your teaching in today's classrooms and to evaluate it in the ways I have suggested, it is helpful to be aware of the range of approaches, and how these have come about, and to recognise and possibly challenge some of the assumptions that have grown up around it.

Historical developments – changes in educational thinking and policy

During the late 1980s and 1990s there was a period of far-reaching change in primary education. An important turning point at this time was the Education Act 1988, which was arguably the most significant Education Act of the last century and brought about radical changes in educational policy and practice. It was this Act that brought in the National Curriculum. Although it did not legislate on teaching methods, as such, it did bring in a new era in education, which was characterised by centralised control. Wide-ranging initiatives were introduced at the level of central government, which had major implications for approaches to learning and teaching in classrooms.

To go further back in time, the 1988 Act was the result of an educational debate which ran through the 1970s. This had grown out of a mistrust and critique of 'child-centred' education – an approach that prevailed at that time in people's imaginations and in the rhetoric about primary education, if not always in reality. Child-centred, or 'progressive' education became widely accepted following the publication of the Plowden Report in 1967 (CEAC, 1967), but it originated much earlier. A significant move towards the progressive position, for instance, was the Hadow Report of 1931. This declared that 'the curriculum is to be thought of in terms of activity and experience rather than of knowledge to be acquired and facts to be stored' (Board of Education, 1931, p. 93). The values inherent in this way of thinking contrasted markedly with those that underpinned traditional forms of education that were often associated with the late nineteenth century and the early days of compulsory education. The didactic teaching methods of that earlier era were caricatured by Dickens in his novel, *Hard Times*, in which the teacher, Gradgrind, insisted on the rote learning of facts which his charges clearly did not understand. There is not space here to discuss whether this was an accurate representation, but it remains a popular view of Victorian elementary education.

By the 1960s, ways of approaching learning and teaching that conformed to traditional ideas of both children and education were being widely challenged. For instance, the common practice of streaming in primary schools (putting children into different classes according to their ability) had begun to disappear, as it had become apparent that children were being segregated more on the basis of their social class than on their ability. The Plowden Report (CEAC, 1967) embodied a different set of values. Children were no longer to be treated as belonging to a category, but were to be seen as having individual needs. The report made extensive, if not necessarily well argued, recommendations about 'good practice' in primary education that placed the child 'at the heart' of the educational process, and promoted an individualised approach to learning. Knowledge, rather than being seen as a predetermined body of information to be passed on from teacher to child, was seen as the achievement of the individual learner through 'learning by discovery'. The typical view of a 'Plowden' classroom was an informal setting where children worked on individualised tasks, possibly self-chosen, with the teacher interacting with individual children rather than formally teaching the whole class.

The popular conception of this 'progressive' approach was that children were not to be 'told things'. Instead, they were to find out for themselves. This led to a perception of schools as undisciplined places where children were allowed to do as they liked, and it was not long before growing concern about falling educational standards came to a head.

The climate of opinion changed and there was a backlash against 'child-centred progressivism'. The Labour leader James Callaghan in the late 1970s initiated what was sometimes referred to as the 'Great Debate' on education to address these concerns, and the Conservatives took up the cause to raise standards during their period of office throughout the 1980s and 1990s. The call was for a return to more 'traditional' methods – which for the government of the day, implied more formal, 'teacher-directed' approaches.

Famously, John Major announced at the Conservative Party conference in 1991 that 'the progressives have had their say and they have had their day'. A return to the values of the past was seen as the way forward.

Research on approaches to learning and teaching

'Progressive' values became a convenient scapegoat as the cause of low standards (though, whether and in which ways standards were low was a matter of dispute). However, it is questionable whether child-centred approaches had ever been as widely adopted as might have been supposed. The prevalence of child-centred teaching was myth more than fact (Richards, 1999). For instance, the observations from the 'Oracle Project' (Galton et al., 1980), showed that rather than being encouraged to find things out for themselves, 'the opposite was taking place. Children were being told what to do more frequently than under any other form of organisation' (Galton, 1995, p. 18). Galton accounted for this in terms of the increased time which teachers using individualised forms of organisation must spend on providing children with instructions about what to do next and giving information which children needed to complete their tasks.

Galton claimed that what tended to be lacking under this form of informal organisation were certain kinds of interaction that the teacher might have with the child which would develop their ability to reason and to think for themselves. For instance, such interactions as asking challenging questions and giving feedback –

making statements that would stimulate thought and enquiry (what are referred to as 'higher order' interactions). These were not, it transpired, the order of the day as might be expected in a setting where 'discovery learning' was supposedly advocated.

The same sort of findings resulted from the research undertaken by Mortimore et al. (1988). Both Galton's and Mortimore's studies concluded that each individual child generally received very little of the teacher's attention, even when they were constantly interacting with children. The studies showed that interactions were very short and did not really engage the child's thinking. Tizard and Hughes (1984), who carried out research with younger children, likewise found that interactions involving 'intellectual challenge' were, alarmingly, less evident in the classroom than they were in the children's homes before they started going to school. In addition, an important evaluation project of primary education in Leeds carried out by Alexander raised many similar issues. In a book that followed up his report of the project, Alexander (1992) commented 'Teacher–pupil talk was often dominated by the teacher's questions, frequently of a rhetorical, closed or token kind. Questions inviting or encouraging the child to think were much rarer' (p. 51).

Engaging and challenging children is the key

It needs to be noted that the evidence of these classroom-based studies carried out in the 1980s do not in themselves undermine any aims or values. What the research does show is what was actually going on in classrooms. It provided evidence about the particular kinds of teaching that were occurring, revealing that teachers tended not to be challenging children's thinking, as well as they might, to promote learning. In reality, while teachers may have adopted individualised approaches, this was not necessarily creating the kind of child-centredness that might have enhanced children's learning. Some of the practice that was going on did not appear to embody the values that might have been espoused by teachers whose central concern was each individual child's educational interests. Or, maybe, it rested on the mistaken belief, perhaps endorsed by Plowden, that children could somehow extract knowledge from their experience in the absence of constructive interaction with others.

In either case, those who were making generalised criticisms of child-centred practice and who might have looked to this kind of research to confirm their views, were making two incorrect assumptions: first, that teachers were actually engaging in such practice and, second, that the kind of practice that was going on showed that child-centred approaches were wrong in principle. Principles such as respect for children as persons, respect for their autonomy and independence and the overriding principle of fairness which would ensure that every individual would be given the opportunity to fulfil their potential to learn, do not stand or fall on the kind of evidence that became available from the research that was carried out.

On closer analysis, it is clear that the values or aims that might underlie a child-centred approach to learning and teaching, and may indeed be the kind of altruistic and caring concerns that would motivate many people to pursue a career in teaching, cannot be shown to be at fault by these empirical studies in themselves. Such studies may provide information that is useful in other ways, but the question as to whether, for example, it is a worthwhile aim to promote the development of autonomous learners is a matter which can only be settled through ethical debate.

There is reason to believe, then, that the politicians' response to what had been perceived to be a decline in educational standards was a reaction that could not lay claim to being justified by the evidence of research, and overlooked the relationship between values and methods. To explain 'falling standards' by polarising approaches along stereotypical lines and to advocate a wholesale return to a more traditional set of values seemed unhelpful and inappropriate.

To illustrate this point, one of the government's priorities was to instigate a return to more 'whole-class' teaching – which is often associated with traditional, teacher-centred approaches. In contrast with the scenario where the teacher moves around the classroom supporting individuals' learning in response to their needs, the teacher addresses the whole group, usually from the front of the class. But, as Galton (1995) pointed out, the Oracle studies showed that 'it was not in itself class teaching or individualised instruction that made the difference, but *the opportunity that the use of a particular method provided for a teacher to engage in certain types of exchanges with children*' (p. 17, emphasis added). The politicians' retreat to a contrasting sets of assumptions failed to address the need to clarify important educational aims and principles. If it is clear that engaging and challenging children's thinking is the aim, then that will inform the teaching approach. Whilst whole-class situations might promote this kind of teaching, the research on classroom practice does not suggest that it does so exclusively. One explanation for the assumption that it does, is the confusion between forms of organisation and methods of teaching. Whilst an individualised form of organisation might be implicit where children are pursuing their own lines of enquiry, this is not necessarily – as Galton showed – going to produce the level of intellectual engagement and challenge that might be desirable, but similarly, nor is a whole-class approach. This will depend on what else the teacher does. The ways of working described earlier in this chapter, where children were working sometimes independently, sometimes with their peers, with appropriate interaction with the teacher, were effective ways of bringing about learning because the teacher was providing the right levels of engagement and challenge.

The influence of central government

As the concerns about standards developed during the late 1980s and the 1990s and the Conservative politicians moved steadily towards centralised government control (see Lawton, 1994), the autonomy of teachers, as well as learners, decreased. Initially, the government's strategy was to focus particularly on the curriculum. Central control of the curriculum would prevent the perceived abuses of professional autonomy which had apparently resulted in children learning what they liked in school. Even though teaching methods remained (and still remain, in law, at least) in the hands of teachers, they did come under increasing scrutiny. In 1992 the government commissioned an enquiry into classroom organisation and practice (Alexander et al., 1992) and, subsequently, began to direct attention towards teaching methods, perhaps realising that this was the only means of achieving the influence it sought. This trend continued with the change of government in 1997. New Labour introduced the National Literacy and Numeracy Strategies, which provided prescriptive guidance on how to teach in these areas and put considerable pressure on schools to adopt the recommended teaching strategies.

Over the decade, the character of primary classrooms was transformed. Timetables, which had been associated with secondary, rather than primary schools, were introduced, so that subject-focused teaching could take place. Teachers were expected to 'deliver' knowledge through programmes that were predetermined. The National Curriculum was reviewed in 2000, and trimmed down, partly in response to the workload that had been imposed on teachers in their efforts to meet its detailed requirements, but also partly in order to accommodate the new National Strategies. However, detailed, prescriptive QCA schemes of work were developed in all subject areas, which were not statutory, but which were widely adopted by schools to provide coverage of the curriculum.

By this time, it was the norm for lessons (again, formerly a feature of secondary, rather than primary education) to be planned to achieve specific, predetermined objectives. The overriding emphasis was on 'outcomes' as the drive to raise achievement in the statutory tests to meet government targets, and to gain high positions in the 'league tables' and good Ofsted reports, set school against school in competition for pupil numbers. The requirement to raise children's achievement led to more 'targeted' teaching, with official encouragement for teachers to classify children, once more, according to their ability. At the time of writing it is common for teachers to divide their classes into low, average and high achievers, and they are encouraged to do so by Ofsted inspectors. The changes that took place amounted to changes in the whole culture of primary education. As teachers were increasingly held accountable for their pupils' levels of achievement there was a clear shift towards a 'performance culture' promoting the kinds of values that did not sit easily with those of many primary teachers.

As a consequence there has been much talk about 'effective' teaching – of giving priority to 'what works'. But the crucial question, which has become eclipsed by the focus on achieving measurable results, is 'effective in terms of what?' In focusing on raising levels of performance there is a danger of losing sight of the questions around the value of what we are trying to achieve. If we make assumptions about what we are working towards, focusing only on the means of achieving the pre-specified end result and neglecting to examine what aims and values underpin these assumptions, then teaching becomes a technical activity rather than a professional one.

Current developments

There are signs, as the twenty-first century progresses, that values within the wider context are changing. The publication of *Every Child Matters* was an important milestone (DfES, 2004), arising out of an enquiry into a particularly tragic case of child abuse. It resulted in the Children Act 2004 which has provided legislation to integrate the different services available to children across care, health and education, with the aim of protecting children from risk and supporting every child so that they can develop to their full potential. The focus is on developing the services available to children around their needs and there is a requirement to listen to children's views. The impact which the new arrangements and expectations will have on schools may well have an effect on learning and teaching in primary classrooms, perhaps leading to a renewed endorsement of child-centred values and approaches. The theme of 'personalisation' permeates all the government's recent proposals and is one of the key principles of reform in the Five Year Strategy (DfES, 2004a): 'Greater personalisation and choice – with the wishes and needs of children, parents and learners centre-stage' (ibid., p. 7). The Secretary of State asserts that 'the learner is a partner in learning, not a passive recipient' (ibid., p. 5).

The Five Year Strategy also claims that teachers will be given more freedom from top-down control and will be given more autonomy in planning to meet individual needs. Whilst this may signal a return to the kind of autonomy that enables teachers to exercise their professional judgement, and to redefine values and practice in primary classrooms, it will need to be seen in the context of the wider range of reforms that are to occur over the five-year period. At the time of writing, certain developments are beginning to take place. Clearly, a new emphasis on creativity in education was established with the publication of the report of the National Advisory Committee on Creative and Cultural Education (DfEE, 1999d). There is now much talk of creative teaching and creative learning, not just with reference to the creative subjects of the curriculum, but in relation to pedagogy across the whole curriculum. The launch of the Primary Strategy (DfES, 2003) indicated a different kind of message coming from central government, one that encourages teachers to 'lead improvement themselves, through their own professional abilities' (p. 12). However, all this remains within a framework of national testing and league tables, which inevitably creates constraints. Nevertheless, the encouragement to make meaningful links across different areas of the curriculum and to focus on learning how to learn, for example, suggest a renewed concern for the child's perspective rather than a demand for performance for its own sake. Similarly, the recent work on 'Assessment for Learning' (Black, 2003) acknowledges the central place of the formative role of assessment, where assessment of the child's learning is seen as the essential starting point for taking it forward.

Despite this, the continuing focus on target setting, testing and league tables, and initiatives such as the Foundation Stage Profile (introduced in 2002/03 as a statutory requirement to record the achievements of 5-year-olds) still tends to encourage the labelling of children in particular categories. (In school you will become familiar with the 'Level 4' child, for example.) By contrast, recent research projects present striking alternatives. Hart (2004) for example, argues that this kind of classification by ability limits the children's potential to learn, by narrowing the learning experiences offered to different groups of children and imposing limited expectations. The research project, 'Learning Without Limits', shows that there are ways of valuing children other than in terms of their ability, and other ways of approaching learning and teaching. This different kind of vision can arise from the kind of questioning approach to the principles that inform your teaching that I have argued for in this chapter.

To return to my earlier point, it is only through analysis of practice in relation to those larger questions of value (what ought we to do) that we can gain some sense of direction in our teaching – its larger educational aims and moral purpose, and the means to critically evaluate what we do in order to improve it. As someone not only learning to teach, but also becoming professional, these are necessary questions for *you* to address in evaluating what you do and developing your own practice. This discussion of changes in educational thinking, policy and practice should help provide a context for understanding your practice and for making your decisions about the best way to teach.

SUMMARY

What I hope has emerged from this chapter is that approaches to learning and teaching are bound up with values. I have presented some illustrations of ways of looking at learning that go beyond a simplistic 'transmission' model. By providing a historical context, I have shown how influences beyond the classroom can shape teachers' values and practice and how important it is to retain a clear sense of aims and principles. What needs to be recognised is the complexity of the teaching and learning process. To maintain their professionalism teachers must take full account of ends as well as means; of the 'why' as well as the 'how' of their practice.

Having described and interpreted your own teaching approaches, identified the values inherent in them and considered whether these are what you would aspire to as a 'good' teacher, you may need to modify your practice. If you find yourself professionally committed to engaging children's minds to develop their ability to think and reason, if you are to respect them as autonomous, thinking people, with equal rights to have their individual educational needs met, what kinds of decisions for action would you make?

ISSUES FOR REFLECTION

Once you have started on some teaching, and you begin to analyse your practice and that of those around you, you may find that the way you or others do things does not conform to the narrower definitions of teaching and learning, but is, instead, valid in terms of wider definitions. In asking yourself what underlying values it reveals, you will need to avoid those assumptions that can so easily be made, given the context I have described. The range of variables you will need to critically address to gain this sort of insight is very wide, and cannot be fully discussed within this single chapter. However, the following list may be helpful as an indication:

- The kinds of relationships which teachers have with children.

- The kinds of interaction between children and teachers. (What forms of interaction are used and for what purposes.)

- The ways in which children are encouraged to think for themselves, to take risks, to be creative, to learn how to learn, to participate and negotiate; to take responsibility for and control of their own learning.

- The kinds of groups children work in. (For what purposes children are grouped – for example: administrative convenience; collaborative work. Which criteria are used for grouping children and for what purpose – for example: ability; friendship; task; interest; gender.)

- The structure of activities in the classroom. (For example: how and when the children work alone, with each other in groups or with the teacher; the pattern of the day; the pattern of a particular session; the kind of time constraints.)
- The way the learning environment is set up. (For example: how the classroom furniture and equipment is arranged so that particular forms of interaction and activity happen; what resources and learning materials there are and how they are made available for children to learn from them.)
- The structure and content of the curriculum. (For example: whether there are set times for different subjects; whether the children are put into 'sets' for specific subjects, taught by specialist teachers in different curriculum areas or always taught by their class teacher; whether 'cross-curricular' connections are made in the content of what the children learn; whether any of the content of the curriculum is linked to children's own interests or centred around questions which they have asked themselves; whether different children do different activities at the same time or do the same thing at the same time.)

Having described and interpreted your own teaching approaches, identified the values inherent in them and considered whether these are what you would aspire to as a 'good' teacher, you may need to modify your practice. If you find yourself professionally committed to engaging children's minds to develop their ability to think and reason; if you are to respect them as autonomous, thinking people, with equal rights to have their individual educational needs met, what kinds of decisions for action would you make?

Further reading

Fisher, J. (2002) *Starting from the Child*. 2nd edition. Milton Keynes: Open University Press. This book provides both theoretical insights into and practical advice on approaches to learning and teaching that start from the child.

Galton, M., Hargreaves, L., Comber, C., Wall, D. and Pell, A. (1999) *Inside the Primary Classroom 20 Years On*. London: Routledge. This book updates the 'Oracle' research, giving a detailed account of children's experiences of learning and teachers' strategies in the classrooms of the 1990s. It sets its discussion of primary practice in the context of changes in policy over the last 20 years and distinguishes what is actually going on in classrooms from rhetoric. It should provide food for thought in developing your ideas about your own practice and primary pedagogy for the future.

Chapter 7

Classroom skills

Rob Barnes

Giving explanations, asking questions, keeping the pace of learning going – experienced teachers often make teaching look straightforward and easy. It is not long before beginning teachers appreciate the challenges and complexities of the task. Here Rob Barnes gives practical insight into the key skills required to be a successful classroom practitioner, including the use – and abuse – of displays!

TEACHING TO EXPLAIN

'Let me explain. You need to take two thropping turns of the sproggit wheel and dank them carefully in benya. Next you'll need a spaffery-doomer and a whiggin. Fix the whiggin to the spaffery-doomer first or it won't work will it? Got it so far? Good, we'll go to the next stage.'

When I don't understand an explanation the words used might just as well be like these because I am lost. I might be listening to a very confidently delivered explanation. Yet in this teacher's explanation there is no context, sequence or meaning, despite the fact that explaining is one of the basic classroom skills expected of any teacher. Confusing explanations can make pupils agitated, tense and apprehensive. Explanations in subjects like science, ICT and mathematics are particularly prone to confused delivery. They involve concepts and processes which by nature are complex. The best advice I ever had about explaining is that some explanations actually need to be developed and honed until they work. Do not be surprised if you begin your career with only a few skills in this department. Explanations are rarely right for every pupil all the time. Most need practice in the classroom before they work well.

Explanations are effective if they use familiar examples (plenty of them), are humorous if possible and memorable. Here is one I use to explain computer programming, where line by line instructions are needed. This is about choosing from a range of possibilities.

```
IF CheeseOnToast = BIG THEN CHEW = 500
IF CheeseOnToast = MEDIUM THEN CHEW = 250
IF CheeseOnToast = SMALL THEN CHEW = 50
IF CheeseOnToast = NOTHING THEN CHEW = 0
IF CHEW > 0 THEN SWALLOW
END
```

If you understood that, you most likely already have a concept of programming, number and sequence. If not, I would need to build that conceptual framework for you and explain the very exact requirements of computer languages.

From there, the main consideration is probably the sequence of my explanation.

CLASSIC EXPLANATIONS AND TOPIC SHIFT

There are classic explanations an experienced teacher uses, but they have not arisen by chance. Experience may tell you that pizzas or cakes are sliced to illustrate fractions, and the order of grid map-references is remembered by the phrase 'along the corridor and up the stairs'. There are helpful mnemonics like 'i before e except after c' for spelling words like the word 'receive'. Useful as these established reminders and analogies are, successful explaining involves much more. It is often a matter of judging when to break things down into smaller parts, when to stop explaining, when to summarise and when best to set children an activity. Too many ideas in one explanation can block pupils' understanding. Animals can be trained to count numbers up to a maximum of seven, and human beings can probably cope with a similar number of items in one go.

Two common faults when you start teaching are to explain everything at great length or to rush your explanation. One reason why explaining at length can go drastically wrong is through the phenomenon of 'topic shift'. You started by explaining one idea and just as that was being absorbed, shifted the topic to something else so that pupils lost the initial thread. An example would be talking about reading a map, but shifting the topic to details about the scale of the map compared with other maps you want to use. The new topic is certainly related to the old, but the explanation has ended at a much less useful point for map-reading. An obvious remedy is to shorten the explanation and stick to the point. When I first started teaching, the deputy head of the school took me aside and said 'Make sure you keep all your explanations to ten minutes at the most'. That advice might have been a little drastic, ignoring the value of interactive teaching, but it keeps an eye firmly on the boredom factor. Might it not be better, for example, to come back to the second half of your explanation after pupils have done a task which exemplifies the first part? There is something to be said for splitting up your explanation into manageable chunks.

Many pupils are predisposed to think about almost anything other than your explanation as they appear to listen to you. If listening requires more than 'looking mute', it requires the ability to attend imaginatively to the other person's words. You may safely assume that not many children will listen meaningfully unless you are ready to check their understanding.

Remember that you are not explaining to adults, where the style of explanation assumes that they have an adult's experience on which to draw. Children do not give their full attention for very long, unless your explanation can involve them or is closely connected with an activity they know they are about to do. It greatly helps if you keep them on track by continually verifying understanding and refocusing their attention.

COMPLEXITY AND AGE-PHASE

Explanations will vary according to the complexity of the material you want to teach and the context in which you explain it. Will you be explaining to 5-year-olds or 11-year-olds? Will you be explaining the effects of static electricity, or how to milk a goat? There is obviously a difference of level and expectation depending on the age of the pupils and their previous knowledge, the level of conceptual difficulty and the depth of understanding needed. Explanations of cause and effect permeate science teaching, while art or music require something more aesthetically driven. There is a difference between asking a pupil to explain why a steel-built boat will float and what is the answer to finding 'two-fifths of 60'. If a teacher says 'Explain why the Vikings invaded Britain' this may be explanation as revision, logical conclusion or inspired guesswork. Some explanations are also given to clear up misunderstandings, such as 'Can you explain again how to do this maths problem?', while others might concern new material, such as 'I'm going to explain how we use our school visit to find out about the Victorians'.

Fortunately it is not necessary to know *all the time* whether your explanation concerns a concept, such as 'evaporation', a procedure, such as converting decimals to fractions, or a process, such as how a washing machine works. Most of your explanations will work if you consider the following features:

- what the children already know

- what they do not know

- what they might reasonably guess or deduce

- where best to start

- which examples might prove useful, including visual aids

- how much explanation to give them at a time.

I headed this list with 'what the children already know' because this is most likely to nudge you away from the fault of talking *at* children rather than explaining *with* them. As Wragg and Brown (1993) put it, finding out what they know 'helps with choice of a language register'. You are more likely to hit the right level of explanation by picking up on the language children use when they try to explain with you. You will find yourself clarifying words, stepping back from your prepared explanation and more easily adapting yourself to the situation. You are also more likely to summarise the explanation so far. This, in itself, can be done by you or it might be done through checking pupils' understanding; for example, by asking 'Who can tell me what we know about evaporation so far?'

Bite-sized and engaging explanations

Experience and professional judgement count when it comes to managing questions, summaries and ideas children offer. For example, a pupil's faltering summary may simply add to the confusion, or be so long-winded and hesitant that you lose the attention of the remaining children. You may find that some children have already grasped the explanation and are bored waiting for the others. You may have enthusiastically taken up what they already know and become side-tracked. This is without taking account of the pupils who may false-foot your explanation by interrupting or making irrelevant observations. All of which points to the need to keep explanations structured and suitably bite-sized. The ten-minute maximum applies until you are more confident in your ability to explain. If in doubt, cut the detail and keep the explanation short. Concentrate on the sequence of ideas which comprise your explanation, not just the detail within each part.

There is a further dimension of explaining to consider, which is the extent to which you engage pupils' minds. Such phrases as 'Imagine this ammonite at the bottom of the sea', 'Imagine what it feels like to be lost in a forest' can trigger the imagination. Problems can also engage the mind, such as 'If I have ten marbles and I give 20 per cent to David, how many have I got left?', and stories, such as, 'There once was a creaky house in a creaky town called ... ' or 'I remember decorating the biggest chocolate cake you ever saw in your life ... '. A visual aid accompanied by a story and questions is also a useful way to put your explanation across. Similarly, a practical demonstration in science or mathematics can engage minds if you use directive language (see Chapter 8). Usually these entertaining parts of your explanation need to be followed up by making clear the point you are trying to make. Even though explanations often come at the start of a lesson, keep your mind on what you want to leave as an impression at the end.

ANALOGIES

Some explanations are rather abstract, such as trying to explain how electricity flows round a circuit. You may, for example, use the analogy of ping-pong balls to represent electrons or water flowing along a stream to represent the direction in which energy flows. These mental images are useful so long as you make it clear they are examples. If you use the analogy of an orange to explain that the Earth's crust is similar to the thickness of orange peel, you do not want children to believe there are enormous pips at the Earth's core. Most analogies fail when closely examined, so you will need to practise using them over time to see if they work. Examples and analogies you use are there to support explanations of *something*, and are rarely self-explanatory. How I wish I could remember that more often.

Analogies are often necessary to explain features of technology and science. There are fewer and fewer pieces of equipment which can be taken apart to see how they work. Many use microchips and computer circuitry so what they do is far from obvious. If you take a mobile phone apart, there is little to show what is going on inside. The best you might manage is to draw a diagram using symbols and pictures to show text messages travelling through space. Remember, though, that you may be the only person who understands your analogy, so you will need to invite feedback from pupils to check they grasped the essentials. Checking out your pupils' understanding in this way is also important because children have the unerring tendency to take in the details of the illustration you use whilst missing the point of the intended learning that is being illustrated!

QUESTIONING SKILLS

Asked what he wished he had learned at school, one of my colleagues replied 'I wish I had learned how to ask questions'. Questioning can be intimidating. Some of your pupils are shy or dislike being in the public eye. Answering can be a lonely experience for pupils unused to doing so, and an unrewarding experience for those pupils whose answers are frequently rejected. Teachers' questions often invite the same volunteers and exclude the shy, uninvolved or lazy pupils who rely on their classmates to provide answers. In school, children learn two unfortunate rules of questioning, even though these are assumptions on their part:

⬤   If an adult asks the same question again, then the answer I gave was wrong.

⬤   The teacher already knows the answer.

One way to break down these assumptions is to make sure that there are conscripts answering as well as enthusiastic volunteers. If you want to create a climate of enquiry, you will need to establish by your responses and actions that more than one answer is wanted. Instead of a 'hands-up' volunteering approach, there is a 'hands-down' one where you ask children by name to give their answer. You might begin by asking 'Steven, see if you can remember the freezing point of water' (implied question). This can be a good opportunity to involve more pupils by asking 'Sarah, do you think that's true?' 'What do you think David?' In each case the style of questioning is to invite pupils by name to involve them. A further refinement is to ask a much more flexible question such as 'Steven, what's your explanation of how water freezes?' or 'Kirstie, what would stop water freezing?'

The dimensions of this involve strategies you are likely to choose intuitively, changing direction moment by moment as you question:

⬤   Do I respond to volunteers?

⬤   Do I ask conscripts by name?

⬤   Do I ask different questions of as many different pupils as possible?

⬤   Do I ask the same question of a few pupils?

⬤   Do I ask for clarification from the same pupil?

⬤   Do I ask for further information, so that answers are comprehensive?

The decisions you make will depend on the context and you can only work intuitively, hoping that you judged the situation well. Some trainee teachers and newly qualified teachers (NQTs) are trapped within a personal style of 'maximum questions to maximum number of pupils', forgetting that shared understanding can be a bonus. It may be more important to follow up answers with another question to the same pupil or simply ask others if they have another view because it illuminates understanding for the majority who are listening.

You probably know that 'closed' questions are those regarded as having only one possible answer. An example is to ask 'How many legs has a spider?', or 'Is it true that London is the capital city of England?' 'Open' questions are those to which there are several acceptable answers, such as 'Why does the weather change?' A useful tip here is to try to turn your questions into 'How?' and 'Why?' For example, as a teacher you might ask yourself, 'Did the pupils understand my explanation?' The answer is inevitably going to be that some understood very well and some did not. An improvement is to ask yourself '*How* well did pupils understand my explanation' or '*Why* might they not understand that part of my explanation?' 'How?' and 'Why?' are more likely to be tougher questions concerning the quality of teaching and learning. 'How?' questions imply 'To what extent?' and 'Why?' questions imply 'For what reasons?', often leading to deeper or more extensive answers.

The importance of an apparently simple question is determined by its context. For example, you would need to know the context in which to understand Hamlet's line, 'To be or not to be? That is the question.' There are more obvious classroom examples of context-dependent questions. A question such as 'What food did Frank eat?' could easily refer to a story children are reading. However, the same question might actually refer to a detailed database about healthy eating (see Chapter 15). If it did, then considerable learning is involved in answering this question because the food data must first be accessed. Questions such as 'Which foods are salty?', 'Which foods are eaten raw?' or 'What percentage of the class prefers apples?' connect with other areas of learning. You may find yourself teaching mathematics and computing at the same time as discussing science. As an experienced teacher, you will devise questions that move learning forward, not just questions that check understanding and memory.

PERSON-CENTRED QUESTIONING AND PRAISE

Although some questions have right answers, many do not. There is a questioning style called 'person-centred' which is different from a style of 'teacher-centred' questions. A 'person-centred' approach has the aim of asking 'What do *you* think Kirstie?', 'Do *you* think that Peter?' rather than 'What's the answer to … ?' A teacher-centred question is 'What is the main reason why the heat is lost from buildings in winter?' and a person-centred version of this is 'Why do *you* think heat is lost from buildings, John?' Locked into a teacher-centred approach there is sometimes a tendency for teachers to ask a question and partly answer it, or pose it in such a way that only one correct answer will do. If you use a person-centred approach, things are different because initially there are no clues and sometimes no praise that might give the game away. Ask for as much information as you can without saying if the answer is good, bad or something between these.

If you want your questioning to grind to a halt, then give praise too early or keep on rephrasing the question. Praise can sometimes alienate pupils because every response is being judged by the praise it receives. 'Excellent answer, Charlene' sets a benchmark others may not reach, so you may be better off collecting answers without implying value judgements along the way. What are you going to say if the answer is less than excellent? Praise, when you give it, is better given for effort and for having the courage to try an answer, as in 'Well done, Charlene, now we're getting some answers'. The error of rephrasing the question is where you asked a question but, before children had a chance to answer, you rephrased it to make it clear (so you believed). If you rephrase, or give too much help with answers, you will probably shift the topic. You thought you asked one question, but you really asked three slightly different ones.

HANDING OVER TO CHILDREN

It would be courageous of you to hand over the questioning to children and there are occasions when you will. When you are in control of questioning, you can decide when to move on and stop taking answers. Teachers do this because it seems an efficient use of time, one more likely to avoid irrelevant answers and fruitless guesswork. Remember though, that children's fruitless guessing can also be the result of teachers' fruitless questioning, which is asking questions to which children could not possibly know any of the answers. Ask yourself, 'Can my pupils *really* be expected to guess the answers to this question? If not, I will need to explain.' I once listened to a teacher trying to find out if 8-year-olds already knew what an ode was in poetry writing. Instead of recognising that her children were clueless, she persisted and the nearest definition we arrived at was 'a bad smell'. Children need some basis on which to answer.

Children are easily side-tracked. When pupils volunteer questions themselves they are just as likely to ask about their own concerns, such as 'Have we nearly finished?', as they are about the topic of study. One of the strongest arguments for organising children into small working groups, such as in science investigations, is that they can learn to ask each other questions and devise further questions for their teacher. They will not usually manage this without some help in formulating useful questions, but the experience is well worth the effort. Like you, they will need to have some idea about 'open' and 'closed' questions, fairness and validity in answers.

MAINTAINING PACE, VALUING WORK

A very good reason for keeping explanations and questions short is so that you can maintain the pace. If you keep back part of your explanation, you can choose another part of the lesson to stop the children and take them further on. Sessions you plan need some variety in terms of how long children sit and listen, involve themselves actively, write, plan, discuss and review their work. Although the pace of teaching and learning cannot be adequately described in a book, there are certain obvious features that can help you. Teaching which has pace often sounds brisk and businesslike. The teacher leads, rather than follows whatever pace the pupils decide to set themselves. There is just a hint of urgency in the voice and low tolerance of pupils' inattention during explanations. The content is not rushed, but neither is it slowly dragged out so that pupils lose interest.

When you plan with 'pace' in mind, remember not to link this too closely with being an entertainer or using 'pace' to control the class. You are not trying to set a hectic game-show pace which you cannot sustain. In Chapter 8, I mention that you can introduce 'settling time' and 'concentration time' into your teaching. Pace is sometimes a question of talking up the level of concentration and making it clear that there are realistic deadlines and targets. By all means make your lessons interesting, but remember pupils need to understand what you and they are doing. In television programmes, camera shots change on average every 20 seconds. Try competing with that and you will burn yourself out in no time. Sometimes work and life are not full of pace. One of the worst messages you can transmit is that learning is *always* interesting, fast-paced and entertaining. If you do, your class will expect you to fulfil these expectations.

One of your skills as a teacher is to try to find interesting ways to teach dull information and processes. Rather than go for fast, bright and breezy, question-and-answer teaching, you may need to aim gradually to increase concentration levels. A higher level of concentration can often help to transform dull material and hard work so that there is a sense of achievement despite the difficulties. Concentration needs effort and you can achieve high levels simply by emphasising the need for quiet sustained effort. Lower the volume of your voice and try to shut out extraneous sounds until you can almost 'feel' the atmosphere of concentration.

STARTING AND ENDING LESSONS

Starting a lesson well is a combination of both a 'selling' and management skill. Few trainee teachers or NQTs can begin a lesson well without giving attention to planning (see Chapter 11). You may discover that you need to plan in detail until you feel not only confident but more interested in teaching the subject matter to pupils. The sequence of a practical good start can then be summarised on something the size of a yellow stick-it label. You need a checklist of the sequence of preplanned items, something short enough to remember and flexible enough to take account of pupils' responses. Assuming that you have gained the attention of the class (see Chapter 8), you need first to involve pupils. For some teachers, a good start begins with a visual aid or collection of objects. For others a good start is a matter of intriguing the pupils with problems, such as 'I wonder why castles have no windows at the bottom and large ones at the top'. Good starts also sell the topic by explaining how worthwhile the learning is. 'We need to know this because … ', and 'We can get better at doing this … ' help to point out the skills and knowledge on offer.

Many pupils can drift through lessons with no idea why they are doing things. Good starts challenge pupils on the basis that if their skills are high and the challenge high there is less chance of apathy. Low challenges and high skills are a poor combination if you want to create a good start to lessons. A good start is one where you know what you want to teach and judge exactly the best way in which you can give just enough challenge to motivate your pupils. No starting point is exactly the same, but the following is a checklist:

- Get the fullest possible attention and eye contact.

- Check you have everyone still with you. Check again.

- Avoid simply announcing what you are going to do (today we're looking at the Viking invasions). Intrigue and challenge instead.

- Sound businesslike as you introduce the session (choosing from a variety of starts such as questions, problem-setting, visual aids or practical demonstration).

- Check again that pupils are still involved, especially if their classmates are answering questions and offering ideas.

- Keep explanations short until you are more skilled at summarising.

Good endings are those which sharpen the lesson content and value what has been achieved. Given that lessons can often deteriorate rapidly, good endings are far harder to achieve than good starts. Even though summarising and giving feedback to pupils can be difficult to do, there is something to be said for creating the habit of a specific timing and style to the finish of lessons. I once used the last ten minutes of a lesson as a really important time for checking that the mathematics children were doing was accurate. Unfortunately a number of children 'corrected' errors that they thought existed, actually reducing the number of correct answers in their enthusiasm to correct as much as possible. I did not abandon the practice, but decided to refine it, rightly believing that it would work in the end.

DEFERRED ENDINGS AND REVISION

You may not always manage good endings to lessons, but that can still be remedied later on. When all children can think of is the lunch they are about to eat, they are in no mood to review the lesson in detail. A good ending for you might be to clear up and ensure pupils are on time for their lunch break. The reality is that a good end to a lesson might actually become the start to the next one, especially if there is a gap of time between the two. The ending of your last lesson might actually be deferred as you start the next one by summarising the content of what was just learned. Praise at the start of a lesson can also be a deferred part of the previous lesson and in itself a motivator for the next session.

My favourite classroom skill is the development of deferred endings by which you can sneak revision into another activity. This is because I see teaching as building on previous knowledge and understanding, which is why I think that pupils need to revise, review and revisit what they learn and understand. How else can you develop formative assessment (assessment which feeds back into teaching)? Overtly you can spend five minutes revising and tell pupils that is what they are doing. An example of sneaky revision would be to point out punctuation marks in the midst of a history text, or the science of forces in the life of Guy Fawkes. Better still, plan your teaching so that you can include a reference to something recently taught. You are trying to be streetwise, maintaining the pace of the whole year by revising 'the story so far' and developing new questions. You revise if you display pupils' work and talk about it. One of the advantages of being a primary school teacher is that you can refer to other subjects, stop and create an interlude, celebrate achievements, run a one-minute quiz or develop a summary of understanding. Reminding and revising can comprise 30-second sound bites for what may be, for some pupils, a lifetime's understanding.

BOARDWORK

Boardwork falls into two main categories. One is that of work prepared before pupils arrive and the other is work generated during an explanation or activity. Many UK schools now use interactive whiteboards, so prepared boardwork may be on a laptop computer and the display be a data projector. I have seen trainee teachers and NQTs give an excellent summary from points listed on a whiteboard during the session they taught. One of the best uses to which boardwork can be put is to act as a record of your teaching. This is easy to achieve using an interactive whiteboard because images and notes can be saved electronically. Try to see if you can to list points, even if your mind has occasional blanks regarding the spelling of some words. If you have already created summaries on a board you can easily embellish these at the end of a lesson by using a different coloured marker or handing one to a pupil to underline points that are important.

Clearly written work on a white or black board is actually a model for pupils. Despite interactive whiteboards, there is still a place for using good quality handwriting on a more conventional board. It also reveals a great deal to anyone else who sees what you wrote. This may come as a shock to you if your personal handwriting is not a very good model for pupils to emulate. You may not even know how difficult it is to read what you just wrote. Very young children can struggle with letter shapes and will not cope with much deviation from an acceptable standard of letter-formation. If your handwriting slopes on the board in several directions as you write, or letter-shapes are hard to decipher, there are some possible remedies. You can of course lightly pencil guide lines on a board, but you are far better off practising keeping your eye on the top edge of the board as you begin to write. Use the top edge as a sightline rather than standing so close to the board that you cannot see its edges. A further device is to make a special effort to write the letters 'a', 'o', 'b', 'd', 'g', 'p' and 'q' more like circles with added lines. Keeping letter shapes rounded can slow your board-writing so it remains legible. A number of trainee teachers and NQTs make letter shapes illegible because they take little trouble to see what letters actually look like in the first place. This observation of shapes is sometimes more a case of joining lines within a letter than it is of joining letters together. A common fault, for example, is to have written a word such as 'down' so it looks like 'clown' because the letter 'd' has gaps in its circle. There will be pupils reading your writing from quite a distance, so try to avoid leaving gaps.

The technical side of lettering can be learned if you invite feedback from staff and it is as well to assume that it needs refining anyway. Like many teaching techniques, you will achieve clear handwriting more quickly by trying to teach your pupils how to produce good quality handwriting themselves. The fact that you attempt to teach them to write clearly can have a salutary effect on your own technique as you take your courage in both hands and act as an exemplar.

DISPLAY

One of the main reasons for producing a display of work is that it presents work in a valued context. Display values what has been achieved, reminds as well as celebrates. Many aspects of work that teachers take for granted, parents do not, so a simple label can be very revealing. Labels and titling can be statements, such as 'Data handling', or they can ask a question, such as 'Which pupils have the fastest heart rate during exercise?'

The relationship between various pieces of work and the space they occupy can affect the final impact of the display and much can be done to make work look special, simply by the position you give it on a display board. Occasionally, however, the mechanics of display are quite out of hand, double, triple and quadruple mounting of work being a major feature. Work looks better mounted but triple-mounted work is really quite unnecessary. Knowing where to place the work within a display is just as important as creating an elaborate border around it.

A common problem in creating a display

In their enthusiasm for display, many teachers put up far too much work in the space they have available. An obvious and understandable reason for this is to try to include work from most of the class without worrying too much about overcrowding the exhibition. You can get round the inevitable chaotic appearance to some extent by careful arrangement of items into well-balanced groups. Yet some choice is necessary and a compromise can be that you decide to display all work from a class project on one wall and use the others for much longer-term displays where you select individual items. Less work can have greater impact. Allow plenty of breathing space around work or objects displayed (a minimum of 50 mm) if they are to be seen to the best effect. The space needed is rather like the space we need between ourselves and someone else in order to carry on a conversation. We need space in which to focus our vision. An overcrowded display board does little for the eye.

Displays which include the original source material as well as the work from which it has grown have considerable impact. An example would be a disused wasp's nest or a honeycomb and the models and drawings made around that topic. We can see what the inspiration was and how inventive the outcomes were. By contrast, displaying two-dimensional work is sometimes like doing a jigsaw. Two alternative arrangements are to consider a symmetrical arrangement (Figure 7.1) or one where work is in vertical columns (Figure 7.2).

Work placed on the outside edges of the display board needs to be considered before that in the middle. Where possible, some attempt should be made to place the top (trimmed) edges of work so that they create a level line to the display. Similarly the bottom edges can be aligned. Alternatively the work can be organised in a symmetrical pattern. A sense of balance is the overall aim. For this reason it is essential not to rely on scissors to trim work. A trimmer or guillotine is necessary because the work can look square when it is being prepared but prove not to be when the whole display has been arranged on a wall.

If work is mounted (for example, on black paper) the margin all the way round generally needs to be about 20 mm. Coloured mounting paper occasionally detracts from the work as does wallpaper especially if it has a strong pattern. Once a piece of work has been put up on a board it needs about 50 mm of space around itself and its neighbour to allow it to be easily seen. Obviously this amount of space will be exceeded for the purposes of balance but is a rough guide to establishing visual 'breathing space' within a display. Headings and questions need a good margin

Figure 7.1   Symmetry

Figure 7.2   Aligned columns

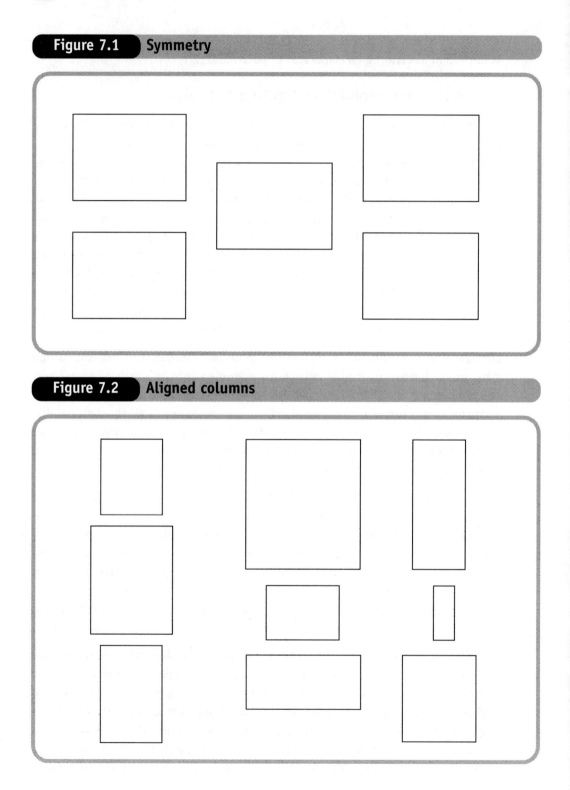

around them to avoid them looking cramped. As much as half the height of the letter is a guide for the margin around a title or label. Paper can always be trimmed off afterwards if the margins surrounding headings are too large.

FEEDBACK AS A CLASSROOM SKILL

Display in itself is a form of feedback for you and other teachers about the work produced. More commonly you can think of using feedback as a way of improving understanding. Feedback, whether verbal, visual or written, often requires prior assessment (see Chapter 10). During a lesson, you can be skilled in using simple verbal and written feedback and gaining it from pupils. Key example questions and requests are:

- What part do you find difficult to understand? (Do not accept an answer such as 'All of it!')

- Which part would it be worth looking at again?

- Talk me through what you're doing.

- If you're really confused, I need to know so I can help. Tell me about it.

Feedback can be expected from discussion and written work (see Chapter 8 concerning 'feedback expectancy'). Simple written feedback from pupils can also be in the form of self-assessments. Older children, for example, can fill in 'help-slips' which are photocopied slips of paper entitled 'I need help with … '. Pupils fill these in and post them in a tin which has a slot in it. I have used these with 8-year-old children and they liked them because they knew that I would try to follow up the misunderstandings they had.

Increasingly, computer programs can provide children and teachers with feedback. A computer maths quiz, for example, can reveal those pupils who have most difficulty. Some programs ask pupils to log in with their name and automatically give them feedback on their progress. As a teacher you are trying to find responses to pupils' feedback that will move them forward and make them feel valued. Tempting though it is to respond to feedback by suggesting practical improvements, do take the time to encourage and praise first.

In some cases, you need to take the trouble to praise and then shut up altogether. There are times when pupils do not benefit from being told what next needs improving because it diminishes the praise you just gave them. Explaining, questioning, maintaining pace and valuing work make teaching not only a blend of skills, but a question of good judgement about when to use them. The experienced teacher is actually a connoisseur in the classroom and can make all these skills look easy to employ. Connoisseurship develops as a result of trying things out with children, but only if you are prepared to take a few risks and fall flat on your face. If you have chosen to work with children, you stand a good chance of developing connoisseurship more quickly than you ever imagined possible.

SUMMARY

- Explanations are effective if they use familiar examples.

- There is a lot to be said for splitting up your explanation into manageable chunks.

- Watch out for 'topic shift' in your explanation.

- Explanations vary according to the complexity of the material you want to teach.

- Examples are rarely self-explanatory. They explain *something* so make that clear.

- Establish by your responses and actions that you may want more than one answer.

- Ask for as much information as you can without saying if the answer is good, bad or something in between.

- You may have inadvertently taught pupils that if they wait long enough, you will answer your own questions.

- Take opportunities to remind and revise within other subjects.

ISSUES FOR REFLECTION

- Observe three teachers' start sessions. What are the similarities? What are the differences? Which strategies worked best? Why do you think that might be the case?

- Think about an explanation you have given in school recently. How might you check whether the children understood it? If you had to give the same explanation again, how might you improve on your earlier performance?

- What classroom skills do you think you will find relatively easy? Which ones might be more challenging? What strategies do you have for building your confidence and developing your teaching skills?

- Think about an occasion when you were not on the same wavelength as someone else – be it a friend, partner, parent, child, colleague. What do you think were the contributing factors to the lack of communication? What did you do – or what might you have done – to break through that impasse?

Further reading

Kyriacou, C. (1991) *Essential Teaching Skills*. Hemel Hempstead: Simon and Schuster Education. Just what the title says. A general classroom handbook covering many useful topics.

Wragg, E.C. and Brown, G. (1993) *Explaining*. London: Routledge. More a booklet than a book – full of exercises to make you think about the topic.

Wragg, E.C. and Brown, G. (1993) *Questioning*. London: Routledge. Similarly, a booklet full of exercises to make you think about the topic.

Chapter 8

Behaviour management and positive ethos

Rob Barnes

Behaviour in the classroom – source of fear and foreboding for the beginning teacher! Well, it does not have to be like this. Here, Rob Barnes paints a comprehensive picture of the positive classroom. He gives a wealth of insight into why children misbehave and describes some tried and tested strategies which can be adopted. Key messages emerge about the need for an overall approach which focuses on your positive relationship with children and your high expectations of them.

INTRODUCTION

'You won't like me. I'm a nuisance.' That was how I was greeted by a boy on my very first teaching practice. First encounters of that kind can make you feel threatened, especially if so far in your life you have not been put to the test by a child. Fortunately, managing a class involves a number of well-tried techniques and attitudes that can be learned. It takes some trainee teachers longer than others, and many experienced teachers will tell you that they still have their moments of difficulty. The most effective of them have discovered that they get much further by remaining rewarding to be with, rather than drifting into nagging, becoming a military dictator or a sarcastic cynic. This takes some doing because you need to be firm and not tolerate bad behaviour while encouraging and praising pupils, and at best inspiring them to produce work of quality. You may find that outwardly you are relaxed and in control, while inwardly at times your emotions are about to reach boiling point. All genuinely positive comments can desert you just when they would be most effective. Rather than controlling pupil behaviour it actually begins to control you. Your smiles begin to look more like sneers and the tone of your voice changes. This is exactly the moment to fall back on sound techniques and established classroom rules to survive, otherwise you may feel you are sitting on a keg of dynamite just waiting for the explosion.

The main change during your early experience of teaching is from a stage where you respond to pupils' behaviour, to a point where you more strongly take the initiative. You become better at seeing their attempts to torpedo your session and quickly involve them in work despite themselves. Most likely the pace of your sessions become better and you have a better understanding of how not to be sucked into their every possible request and demand.

You cannot do this at first because it takes time to discover the many ways in which pupils say and do things. Children can sound friendly when they are really being cheeky and you may not know the difference when you begin teaching. You may wonder why experienced teachers can seem rather hard on their pupils. They know that if they deal with small problems early, they will have fewer serious difficulties. As soon as you possibly can, develop a teaching style where you are active, rather than passive, determined and quietly insistent, rather than pleasantly tolerant of behaviour which adversely affects pupils' ability to learn.

The best pupil discipline is 'self-discipline', and you will find this a useful longer-term management goal. One of the anomalies of teaching is that you need to manage your class yet encourage them positively to develop the social skills to do most of the managing without you. Four pieces of survival advice helped me when I started as a teacher:

- Make sure your teaching is well prepared.

- Don't overreact to bad behaviour.

- When in doubt focus on work to be done, rather than on bad behaviour.

- Get involved in pupil clubs, football, netball or anything that helps you to be seen in a positive light by your pupils.

Some of the ideas which follow need translating for the age range of pupils you are teaching.

THE FIRST VISIT TO A SCHOOL

When you arrive at a school for the very first time, children are naturally curious about you. This is true however experienced you are, though by the time you are an NQT you have learned what to expect. Even if you want to appear confident it is usual to feel quite the opposite. If you have been invited to the school as a trainee to observe, there are still ways to make a good impression rather than be like a cardboard cut-out. Few teachers are going to take you aside and tell you what to do, so try to involve yourself from the start. Offer to help teachers and start talking with children, showing a genuine interest in their work. If you are a real beginner, talk to teachers concerning your observations about teaching and ask in particular what they do with a new class in September. They may not remember they have a share in setting your programme, but you are likely to want to ask about how lessons start and finish, how teachers get attention and how they keep things going. Be ready for experienced teachers' notorious 'gallows' humour, by the way, as they gently tease you about the stresses of teaching.

Before you arrive at the school, be clear about what you are meant to do. You may think you are there only to observe, but this does not mean hovering silently in classrooms and corridors. Headteachers vary in their preferences, but I have met many who were impressed by the fact you said 'Good morning' and introduced yourself before they asked what you were doing on the premises. Ask questions, but pick your moment. A busy teacher or headteacher does not want to hear the stream of your consciousness including a description of your journey to the school. You will need to find out where equipment is kept, how the school behaviour policy works and what classroom rules there are. It is also worth arriving with *something* you could do with children (such as read a story) if the teacher is called away for a few minutes or there's a spare five minutes. No teacher wants a passive trainee whose idea of action is to be like a vacuum cleaner sucking up information. Rather than hover over individual children, divide your observation clearly between writing things down and becoming involved in talking with groups and individuals. You do not want to stop pupils working, but you still need to establish a presence in the classroom by giving something back. If you fail to establish a presence, you will become like wallpaper in the room.

Sooner or later comes the moment for your very first talk with pupils. Some of them will be wary of you and some ready to try out their brand of minor cheekiness to see what you will do. This can be one of the most difficult moments because you probably want to be liked, yet have heard that it may be wiser not to smile until Easter. On your first visit, keep most of the conversation with pupils to the topic of their work because it is a relatively safe area of discussion. Show enthusiasm for what pupils are doing, but deflect personal questions as best you can ('Are you married?', 'Are those your own teeth?'). Your main aim is to become used to sounding professional, as opposed to behaving like an older brother or sister. It will be some time before you can pitch this exactly right, so far better at this early stage to err on the side of caution and keep steering conversation towards work. You will look and sound like a teacher if you do what teachers frequently do. Teachers spend most of their day talking about school work and pupils expect them to do just that.

GETTING THE PUPILS' ATTENTION

When you listen to the radio, you can probably do many other tasks at the same time, whereas television demands eye contact. If you give only passing attention to the television, you will inevitably look away, unless you hear something which signals that you need to look again. Eye contact from pupils might at worst be a glazed look of inattention, but more likely it indicates some level of involvement. It is not a foolproof signal they are attending, but more convincing than the backs of their heads.

The most common problems I see in beginning teachers concern signalling effectively that they want attention, then making sure they have eye contact with their pupils before continuing. I have listened to trainees complain that it is impossible to get pupils to turn towards a whiteboard or to give full attention. If you really want to be effective, insist on full attention from the very first moment you stand in front of a class, however long it takes. Why would you want that? When you explain, or ask questions, your facial expression is very important, as is your tone of voice. If there is no eye contact, then having a good rapport with your pupils is almost impossible. Facial expression, a raised eyebrow or a smile communicate with your pupils, and no pupil is going to engage with these unless they are looking at you. You may not always achieve 100 per cent eye contact, but there are known bad habits pupils will display if you ask them to listen without looking.

At worst, pupils sit with their backs to the teacher, chatter while the teacher is speaking and fidget with equipment in their hands. Sometimes their idea of paying attention is a half-turn towards the teacher or board. The general 'under-chatter' then becomes accepted with the teacher's voice loud enough to drown it out. Children fiddle with pencils, paper and anything else you care to imagine. One pupil might even be seen rearranging another's hairstyle. Another has wandered over to another part of the room for no good reason. Two more are playing a subversive touch game of 'You're IT' and another is constructing an abstract piece of origami with scrap paper. Contrast this with pupils who, in the first few seconds of your teaching, realised you meant business and were not prepared to let them continue with their private agenda of non-attention.

GIVING A CLEAR SIGNAL

The first stage in getting attention is to give a very clear signal that pupils can hear. Many trainee teachers are quite unused to a public style of speaking to a large group and are surprised to hear the words come out of their mouth. If the signal is your own voice, then have a consistent strong way of stopping the class or group. Stand in one place and keep still, because pupils find it very difficult to listen to someone who is walking round the classroom as they give instructions. Give a clear, loud signal, wait and drop the volume of your voice. How does this work in practice? Imagine a typical situation where there is some general class chatter going on, too loud for the teacher to be heard using a normal speaking voice. One teacher's method of signalling is to shout 'Thank you', another might be 'Everybody stop. Things down, and look this way.' Another claps his hands three times and says 'Looking and listening please.' Another taps on a chime bar, another a small bell and yet another slams a piece of wood on a desk (a little over-dramatic for my taste, but it is still effective). You may not need to rush out to buy a gavel, but whatever signal you try, you may be sure of one thing: it is not the signal that matters so much as what the pupils have learned it *means*.

If your signal means nothing to them you can stamp and scream all you like to no effect. If you want to use your voice, your speech signal must be the same each time, generally loud, followed by a pause, followed by a drop in the volume of your voice. You may even need to rehearse what this means with pupils, something like 'When I say/do ... it *means* that you turn round, face me and put everything out of your hands. Keep your hands and feet to yourself, and do any talking inside your head. All eyes this way and ready to concentrate.' Knowing what the signal actually means will work for most pupils if you are consistent. The time to do all this is the very *first* time you ask a class to pay attention.

Technically, the crucial feature of getting attention is to pause after the attention signal, and insist on attention until you have eye contact and all chatter, 'pen-maintenance' and fidgeting has stopped. It is tempting to settle for less (seriously disturbed pupils notwithstanding) but in time you will undermine your signal. Insist, insist and insist by saying the same phrase, such as 'I can't see everyone's eyes'. Pause, repeat the phrase with slight surprise in your voice, and insist. You may not succeed in this every time, but you are developing and honing a basic classroom skill. There is also a curious effect here, which I have yet to disprove. If your signal is to clap your hands or bang an object three times, the pace of this has to be right. Three overly rapid sounds really count as one. You need to clap your hands at a pace of one loud sound per second, not four sounds or two sounds and always followed by a one or two-second pause before instructions. If you want to avoid pupils clapping in imitation of you, give clear and loud commands ('pens down, looking and listening') at the same time as you clap.

POWER STRUGGLES

Some pupils want to be the last to give their attention. This can be refusal to give eye contact, sometimes it is under-chatter and sometimes a power struggle with the teacher over being the last to close a storage drawer or put down equipment. Some pupils (very few in fact) may need to be ignored if they are known to be extreme in behaviour. Whatever the ploy, very early intervention for the majority of pupils is more effective than endless patience and a frustrated 'I'm waiting' expression on your face. This might take the form of a sharp reprimand backed up by a threat of losing five minutes at break/playtime. More likely a threat of losing some opportunity to do something very enjoyable that the rest of the class is going to do will have a desired effect. Give a warning, though, and a choice such as 'You're choosing to lose some of your time if you … '. Some teachers have a plan for pupils to earn time back by the break: 'You might earn break time back if you're sensible for the rest of the lesson.' Alongside this I would consistently remind pupils about 'being co-operative', 'concentrating', and spell out as positively as I could the classroom social skills I wanted to develop.

Perhaps your greatest fear is of blank refusal to give attention or to stop disrupting. Imagine that a power struggle develops when you ask a pupil called Daniel to move to a seat nearer you. A confrontation is imminent as he refuses for the second time to move. At this point you may need an escape route because Daniel is enjoying the confrontation. A solution is to keep calm, give him a third chance to move/stop activity, and back this up with a consequent threat of loss of time. At the third refusal, all you can do is put life on a backburner because there is no way you will win in a confrontation. You can say something like, 'You've chosen to refuse and you've chosen to ignore me, so we'll need to look at that later. Sit there and do nothing or choose to work and let me know if you need help'. You then try to keep the rest of the class on your side, turning away physically from Daniel if you can and saying something like, 'We may need to ignore Daniel's behaviour until it changes'. In the final analysis, with extremely difficult pupils, you may be thrown back on your supervising teacher's help and the behaviour policies of the school. There is no shame whatever in seeking help from more experienced teachers.

RAPID RESPONSE

More positively, there are ways to encourage pupils to co-operate rather than having to discipline or punish. One teacher I know awards points for 'rapid response' to her requests to pay attention or to stop what is being done and look at the board. This teacher puts marbles in a jar and shakes them as her loud attention-getting signal. If the response to this is rapid (all eyes on the board, nothing in their hands) another marble is put in the jar. Ten marbles gain a team point or reward and these are tallied at the end of the day. Some teachers are scathing about the use of rewards and stickers, but pupils respond to them remarkably well.

The oldest reward system I know of is to give three silver stars and then a gold. You might be surprised how much attention children take of stickers, certificates and 'black mark' punishments. Schools who take rewards seriously often have 'good work' assemblies and a hierarchy of rewards. There is nothing quite like having reward certificates given out in assembly, rather than in the classroom. Most children feel much more important being recognised publicly, even taking certificates and stickers home. The power of such symbols is also effective when used as the traditional 'black mark'. One school I know of uses a system of green stickers for disruptive behaviour. Being given a total of ten green stickers automatically triggers a letter home to parents.

So, these are examples of a range of strategies that successful teachers have used. Not all will appeal or feel right for you to adopt, and you will decide for yourself the approach that best fits in with the classroom that you manage. There is another important thing to remember when employing whatever range of behaviour management techniques you choose. Strategies are often perceived to have failed when in fact the teacher has simply not been consistent and persistent in using them. The lack of tenacious application of a strategy is one of the main reasons why it can become ineffective. In a very busy and often stressful teaching environment, it can be very demanding to maintain such an approach when there are many other demands being made of you. However, children can be very adept at taking advantage of any inconsistency in behaviour management strategies, and you also run the risk of losing credibility in their eyes when you later introduce other ones. Although it can be time-consuming, failing to 'follow through' on behaviour management techniques can be far more costly in time and energy in the long run.

SETTING GOOD BEHAVIOUR PATTERNS

You are trying to set patterns of behaviour when you are new to the class. You do not want to adopt techniques too different from your teacher because that could unsettle pupils. Even so, you are actually out there on your own terms. A useful phrase for establishing new working patterns is to preface your instructions with 'When you are working with me … '. You will need to practise consistently doing things the same way and be very fussy about clamping down on children playing with pens, pencils and whatever takes their fancy. Clamp down firmly on any 'pen-maintenance' and under-chatter if you want to avoid further disruption, such as pupils wandering around the room aimlessly. Children disrupt in stages according to your tolerance of what they just did.

Every trainee teacher makes mistakes in the way instructions are phrased. Your hope may be that pupils have developed social skills and are self-disciplined, but many are not at that stage. For example, if it is approaching lunch time, you might have decided to let the best behaved table or row leave first. How you do this is up to you, but certainly in upper primary age ranges, there is a difference between saying 'You can go now' and 'That table of children can put chairs underneath'. If you say 'You can go', pupils will most likely make a rush for the door, unless you have already established a polite way of room-quitting. If all you say is 'Put your chairs under the desks', there's nothing much they can do but wait for the next instruction, 'Quietly walk out'. Unfortunately, a great deal of class management is a matter of using the exact words for the effect you want. It is a common foible of experienced teachers to be heard saying '*Quietly* walk out', rather than 'Walk out quietly' so that pupils (in theory) register the operative word before they hear the remainder.

VOICE TONE AND POSITIVE REMINDERS

Reminders about social skills and concentration are far better delivered in bright good humour than in anger or boredom. You may not realise why some very popular teachers can be quite aggressive in voice tone when they deal with trouble. I have noticed that they are able to return to a positive sound in their voice almost immediately after giving pupils a sharp ticking off. Their pupils know that 99 times out of 100 the teacher is positive, so they respond without resentment to the odd occasion they are on the receiving end of a rebuke. By contrast, there are teachers and pupils for whom classroom life is an unnecessary war zone. A pupil who is only ever spoken to in negative terms will respond accordingly. Difficult pupils will inevitably invite negative responses from teachers and other pupils. The hard part is to ignore that and give positive encouragement when a difficult pupil least expects it. When you first start teaching you might expect pupils to realise that by being co-operative they would invite your better nature. Unfortunately they rarely realise that.

It is up to you to turn the situation to everyone's advantage, by being rewarding as well as demanding of pupils. Nobody can make you teach with a sense of fun, but an attitude of humourless, pained and patient tolerance is a poor alternative. From time to time, try to analyse how generally positive or negative you have become in the classroom. The co-operative pupils are easy to praise, but difficult pupils sometimes want the public glare and drama of a ticking off. They want to be good at being bad. Even so, you are trying to remain rewarding to be with and will need to take disrupters by surprise with your praise whenever you can.

In time you can minimise what you want by using signals instead. For example, one teacher I know walks to the front of the classroom and sits in a chair with the register in her hand. This, it has been firmly established, means that within 30 seconds, the pupils are to begin silent reading, or check spellings silently. The register is called without fuss and the class is ready to listen when the last pupil has responded.

Another teacher draws his signals on the board. He draws an oval with two eyes (look this way) and pupils hear him clear his throat over-dramatically, which is a signal to look at his drawing. He next draws a mouth with a cross through it and stares at his pupils with fixed gaze (no talking).When the noise settles, he pauses and draws two ears on the face (everyone listening). He has signals for 'four chair legs on the floor, not two' and signals for 'maximum concentration'. The ultimate signal is called 'the teacher's look', which is a reproachful way of looking at a pupil, head half turned, but with a strongly focused eye. Alongside such odd teacher-phrases as 'quietly walk', this may have you easily spotted as a teacher at Tesco's supermarket checkout. If your non-verbal signal is not effective, re-examine your explanation to pupils of what it means and reinforce the consequences for not responding.

PROXIMITY PRAISE

If you want to encourage pupils' self-discipline in giving attention, you can use 'proximity praise'. This is a technique of quite genuinely thanking (praising) pupils who are sitting nearest to those who are not yet ready. 'Thank you Kirsty. Thank you Peter. Thank you Sarah' can be said in warm tones as you notice pupils are ready. Pick the pupils who are in proximity to the most difficult children. Gradually reduce the volume of your voice as an increasing number of pupils give their attention and make sure that you thank pupils by name. You need to be heard loudly enough for all to hear you, so this is a technique you might use immediately following the *pause* after your attention signal. The technique works partly because you deprive inattentive pupils of their audience, partly because you repeat the same positive praise, and partly because it is personal.

The repetition is similar to that used when you want a child to do something they may not want to. You will achieve more by saying 'I need you to … ' and repeating it, even if they complain and mutter, rather than being drawn into an argument. Simply repeat the same phrase, giving eye contact and refusing to say anything else except *exactly* the same phrase. Proximity praise can also include descriptions of good responses. These are powerful and here are some examples that could be used either when pupils are waiting, or when they are working at a task:

- I can see Kirsty has her book open and ready to read.

- I can see that Peter has arranged the space on the desk so nothing gets in anyone else's way.

- There's litter on the floor and two of you near the window have picked some of it up.

● John, Sarah and David are making a real effort and I'm waiting …

● I really like the way this group/table has realised we're ready.

KEEPING ON TOP OF A GOOD START

When you have achieved your attention signal, sustaining attention requires more subtle management. You will need to engage children's minds in several ways because managing a class cannot be separated from different styles of teaching and learning. Here is where three techniques come to the fore. The first of these is to refocus attention as it wanes. Typically, you will begin to explain, question or instruct and three or more pupils will look away or chatter. Within a nano-second of this happening, refocus attention in as unobtrusive a way as you can. You do not want to stop and remonstrate or you will lose the thread of your lesson. A sharp 'Simon. Looking this way' will work if it is done soon enough. Avoid constant interruptions to the flow, but keep refocusing attention periodically as you go.

The second technique is to 'engage' pupils' thinking and the third is to use 'directive language'. When teachers engage minds, they typically use classroom language like:

● Imagine …

● I want you to think about …

● If I had twelve pieces of pizza and …

● I wonder who knows if …

● Here's a problem we need to solve …

● And the third planet from the Sun is … ?

● If you were on the bottom of the sea and …

● If the hands on this clock said …

Directive language makes what teachers say more specific by asking precisely for the behaviour and action wanted. A familiar example is when you deal with the eternal problem of children calling out, rather than allowing turns or putting up a hand to answer. If you want to waste your breath say 'Don't call out', or worse still, 'How many times have I told you … '. This does not direct their behaviour. Directive language includes physical actions, such as 'Hands up, who can tell me … ' which is different from 'Tell me who … '. Hearing the word 'tell' may invite calling out (telling) unless the pupil has the wit to remember to put up a hand.

Here are some more examples which *specifically* direct mind, eyes and ears. Most experienced teachers, by the way, would probably do this without realising that they did.

- Look at the speech bubble halfway down the page (rather than 'Look at the page').

- Look at the top left line on the board where it says (rather than 'Look at the board').

- Look carefully at the shape of these ammonite fossils and imagine them lying on the bottom of the sea (engages imagination).

- Listen to this sentence/story and see if you can pick out … (specific items).

- David, tell me what you think … (specific pupil directive).

- Why do you think he's right, Sharon? (specific pupil question).

The very first teaching practice is a good opportunity to tune in to and observe 'teacher-talk' picking up the specifics of directive language. There are hundreds of examples to add to these.

HOW A GOOD START FALLS APART

Classrooms are full of good starts, many of which lead nowhere. As a trainee your one thought may be just to survive until the end of a lesson. This is almost impossible if you do not think about what comes next in a lesson, something which seems so obvious it is hard to imagine you would forget to plan for it. If you want your session to fall apart it can happen in these ways:

- Poor planning (work is too easy/too hard and boring).

- Failing to give and get eye contact when you need to.

- Introducing work in a frivolous manner.

- Forgetting to refocus attention immediately when you/pupils are talking.

- Forgetting to remind pupils frequently what they are trying to achieve.

- Not setting deadlines and targets (pupils stretch the task to fit the time).

- Failing to scan the room to see if pupils are still on task.

- Trying to do the same activity for too long.

- Not taking action with pupils who are about to finish or who are off task.

- Ignoring pupils who are not putting in any effort.

- Not planning so that there is variety within an hour's work.

- Rarely giving praise.

- Forgetting to tell children what they have achieved.

A shorthand for all of this is that you may unwittingly make your classroom an unrewarding and dull place to be.

THAT MID-SENTENCE PAUSE

At any time, whenever you are explaining, asking questions and doing your best to keep attention you may be torpedoed. One way pupils do this is by asking irrelevant, sometimes silly questions or making silly or cheeky remarks. Noises can be another torpedo, fidgeting another. The general aim is to wrong-foot you as you teach. When you are a trainee, a pupil might say 'You're not a proper teacher are you?' which can be deflected by a very firm 'That's not a helpful remark just now. Tell me what work should you be doing?' This is safer ground than attempting witty replies and refers the pupil back to the work under way. You have a number of other counter-strategies available. You could, of course, ignore the interruptions and simply press on. Sometimes this actually works because the rest of the group is involved and the disrupters are pulled along by the others (they have lost their main audience and settle down). More likely you will use a strategy such as the 'mid-sentence pause' for effect. Up and down the country teachers pause mid-sentence in mock astonishment that they have lost a pupil's attention or that there is unacceptable behaviour.

Alternatively, you can admonish and cajole pupils in a low-key way, aside from your main explanation or direction. The voice tone for these asides needs to be 'matter of fact' and unobtrusive. Try not to give eye contact to the disrupter, but use their names instead, showing that you are aware of them but determined to keep your focus on teaching. The following example goes some way towards explaining the unobtrusive admonishing and corrective language. Bold type is my main teacher-talk and the rest of the text is woven between as low-key insistence on social skills. Overdone this would be ridiculous nagging, and this is just an example compressed into one sentence. The aim is not to disturb the flow of the explanation.

> *(In adult tones, no sarcasm when you use the pupil's name)* **So you can see that the candle** – Stephen, looking and listening – **burns blue at the base, but yellow higher up. Hands up if you** – Karen, sitting properly thanks – **can see any other changes to the flame.**

This only works if pupils know that there are consequences for not giving their attention. It fails if you punctuate your entire explanation with these incidental directions. Whether you employ the 'mid-sentence pause', incidental directions or other strategies, you will need to intervene early and briefly, making sure there are consequences for poor attention. Keeping attention is a matter of anticipating the fidgets.

MANIC VIGILANCE

A word of warning here about striking a balance between being vigilant and being aggressively 'manic' in your vigilance. The manically vigilant teacher treats each infringement of attention or pupil disruption as a personal threat, barking at pupils in return. The teacher's eyes widen, the forehead furrows and the head darts in quick movements in search of the next infringement of a rule. Two effects of being manically vigilant are that you will shift the focus towards pupils' behaviour (rather than concentrating on your teaching and the pupils' learning) and you will invite pupils to try you out. If you are looking for the next infringement of discipline, you may be sure they will begin to provide it. There is a marked difference between noticing a pupil is not attending, and overreacting to the extent that you lose sight of your teaching. Think about where you want children's minds to be focused.

MINIMAL INTERVENTION

The way to waste emotional energy, time and lesson pace is to turn minor infringements into an opportunity for a major admonishing speech. What usually happens is that you will make a meal of dealing with 'You should know by now to put your hands up ... ', 'I don't expect that from you Stephen. How many times have I told you?' (which are not very effective because they refer to the past). You probably began with a quick rebuke, but now it has become a 20 or 30-second speech which actually destroys the flow of your lesson. You really need a more effective shorthand method which still keeps your teaching on track. Phrases such as 'Hands up only', 'Listening means you, David' are better because they do not so readily interrupt essential explanations and pupils' responses. You can make the shorthand up as you go along ('Eyes, Rachel', 'First warning, John', 'Sitting properly please, Sarah', 'Pen down, hands on the desk, Peter'). The rule of thumb here is to abandon management techniques which are so long-winded that they shift focus. By all means stretch a pregnant pause to an interminable ten seconds or so, but avoid the long nagging reminders. Go for a pithy phrase and press on, engaging pupils' minds. The children you over-lecture about infringements are most likely those who get up your nose because they deliberately flout your authority. You may unwittingly reward them with your major (and personal) speech, delivering exactly the payoff and attention they wanted. The result is that you lose the rest of the class.

Reduce your behaviour management to signals as often as you can. For example, the 'Hands up' command can be accompanied by a signal using your own hand with the flat of the palm facing the child calling out. After a few days, you will find that all you need do to the pupils who call out is show them the non-verbal signal of the palm of your hand. At the same time, turn towards a pupil who has a hand raised. The combination of hand signal to the pupil calling out and turning to the pupil who has a hand up is also another signal.

SETTING ABSORBING TASKS

The best teacher-talk in the world is no substitute for absorbed and interested pupils (see Chapters 5, 11, 12, 13 and 14). You will obviously have fewer management problems if the tasks you set are interesting and worth doing. Pupil behaviour is affected by whether there is enough variety to keep them involved. Are your pupils going to be doing exactly the same thing the entire lesson? Are there important changes of direction? Are there opportunities to summarise what they have learned? I sometimes wonder whatever happened to using a tone of voice that signals challenge, interest and a sense of 'making progress'. As the numeracy questions roll out, one after the other, I long to hear a trainee teacher say 'Well done. You got that. Now let's see if you can do something difficult like – if I had twenty-seven and there were ...', or 'I wonder who can work out what we would need to do if the perimeter changed to ... '. The challenge is partly in the eyes and voice as you transmit a sense of curiosity, wonder and puzzle-solving rewards.

The following features of teaching help maintain interest and good pupil behaviour management:

- Having minimal but well-established classroom rules in the first place.

- Explaining briefly and clearly what you are trying to achieve.

- Explaining briefly and clearly what they are trying to achieve.

- Setting challenging tasks which are active and rewarding.

- Sounding as if you are challenging the pupils, daring them to solve problems.

- Setting a reasonable but demanding deadline for completion.

- Summarising the main points they have learned.

ON-TASK BEHAVIOUR MANAGEMENT

So far I have mentioned techniques you can use when discussing, explaining and giving direction. Styles of teaching vary, but at some point children will begin a task, individually, in pairs or in groups. When you first start your teaching practice, you will probably work with small groups rather than be responsible for the whole class. This has the advantage that you can study children's learning, but the disadvantage that you may not learn to scan the entire classroom effectively. Maybe you become absorbed with individuals at the expense of scanning the whole classroom every few minutes to see what is happening. You probably forget the children furthest from you and you may miss seeing their hands go up or miss being aware of problem behaviour. Worse still, if you become too absorbed with individuals, you actually turn your back on the rest and see very little that happens. Try to position yourself strategically, with your back to the wall or window, where you can easily scan the room to see who is working, even if you are bending over an individual child's work. If you stand in the centre of the room and need to speak to a class, turn round and establish eye contact with pupils at a distance from you. Try not to bawl at pupils loudly across the room, or so might they. If you push up noise levels yourself, do not be surprised if you consequently have a noisy class.

During on-task behaviour, it is worth putting in some effort to set the social tone of your classroom so that you can easily refer to the behaviour you prefer. You will need to set noise levels to a low level that *you* decide is acceptable. Some teachers announce 'partner voices' or 'whisper-level' voices. My preference is to establish a pattern of two minutes 'settling time', after which the class is into 'concentration time' or 'thinking time'. Has it ever occurred to you that children *do* need an atmosphere in which they can concentrate? Personally I do not subscribe to the view that children can always talk and work at the same time. Even if it sounds like propaganda, use the words that emphasise the behaviour you want, words such as 'concentrate', and 'think carefully'. Talk about 'accuracy' if it is appropriate, and certainly use any words you associate with 'quality' in pupils' work. Quality, by the way, is not the same as 'neatness of presentation' and you will need to think about what you are trying to achieve. It may take some time for words like 'concentrate' and 'quality' to have an effect, but over a period of time they will.

When pupils begin a task, this is often the very time to leave them alone. Some teachers stand quietly watching to ensure that pupils engage with their work. Others simply expect pupils to sort themselves out, knowing that there will soon be a check on how far they have progressed. It is tempting to assume you must teach all the time. On-task behaviour is exactly that and not particularly helped by interruptions from you or anyone else. If you were astute enough to set manageable (differentiated) tasks, deadlines and targets, your success could be measured by being redundant. This takes forethought in planning (see Chapter 11).

HIGH EXPECTATIONS AND BEHAVIOUR

Behaviour during tasks is often driven by the expectations children have. A useful way to keep children involved, for example, is to put in a measure of 'feedback expectancy'. Imagine you are about to show a video of 'The Victorians'. If you just announce this fact to the class you will probably get a groan from them. By contrast, if you were to compare a Victorian lace iron with a modern electric one and ask the children to look out for examples of how Victorians lived *without electricity* you would be halfway there. 'Feedback expectancy' is when you add 'At the end of the video, you should be able to tell me about … ' or you indicate you're going to collect work in or ask some of them to explain. 'Feedback expectancy' is a matter of building in an *early* expectation of feedback from pupils. Alternatively, you set a deadline and a target concerning what you expect in the time available. The messages you are trying to transmit are that you expect children to be industrious, there are deadlines, feedback and that their concentration is well worth the effort.

By contrast, off-task behaviour consists of almost anything which is a diversion from work. Examples are calling out to other pupils, back-chatting indirectly by commenting on what is happening, wandering about the room, interfering with other pupils, carrying on conversation concerning gossip, social comment about relationships, flicking things, antagonising, pulling someone's chair, kicking someone, demonstrating how to reorganise a pencil case, constructing a model aircraft from a ruler (the wings) and pen (fuselage with pen clip holding the ruler in place), sharpening pencils, preening hair and nails, and becoming drawn into abusive exchanges with other pupils. If you do not make it clear that there are agreed rules, acceptable and unacceptable behaviour, then you have no reference point.

CLASSROOM RULES

There are obvious class rules, such as 'We listen to one person, not talk when they are', and 'We keep our hands and feet to ourselves'. Beyond these are a number about politeness, concentrating, making sure 'We do not interfere with another pupil's right to work'. More important than a minimal set of classroom rules is how they are used. You can throw responsibility back where it belongs by referring to the rules, backed up by there being consequences:

- You know we keep our hands and feet to ourselves. How are you going to solve that problem?

- I'll give you one minute to find a way to sort that out.

- What are you asking me for?

- You two tell me in five minutes what your solution is to this.

- We respect each other's work and look after it. What could you do to show you understand that?

- Tell me how you've helped another pupil today.

Rules are particularly effective if you offer pupils a choice, the obvious one being: 'You can lose five minutes of your time, or you can settle to some work. You choose.' When you follow this up as a consequence, you are then able to refer back by saying: 'You're choosing to lose five minutes break.' It is also possible to say this either as a warning or as a threat. During activities you could dwell on the negative side by concentrating on all the things you do *not* want the individual pupil to do. But there are far better ways. It is better to caution the action rather than the actor. You can do this by using the third person as in 'That isn't the kind of behaviour *we* expect here', distancing you from getting too personally involved (compared with 'You're a pest. Why can't you behave yourself?'). Usually pupils already know what is unacceptable, so it is better to remind them of established consequences. As a trainee teacher you may occasionally find that you want firmer rules than your teacher does. Your solution with pupils is to adopt a 'When you're working with me … ' approach so that neither your position, nor that of the teacher is compromised.

When you follow up rules with consequences, always offer a chance or a choice. The football referee's yellow card is preferable to an instant red one. Give a warning with consequences spelled out, consequences you are prepared to follow through consistently. Alternatively, give children choices. They can choose to work *now*, have to catch up later or lose privileges. Ideally, you want children to choose the option of behaving well, rather than your continually imposing sanctions and minor punishments.

In one school, the following rules were agreed:

Rules
Look at and listen to talker
Follow instructions carefully
Treat others as we would like to be treated
Move carefully and quietly in class
Respect own and others' property

Consequences
Warning
Isolation
Lost play
Detention
Headteacher
Contact parents

Rewards
Praise
Treats
Teacher awards
Free time
Headteacher awards
Contact parents

ATTENTION-SEEKING PUPILS

Some children are addicted to gaining the maximum attention they can from any situation. Occasionally this can be channelled positively but more usually it creates a problem for teachers. Attention-seeking children have more ways of becoming noticed than a teacher can imagine. They are experts at disturbing the flow of a lesson. The system of being 'on report' is well known in upper primary schooling as a consequence for the pupil of behaving unacceptably. Disruptive pupils are given ticks or a grade on the report for behaving well each lesson. This is often seen as being the only way forward, but it can have consequences the teacher does not want.

A pupil, I will call her Keeley, was on an intensive programme of support for behaving badly. She did so well with a personal behaviour plan for two weeks that she was praised and told she was 'off report'. She saw other pupils on report going to the teacher for individual attention at the end of lessons and asked why she could not do the same. She liked the ticks and point system so she wanted to go back on report for the attention it gave her. When she was told she was behaving so well that it was not necessary, she promptly began to behave badly. Recognising that Keeley's real need was for attention, the teacher devised an alternative, challenging, target report with ticks, rewards and a minimal low target with a consequence. Keeley had to score above the minimum target or would be kept in for 30 minutes. If she reached her numerical target, with ticks for quality work and behaviour, she received a certificate to take home. Teachers occasionally need to do such very strange things.

Attention-seeking pupils seem deliberately to forget any systems and rules there are, in order to be seen and noticed. This can sometimes be undermined by praising them when they least expect it, and refusing eye contact when they are seeking attention. It is worth remembering that they live rather inside their own bubble of space where the needs of other pupils are of little concern. Imagine I have a 9-year-old attention-seeker called Daniel, who calls out and becomes angry if he is ignored. He frequently shouts 'Is this all right?' and holds up his work. He stops other children working and wants to be the centre of attention. What are some of the options for dealing with him?

- I can give Daniel time out or remove him and say 'I'd like you to be involved in this Daniel, but it's too expensive to teach you all by yourself. So when you're ready to co-operate, you can join us because some of this is worth doing. Otherwise you'll have to be by yourself and do nothing, which is very boring.'

- I can say to the class 'Daniel has had enough of my attention now and I need to teach all of you, not just one person, so we might need to ignore him until he settles.'

- I can use a deflective statement to avoid confrontation and say 'I can see you're wanting a lot of my time Daniel … so we'll need to talk about this later.'

- I can restate classroom rules. 'Daniel. You know the rule about stopping other people from working.'

- I can state how I feel. 'I feel angry because I can't give my attention to other people who need it. I get very annoyed Daniel if I have to re-explain things.'

Daniel might well like the fact that I feel angry, but it is still worth letting Daniel know the effect he has on other people. You are trying to keep the rest of the class on your side while they and you cope with Daniel. You are trying not to respond directly to Daniel's demands. His need is so great that he is unlikely to give up seeking attention. You can contain Daniel, but a cure is more difficult.

CREATING A POSITIVE ETHOS

When you reach your final teaching practice, you will find that far more of these strategies are ingrained in your teaching. Your aim is to minimise the need to discipline pupils and maximise your chances to interest them. With luck, you will learn to laugh in the face of adversity. You will know by then that to teach with good humour has made you more rewarding for your pupils to be with. Above all, try to improve their sense of self, their sense of achievement and their positive work habits. That route offers more than a nagging disciplinarian ever can. Children need recognition. As an ancient piece of Cherokee wisdom summarises: 'Learn to listen or you will deafen yourself with your tongue.'

There are several ways to create a negative or positive ethos in your classroom. Few teachers are intentionally negative, but the following contrasting attributes may help.

Negative

- Continually telling children their work is not good enough (using standards as an excuse).

- Making negative comparisons with pupils you regard as better.

- Using labels such as 'intelligent' and 'stupid'.

- Creating an atmosphere of mistrust and lack of value.

- Being bad-tempered and nagging.

- Using sarcasm and misguided teasing.

- Building most of your teaching around photocopied worksheets, rather than making an effort to interest pupils.

- Slowing the pace of lessons to a crawl.

- Using equipment that is badly organised, broken/blunt or with parts missing.

Positive

- Creating an atmosphere where pupils feel valued.

- Engaging minds and giving lessons pace.

- Taking time to praise effort and performance, rather than intelligence.

- Becoming excited yourself about the subject you are teaching.

- Emphasising politeness, caring and co-operation.

- Giving rewards for pupils' rapid response to attention (discussed above).

- Learning to listen to pupils.

- Teaching pupils the value of listening and responding.

- Being proud of what you and your pupils can do and be.

- Taking care to value and display pupils' work.

SUMMARY

- Expect to be tried out, but do not overreact.

- Give a clear signal for getting attention, followed by a pause. Establish what this *means*.

- Insist and persist in getting attention.

- Learn to refocus attention quickly after you have gained it.

- Intervene early, dealing with problems before they escalate.

- Be vigilant, but not 'manic-vigilant'.

- Set noise levels and establish what they mean.

- Look, sound and be someone who sets challenges.

- Praise attention-seekers when they least expect it. Deal with attention-seeking by not responding to their demand for attention.

- Experiment with 'proximity praise' to see its effect.

- Be consistent and persistent in the application of the behaviour management technique you employ.

ISSUES FOR REFLECTION

- Observe two teachers' verbal and non-verbal strategies to gain the attention of their pupils. Which of these strategies might work best for you? Why? Are there other techniques you might usefully develop?

- Reflect on which social skills you definitely want to encourage in your children. Discuss these with a friend, explaining why these skills are so important and how you might encourage your pupils to develop them.

- Sometimes inappropriate behaviour is best ignored. Why might this be the case? Ask yourself, 'When I intervene, am I creating difficulties or minimising them?'

- Observe a teacher manage undesirable pupil behaviour. Ask yourself 'Am I able to treat children with respect, yet still let them know there are consequences for poor behaviour?' Why is it so important to focus on the child's actions rather than on them as a person when they have misbehaved?

Further reading

Barnes, R. (1999) *Positive Teaching, Positive Learning*. London: Routledge. This book outlines a number of ways to encourage positive classroom feedback from children and teachers.

Faber, A. and Mazlisch, E. (1989) *How to Talk so Kids Will Listen & How to Listen so Kids Will Talk*. London: Avon Books. A detailed look at responding to children's feelings and developing their independent social skills.

Galvin, P., Miller, A. and Nash, J. (1999) *Behaviour and Discipline in Schools*. London: David Fulton. A broad look at the topic of behaviour and discipline.

McManus, M. (1989) *Troublesome Behaviour in the Classroom*. London: Routledge. General coverage of the topic with some practical ideas.

Rogers, B. (1998) *You Know the Fair Rule*. London: Pitman. Ways to establish 'least-intrusive' classroom control by establishing rules and responsibilities.

Chapter 9

Reflective practice

Jenifer Smith

> Reflection can be a highly effective way to enhance the quality of your teaching and learning. In this chapter Jenifer Smith conveys inspirational messages about teaching with 'your whole self' and becoming the teacher you want to be. She describes a range of techniques which others have found both challenging and useful. You are invited to consider how you have reflected on your actions in the past and how you might develop this practice in the future.

INTRODUCTION

Reflection is about slowing down, thinking more deeply, asking questions, being willing not to have complete answers, learning to live with uncertainty, seeing patterns, making links between experience, reading, writing and talk. This chapter considers why reflective teaching is important. It suggests ways in which you might begin to reflect on practice and how to focus reflection in the classroom.

WHY REFLECT?

Do you swim? Can you ride a bicycle? Do you improvise with other musicians or use a screwdriver? Could you tell someone else how to do any of these things? You can give them pointers, you can tell them the rules or how things work, you can demonstrate, but they must get the sense of *how* to do it themselves. They have to hold the screwdriver and feel how it is in their hand. They have, somehow, to let go while taking note of how the successful movements feel. And they must carry that sense with them so that they can use that knowledge again. If you were to think in too much detail about how you ride a bicycle as you are riding, the chances are that you would fall off – or never get started. You can help others learn to do these things, but it is hard to find the words to describe just what the knack is. Swimming, riding a bicycle, wielding a screwdriver are activities which depend heavily on knowing through the body. Improvising in music demands not only the skills of playing an instrument and knowledge of harmony, melody and rhythm, but also an awareness of others and the sounds they are making, or, even, about to make, a sensitivity to what is going on around us and the effect that we are having on our surroundings. As we are in the midst of cycling or improvising we may not be thinking consciously about what we are doing, but we can take time outside that activity to reflect upon our actions.

Teaching is a highly skilled activity which requires us to anticipate and respond to the complexities of the classroom, to make judgements and to act upon them, and to be aware of the consequences of our actions. Others can talk with us and share their experience of teaching and we can learn from practical advice. However, becoming a teacher, and the process of teaching itself, is something we must each grow to understand and know for ourselves. As we learn to teach and continue to develop our skills, we respond to the many, many tiny events of the classroom and we draw upon an intricate web of knowledge and experiences to help us. It is not always easy to articulate this complex activity, and sometimes advice given or theory proposed does not match or seems too easy by comparison with the messiness and unevenness of the experience itself. Reflection helps us to make better sense of our teaching and learning, and in so doing helps us to grow in skill and understanding.

WHAT PLACE DOES REFLECTION HAVE IN TEACHING AND LEARNING?

We learn about teaching by teaching, by learning how it feels and what the signs are; but we also learn by reflecting on our thoughts and actions, and by relating our thoughts to the advice, written and spoken, of experts, and to other analogous experiences of our own. When we are in the midst of the situation we do not necessarily think consciously about what we are doing, particularly as we become more skilled. It is what Donald Schon describes as knowing-in-action.

> Our knowing is ordinarily tacit, implicit in our patterns of action and our feel for the stuff with which we are dealing. It seems right to say that our knowing is in our action.

> Similarly, the workaday life of the professional depends on tacit knowing-in-

action. Every competent practitioner can recognise phenomena – families of symptoms associated with a particular disease, peculiarities of a certain kind of building site, irregularities of materials of structures – for which he cannot give a reasonably accurate or complete description. In his day-to-day practice he makes innumerable judgements of quality for which he cannot state adequate criteria, and he displays skills for which he cannot state the rules and procedures. Even when he makes conscious use of research based theories and techniques, he is dependent on tacit recognitions, judgements and skilful performances. (Schon, 1991, pp. 49–50)

Skilled teaching calls upon every aspect of our being, the whole person: physical presence and action, physical awareness of the activities and actions of the classroom, smell, sight, sound, intellectual understanding, emotional and moral awareness, and social consciousness. As we gain experience in the classroom we learn to read the signs. We also need to think about the context in which we work and which we create. A teacher is making judgements about how to act, every moment of the day, and planning is based upon a range of understandings. When you begin teaching there seem too many things to hold in the mind at one time. In the moment, in the classroom, the teacher calls upon a complex web of experience, knowledge and understanding. You will notice that some things 'work', and others can lead to horrible, toe-curling disasters. Some things are just 'OK'. As you respond to children, or adjust your actions in the classroom, as you think consciously about your presentation or the way you are asking questions, you are drawing on any number of sources to inform your action. A memory of a piece of advice, or of the actions of a teacher you have observed may come into play as you deal with the events of a lesson. You may be consciously trying out an idea or you may find yourself drawing on your own experience of the last time you were in a similar situation. In the classroom, you must act. Later, with a little time to reflect, you are able to begin to see patterns, and to articulate what you are doing or might do.

Professional practitioners do not merely act without thinking. They reflect on their actions both in the midst of acting, and later. Reflection can help us to identify the strengths and shortcomings of our actions, so that we can make changes or capitalise on a success. Reflection can help us solve problems, and reflection can offer us a moment of stillness in a job which is never finished, where there is always something more that could be done. Schon suggests that 'thinking-in-action' is sparked by surprise. Indeed, our surprised pleasure at things that go well is one thing which prompts us to look back and consider how that success was achieved: why did we judge it successful? What were the conditions? What did we do? What was our thinking and our intention? Teachers also reflect on the curiosities and the discomforts of the classroom. How will I respond to what this child's actions are telling me about her understanding of pattern? What is preventing this child from making progress in reading? Why is the class so unsettled after lunch – and what shall I do about it? How might I engage more children during whole-class shared writing? And teachers may choose to reflect on the everyday happenings of the classroom, perhaps the actions of a child who often goes unnoticed, to help them learn about teaching and about learning. (You may want to eventually develop some of these issues into specific questions for more systematic enquiry and research – see Chapter 2.)

A class of children constantly presents the teacher with intriguing puzzles. It is one of the real pleasures of teaching to engage with these puzzles. Indeed, I would suggest that a careful awareness of what children tell us through their speech and actions, and our subsequent reflections on that knowledge is central to the act of teaching. Children are not the only presence in the classroom. There are other adults, both within and powerfully on the fringes of the classroom: teachers, classroom assistants, parents, governors, other professionals. Sometimes you may wish to reflect on the roles they play and upon your relationship with them. However, the other key presence in the classroom is you, the teacher or trainee teacher. Teaching is a part of who we are, and our actions in the classroom are informed by our beliefs, our understandings and our prejudices. Reflection has an important part to play in helping us resolve the part the self plays in teaching, and in helping us to identify the blind spots and troublesome areas which make our teaching less effective for some children.

THE TEACHER WE MIGHT BE

It is quite likely that you have some sense of the kind of teacher you want to be, although this picture may change with experience. It will be drawn from any number of images. We are shaped, as teachers, by our own experiences of teachers and of learning. Thinking about teachers, those who have taught us, and others whom we have observed, can help us think about some of the ways we behave when teaching, and about our beliefs and assumptions. There may be others, who are not teachers in schools, but who have, nevertheless, taught us about ways of being with children, and about teaching. It is worth reflecting on such influences, attempting not only to recall and describe carefully how these people behave, and your responses to them, but also to think about what it was, in particular, that made them so effective, or so destructive, and how that is present in some of the ways you behave or aspire to behave.

We can also draw upon our own experience of childhood. Reflecting on our learning in different contexts can help us think about ourselves as learners and as children experiencing school. There are two main reasons for reflecting on our history as learners and on our learning processes. Reflecting on our own processes of understanding can be helpful in finding ways of explaining something, setting up a series of activities or creating a context for learning. It can help us to place ourselves in the position of learners. It can also help us to remember and recognise differences and extend the possibilities we offer in our classroom. We need to be aware of different styles of learning, know that we are likely to favour our own preferred style, and be able to think about planning for a variety of approaches.

KNOWING OURSELVES

Knowing ourselves is important in a classroom. Self-knowledge can help us to be more open to others and be open to other ways of thinking and behaving. Look back over your history as a learner. Think about the rhythms and impulses of that history. What were your passions? What have you found easy, and why? What did it feel like to be able to run fast? Write a beautiful script? Make others laugh? What fostered those things? What hindered you? Have there been changes in enthusiasms and feelings of success? Think about the images and stories which stay with you. Make a list of the stories which you tell, or could tell which you think help to define you, as a person, as a teacher.

It can be interesting to write a history of yourself in some particular area of learning: as a writer or reader or mathematician. What is your history in relation to physical exercise and sport? Art? Music? Science? Often teachers, when writing about their history as learners, find that they have not included significant experiences in their classrooms; others, recognising real difficulties or prejudices, are able to think about how to prevent those from spilling into the experiences of the children they teach.

CONTEXTS FOR REFLECTION

Reflecting is a way of thinking about things which pushes beyond the superficial and beyond incapacitating worry, although it cannot be guaranteed to be a comfortable process. Of course, one way of reflecting is in your head as you walk or drive or do household chores. But there comes a point when we need something more. We might want to read something, to talk with others, try our ideas out, or we might wish to write them down, stop them slithering about, forcing us to be more complete, rather than leaving difficult things on one side.

Conversation

The act of speaking, and of writing, can offer the opportunity to move beyond the surface, and beyond the nagging worry. It helps us move into reflection, exploration and action. Talking with others can be crucial to reflection, and it is worth finding colleagues, fellow trainees and teachers, with whom talk can go beyond the initial sharing of adventures and letting off steam. Letting off steam and recognition of similar problems and pleasures remains hugely important throughout your teaching career, but the very best conversations are those which allow you to take a broader view of what is happening, or to engage more deeply in what concerns you.

During the period in which you are training, some of the best reflective conversations will be with the class teacher with whom you are working. Sometimes they will have been present when events have occurred that have intrigued or frustrated, or really pleased you. Class teachers know the children with whom you are working very well, and it is often a pleasure, and a help to them as much as it is to you, to talk about these things at the end of the day or during breaks. Not all teachers wish to talk in this way, and many are busy with other commitments in school. However, teachers are often glad to talk to trainees about what is going on in the classroom. When we are first learning we are more likely to be self-conscious about what we do and to reflect on it. Sometimes teachers do not have the opportunity to talk with others about the business of teaching, and find that having to articulate practice for a trainee teacher is helpful to them as well as the trainee.

If you work with a teacher who is willing and who enjoys reflecting on the day's events, enjoy and appreciate the opportunity this offers. Talking forces you, as writing does, to formulate your ideas, though, perhaps, with more allowance for gaps and incompleteness than writing. As you describe a situation you are forced to think about it again, and the very presence of a listener can make you aware of what you saw, your perceptions of it, how you are presenting it (what are you hiding, or exaggerating?). A conversation can allow you to test your hypotheses and to try out different approaches. The teacher's experience and particular knowledge of the children you are teaching can give you a deeper insight into their learning. Teachers can suggest a different way of looking, and can give you more information which you can use to adapt and develop your thinking. Try to be open and contemplative, rather than rushing to solutions.

It is possible to plan reflective conversations with both teachers and tutors on the basis of focused observations of your teaching. When you know that you are to be observed, you might identify an area of teaching or class management that you would like the observer to take particular note of. This may well be an area that you have been thinking about already. The perceptions of an observer can bring a new perspective to your thinking and understanding. This opens up the possibility of professional conversation about shared concerns. You may have specific questions to ask teachers or tutors. Try not to want a definitive answer to some of the more complex questions. See how your own experience and the observations and thoughts of others can weave together with your thinking to make something that you, personally, can work with.

Apart from the experienced practitioner, perhaps the most influential, lifelong partner in conversation can be a fellow trainee. You share the experience of learning together. You are faced with similar challenges in terms of practical teaching and getting to grips with new curriculum areas and teaching theories. You will have your own ideas and understandings of education, and you are in a position to support and challenge each other on an equal footing. You may be lucky enough to get to know someone well enough to be able to talk openly about each other's qualities and blind spots and to test out new ideas without fear of embarrassment.

Talk opens possibilities and, like the experience itself, is mercurial. Writing can hold the moment so that you can return to it.

Writing

We can write something down and then return to it when the heat of the moment has cooled. Writing forces us to find words, to slow down, to look at the situation more carefully and in greater detail. During school placements, whether you are observing, working with a teacher, with small groups or teaching the whole class, it is helpful to make notes of things that you notice, that you do, that raise questions for you. There is so much going on in a classroom that it can sometimes be difficult to know what to note down. For that reason, you may find it useful to have a focus for your written notes and I shall return to that later in the chapter. When you are teaching, whether it be small groups or a whole class, the kind of notes you make should help you to think about your practice. You need to make useful notes in a way that does not make you feel as if you are simply fulfilling a requirement made of you by others. The notes should help you to consolidate and develop your own practice. Writing evaluations of your teaching can be very time-consuming. Sometimes trainees feel that these are a distraction from the job of planning for the next day and marking children's work. They need to be a part of that thinking and planning.

There is a real value in writing down notes during the day and at the end of the day before you go home. These may take the form of an aide memoire, or questions, or a description of something that happened which puzzled you or which you think may be part of an emerging pattern. Notes written during the day can be useful, because they catch that moment and can serve as a reminder of how you felt and of things you want to think about at leisure. Notes written on teaching plans are helpful because they relate directly to the lesson and can be used when planning. Often, these notes will refer to a child or group of children, or to a response made by the class to something that you have done. You may wish to replicate that event, you may wish that it never happens again! Either way, your noting it down gives you a chance to think about it later. It is surprising how easily we forget things that seem very memorable in the classroom. Things move so rapidly. There can be many remarkable moments in a single day.

You may wish to choose a focus for what you write down, so that you have some aspect of teaching or learning uppermost in your mind while you are working. You can look back over a week or more of such notes and see how things have changed, or consolidated; see whether there is a pattern to what you are writing, your preoccupations, things that you are noticing about the way children respond, and the ways in which they reveal what they are learning. It is worth writing things down, because our feelings and perceptions change, and it is useful to be reminded of how we saw things at different stages in a day, week, or school placement. A record of observations and your responses to events can chart your progress. It can also help you to celebrate success, or see that things are not as bad as you thought they were at the time!

Journals

A teaching journal can become a powerful part of a teacher's continuing professional development. It can provide a space for reflection, an opportunity to make sense of what is happening in the classroom and in your teaching life, and to move beyond the surface, to acknowledge things, and to make connections. 'The journal holds experiences as a puzzle frame holds its integral pieces. The writer begins to recognise the pieces that fit together and, like a detective, sees the picture evolve' (Holly, 1984, p. 8). A journal is a place for reflecting, speculating, wondering, worrying, exclaiming, recording, proposing, reminding, reconstructing, questioning, confronting, dreaming, considering and reconsidering. It is a space for thinking.

A journal is usually a personal document. There are no hard and fast rules about how it is kept or what is written there. Some people like to use a special notebook that can be carried around. Others prefer a loose-leaf folder. It usually combines a written record of events with a record of thoughts, feelings, ideas and questions. It can include drawing and other visual ways of recording and thinking, although I believe that extended writing in a journal can be of enormous value professionally and personally. Mary Louise Holly suggests that a journal is something like a cross between a log and a diary.

> Journal writing can include the structured, descriptive, and objective notes of the log and the free flowing, impressionistic meanderings of a diary. That is, it can serve the purposes of both logs and diaries. It is a more difficult and perhaps more demanding document to keep – indeed, it is more complex. Its advantages are also greater: it combines purposes and it extends into other uses. The con-

tents of a journal are more comprehensive than those of either log or diary, has both objective and subjective dimensions, but unlike most diaries, there is a consciousness of this differentiation.

In a journal, the writer can carry on a dialogue between and among various dimensions of experience. What happened? What are the facts? What was my role? What feelings and senses surrounded the events? What did I do? What did I feel about what I did? Why? What was the setting? The flow of events? And later, what were the important elements of the event? What preceded it? Followed it? What might I be aware of if the situation recurs? This dialogue, traversing back and forth between objective and subjective views, allows the writer to become increasingly more accepting and perhaps less judgmental as the flow of events takes form. Independent actions take on added meaning. (Holly, 1984, p. 6)

How might I write in a journal?

Write in a way which pleases you. Don't worry about formal language conventions; abbreviations, incomplete sentences, lists, lots of exclamations are all fine. Take risks with the writing, explore your own voice. Write long entries as often as possible to develop ideas fully. Sometimes try and write in great detail. Toby Fulwiler (1987) believes that quantity is the best measure of a good journal. Sometimes you need to write your way into understanding or insight. Sometimes you won't know, until you start writing, what it is you need to write about. Give yourself time. Good things will emerge!

What might I write in my journal?

Write to record. Write to remember the detail. Write to explore and to discover. Write speculatively, analytically, imaginatively. Write in immediate response to something, capturing the moment. Write later, reflectively. When you are working in the classroom, you react in the moment. When you have the opportunity to step back and view the same events from a distance your perceptions can change and you are able to consider other possibilities and to probe a little, challenging and affirming your actions, considering the behaviour of children more tranquilly. Mary Louise Holly says:

Unfortunately once we move beyond perplexing events, we often dismiss them until they recur (sometimes in a slightly different format), and as they often relate to the same underlying problem, we are likely to continue to cope with our circumstances on an *ad hoc* basis. This sometimes solves the immediate problems; sometimes it does not. If we could freeze our perceptions *at the time of our action*, we might be able to identify and understand better the underlying problems and contributing factors that are ordinarily only vaguely 'felt'. And we could prevent many problems from recurring – we could learn from our experience.

Keeping a personal-professional journal allows us to do just that. (Holly, 1984, p. 18)

Writing to evaluate

As trainee teachers, you are likely to be much more rawly conscious of your actions than a more experienced teacher who has much experience to draw on. A journal can bring a sense of perspective to some things that can feel potentially overwhelming as you begin to work in a classroom. A journal can also help you to begin to formulate and clarify some of your underlying beliefs about teaching and learning, and to relate the theory you are learning to the practical experience of the classroom. Some of the most difficult things to think about are our overarching aims in teaching. These and underlying principles are often the hardest things to identify when preparing plans for teaching placements but reflective teaching suggests an approach which goes beyond simply becoming competent in certain techniques. Writing about the events of the classroom gives you the opportunity to consider why you did certain things. This kind of reflection, rooted in the events of the classroom, can help you identify aims and principles. These in turn can be drawn upon effectively when you are planning.

Keeping a journal can also play a significant part in self-evaluation. During training and then as a member of the teaching profession, you will be evaluated by others, and their observations and insights can make a significant contribution to your development. However, ultimately, the responsibility for your growth as a teacher lies in your hands, and a journal can provide the opportunity for you to think about your practice. I often think of reflecting in teaching as a bit like the growing of fertiliser crops. You grow clover, high in nitrogen, and plough it back into the ground. You take note of actions, feelings, responses, failures, successes. You think about them, try and make sense of them. Then that experience can be ploughed back into your teaching.

Reflecting on the life of the classroom

When I introduce the idea of a journal, I often use the notion of a 'disturbance', at which point newly qualified teachers often laugh ironically. I have tried using other words to avoid the negative connotations of disturbance, but keep returning to it, because I think that the things we are drawn to reflect on are often those which have disturbed our view of the world in some way. These need not be negative things. When a child acts with unexpected success, or suddenly makes a breakthrough, there is often the element of surprise and then the puzzle of how that success was achieved. Sometimes there seems no rhyme or reason to it. Sometimes we have a hunch as to why it might have happened, but we want to know more, to explore the conditions and actions which contributed to that happening. So a disturbance might be a surprise, a moment of great pleasure, a nagging worry about why a child does not seem to be making progress, the sneaking feeling that, although they are all sitting quietly and answering the questions, nothing much seems to be happening in the way of learning, the horrible feeling when a class just won't settle or the moment when anger catches you unawares. When you begin writing a journal you might begin with a moment such as one of these. Begin by describing that moment. Tell the story. Recall the detail. And then let the pen go. Write whatever comes into your mind as you think about the event you have described. Later, come back to the writing, and write again.

There are any number of ways of writing about teaching which may or may not be a part of your journal. Some people like using a journal very much, others feel less comfortable with it. Reflective writing can be very fruitful, but you may not always wish to write. Sometimes things which you wish to reflect upon can be represented in different ways. Reflection is about slowing down, pausing. Drawing can be helpful. You may exclaim, 'but I'm no good at drawing!' You do not have to be a consummate artist to make a visual representation of various aspects of your classroom practice.

You might try maps, drawings or diagrams of:

- a lesson
- something you are reading, relating it to your classroom experience
- children in the class you are teaching
- your feeling through a lesson or series of lessons
- you and your relationship to the class
- the way the classroom looks at different times of the day, or at the moment of one particular event you would like to think about.

Although I have suggested that a journal is a personal document, there is also real value in sharing your thoughts with others. By doing so you broaden the professional conversation and bring other perspectives to bear on your experience. I am not suggesting that you share everything that you write in a journal because there can be a real value in the sense of privacy it brings, but there are aspects of a journal which can be very useful in focusing conversations with other teachers, with your tutors and with peers. You may choose to use the journal in an extremely personal way, and touch on things that you do not wish to share. However, a professional journal can make a significant contribution to your evaluation of your progress, and an assessment of your learning.

REFLECTING ON TAUGHT SESSIONS AND WORKSHOPS

Lectures and workshops often occur before you have had a great deal of experience of teaching. They should support your classroom practice. However, you may find that you need to return to lecture notes with the knowledge and questions that you have once you have begun to teach. Sometimes work outside the classroom can seem irrelevant to you as you grapple with the practicalities of managing a large class. Reflective practice involves making links between theory and practice. Lectures should raise questions for you. You may begin lectures with particular questions in mind, and more will be raised. Discuss these with colleagues and with the tutor. Relate these to your reading. Try and respond to the lecture as well as recording information. Think about issues that are raised by the lecture and which you would like to explore further when you are in school.

Some trainees find it useful to jot down two or three questions they have about the subject of the lecture before it begins. These can help you to engage with what the lecturer has to say in a more active way. It is to be hoped that some lectures will challenge your thinking or offer you a different way of looking at a subject. Sometimes you will need time to reflect on what a trainer has to say in order to make sense of it. It is worth thinking about what to record during a lecture or workshop and how to do so. You may wish to capture key words and phrases, or to make a note of references you wish to follow up, but very often these are repeated in notes accompanying a taught session. You might like to think of ways of engaging with the subject matter in a more personal way. Mind maps and drawings are good ways of transforming what you hear into something that is your own. The diagram or map you draw and the links you make may not be those the lecturer had in mind, but they will make sense to you.

Linking lectures and workshops to experience

As you sit in a lecture or take part in a workshop, it can be very useful to see if you can find examples of what is being proposed within your experience of classrooms. One way of doing this is to write a key phrase and link it immediately, or later, to an example from your experience of schools. By making connections, you can properly confront the information and ideas you are being presented with. Whether you find confirmation, contradiction or puzzling anomalies, the making of links with experience helps you to reflect on both theory and practice.

You may return from school placements with any number of questions in your mind. Use these questions to focus your thinking. Ask them of your tutors and your peers. Use them to set agendas when working in small groups. Use questions also to harvest ideas. It can be useful to write down the questions you have about a particular topic, and perhaps even ask others to do so, and then to find out what a number of different people have to say. When you are thinking about teaching, the spaces, the contradictions, the matching of ideas and the slightly different viewpoint can work productively together to help you reach your own way of proceeding. Ask the questions. Engage in debate. Take time while you are alone, to reflect on the differences and similarities, and to think about what you wish to try, and what you feel comfortable with at the moment.

If you are following one of the adult-based training routes into teaching such as the Graduate Teacher programme, or are being trained within a School Centred Initial Teacher Training (SCITT) consortium, then there is likely to be a much more immediate link between taught sessions and *in situ* coaching, and your practice within the classroom. This can sometimes be very useful but it may not always give you the time you need to reflect sufficiently on what you have seen and heard.

RESPONDING TO READING

During your training, reading may seem like an impossible demand, even a luxury. You are more than likely to limit your reading to texts which will answer the immediate demands of the course. However, reading can help you make the best possible use of your school placements. Reflecting on experience is crucial to your development as a teacher. Making links to the experience and theories of others enriches, broadens, affirms and challenges your thinking. Ask others, especially tutors, about books and articles which might help you think in greater depth and with finer purpose about the issues which are engaging you.

Whatever you choose to read, make links between your own thinking, your experience of teaching, and what you are reading. Theory on its own is hardest to deal with. The challenge is to make sense of it in terms of what you are learning through experience and to translate the theory into the practice of the classroom, or to use it to help you interpret what happens there. Always be prepared to test ideas out, to test them against your observations and experience, and to challenge your own perceptions. Books which are full of practical ideas for teachers can be really useful, but if you like an idea, be prepared to think it through, decide what is its purpose and why you want to use it. Sometimes books which emphasise experience, which may be autobiographical, strongly narrative, or even fiction, can help you think around situations and get a sense of them. Sometimes they can help you picture yourself in similar situations or aiming to achieve similar outcomes. Talk with others about what you are reading. Use writing to help make sense of it, to develop it into a shape you can use and make your own. Many books about teaching tell some kind of story.

More often than not it is a smooth and successful story. Rarely do books and articles reveal the messy reality of a classroom, the unsatisfactory ragged nature of much teaching. Sometimes such smoothness can make even experienced teachers feel inadequate or guilty. Stories can be useful touchstones. Records of successful practice have embedded in them ideas which are useful to practitioners. Always, though, trust the reality of your experience, make links with what you read, and keep moving between the two. It is especially useful to identify themes, questions, interests which arise directly from your practice and seek out the books and articles which will help you to explore them further.

REFLECTING ON TEACHING

Although, at first, you may feel that your emphasis is on the *how* of teaching, reflective teaching implies an active concern with aims and with what happens as a result of your actions. When planning, the underlying question of why you are choosing any course of action or sequence of activities is fundamental. When teaching, and when observing the classrooms of others, you may find it useful to have particular questions in mind. Mary Jane Drummond (1996) refers to six 'deceptively simple' questions suggested in the Open University publication, *Curriculum in Action: An Approach to Evaluation* (CACT, 1980):

1. What did the children actually do?

2. What were they learning?

3. How worthwhile was it?

4. What did you (the teacher) do?

5. What did you learn?

6. What will you do next?

To these six questions, I would add: 'How did you know?' Think about the evidence that is leading you to draw certain conclusions. Check whether you are seeing what is there, or what you would like to see! In her article 'Teachers asking questions', Mary Jane Drummond (1996, p. 12) goes on to say:

> A simple question about classroom things may tell you something about people; a question about children may tell you a lot about teachers; a question about learning may tell you more than you wanted to know about teaching. Linked to this proposition is my belief that children are expert witnesses in our search for evidence of teaching and learning.

LEARNING FROM CHILDREN

While you will learn a great deal from the practice of other teachers, the close observation of children and reflection on their actions seem to me to be central to the art of teaching. Learning from children's behaviour and from their responses to the activities you prepare for them is closely linked to the everyday assessment of children and to your day-by-day adaptation of your plans for individuals and groups. David Hawkins, in his essay 'I, thou and it' (Hawkins, 1974), talks about the notion of a 'feedback loop'. The teacher provides a context, materials, an activity for children to explore and work with. Children's actions and responses can tell you about what they already know, what they are interested in, and can give you clues as to what you might offer them next in order to build on that. At its simplest, you notice that some children still have difficulty dividing by ten, then you make a mental note that that is an area you must continue to focus on for them.

However, you may want to look beyond the surface and think about what a child is telling you through what they say, and write and draw, and how they do those things. Listen carefully to what children say and what you notice them doing. Sometimes you might take the opportunity to watch one child or a group of children very carefully. Notice exactly what they are doing, the detail of it. How are they sitting? How do they hold their pencils? Where are they looking? And then, later, think about what that tells you, about the nature of the task, the subject, the children. When you are observing or assisting in the classroom and working with small groups, take as much opportunity as you can to find out more about children, what they know and how they set about tasks in different subject areas. You will have opportunities to learn in much greater depth than you are able to do when working with the whole class. Ask children to try and explain to you their thinking and the processes which they are using to perform whatever activity they are engaged in. Such close attention to what children have to say can be significant in your assessment of children. (Note, in Chapter 2 Graham Handscomb refers in detail to developing the practice of actively listening to the 'pupil's voice' and consulting children.)

Michael Armstrong (1980) suggests that we can think of children as apprentices, who behave as writers, artists, mathematical thinkers, scientists. He argues that they use their limited experience and knowledge to its maximum, using the same processes as an adult practitioner. His detailed observations and analysis of children working in the classroom offer a way of looking at what goes on in the classroom which invites reflection. When looking at children's work it is always worth asking the question: 'What does this tell me about what the child knows?' 'What is their achievement?' And then, 'Did the task set give the child the greatest opportunity to reveal their knowledge and understanding?'

SUMMARY

During your training you are learning about classroom skills, about ways of behaving with children, both socially and as a community of learners. At the beginning of the year you are likely to be very conscious of yourself as a key player in the classroom. As you become more experienced, awareness of the children you are teaching will become increasingly important. However, you remain, always, a significant figure in the classroom. Part of learning to be a teacher is knowing how and when to intervene, when to act and when to stand aside. Self-knowledge, or self-awareness, is a fundamental part of creating the context for children's confident growth as learners and as people. Reflection is partly about moving away from self. It is not always comfortable, but nor should it be negative.

Reflection is, or can be, an integral part of teaching. The way we reflect and the focus of our reflections can change as we change. Reflection at the beginning of your training is likely to be different from reflection at its end, as you start your career, and later as you continue to gain experience. Teaching is a complex activity. It is full of uncertainties and indeterminacies. The more we write and reflect, the more we learn about our teaching, and the more comfortable we become with the uncertainties of the classroom.

ISSUES FOR REFLECTION

- Why do *you* think this book places so much emphasis on reflective practice? Why might some people find this challenging? Do you? How might you overcome this fear?

- Think about a recent success. Why was it a success? What did you learn from the experience?

- Take a minute to reflect on your latest experiences as a teacher and as a learner. What insights do you gain by comparing the one with the other?

- What strategies do (might) you use to reflect on your practice? Are there other methods you could add to your repertoire which might encourage greater reflection? Why/why not?

Further reading

Drummond, M.J. (1996) Teachers asking questions: approaches to evaluation, *Education 3–13*, October. In this useful article Mary Jane Drummond focuses on how asking questions can contribute to evaluation and development and includes a health warning about the potentially unsettling nature of asking questions.

Holly, M.L. (1989) *Writing to Grow*. Portsmouth NH: Heinemann. A useful guide to writing reflectively using a journal. It includes a rationale for using a 'personal-professional journal', examples from teachers' journals and practical suggestions for keeping a journal.

Pollard, A. (1999) *Reflective Teaching in the Primary School: A Handbook for the Classroom*. 3rd edition. London: Cassell Education. This handbook offers very many suggestions of ways of looking at the classroom. You might find it useful to look at this book if you are wanting to find ways of investigating and thinking about different areas of classroom practice.

Pollard, A. (ed.) (1996) *Readings for Reflective Teaching in the Primary School*. London: Cassell Education. This is a companion volume to *Reflective Teaching in the Primary School*. It is a collection of readings referred to in the handbook and covers a wide range of subjects. It is not only useful in terms of reflecting on practice, but also introduces the reader to a range of interesting and thought-provoking texts.

Website: http://learnweb.harvard.edu/alps/reflect/index.cfm. This is part of the Active Learning Practices for Schools website that is linked to Project Zero at Harvard University. Project Zero lays its emphasis on creativity and practitioner-based research. This particular site offers tools for reflection and for curriculum planning that are engaging and easy to use, and might be an attractive introduction to reflective teaching.

Chapter 10

Assessment

Derek Haylock

Let's test the children! But why? Assessment can range from being a very simple process to a surprisingly complex one. It also generate lots of heat and controversial debate. In this chapter Derek Haylock tackles all the issues head on, whilst giving a very comprehensive practical guide on how assessment can be used as a tool to inform teaching and learning.

INTRODUCTION

There are two things that are transparently clear about assessment. First, assessment is an integral and essential part of teaching. Second, assessment is difficult. The following discussion of these two points outlines some of the ways teachers assess pupils as part of the everyday process of teaching and also introduces some key ideas in assessment theory: reliability, validity, and criterion- and norm-referencing. The ideas of formative and summative assessment and reasons why primary teachers assess their pupils are then outlined. This wide-ranging discussion includes some details of statutory requirements for baseline assessment, reporting to parents and end-of-Key-Stage assessment. The ideas are then brought together in a model of what good practice in assessment in a primary school might be like. Finally, I make some suggestions about how trainee teachers might develop and demonstrate their personal standards in this area.

THE TECHNICAL LANGUAGE OF ASSESSMENT

The word *assessment* in education refers to the process by which we attempt to measure the quality, quantity or level of a pupil's learning. Any discussion of assessment inevitably involves the use of some technical language, so it is important to clarify the meaning of some of these key terms from the outset.

Formative and summative

Two key words in any discussion of assessment are *formative* and *summative*. 'Formative' describes an assessment where the main purposes are to inform the teacher's planning and teaching in order to promote the pupils' learning. 'Summative' describes an assessment where the main purpose is to make a judgement about the achievements of the pupils being assessed. Formative assessment is likely to be an ongoing part of the teacher's work, whereas summative assessment is likely to take place at the end of a block of teaching.

These ideas indicate that there is a wide range of reasons why teachers might assess their pupils. At the formative end of the range teachers perceive assessment as being integral to their day-to-day teaching. In discussions with pupils in the classroom they will pose questions to generate evidence of how much the pupils understand particular concepts and principles, both to inform their teaching there and then, and to help the pupils themselves to recognise explicitly the learning with which they are engaged. Assessment understood like this is something that most teachers embrace enthusiastically. At the summative end of the range teachers may be required to make arrangements for their pupils to do statutory national tests in order to provide the Department for Education and Skills (DfES) with statistical data about their pupils' achievement that can be used to monitor and evaluate the work of the school. Not surprisingly, teachers tend to be less enthusiastic about assessment perceived in these terms.

Reliability and validity

One of the key ideas in discussing the formal theory of assessment is *reliability*. Can we *rely* on the results of an assessment? If I were to measure your weight, for example, using my bathroom scales, you might ask the following questions about the process: is the instrument accurate? Does it give the same result every time you use it? Can we be sure that it has been used correctly? Has the assessor interpreted the outcomes correctly? These are precisely the questions that have to be asked about any formal assessment instrument to convince us of its reliability. Unfortunately, it is often very difficult to provide answers to these questions. A proper discussion of how reliability may be measured or enhanced is beyond the scope of this chapter, but we might note that the most frequent mistake in this field is to ascribe too high a degree of reliability to tests and examinations used to make summative assessments of pupils.

A second key idea in discussing the formal theory of assessment is *validity*. Does the assessment actually assess what it purports to assess? Primary teachers are acutely aware, for example, that written tests can often be more an assessment of the pupil's ability to read and interpret instructions than of their understanding and skills in the subject matter of the test.

In general, validity is easier to achieve in the assessment of lower-order categories of learning. The more that the area being assessed can be couched in terms of very specific, behavioural and demonstrable objectives, the more straightforward it is to devise a valid form of assessment. For example, we might ask if the driving test is a valid assessment of whether or not you are a safe and competent driver. This is difficult to answer because 'safe and competent' are not very precise terms, although they refer to valued and important principles. However, what we could argue convincingly is that the test is a valid assessment of your ability to carry out the small subset of specific driving skills that have to be demonstrated in order to pass, such as being able to reverse a car round a bend.

So it is easier to devise valid assessments of lower-order learning, such as the recall of specific facts, the knowledge of specific conventions, the rehearsal of specific skills, than it is of higher-order learning, such as understanding, application, problem-solving and creativity. For example, it would be easier to devise a valid assessment of whether pupils can apply consistently the rule for dropping the 'e' at the end of a word when adding 'ing', than it is to make a valid assessment of their ability to use language imaginatively in a descriptive piece of prose.

In general, summative assessments of attainment in an area of the curriculum that are based on the accumulation of a wide range of evidence gathered over a period of time on a number of different occasions are likely to be more valid than those based on a pupil's performance on a particular day on a limited selection of assessment items. This means that a teacher's summative assessment, if genuinely based on an informed evaluation of a substantial portfolio of evidence for the pupil concerned, should be a more valid assessment of the pupil's attainment than a national or commercially produced test paper. The problem is convincing teachers that this is the case.

Criterion- and Norm-Referencing

There are two different kinds of inferences that might be drawn from an assessment. In a *criterion-referenced* assessment we are setting out to determine whether or not the person being assessed meets one or more criteria. The driving test is a good example of criterion-referenced assessment. If you can meet each of the stated criteria by demonstrating the required skill then you pass. Teachers use criterion-referenced assessments when they determine very specific objectives for their pupils' learning and then assess which pupils have met those objectives. Their record-keeping can then be a simple system of ticks against pupils' names, under a heading referring to the objective assessed.

In a *norm-referenced* assessment we are making inferences about a person's performance compared to other people. Commercially produced standardised tests often provide normative data, enabling the teacher to interpret a pupil's performance in terms of how it compares with that of the population of similarly aged pupils. For example, a standardised comprehension test might give a pupil's score as being at the 67th percentile: this means that 67 per cent of pupils of the same age would not have scored higher than this on the test. Teachers use a kind of norm-referencing when they record the marks that pupils have scored in tests. For example, to put in my mark book that Jack scored 14 out of 20 in this week's spelling test records very little useful information about what Jack can or cannot do, but it does allow me to see at a glance how Jack has done in that test compared with other pupils.

For teaching and learning purposes, criterion-referenced assessments and records are the more useful since they provide specific information that can inform the teacher's planning and teaching and inform the pupil of their progress towards specific learning goals. However, norm-referenced assessments are frequently required for reporting purposes: parents, for example, quite often like to know how their children are doing compared with others.

ASSESSMENT FOR TEACHING

The process of teaching involves an obvious cycle, in which assessment of pupils' learning is an integral component:

- planning what you want the pupils to learn

- deciding how you will determine whether they have learnt it

- teaching them

- assessing them

- using the information from your assessments to inform your future planning.

But this is not to suggest that assessment only happens at the end of a period of teaching. Teachers assess their pupils and monitor their progress all the time, at every stage of a lesson, in every interaction and observation that takes place in the classroom. Teachers are constantly making judgements about their pupils' recall of specific knowledge, their ability to perform particular skills, their understanding of key concepts and principles, their attitudes and personal qualities, their social skills, and so on.

They do this in a variety of ways, both formal and informal, both planned and unplanned. It is important for trainee teachers to grasp the idea that assessment is not just about giving pupils written tests. For example, primary school teachers gather evidence about their pupils' learning by:

- listening carefully to the children's oral responses in class and group discussion

- engaging in one-to-one discussions with them about their work

- listening to them read

- scrutinising and marking their written work

- getting pupils to make their own self-assessments of their learning

- observing them in practical and group activities

- giving them occasional written or practical tests

- analysing their results on formal, national or commercially produced tests.

Below are four reasons why assessment is an integral part of teaching.

To provide the teacher with information about the pupils' progress to inform their teaching and planning

This is the primary purpose of formative assessment. Put simply, teachers need to know the extent to which their pupils are actually learning the material they are teaching; whether they are achieving the learning objectives they have specified in their lessons plans. To help in their planning of the next teaching session, teachers *in every lesson* need to make some kind of assessment of their pupils' progress with the material in hand. This does not mean that they have to give their pupils a written test in every lesson. Teachers can get this feedback by a variety of means, as I have indicated above.

Trainee teachers are sometimes surprised to discover that just because you have explained something clearly and thoroughly you cannot assume that the pupils have learnt it! Continuously we need to be assessing whether our pupils have acquired the specific knowledge, mastered the various skills, understood the key concepts and grasped the general principles in what we are teaching. This information then helps us to make judgements about whether or not we can move on, whether we should give more time to particular aspects, or whether we need to revisit them later with particular groups of pupils.

It is essential therefore for effective teaching that a primary school teacher ensures that their lessons have clear objectives, that they plan how they will assess the pupils' learning of these objectives and that they make subsequent curriculum plans in the light of this assessment.

To diagnose an individual pupil's problems

Sometimes teachers feel they need to try to sort out why an individual pupil is having particular problems with some of the material they should be learning. They might then try to assess very carefully and in detail the precise nature of the pupil's problems. The distinctive nature of this diagnostic assessment is that it does not just determine that a pupil has failed to learn something, but attempts to determine the reasons why. Diagnostic assessment is especially important therefore with pupils who have particular learning difficulties in one or more areas of the curriculum.

Diagnostic assessment is inevitably time-consuming. In practice, unfortunately, many teachers are rarely able to give to individual pupils the time they need to get to the bottom of their difficulties. However, trainee teachers, particularly early on in their training, are often in a position where they can sit and work with individual pupils. This can be an invaluable opportunity to get close to the way the pupil's mind works on particular tasks and to get some experience of trying to diagnose the underlying reasons for any difficulties encountered.

To group pupils for teaching purposes

Primary schools with more than one class in a year group sometimes decide to group pupils across classes into sets according to their ability for various subjects. This is particularly common in mathematics where teachers find the difficulties of teaching the whole range of ability in one class to be especially challenging. Because the range of attainment in this subject can be so marked, some primary schools set their pupils for mathematics across a number of year groups. Even where setting is not used it is very common for pupils within a class to be put into groups according to ability for various lessons. This enables the teacher to make different provision for the different ability groups at certain stages of the lesson. In order to undertake any such grouping or setting, teachers must inevitably assess their pupils.

Such assessment can be done using a wide range of evidence, such as the teacher's own records of the pupils' progress against specific key objectives, portfolios of evidence from the pupils' work over a period of time, the pupils' performances in various planned assessment tasks devised by the teacher, or the pupils' scores on some commercially produced or national tests. However it is done, since the implications of setting or grouping for teaching purposes can be very significant for an individual pupil, it is essential that the process is based on assessment evidence that is substantial, objective, systematic and up to date.

To contribute to the teacher's evaluation of his or her teaching

The best teachers reflect continually on their teaching, analyse what goes on in their classrooms and systematically evaluate their own performance. Information obtained from the assessment of their pupils is clearly one of the most significant components of the teacher's personal evaluation of their teaching. In making judgements about the effectiveness of their choices in teaching content and methods, their approaches to classroom organisation, their teaching style, their communication skills and so on, teachers will be informed by the extent to which the evidence from their assessments suggests that these have resulted in pupils learning what was intended. The temptation for trainee teachers in evaluating their teaching is to focus mainly on how well the pupils behave and whether or not they enjoy the lesson. These are important, of course, but the ultimate question in evaluation must always be: are they learning anything?

ASSESSMENT FOR LEARNING

An exciting recent development promoted by the Qualifications and Curriculum Authority (QCA) in England has been the emphasis on formative assessment as an effective means for promoting learning. This has been a welcome counterbalance to the emphasis on summative assessment as a means of generating data about school performance that has dominated education since the introduction of the National Curriculum. The new emphasis is the result of the work of the Assessment Reform Group, which has built on the extensive review of research into formative assessment by Black and Wiliam (1998), proposing ten principles for assessment for learning (Assessment Reform Group, 2002). These encapsulate an approach to assessment and learning that involves the pupils themselves in understanding their learning goals and being actively involved in assessing their own progress towards these. In summary the ten principles are that assessment for learning:

- is part of effective teaching

- focuses on how students learn

- is central to classroom practice

- is a key professional skill

- is sensitive and constructive

- fosters motivation

- promotes understanding of goals and criteria

- helps learners know how to improve

- develops the capacity for self-assessment

- recognises all educational achievement.

Primary school teachers who include this emphasis in their approach to assessment, as a matter of course, share their learning goals with pupils. They ensure that pupils understand these goals and are clear about how they will know if they have achieved them. They give time to discussing the assessment criteria with their pupils, using language the pupils can understand and examples to clarify what counts as success. They plan assessment opportunities within their lessons, using a variety of means to enable both the teacher and the pupil to gain insights into how the pupil's learning is progressing towards the goals. They provide pupils with feedback that highlights what they have achieved and that is clear and constructive about their weaknesses and how these might be addressed. The evidence from research into formative assessment is that when pupils are actively engaged in this process of reviewing their own progress then learning is enhanced and pupils are empowered to take action to improve their own performance (Assessment Reform Group, 1999). So, in focusing on assessment for learning, we can identify three further purposes in teachers assessing their learners.

To provide pupils with feedback on their progress towards agreed learning goals

It is not just teachers who need to know how the pupils are progressing. The pupils need to know as well. The findings of the Assessment Reform Group indicate that engagement with the process of formative assessment and constructive feedback on their progress enable pupils to learn more effectively. Good teaching will ensure that pupils understand clearly what they are supposed to be learning and how they are to demonstrate that they have learnt it. As a consequence it must also ensure that pupils know the extent to which they are meeting their individual learning objectives. So teachers assess pupils in order to be able, through constructive feedback, to make pupils explicitly aware of the learning that they are achieving.

To motivate pupils to do their best work

The feedback they get from their teachers about their progress is one of the principal components of motivation for pupils in school. Most pupils in primary schools want to please their teachers and to do well in school. All kinds of feedback from teachers' assessment of their work and achievements are therefore important to the pupils and will usually contribute to their motivation: marks, grades, stars, smiley faces, oral feedback, written comments, praise and so on. Not all primary school pupils would have sufficient motivation to do their best work in school if they knew that their efforts were not to be assessed in some way or other by the teacher. Assessment linked to specific objectives that are attainable in the short term can be particularly effective in motivating lower-attaining pupils who can in this way be encouraged and enabled to see that they are making real progress, albeit in small steps.

But just as constructive feedback can be a powerful means of motivating pupils, teachers must also be aware of the impact that negative comments and low marks can have on a pupil's confidence and enthusiasm. In particular, it is important to focus comments about failure on the work itself and how it could have been better, and not on the individual pupil.

To develop pupils as independent learners with skills of self-assessment

An important aim for all teachers is that their pupils should take responsibility for their own learning and be able to learn independently of the teacher. Engaging the pupils with the whole process of formative assessment, as described above, encourages the pupils to do just that. To be an independent learner you need to be able to recognise what you do understand and what you do not understand, which skills you have mastered and which skills you need to focus on next. This describes precisely what pupils are engaged in when they are involved in self-assessment of their own learning. So the impact of assessment for learning is more than just helping pupils to learn some specific knowledge or skills more effectively: it is also helping them to develop more general strategies for independent learning per se.

ASSESSMENT FOR REPORTING

Apart from the teacher and the pupil, there are others who want to know about the pupil's progress in school and to whom summative assessments of the pupil's achievements have to be reported. So we can add at least three other purposes for assessment in education.

To provide parents with information about their children's progress

The 1988 Education Reform Act established a statutory requirement for schools to provide annual written reports to parents on their children's progress – and most parents will actually want to know how their children are progressing in various aspects of learning at school. Teachers' assessments of their pupils therefore must provide them with the data they require to provide parents with the information they require. Interestingly, many parents are as much concerned with teachers' (informal, subjective) assessments of their children's attitudes and behaviour in class as they are with their assessment of their academic attainment.

There is a statutory requirement for schools to provide at least one annual written report to parents. Government guidance for teachers about report-writing (QCA/DfEE, 2000a, 2000b) suggests that most parents will want to know:

- how the child is performing in relation to their potential and past achievements

- how the child is performing in relation to the rest of the class and national standards

- their child's strengths and any particular achievements

- areas for development and improvement

- how they can help

- whether their child is happy, settled and behaving well.

● To determine levels of attainment in the National Curriculum

Since its inception following the 1988 Education Reform Act, the National Curriculum in England and Wales has been assessment led. Significantly, the first group set up by the government to get the process of establishing a National Curriculum for England and Wales under way was the Task Group on Assessment and Testing (TGAT). The result of the TGAT report (DES, 1988) and subsequent versions of the curriculum is that each subject is structured for assessment purposes into one or more attainment targets (ATs) which are themselves broken down into a series of levels of attainment. Mathematics, for example, has four ATs (Using and Applying Mathematics; Number and Algebra; Shape, Space and Measures; Handling Data), English has three (Speaking and Listening; Reading; Writing) and science has four (Scientific Enquiry; Life Processes and Living Things; Materials and their Properties; Physical Processes). But each of the other subjects – the foundation subjects – art and design, history, geography, and so on, has just one (DfEE/QCA, 1999a).

Arbitrarily, there are for each AT in each subject eight levels of attainment covering Key Stages 1, 2 and 3, plus an additional level representing 'exceptional perform-ance above level 8'. Equally arbitrarily, the expectation (of the government, at least) is that most pupils will achieve at least level 2 by the end of Key Stage 1 (that is, at age 7, in Year 2) and at least level 4 by the end of Key Stage 2 (that is, at age 11, in

Year 6). Pupils are therefore assessed at the end of each Key Stage to determine their National Curriculum levels for various subjects. At the end of Key Stage 1 and at the end of Key Stage 2 there is a statutory requirement for assessments of their levels of attainment in English, mathematics and science. The pupils' levels of attainment in these subjects are determined separately by their performance in the national tests and also by teacher assessment, although at Key Stage 1 science levels are determined only by teacher assessment.

Teacher assessment in each attainment target involves making a judgement about which of the 'level descriptions' provided in the National Curriculum best fits the pupil. To enable them to do this, teachers will often assemble a portfolio of evidence of each pupil's attainment over a period of time. There is also guidance made available by the QCA in the form of exemplification of standards. Since teacher assessment at the end of Year 2 for attainment targets in mathematics and English and at the end of Year 6 for those in mathematics, English and science is a statutory requirement, teachers in these year groups have this additional reason for assessing their pupils systematically and regularly. Many primary schools are now assessing their pupils against the National Curriculum level descriptions in at least mathematics and English at the end of every year. Often they make use of non-statutory tests produced by the QCA to assist them in this. It is important to note that an average pupil will take about two years to move up one level for any given attainment target.

Because the attainment levels are assigned numbers (0, 1, 2, 3, 4, and so on) there is a tendency for people to do arithmetic with them. This is usually quite unjustified and simply produces other numbers that are essentially meaningless. For example, to determine an overall level of attainment for science at Key Stage 1 teachers are required to multiply the level of attainment for Scientific Enquiry by three, to add on the levels of attainment for the other three ATs, divide the answer by 6 and round to the nearest whole number (QCA/DfEE 2000b). To see how meaningless this process is, note that it would result in two pupils with AT levels of 2, 4, 5, 5 and 3, 2, 2, 2 for science both getting an overall level of 3. But this kind of arithmetic can only be used on a 'ratio scale' (see Haylock and Cockburn, 2003), where it can be assumed, for example, that the numbers on the scale represent entities that are spaced at equal intervals and that zero represents nothing. Clearly, levels of attainment are not like this. For example, the difference between what a level 2 pupil can do and what a level 3 pupil can do is in no meaningful sense 'equal' to the difference between a level 3 pupil and a level 4 pupil; and no one would suggest that a pupil who is not yet at level 1 (and scores 0) knows 'nothing'! The attainment levels constitute only an 'ordinal' scale, allowing us to do no more than use them to state that the attainment of one pupil is higher than, lower than or broadly the same as another. Any aggregation of levels or calculations of average levels, for example, is unacceptable for the kind of measuring scale being used here, yet government reports and documents do this kind of thing endlessly.

⬤ To enable partner schools to inform fed-schools about pupils' attainment

Liaison between different phases of schooling, such as when pupils move from nursery to primary, from infant to junior or from primary to secondary, will normally include the partner-school passing on records of pupils' attainment in various subjects. This provides the recruiting schools with information that can be used to plan their provision and to group pupils for teaching purposes. This is another reason why teachers must assess their pupils.

⬤ To enable authorities to monitor standards and for schools to set targets

Teachers in primary schools are required to assess their pupils formally and summatively because national government and local education authorities are committed to monitoring standards being achieved by pupils in schools. They do this mainly through the school's performance in the statutory assessments undertaken at the ends of Key Stages, as we have discussed above. As part of the process of monitoring standards, the Standards Unit at the DfES sends annually to schools in England a substantial package of information about national assessment, which includes their individual Performance and Assessment Data (referred to as a PANDA). For each of the areas assessed, schools can use these data to compare their performance with national standards and with standards achieved in 'similar' schools. (At present, 'similar' schools are determined by the proportion of pupils who receive free school meals.) The intention behind the provision of all these data is to enable schools – and hence individual teachers – to set targets for their pupils' progress, in terms of National Curriculum levels, as part of the government's drive to raise standards (DfEE, 1998b). It should be noted that 'standards' in this context means nothing more than the summative assessment of pupils' achievements measured by their performance in the formal, statutory end-of-Key-Stage assessments.

⬤ THE CLASS TEACHER'S RESPONSIBILITY FOR MARKING

Marking of written work is a chore for most teachers, increasingly so as the pupils get older and generate more and more written work each day. But teachers generally recognise that this marking is an important component of the assessment and learning cycle. Clearly, the information that the teacher gleans from their evening spent ploughing through today's pile of exercise books contributes to their ongoing, informal assessments of how well the pupils are learning the material being taught. The marked work also provides a written record that can be consulted for summative assessment purposes. Effective marking will contribute directly to the pupils' learning. It will provide pupils with clear feedback on both the strengths and weaknesses in their written work. At times this is selective: pointing out all the weaknesses in a piece of work might be discouraging for pupils, confusing and counterproductive. The teacher must remember that, if a pupil produces work littered with errors, then it is probably the teacher who has made the biggest error in setting the child a task that is not appropriately matched to their ability. Most teachers aim to find every opportunity for encouraging and rewarding effort and progress in their feedback on pupils' written work.

Teachers are also very conscious of the fact that the audience for their marking will often include parents. As well as ensuring that teachers are conscientious and careful in what they write on the pupils' work, this aspect makes marking a useful mechanism for helping parents to understand the strengths and weaknesses in their children's written work. Written comments on pupils' work can have different purposes (SCAA, 1997). Sometimes they are intended to be the basis for discussion between the teacher and the child. Other times they are simply intended to be read by the pupils, to encourage them or to challenge them. In this case pupils need time and opportunity in the lesson to read the comments and to reflect on them. Some comments are intended to give specific guidance for how the pupil should approach future written work. Others are simply to correct or improve an existing or ongoing piece of work. It is important therefore for the teacher to be clear about the purpose of their written comments and to shape them accordingly. As part of assessment for learning practice and of pupils' self-evaluation, there is also a growing development of using children's own marking as part of the assessment process.

Many schools have guidelines for teachers in their marking, outlining expected standards of presentation in children's work and giving, for example, advice such as:

- relate comments to specific learning objectives

- ensure that comments are legible and clear in their meaning

- be positive and encouraging about the pupil's achievements

- provide an indication of what needs to be addressed in the future.

Trainee teachers should ask to see any guidance on marking children's work that is given to teachers in their placement schools, ensure that they are familiar with it and then implement it in their own day-to-day marking.

ONE MODEL OF GOOD PRIMARY SCHOOL PRACTICE

In this section I bring together some of the ideas about assessment discussed above and outline a model of good primary school practice. This model identifies four aspects of the primary school teacher's responsibilities for monitoring, assessment, recording, reporting and accountability:

1. Informal, ongoing teacher assessment.

2. Planned assessment opportunities.

3. Statutory teacher assessment.

4. National Curriculum tests and tasks.

Each of these is considered in terms of timing, main purposes, subsidiary purposes, possible methods, and recording and reporting. It is important to note that the categorisation of some of these different aspects of assessment is not hard and fast. But the model demonstrates the range of assessment activities and the purposes of these.

1. Informal, ongoing teacher assessment

Timing

- Every day, every lesson even, as a normal part of teaching and planning.

Main purposes

- To inform the teacher's short-term and medium-term planning.

- To keep track of children's coverage of programmes of study and progress through the school's curriculum.

- To diagnose children's individual problems and to identify areas needing more general attention.

- To engage pupils in the process of assessment and thereby to enhance their learning.

Subsidiary purposes

- To contribute to teacher assessment of National Curriculum levels of attainment.

- To monitor pupils' personal and social development.

- To provide the teacher with data for the evaluation of the quality of their own teaching and the quality of the pupils' learning.

- To provide the teacher with informal data for feedback to parents throughout the year.

Possible methods

- Scrutiny and marking of pupils' written work.

- Watching and listening to pupils as they engage with their classroom activities.

- Question and answer as part of everyday teaching with groups or the whole class.

- Talking with individual children.

- Pupils writing their own self-assessments of their strengths and weaknesses, or their progress towards their learning goals.

- Interviews with parents, carers.

- Discussion with other teachers.

Recording and reporting

- Recording informal notes as part of personal planning.

- Maintaining a system for keeping records of work/tasks/activities completed.

- Contributing to the pupil's personal portfolio occasional 'significant pieces of work' in English, mathematics and science, annotated by the teacher, or pieces of evidence of significant learning (not necessarily just written work).

- Reporting to parents via formal and informal meetings.

2. Planned assessment opportunities

Timing

- Opportunities planned at fairly regular intervals (for example, every two or three weeks per core subject) specifically to generate data about children's learning of key objectives or aspects of the level descriptions.

- Such assessment opportunities would be incorporated into medium-term planning.

Main purposes

- To make summative judgements about pupils' learning at the end of a block of teaching.

- To contribute to teacher assessment of National Curriculum levels in the core subjects.

- To inform the teacher's short-term and medium-term planning.

- To give pupils constructive feedback on their progress towards their personal learning goals.

Subsidiary purposes

- To diagnose problems and identify areas needing attention for individual pupils.

- To provide data for the evaluation of the teacher's teaching.

- To motivate pupils.

- To record information about pupils' attainment for their next teacher.

Possible methods

- Activities that would anyway form part of a normal teaching session, but which are designed to generate evidence of learning of specific objectives by individuals.

- Group tasks, focusing on specific aspects of the level descriptions, with structured observation by the teacher.

- Small-group teacher-led discussion sessions, focusing on assessment of key objectives or aspects of the level descriptions.

- Individual written work designed to generate evidence for assessment of the level of attainment on specific attainment targets.

- Teacher-devised tests, focusing on specific key objectives or aspects of the level descriptions.

- Commercially produced (often criterion-referenced) tests.

- Diagnostic interviews of individual children.

Recording and reporting

- Recording performance on tests or tasks in a class record, preferably showing which pupils achieved or failed to achieve specific objectives.

- Contributing 'significant pieces of work' in English, mathematics and science, annotated by the teacher, (not necessarily just written work) to the pupil's personal portfolio.

- Reporting to parents at parents' meetings.

- The pupil contributing to their personal record of achievement.

- Reporting to parents via the annual written report.

- Passing on records to the next teacher.

3. Statutory teacher assessment

Timing

- The statutory requirement is for teachers to make a teacher assessment of levels of attainment towards the end of each Key Stage.

- Many schools now do this towards the end of each academic year.

- There is also a statutory requirement for assessment for 4–5-year-olds starting school through the compilation of a Foundation Profile.

Main purposes

- To meet the statutory requirements for teacher assessment.

- To provide data for statutory requirements for reporting to parents, school governors and other authorised audiences.

Subsidiary purposes

- To contribute to the school's evaluation of their curriculum policies.

- To provide summative information to pupils about their achievements.

- To provide data for liaison with other schools or teachers at the point of transfer.

Method

- Teacher makes a 'best-fit' judgement of the level of attainment for each AT in science, maths and English, based on the level descriptions, drawing on class records and the individual pupil's portfolio of work, and using as guidance and moderation: (a) the portfolio of pupils' work; (b) the exemplification of standards materials provided by the QCA; (c) discussion and comparison of standards with other teachers.

Recording and reporting

- Completing whatever formal systems of recording and reporting of teacher assessments the school has in operation (as detailed in the school's policy statement for assessment), including pro formas for recording levels of attainment, report forms for parents, and individual pupils' records of achievement.

- Using data about levels of attainment for liaison with other schools and teachers at the point of transfer.

4. National Curriculum tests and tasks

Timing

- The external, statutory, end-of-Key-Stage tests and tasks are administered to pupils towards the end of Year 2 and Year 6.

Main purposes

- To determine the 'test' level for each pupil for English, maths and science attainment.

- To provide data for formal requirements for reporting to parents, school governors and other authorised audiences.

Subsidiary purposes

- To provide data to complement statutory teacher assessments.

- To contribute to the school's evaluation of their curriculum policies.

- To provide feedback to pupils on their progress.

- To provide data for liaison with other schools or teachers at the point of transfer.

Method

- Prepare pupils appropriately for the tests and tasks.

- Administer the national tests and tasks as instructed by the QCA.

Recording and reporting

- Completing whatever formal system of recording and reporting of national test levels is required both externally and internally, including the pro forma for recording marks and levels of attainment, report forms for parents, and individual pupils' records of achievement.

● Using data about levels of attainment for liaison with other schools or other teachers at the point of transfer.

DEVELOPING AND DEMONSTRATING STANDARDS IN ASSESSMENT

Below is a summary of what a trainee teacher might aim to do during their initial teacher training in order to develop their skills in monitoring, assessment, recording, reporting and accountability, and to demonstrate to tutors or mentors that they are achieving the required standards.

1. Make sure that all lesson plans have clearly stated objectives: the more specific and observable these are the easier it will be to make valid and reliable assessments of them. Make these explicit to the pupils and ensure that they understand how these objectives might be achieved.

2. State in all lesson plans how you intend to monitor and assess pupils' learning, such as question-and-answer sessions, marking of written work, observation of pupils, and make sure that pupils know that this is how they will be assessed.

3. Keep brief notes on your day-to-day, informal assessments, organised by subject, adding to this after each lesson. Note to what extent the objectives for the session were achieved – based on evidence from monitoring and marking of pupils' work, observation of the pupils engaging with their classroom activities, responses in question-and answer sessions, and so on; note any significant learning or difficulties shown by individual pupils or groups of pupils. Here is an example of such an assessment note written after a Year 3 numeracy lesson:

   Evidence from the question-and-answer session with the lower group indicated that they seemed to have got the basic idea of what you had to do with counters to work out a division and to find a remainder. Marking the middle and top groups' written work showed that the learning objective for the main part of the lesson had been achieved [using counters if needed, pupils will be able to work out a simple division of a number up to 40 by 2, 3, 5 or 10 in cases where there is a remainder, using grouping, and identify the remainder], although my observation indicated that some of them (particularly Jack and Anne) did not use grouping. Sue and Tom in the top group found even the harder examples to be very easy and are ready to experience remainders with division by a wider range of single-digit numbers.

4. Have a list of the names of the pupils you are teaching and against each name write the date of any assessment note that refers to them by name. This will enable you to access quickly the assessment evidence related to individual pupils and to spot any pupils for whom you are not collecting much evidence.

5. Maintain the class teacher's existing systems for record-keeping, but put a photocopy in your own file to demonstrate that you are doing this.

6. Include in your medium-term planning a number of 'planned assessment opportunities' in the core subjects and any other specialist curriculum area: about once every two weeks for maths and English, and about once every three weeks for science and any other specialism. These planned assessments should be for all or most of the pupils in the class. They should also normally be just one of the activities taking place in a normal teaching session. The distinctive feature of such an assessment should be, however, that it is clearly focused on providing evidence of learning in relation to one or more key objectives or aspects of the level descriptions. It need not be a written test: it could be any kind of focused activity that will generate evidence of learning in relation to the objective(s). The evidence may be written work, but it could also be other kinds of evidence systematically recorded. The activity providing the evidence does not need to be completed by all pupils on the same occasion.

7. Keep up to date with marking of pupils' written work and give them constructive written feedback on their work.

8. Record the outcomes of these assessments in a way that shows which pupils have demonstrated evidence of learning in relation to which specific key objectives.

9. Make sure that your lesson planning clearly shows how your ongoing assessment is informing your planning.

10. Trainee teachers do not usually have sufficient time to put together enough evidence to make summative judgements of levels of attainment for all the pupils in the class so compile substantial portfolios of evidence of learning for perhaps two or three pupils in the class. Add evidence to these portfolios at the rate of about one entry per week for each of the core subjects and any other specialist curriculum area.

11. For these pupils, towards the end of your time working with them, use the evidence from the portfolios to make a best-fit judgement of their level of attainment for each attainment target for the core subjects and any other specialist subject.

12. Also for these pupils, write brief summaries of their attainment in a form that can be incorporated into a report for parents; discuss these with the class teacher and pass them on to them when you have finished them.

13. Take any opportunities to work with the class teacher in preparing written reports and in making informal or formal oral reports to parents.

14. Take any opportunities to participate in the administration of end-of-Key-Stage national tests and tasks.

15. Ask to see the school's PANDA and discuss with the teachers how this information is being used to assist long-term planning and to set targets.

SUMMARY

- Key ideas in assessment theory include reliability, validity, criterion- and norm-referencing, formative and summative assessment.

- There is a wide range of purposes in teachers assessing pupils, both formative and summative, both non-statutory and statutory, covering assessment for teaching, assessment for learning and assessment for reporting.

- Monitoring, assessment and recording are integral parts of the cycle of everyday teaching.

- Involving pupils explicitly in every aspect of the process of formative assessment contributes powerfully to their learning.

- There is a wide range of methods available for teachers to gather evidence of pupils' learning: assessment is not just about giving pupils written tests.

- Trainee teachers must ensure that they plan their monitoring, assessment, recording and reporting of pupils systematically and thoroughly in order to demonstrate that they are achieving the required standards.

ISSUES FOR REFLECTION

- Consider how you might put into practice the ten principles for assessment for learning.

- 'You and I both know that this is not your best work.' Come up with other examples of comments on poor work which focus on the work without being negative about the pupil.

- How can trainee teachers convince those who are assessing them that they are using assessment to inform their planning?

- Consider the different kinds of records of pupils' work and attainment kept by the teachers with whom you work. What information do these records provide? How useful is this information for planning? For making summative judgements? For reporting? For meeting statutory requirements?

Further reading

Assessment Reform Group (2002) *Assessment for Learning, 10 Principles*: *Research-Based Principles to Guide Classroom Practice*. Assessment Reform Group (down-loadable from www.assessment–reform–group.org.uk). This leaflet is a handy summary of the ten principles for assessment for learning.

Black, P. and Wiliam, D. (1998) *Inside the Black Box: Raising Standards through Classroom Assessment*. London: King's College (reissued 2004 by NFER Nelson). This important report is based on an extensive review of research into the effectiveness of formative assessment. The authors argue convincingly for the contribution of formative assessment to effective teaching and raising of standards in learning.

Conner, C. (ed.) (1999) *Assessment in Action in the Primary School*. London: Falmer Press. A comprehensive and practical guide to assessment for primary teachers, this will be a useful reference book for those training to teach in primary schools.

Dockrell, B. (1995) *Assessment and Evaluation*, Part IV of C. Desforges (ed.), *An Introduction to Teaching: Psychological Perspectives*. Oxford: Blackwell. The two chapters here that deal with approaches to educational assessment and assessment, teaching and learning will help trainee teachers be clear about how the principles of good assessment can be applied in the classroom.

Headington, R. (2000) *Monitoring, Assessment, Recording, Reporting and Accountability: Meeting the Standards*. London: David Fulton. This is an accessible and straightforward guide for trainee teachers, a good mix of theory and practice, with effective illustrative use of examples of children's work and trainees' assessments.

Chapter 11

Planning

Derek Haylock

Making lessons work? It's all in the planning! Good planning is important for a whole host of reasons, not least of which is that it generally gives you confidence and results in more successful sessions. Different schools and different teachers plan in different ways. Here Derek Haylock describes some of the fundamental principles, and gives detailed guidance to help you plan effectively.

INTRODUCTION

The principles of good lesson-planning are to have clear statements of what the pupils are supposed to learn, to ensure that the teaching and pupil-activities are focused on these, and to determine in advance how you will assess whether or not the children have learnt what was intended. This chapter shows how these principles might work out in practice for a trainee teacher in developing their skills in planning and preparation. It is based on the conviction that teaching is not about giving pupils nice things to do: it is about promoting learning. If this is successful, children will recognise it and will enjoy the experience.

LONG-TERM, MEDIUM-TERM, SHORT-TERM: PLANNING AND PURPOSES

Clear purposes in terms of 'learning outcomes' are essential for good teaching. Without them teaching and assessment of pupils are unfocused. With them the teacher has the basis for ensuring that the pupils are learning and progressing.

Confusion of terminology

In the literature about teaching and learning we find a wide range of terms used to describe purposes in teaching, not always used in the same way. For example, Waring (1999) and Petty (2004) refer to *educational objectives* and *learning outcomes*, using these terms synonymously. Headington (2000), in a discussion about *teaching intentions*, makes a distinction between objectives (what the teacher intends) and learning outcomes (what the pupils actually learn). Petty also refers to the term *SMART objectives* (learning outcomes that are Specific, Measurable, Agreed, Realistic, Time-bound). The word *target* is often used in relation to planning the progress of an individual pupil. For example, much of the guidance about planning the provision for individual pupils with special needs uses the concept of *SMART targets*. Many authors, such as Heywood (1982), make use of Bloom's (1964) distinction between *cognitive* objectives, referring to intellectual skills and abilities, and *affective* objectives, referring to attitudes and values. Bloom was one of the pioneers of the move towards teaching objectives being specified in *behavioural* terms, that is, as specific, observable behaviours rather than as things that we imagine to be happening in the learner's mind. Gagné, (1976) showed how this approach could be used to describe a hierarchy of learning outcomes, from lower-order motor skills (such as forming numerals correctly), through to higher-order cognitive strategies (such as problem-solving).

Most authors make a widely accepted distinction between longer-term *aims* and shorter term *objectives* (for example, Kyriacou, 1998). Cole and Chan (1994) talk about *general goals* for medium-term planning and *instructional goals* for lesson planning. Macharia and Wario (1989) illustrate well the potential for confusion: 'Sometimes in the beginning of a syllabus there may be an outline of the broad objectives (goals or aims) of education ...' (p. 18).

At the risk of adding to the confusion, I will use three terms in this chapter to describe our purposes in teaching: aims, goals and objectives. Respectively, these correspond to the three levels of planning in which teachers have to engage: long term, medium term and short term.

Long-term planning

Long-term planning is what the school staff will usually undertake collaboratively, under the guidance of the curriculum co-ordinator for a particular subject. The result of long-term planning will be a school curriculum statement and syllabus for that subject, covering all year groups in the school. Trainee teachers should expect to have access to a school's long-term plans for each subject they have to teach, but are unlikely to be involved in the production of such plans. A school's long-term plan is likely to include some general *aims* for each subject, often giving an indication of the school's philosophy of teaching. These will be statements that indicate what the teachers collectively hope to achieve in the long term; they may therefore have a pervasive, but rather unspecific, influence on what actually happens from day to day in the classroom. These are not things which we will *achieve* over a specific period of time with a particular group of children, but they may be influential in directing our thinking when we are undertaking medium-term planning. Particularly important across the curriculum are *affective* aims related to personal, social and emotional development, including attitudes and values. Here are some examples of long-term aims:

- *Pupils should have a positive attitude to mathematics, enjoying it, valuing it and recognising its importance in a wide range of applications.*

- *Pupils should have high standards of presentation in their written work in English, including handwriting, spelling and punctuation.*

- *Pupils should develop an awareness of the principles of scientific enquiry, including being able to plan an investigation, carry it out systematically and evaluate the evidence obtained from it.*

- *Pupils should learn to listen to and to respect other people's points of view.*

Medium-term planning

Medium-term planning is what an individual teacher undertakes at the start of a block of teaching. It might, for example, involve planning for half a term's work for a class. For a trainee teacher it is likely to be the production of a scheme of work for a teaching practice of a number of weeks in duration. A medium-term plan is likely to contain some indication of the major *goals* for what the pupils should learn during the block of teaching in question. The major sources for determining the goals for a block of teaching will be the school's long-term plan and the government curriculum documents such as: the National Curriculum Attainment Targets, the Early Learning Goals, the frameworks of the National Numeracy and Literacy Strategies. Here are some examples of such medium-term goals:

- *For text-level learning in English, pupils will develop their ability to discuss the feelings, behaviour and relationships of a character in a story.*

- *Pupils will develop their confidence in using a wide range of mental strategies for addition and subtraction with whole numbers up to 1,000.*

- *Pupils will develop their understanding of the idea of a fair test in science and be able to apply this in designing their own experiments.*

> *Pupils will learn the major differences between Islam and Christianity.*

Good medium-term planning by teachers will also include some specific goals in the affective area, such as:

> *This half-term one of my goals is specifically to improve the pupils' appreciation of the joy of reading fiction.*

> *One of my goals is that pupils will value mental strategies for doing calculations and not regard them as inferior to formal written methods.*

Short-term planning

Short-term planning refers to the planning needed for each lesson. Trainee teachers have to accept that more detail will be required of them in lesson planning than would be the case for most practising teachers. This is, first, because they are relative novices and cannot rely on years of experience, and, second, to provide evidence that they are meeting the required standards for planning and preparation and thus to satisfy those who are assessing them.

Our short-term *objectives* are what we hope to see some pupils achieve as the result of our teaching and their activities in a particular lesson or over a series of a few lessons. These will focus mainly on *cognitive objectives* such as: knowledge of facts, terms, conventions; mastery of skills and techniques; understanding of concepts and principles; application of knowledge, skill and understanding. The more specific and behavioural we can make these objectives the more we will be able to demonstrate that we are achieving our teaching intentions. *Behavioural objectives* are those that refer to learning outcomes that are precise, specific, observable and therefore assessable behaviours. They normally begin with the phrase, 'the pupil will be able to ... '. This is then followed by a verb that represents a behaviour, such as: recall, state, select, draw, describe, illustrate, construct, summarise, and so on. For example, some specific, assessable, short-term behavioural objectives might be:

> *By the end of the lesson the pupils will be able to state correctly three ways in which they ensured that their experiment was a fair test.*

> *By the end of the lesson the pupils will be able to use the strategy of compensation to add a two-digit number ending in 9 to any other two-digit number.*

> *By the end of the lesson the pupils will be able to apply correctly the rule for dropping the 'e' at the end of a verb when adding 'ing'.*

Note that words such as 'understand', 'grasp' and 'appreciate' would not appear in behavioural objectives. The behaviourist would ask you to tell us how you would know that the pupil understands a particular concept, grasps a principle or appreciates something. How you answer this question will then suggest ways in which you could turn the objectives into behavioural statements. For example, I might say: I will know that the pupils understand the principle of place value if they can write down correctly a set of numbers up to 1,000 that I read out to them and then put them in order from smallest to largest. The behaviourist would reply, 'So these are your objectives!' The advantage of this approach is that it is fairly apparent how the teacher might plan to assess for which pupils a specific, behavioural objective is achieved. Most teacher training institutions encourage trainee teachers to write their short-term lesson objectives in this way as far as possible.

However, there are disadvantages to the behaviourist approach. One is that many of the things that we are trying to achieve in a particular lesson or series of lessons cannot easily be put into this kind of language, without it becoming extremely cumbersome. Words such as 'understanding' – although somewhat vague in meaning – are, in practice, very useful abbreviations for a collection of specific behaviours. In addition, we usually have to revisit skills and concepts several times in order to be confident that the pupil has learnt them, so that the phrase, 'by the end of the lesson the pupil will be able to' sounds somewhat ambitious. So, my view is that it will often be appropriate – and quite acceptable – for lesson objectives to indicate that we are contributing to the development of some key aspects of learning. Such objectives might appear in a session plan as a statement beginning with the phrase: 'This session will contribute to the development of'. For example: *this session will contribute to the development of the children's understanding of what constitutes a fair test in science.* It is also appropriate and important to include in lesson planning objectives related to the development of aspects of personal, social and moral education. For example: *this session will help the pupils to develop their skills of co-operating in small groups.*

It is not acceptable merely to state what the children will do in the session as its objective. This is a common shortcoming of trainee teachers' lesson plans. For example, these are *not* learning objectives: the children will write an acrostic poem about winter; the pupils will write up their reports on their investigations from yesterday; the yellow group will complete the exercises on page 27 in the mathematics scheme. The objectives of the session should be specified in terms of what the children are supposed to be *learning*, not what they will be doing.

COMPONENTS OF PLANNING: WHY? WHAT? HOW? HAVE I?

For the reasons outlined above, attempts to plan teaching and learning entirely in terms of behavioural objectives have not been entirely satisfactory, although their strength is the clear emphasis on *attainment*. The weakness is that teachers still feel that the quality of pupils' *experience* in school is equally important and that this is not reflected in an objectives approach. Other approaches, such as those based on the enquiry-based principles that underpinned the educational philosophy of Stenhouse (see, for example, Stenhouse, 1971), have planned the curriculum principally in terms of the kinds of experience that pupils should have. Inevitably such an approach is criticised for not being systematic enough about monitoring and assessing pupils' progress. The best advice therefore is that good planning must maintain a *balance* between having clear objectives, with an emphasis on *attainment*, and the consideration of the kinds of *experience* that we consider valuable for our pupils. The National Curriculum Orders (DfEE/QCA, 1999b) reflect this balance. Each subject includes statements of the specific knowledge, skills and understanding to be learnt by the pupils, written in the form of objectives. For example, for Key Stage 1 mathematics, 'pupils should be taught to … know doubles of numbers up to 10 and halves of even numbers to 20' (DfEE/QCA, 1999c p. 17). These objectives are then followed by a section headed 'Breadth of study', which outlines the range of activities, contexts and experiences through which the pupils should be learning the subject. For example, again for Key Stage 1 mathematics, 'pupils should be taught the knowledge, skills and understanding through … using mental images of numbers and their relationships to support the development of mental calculation strategies' (ibid., p. 20). These two very different kinds of statement demonstrate clearly that, in talking about what we want pupils to learn, we need to retain this balance between attainment and experience.

Whatever model of the curriculum is adopted, inevitably systematic planning will involve addressing what we might call the four curriculum questions: Why? What? How? Have I? I will consider these in this order but, in practice, we often find ourselves addressing all four questions simultaneously in our planning.

Why?

This question is about purposes. Why am I doing this? Yes, you will ask yourself that question many times during your teacher training and, no doubt, throughout your career! But in this context, the question refers to having clear purposes for some planned teaching. Why am I teaching this material in this way to these pupils? This question raises all the issues of aims, goals and objectives discussed above.

What?

This question is about content. What am I planning to teach the pupils? What are the specific facts, conventions, terms, skills, techniques, concepts, principles, strategies, applications, and so on, that I want the pupils to learn? What are the attitudes, personal qualities, social skills and so on, which I want to develop?

How?

This question is about methods. How am I going to teach them in order to achieve my intentions for their learning? What are the specific experiences, activities and materials that I will use? What teaching style or teaching methods will I employ? How will I organise the class for teaching and learning?

Have I?

This question is about evaluation. Have I achieved what I set out to achieve in my teaching plans? Have the pupils learnt what was intended and developed in the areas planned? In the planning stage, the question is, 'How will I know whether the pupils have learnt what was intended?' In the evaluation stage, after the teaching, it becomes, 'What is the evidence that the pupils have learnt what was intended? If not, why not? Is the problem in the appropriateness of the learning objectives or in choices of teaching method? Or does it relate to my own effectiveness in classroom teaching skills at this stage of my professional development?'

MEDIUM-TERM PLANNING FOR TRAINEE TEACHERS

For trainee teachers a scheme of work is the written, medium-term planning undertaken for a particular subject (or any other discrete component of the pupils' curriculum) prior to a block teaching practice. This should show that, in advance of the period of teaching, the trainee teacher has addressed the four basic curriculum questions discussed above: in other words, they have considered purposes, content, method and evaluation/assessment. A scheme of work should contain sufficient detail and substance for the trainee to use it for their daily, short-term planning of lessons, with coherence, progression and clearly stated objectives for the pupils' learning.

Nowadays it will be rare for a trainee teacher to be given a completely free hand for planning their schemes of work for a teaching practice. The class teacher will almost certainly already have their own medium-term plans in place and will probably – and rightly – expect the trainee teacher to implement these. Trainee teachers should therefore expect to prepare their own schemes in conjunction with the class teacher, possibly drawing on advice from curriculum co-ordinators. If possible, trainees should be involved in any curriculum planning meetings taking place during their time based in schools. For the core subjects and for any other specialist curriculum area trainees will be required to demonstrate that they can do medium-term planning. They must therefore be prepared to take the existing plans of the teacher and somehow 'make them their own'. However, trainees should not expect to have to duplicate material in order to satisfy the differing demands of the school and the training institution. It is sensible for the existing plans to be photocopied and included as part of the trainee's scheme. But there should be evidence in the trainee's own planning that they have got to grips with the structure and content of the material; that they have thought through the purposes and principles; that they have considered organisational aspects; and that they have added some substantial ideas or emphases of their own, particularly in terms of activities, resources and outputs.

It is not possible to lay down one structure or framework for a scheme of work that will apply in all circumstances, because schools, classes and curriculum subjects vary in their nature. Any structure which shows that the four curriculum questions (Why? What? How? Have I?) have been addressed should be acceptable.

A sensible and professional set of requirements for medium-term planning of a scheme of work for a trainee teacher on a block teaching practice, which gives the trainee the opportunity to take ownership of the planning, might be as follows:

- A photocopy of the teacher's medium-term plans for the period that includes the teaching practice.

- An indication of the sections of the teacher's medium-term plans that are to be covered in the teaching practice (this could be done by highlighting on the photocopy).

- An indication of how the material to be covered relates to the National Curriculum, the National Literacy or Numeracy Strategies, or the Early Learning Goals.

- A statement of the medium-term goals for the pupils' learning: the key knowledge, skills, concepts, principles and so on, that the pupils should learn during the period of teaching practice.

- A brief statement of how the content of this scheme builds on any related previous experience the pupils have had.

- A set of key activities or learning experiences that will probably be used during the teaching practice. (Some flexibility is necessary here, because short-term planning will have to respond to your ongoing assessment of pupils' learning.)

- A description of how the pupils and the space are usually to be organised for these lessons for different kinds of activities, including how the trainee teacher intends to differentiate for the range of ability within the class.

- A list of the main resources that will be required.

- A statement of how information and communications technology will be incorporated into the teaching of this subject.

- An indication of what opportunities for assessment are planned (see Chapter 10 for a discussion of 'planned assessment opportunities') and how the outcomes of these will be recorded.

- At least the first lesson plan.

- A statement by the trainee teacher of five or six *curriculum principles* that will guide their approach to teaching this area of the curriculum and the selection of material and activities.

This last suggestion is to give the trainee teacher the opportunity to engage in some reflection related to their longer-term aims for their teaching of the subject and to think through a little of their own developing educational philosophy. These are intended to be the kinds of things you might say at interview if someone asked you questions such as: 'What's your approach to teaching science?' 'What's your personal philosophy for teaching English?' 'What are the key principles that underpin your teaching of mathematics?' Some examples of curriculum principles to guide the approach to teaching an area of the curriculum and the selection of material and activities are given below:

- *Mathematics: Pupils should see the mathematics they are learning in school as relevant to the real world and their lives outside school.*

- *English: It is important that all pupils develop positive attitudes to reading and writing and see these as useful, enjoyable and productive experiences.*

- *Science: All science planning must ensure that pupils make progress in the skills and principles of experimental and investigative science, as well as in their understanding of key science concepts.*

SHORT-TERM PLANNING FOR TRAINEE TEACHERS

During a block teaching practice the planning of each teaching session should be clearly derived from the medium-term plan. Trainee teachers should also ensure that they use the feedback from their ongoing and planned assessment of pupils to inform their short-term planning – see the discussion of the relationship between assessment and planning in Chapter 10.

There is no single format that is appropriate for planning every teaching session. Tutors and teachers will suggest different approaches. Different formats will be found to be more useful for various situations, depending on the ages of the children, the style of curriculum organisation, the subjects being taught, the size of the group, how the children are organised for learning and the range of abilities.

But, however it is laid out on the page, short-term planning of lessons or teaching sessions might include the following:

● details of the class/set/group, number of children, subject or topic

● date, time and length of the session

● a clear statement of the specific learning objectives for the lesson

● how this session relates to previous and subsequent lessons

● the content, structure, timing and organisation of the lesson.

This last section is the bulk of the lesson plan. Once again, there is no standard format that suits every session in every subject with every class or group of children. But good planning will always consider at least the following aspects *for each stage of the lesson*:

● what the teacher will be doing

● what the children will be doing

● what noise level is appropriate (plan this!)

● how the children will be grouped and organised

● how the space will be used

● the approximate timing of various phases of the session

● what resources are needed and how they will be accessed.

At the end of a teaching session it is useful to make some brief 'working notes' at the foot of your lesson plan. This would just be a note of anything you need to remember that will help you with planning subsequent sessions; for example, any activities which were not completed, particular organisational problems that need to be addressed, points which turned up in the session that should be taken up later with the class, a group or an individual. These working notes are not assessment notes, nor are they an 'evaluation' of your teaching. There will be expectations for trainee teachers to undertake ongoing and planned assessments of their pupils' learning and to record these appropriately. Some suggestions in this respect are given in Chapter 10.

There will also be expectations for trainee teachers to do formal evaluations of their teaching. The information derived from their assessments of pupils constitutes the starting point for the trainee teacher's evaluation of their work. This leads on to evaluation of their choices in the classroom: the effectiveness of their teaching methods, their organisation of pupils for learning and their selection of materials; the appropriateness of the specified learning objectives; and their personal professional development as a teacher. As a trainee teacher you will find it important to evaluate your developing skills in planning, teaching and assessment against the standards that you will be required to demonstrate in order to achieve Qualified Teacher Status.

WEEKLY PLANNING: LITERACY AND NUMERACY

The introduction of the National Literacy and Numeracy Strategies (DfEE, 1998c; 1999a; 1999b) has prompted many teachers to adopt the recommended frameworks for weekly rather than daily planning. It is unlikely that the detail involved in a weekly plan will be sufficient for a trainee teacher to use for their teaching day by day. But it is also unrealistic for trainee teachers on teaching practice to finish up having to do three levels of planning: a medium-term scheme, weekly plans and daily lesson plans. It is probably best therefore for Numeracy and Literacy for a trainee teacher to prepare weekly plans using the weekly planning formats suggested by the Numeracy and Literacy Strategies, but to regard these as an alternative to a medium-term scheme of work.

SUMMARY

- Planning can be discussed at three levels: long term, medium term and short term.

- Long-term planning is usually undertaken by the whole staff and results in a curriculum policy statement and syllabus for the school.

- Medium-term planning is what a teacher does for a block of teaching: for a trainee teacher this will be a scheme of work for a curriculum area for teaching practice.

- Short-term planning is the daily planning of individual lessons.

- Corresponding to the three levels of planning are three levels of teaching purposes: long-term aims, medium-term goals and short-term objectives.

- Weekly planning has replaced daily planning for Numeracy and Literacy for many teachers, but trainee teachers will probably still need to do short-term planning on a daily basis.

- There are advantages in terms of assessment of pupils and focused teaching if short-term objectives can be as specific as possible and written in behavioural terms.

- As well as dealing with knowledge, skills and understanding, a teacher's aims, goals and objectives in planning should include the affective area, relating to attitudes, personal qualities, social skills and values.

- Planning should address both the pupils' attainment and the quality of their experience.

- The four basic curriculum questions to guide planning are: Why? What? How? and Have I? These address issues of purpose, content, method and evaluation/assessment.

ISSUES FOR REFLECTION

- What are the planning issues related to organising pupils in a class for group work where not all the groups are doing the same task?

- In your lesson planning how do you deal with the problem that different groups within a mixed-ability class may require different sets of objectives?

- *One of my objectives in this lesson is to improve the ability of the pupils to work together co-operatively in groups.* Is it possible (or helpful) to rewrite an objective like this in more precise, behaviourist terms? Would you then be better able to determine to what extent the objective had been achieved? What evidence in terms of pupil behaviour would indicate that they were learning to work co-operatively?

- What would be the 'curriculum principles' that would guide your personal approach to teaching and the selection of material and activities, for English, mathematics and science?

Further reading

Cole, P. and Chan, L. (1994) *Teaching Principles and Practice.* 2nd edition. New York: Prentice Hall. Chapter 3 of this book provides a very systematic and thorough discussion of planning and preparation for teaching. The authors discuss clear principles that underpin good planning, illustrating their points with both good and bad examples.

Kyriacou, C. (1998) *Essential Teaching Skills.* 2nd edition. Cheltenham: Stanley Thornes. This book is one of the best general guides for trainee teachers at both primary and secondary levels. The second edition has provided the author with an opportunity to rewrite his material in the light of recent developments. Chapter 2 is a very useful guide to planning and preparation, written in a style that suggests the author understands the realities of classrooms.

Petty, G. (2004) *Teaching Today: A Practical Guide*. 3rd edition. Cheltenham: Stanley Thornes. This very practical book provides useful guidance on thinking through aims and objectives for teaching and some helpful models for lesson planning.

Waring, M. (1999) Plan and prepare to be an effective teacher. In G. Nicholls (ed.), *Learning to Teach*. London: Kogan Page. This chapter provides straightforward guidance for trainee teachers to help them to meet the requirements for planning and preparation for teaching practice.

Chapter 12

Teaching English

Ann Browne

What's the secret of successful teaching of English? Well, as Ann Browne demonstrates in this chapter, it lies in clear thinking and careful organisation. She explains that learning to teach English well can be a very rewarding and exciting challenge. She describes, step by step, what you might expect at various stages of your training and how to capitalise on the available opportunities.

 ## INTRODUCTION

Teaching English well on school placements is the result of understanding the subject to be taught, understanding how children learn, being able to employ a range of teaching techniques, making use of assessment data and reflecting on classroom events. This chapter describes how trainee teachers can have successful and rewarding teaching practices by making good use of course- and school-based work in the early part of their training, and planning and preparing carefully for the final practice. It covers the following topics:

- the way in which the taught course- and school-based elements of training complement each other

- how to make best use of initial periods of school experience

- successful English teaching on final practice.

WHAT IS EXPECTED BY THE END OF THE COURSE

By the time trainees become newly qualified teachers they are expected to know and understand a great deal about the teaching of English. The expectations are specified in *Qualifying to Teach: Professional Standards for Qualified Teacher Status and Requirements for Initial Teacher Training* (DfES/TTA, 2002). By the end of their course trainees should:

- know what should be taught to children at different ages and stages of education

- be able to plan a coherent scheme of work for English

- employ a varied range of teaching and learning methods appropriately

- be able to monitor and assess children's progress informally and formally

- recognise that learning occurs through a circular series of actions, which include planning, implementation, evaluation of teaching and assessment of learning.

At the beginning of a training course these requirements may seem quite daunting. The purpose of this chapter is not to overwhelm you. Rather, the intention is to show how courses, assignments, time spent in school and guidance from tutors and teachers all work together to provide experiences that develop trainees' knowledge, understanding and skills so that by the end of your course you will have the necessary competence and confidence to teach English with success.

PRELIMINARY VISITS

Before the first sustained period of teaching practice there is usually an opportunity for you to become familiar with the class you will be teaching and with the teacher with whom you will be working.

Observation

You and your school may be provided with guidance on how to make best use of this time. This is a good opportunity to find out as much as possible about the school by reading school policies and other information. It is also a good time to find out as much as possible about how the curriculum is taught. You will learn a great deal by observing teachers at work (see Chapter 4) and noticing how the teaching of English is organised. You might try to find out the answers to the following questions:

- Does each class have a daily literacy hour?

- Do children engage in shared reading, shared writing, group reading, group writing and individual literacy activities throughout the day?

- Does the class follow the literacy hour format for part of the week but have different arrangements on certain days?

- Do children have access to literacy activities as they play?

- Do children use literacy resources such as the writing area throughout the day?

- Are there periods of sustained silent reading?

- Does the school have writing workshops?

- How is literacy developed across the curriculum?

- When and how are speaking and listening taught and learned?

You might notice how children are grouped for English.

- Are the children placed in ability groups?

- Are children from different classes grouped together in ability sets?

- Do the children work collaboratively in their groups?

You may also notice the kinds of resources that are used to develop language and literacy.

- Are computers used as an aid to developing writing, reading, speaking and listening?

- Do children have regular, planned access to the listening station to listen to tapes as they read new and unfamiliar books?

- Do children use tape recorders as part of the speaking and listening programme?

- Does the teacher follow a commercial language and literacy scheme to teach reading, writing, spelling or handwriting?

- Do the class follow a reading scheme?

- What use is made of the library or the class reading area?

- Does the class have a writing area?

- Does the teacher use worksheets to develop or monitor writing and reading?

 ⬤   Do the children have word books or spelling journals?

Observation and reading the school's English and related policies will give you an insight into how English is taught and the methods teachers use to develop children's abilities in English. All of this information will be invaluable when you are planning for your first period of school practice.

⬤ Assignments

In order to help you to understand the significance of what you are observing, hearing and reading about in the early stages of your course, trainees often undertake a number of English activities in school. These may include:

 ⬤   listening to children reading and analysing what children do when they read

 ⬤   carrying out a writing activity in school and analysing samples of written work

 ⬤   selecting books to share with or read to pupils

 ⬤   telling or reading a story to a class

 ⬤   compiling a portfolio of work and observations of a pupil over a period of time

 ⬤   designing a resource to be used with a group of pupils when teaching English.

These or similar activities are intended to familiarise you with how children learn language and literacy, the processes that are involved and the factors that teachers need to take account of when they are planning for English. For example, analysing the reading of one child may help you to recognise how children draw on word, sentence and text level strategies in order to read. Reflecting on your own interventions as the child reads may help you to see how you need to employ a range of support strategies in order to develop the range of cues that children use.

In order to fit assignments and set tasks into the schedule of placements and the teacher's teaching programme it will be necessary to discuss the timing of course work with the class teacher. If possible, plan for them to occur fairly early on in the placement so that if anything goes wrong or you are not able to complete the assignments you will be able to repeat them later. After deciding when to do the tasks find out whether they need to be linked to the work the teacher has already planned. For example, if you are expected to undertake a writing activity this may be linked to the type of writing that the children are learning about as part of their literacy hour work. Writing in the nursery can be linked to the theme and be planned for imaginative play areas. You will need to know how this is to be organised in order to plan an activity that is appropriate. If you have been asked to select and read a story to the class, you may want to choose one written by an author the children have been studying or with a theme that complements the current class topic. It is useful to show your plans to the class teacher before you work with the children.

Having identified when you are going to carry out your tasks you will need to plan them. Considering the following questions might help you to design a worthwhile activity that will interest the children:

- Which children will be involved in the activity?

- What starting point will appeal to this group of children?

- How long will the session be?

- What can the children do in English?

- What have their recent experiences in English been?

- How does the teacher normally organise English sessions?

- Do I need to follow the usual format?

When you have decided what you want the children to do and why, you may think about how you will organise the session.

- What resources will you need?

- Are these in school or will you have to bring in materials from home?

- How will you introduce the activity?

- How will you support the children when they are working with you?

- How will the session end?

- What will happen to the work the children have produced?

Course tasks are often undertaken with individuals or groups of children. This may seem quite removed from how class teachers normally teach language and literacy. However, they are valuable for two reasons. First, going through the stages of preparing, planning, teaching and evaluating an activity in this way is excellent preparation for producing session plans that will be required later. When undertaking course tasks you may decide not to write down everything you and the children will do but you will have rehearsed all the elements that need to be included in a session plan. Second, effective teaching depends on being able to assess children's abilities and match work to their learning needs. Working with small groups and analysing their work and their behaviour reveals a great deal about what children can do, and will help you to have realistic expectations and to plan appropriate work.

EARLY PRACTICES

Most trainees complete a brief period of teaching practice quite early on in their training. Although during this time trainees are expected to take some responsibility for teaching the class and planning the work, they generally do this with the teacher's guidance and have a fairly small teaching load.

If English is one of the subjects that you are expected to take some responsibility for you may have to plan and implement a number of whole-class and group sessions. As many schools have now adopted the literacy hour for teaching English most trainees working in Key Stage 1 and 2 classes will base their planning and teaching on this format and use the literacy strategy objectives as a starting point for their planning. In Nursery and Reception classes trainees will be working with the *Curriculum Guidance for the Foundation Stage* (DfEE/QCA, 2000) and will be linking many of their English activities with play, existing resources and working areas.

Although you may be quite anxious about your first experiences of teaching, the aims for early practices are usually modest. At this stage, typically the intention is for trainees to:

- use their developing subject knowledge of English to inform their planning and teaching

- gain experience of planning short sequences of work and daily sessions

- use a range of techniques to teach English

- explore organisational strategies such as different forms of group work and whole class management techniques

- devise appropriate and meaningful activities to develop children's language and literacy

- become more familiar with the Early Learning Goals, the National Curriculum programmes of study and the objectives in the National Literacy Framework.

In short you are continuing to extend your own learning about the English curriculum, how children learn English and how to teach English. Neither teachers nor tutors will be expecting to see perfect teaching. They know that beginning teachers in the early stages of their training make mistakes but they also know that these can be valuable learning experiences. They will want to encourage you to take risks and use these early encounters with the class and with groups to experiment with activities and procedures.

GETTING THE MOST OUT OF EARLY PRACTICES

Preparation

Much of the preparation for the first teaching experience will have been completed during the lead-up to the practice. You will have become familiar with the school's approach to English, the way sessions are organised and the resources that are used. You will also have become familiar with the children you will be teaching and have some idea of their abilities and interests. You will know who in the class requires or receives extra help and which children need stretching. You will need to draw on this information when you are planning and devising activities for the class.

Planning

Your class teacher will probably make a date to discuss your planning a few weeks before the practice begins. You will probably be given a copy of the medium-term plans and identify what the class is expected to have covered before you assume responsibility. At this stage you might want to relate the teacher's planning to the Early Learning Goals, the National Curriculum programmes of study and the National Literacy Strategy objectives. This will give you a sense of what the children will have already covered and add some details to what the teacher has written. You may be able to start thinking about what you will be expected to do and how you might arrange this. You may begin to collect resources that will be helpful; for example, a collection of texts which exemplify a particular genre.

You will have a more exact idea of what you will need to teach as the time for your practice draws nearer. About a week before the practice you will need to check exactly what work the class have completed and what the teacher has identified as the next step. At this stage the teacher will probably give you a copy of the weekly planning and identify the sessions, the activities and the objectives for which you will take responsibility. For English this might begin with you working with groups of children on guided group reading or writing or other activities during the literacy hour, then involve taking responsibility for the whole-class work and one or two groups during the hour and, towards the end of the practice, taking responsibility for all aspects of the literacy hour. In addition you may be expected to read or tell a story to the class each day or organise sustained silent reading sessions. You may also be expected to plan to cover certain aspects of the speaking and listening curriculum within English sessions and other activities. In the nursery you may have to plan a language activity, take some responsibility for the writing or reading area, plan to develop language through imaginative play and other regular activities and read stories. You may also be working with individual children, sharing books with them and discussing their early attempts at writing.

Once you know when you will be in charge and what you have to teach, you can begin to prepare detailed plans. The starting point for these is the learning objectives that are to be covered. The series of session plans that you produce should reveal how the children will address the objectives in different ways over a number of days, how you intend to introduce children to the new learning and allow time for them to experiment with and explore the new concept, and how their work will result in an outcome or product that is satisfying to the children. The final piece of work should also indicate to you how well the children have achieved the objectives you set at the start of the period of teaching.

Whole-class work

Working with the whole class is a time when you can instruct, model and explain to large numbers of children. It is an efficient and often effective way of introducing new learning if the teaching is clearly focused and well paced. In order for it to work well, the children have to find the work interesting and motivating. They need to be actively involved and challenged through high-level questioning. During whole-class times children can also be given clear feedback about their responses and any misunderstandings can be clarified quickly. Whole-class sessions are usually pitched at the middle of the ability range in the class, with only limited opportunities for differentiation when questions are directed to specific individuals. Consequently, whole-class times are good for introducing new concepts or revising familiar ideas.

In the literacy hour the initial whole-class period should cover text- and word-level work and include sentence-level work when appropriate. Text-level work in reading may involve shared reading or discussion of response to a text or the characteristics of a particular text type. In writing the shared composition of a piece of writing or a demonstration of planning strategies are text-level work. Sentence-level work is concerned with grammar and punctuation and word-level work covers phonics, spelling and vocabulary. Whole-class work at sentence and word level will include explanation, demonstration or instruction about grammatical items such as classes of words, the use and form of punctuation, spelling patterns and common words taken from the lists in the appendix of the *National Literacy Strategy Framework for Teaching* (DfEE, 1998c), vocabulary extension and handwriting.

Although the whole-class period is a time for teaching children it should include opportunities for the children to actively participate. It is possible to vary the nature of their participation depending on the objective that is being taught. Guidance about teaching the literacy strategy (DfEE, 1999a) suggests children can be given letter and word fans to hold up or personal whiteboards on which to write down their answers to the teacher's questions. These enable all the class to respond when questions are asked.

In the nursery there are times when all the children or large groups are gathered together and when all the children can be taught at once. The children may be introduced to the elements of a story through the use of story props depicting the characters and settings in a familiar text. They can be offered demonstrations of writing through the shared writing of notices, captions or a brief letter. The children can be actively involved through questioning, participating in a story or having a go at writing.

Plenary sessions

Plenary sessions are one of the elements of the literacy hour but they may occur at other times in the school day. These are times when some children can present their learning to the remainder of the group. The children's presentations and their reflection on their work need to be carefully organised by the teacher. Those children who are going to make a contribution to a plenary need to be identified and prepared ahead. They can be given a framework such as:

- describe what you found difficult and how you solved your difficulties

or

- list three things you found out about …

During plenary sessions the teacher may be assessing the contributing children's learning or intending them to use aspects of the speaking and listening curriculum. If so he or she will be observing and listening carefully to the participants. He or she may also need to take a more active role. Plenary sessions are a time for teachers to reiterate and clarify what children have been learning and show children how what they have been doing relates to earlier experiences. These uses of a plenary session may be realised through providing a brief summary or through questioning the children.

Group work

Teaching children who have been grouped together because they share a similar learning need is an effective way of using adult time. The teacher's instruction, demonstration, explanation, questions and feedback can be planned to meet the particular needs of the group, rather than addressing a general need as is the case with whole-class teaching. Guided reading and writing are group activities that benefit from the careful targeting of support for the children.

If you are working with a group of children the remainder of the class need to be involved in productive activities that they can do without adult support. Devising and organising activities that are matched to the children's abilities and that can be completed with minimal adult intervention can be one of the most difficult aspects of planning and teaching for inexperienced teachers. In order to do this you need to:

- have an accurate appreciation of what the children can do

- recognise the next step in reading, writing and oral language development

- provide all the resources that children will need in order to complete their tasks

- have a sense of how long activities will take

- give clear, easy to follow explanations.

Although you will be familiar with the class and will have worked with the children, your knowledge of their abilities will still be fairly limited. You may still not know about all the resources that are in the class and whether all the children can make use of them. At this stage in your training your knowledge of English and progression in English will still be incomplete. Because of all the potential pitfalls that can occur with group work it is best to assume responsibility for managing group activities slowly. Planning for group reading or writing at the start of the practice, which enables you to work closely with a group of children, will reveal the difficulty level of the task you have set, whether it was well matched to the children's needs and whether the resources and your initial explanation helped the children to complete the task easily. If you are working with the group and the activity is too easy, too difficult, too long or too short, you may be able to adapt the activity. You will certainly learn valuable lessons about how to plan independent work for the group.

Once you have worked closely with two or more groups you may be ready to take responsibility for the teacher-led group and an independent activity. This will be easier if the independent group is one that you have worked with and if the activity is linked to the work they did with you earlier in the week. The examples of session plans which follow illustrate how a trainee planned a guided writing activity for groups of children throughout the week. She was in charge of this session for two days and after that the teaching assistant took over (Figure 12.1). After the first day the trainee introduced an independent activity (Figure 12.2). This was simply to complete the writing that had been started during the guided session. On the third day the trainee designed a second independent activity for the first group with whom she had worked (Figure 12.3).This was to make a lotto game using ten of the words taken from the appendix in the *National Literacy Strategy Framework for Teaching* (DfEE, 1998c).

Slowly increasing the number of groups that you plan for and manage allows you to prepare activities that are well matched to the children's needs and that are successful. This enables you to build up your confidence and your teaching skills so that by the time you are working with the whole class you are likely to feel that you are teaching well.

Figure 12.1 Session plan for guided writing activity

Session Plan

Curriculum Area English – Writing
Date 31 01 2005
Time 20 minutes
Group 6 children, mixed ability
Reference NLS Year 2 term 2 text level objective 20

This lesson will be repeated with each of the 5 groups of children in the class over the course of the week. I will take the groups on Monday and Tuesday and Mr D (teaching assistant) will work with the groups on Wednesday, Thursday and Friday.

Learning objectives
To be able to compose a definition of a familiar object
To consider how to write a clear definition
To begin to think about the needs of an audience

Relationship to previous sessions
The children have been investigating toys and playthings. The definitions will be of toys. The children have been writing personal accounts of toys. This session is intended to introduce them to a factual style of writing.

Relationship to subsequent sessions
I would like the children to 'publish' their definitions either in a large class dictionary or on a display. The writing may need to be revised before this is possible.

Content and structure
Look at a collection of toys
Give an oral definition of one toy (puppet)
Ask each child in turn to select one toy
Each child to give an oral definition of the one they have selected
Help the children to phrase the definition
Write up part of an opening sentence on the flip chart, 'A .... is a ......', to be used as a starter
With the children write up the name of each selected toy
The children begin their writing

Organisation
Teacher-led group
Individual writing
Teacher support – focus on the structure of the writing

Working notes
It took longer than I expected to introduce the session and allow the children time to give an oral definition. It might have been more effective to have used shared writing to produce a group definition and have left the individual writing until next session. The writing was unfinished. The children should be able to continue it tomorrow. I think that they will be able to do this independently, although I will ask Mr D (teaching assistant) to keep an eye on the children while I work with the next group.

Informal assessment
With help all the children, apart from Sally, gave a reasonable oral definition of their toy. They could all see that a definition needs to 'stand alone' if it is to make sense to others. They moved from 'It's furry and soft and I like it' to, for example, 'A teddy is a soft toy' (contributed by Terri).
Sally might benefit from joining the group that start this work tomorrow in order to get extra practice at oral rehearsal before starting her writing.

Figure 12.2   Session plan for independent activity

Session Plan

Curriculum Area English – Writing
Date 01 02 2005
Time 20 minutes Group 6 children, mixed ability
Reference NLS Year 2 term 2 text level objective 20

This lesson will be repeated with 4 groups of children in the class over the course of the week. I will take responsibility for this activity although the children will be working independently.

Learning objectives
To write a definition of a familiar object
To consider how to write a clear definition
To begin to think about the needs of an audience

Relationship to previous sessions
The children will have produced a partial or completed definition related to one of the toys on the display.

Relationship to subsequent sessions
The finished definitions are to be displayed in a large class dictionary. The writing may need to be revised before this is possible.

Content and structure
Remind the children about yesterday's writing
Remind them to collect their toy
Remind them about the list of words we prepared yesterday
Children to finish their definitions, working independently
If the children complete their writing they have to carefully draw their object and head the piece of writing with the name of their object. This can be written in bold or ornate writing.

Organisation
All the resources should be ready either on or near the writing table or available for the children to collect
Individual independent writing
Mid way through the session check that they are completing their work

Working notes

Informal assessment

When you are planning your sessions you will need to bear in mind which teaching strategies to use during the whole class sessions, and how to arrange group sessions depending on whether you want children to explore, rehearse, practise, consolidate, extend or revise their learning. During your early practices you may only have an embryonic awareness of teaching and organisational strategies and their different uses but you should experiment with different formats so that you can find out about their effectiveness and your own preferences.

Figure 12.3   Session plan for an independent reading activity

Session Plan

Curriculum Area English – Writing
Date 02 02 2005
Time 20 minutes
Group 6 children, mixed ability
Reference NLS Year 2 term 2 word level objective 6
QCA Framework for planning speaking and listening Year 2 term 2

This activity will be repeated with 3 groups of children in the class from Wednesday until the end of the week.

Learning objectives
To learn to read on sight 10 of the words from list 1 in the Appendix of the NLS Framework
To learn how to spell 10 of the words from list 1 in the Appendix of the NLS Framework
To use talk to allocate tasks and pool ideas

Relationship to previous sessions
The children regularly engage in activities that help them to read and spell words taken from the NLS Framework. I have decided to arrange the activity in the form of making a lotto game. This fits in with the work the children have been doing on toys and playthings.

Relationship to subsequent sessions
I would like the children to play their game. I intend that the games will become a useful resource for the classroom which all the children can use.

Content and structure
Words to be learned – ball, boy, have, home, love, made, name, new, old, when
The words have been written on cards
Each pair will choose six words to copy onto two base cards which have been divided into six sections
The children need to take care with their writing
They will cut one of the base cards into six pieces
Each pair needs to check that between them they have used all the words at least once

Organisation
Independent group work
The children will work in pairs to complete their lotto bases and cards
The pairs are David and Tuesday, Dean and Matthew, Holly and Omar
I will monitor but not supervise the activity
If the children complete the game they can play it
If only one pair finish quickly they can draw a toy and label it with its beginning letter for the cover of the class dictionary

Working notes

Informal assessment

Play

Play can provide a rich context in which children can explore, rehearse, practise and consolidate their understanding and knowledge of reading, writing, speaking and listening. Situating learning in meaningful contexts helps children to appreciate the purposes of reading and writing, the effect audience and context can have on writing and talk, and the different uses of the written and the spoken word. Play is often undertaken by groups of children who work co-operatively. This enables children to learn from each other and, acting on each other's suggestions, explore ideas further than when working alone. Play is a natural venue for the use and development of speaking and listening.

Play activities are an accepted means of developing literacy and language in nursery classes but there is often less evidence of them being fully exploited in the later years of schooling (Ofsted, 1993). Play also helps teachers when they are organising group activities, as play can often be undertaken independently or with limited adult involvement.

When you are planning for English try to incorporate play activities into your programme. Think about ways of resourcing the imaginative play area to allow children to act out a familiar story and so gain experience of plots, characterisation, dialogue and story language. Resource the home corner with materials that will enable them to make different sorts of lists or to record information alphabetically when you are teaching the class about non-fiction texts. Let the children use story props or collections of items to retell stories. Even older children can learn about English through play. For example, turning a corner of the classroom into a TV or newspaper newsroom would enable the children to produce writing that would address most of the NLS objectives for writing composition in Year 6 term 1.

Working in the Foundation Stage

In Nursery and Reception classes the planning may take a different form from that required in Key Stages 1 and 2. Your learning objectives are more likely to be located within the resources and play activities that are commonly found in the classroom. In English it is likely that there will be more emphasis on developing oral language than on developing literacy. The children will complete many of the activities independently and so they need to be carefully resourced in order to support the learning that you intend. Figure 12.4 shows the way some practitioners plan in the nursery.

Evaluation

Evaluating sessions helps you to learn about organisation, how to use resources and how to make your intentions clear to the children. Reflections on teaching skills can

Figure 12.4 Sample planning sheet for language and literacy in a nursery class

Theme: Bears

Objectives	Activity and resources	Children	Adult role
to use language in role	IPA resourced as a picnic area in a forest	any who choose to participate	play alongside the children
to use story language	as above	as above	as above
to foster enthusiasm for books	make a collection of books about bears	as above	read from the collection at storytimes and share books with individuals
to practise writing names	drawing and labelling bears	Esin, Charlie, Pip, Calum and Tim + any others who choose to join	introduce activity, encourage children to talk about names, reinforce during large group time

be recorded as working notes (see Figure 12.1). When evaluating you will also find out whether the children learned what you intended and whether your aims for their learning were appropriate to their needs. Notes about children's learning can be recorded under the heading 'assessment of children's learning' (see Figure 12.1). Using evaluations to reflect on your teaching and on children's learning should help your development as a teacher. It should help you to decide what you need to teach, to whom and in what ways.

During your early periods of teaching you will be learning a great deal from your own experiences of planning and teaching, and from feedback from your teacher and tutor. The process of experimentation, evaluation and discussion should mean that by the end of your early placements you have learned a great deal about how to teach and what makes effective teaching and learning. This is a foundation on which you will build in your later, more extended periods of teaching.

FINAL PRACTICE

By the time you begin to prepare for final teaching practice your knowledge of English and the English curriculum, understanding of learning and your teaching skills will have developed a great deal. Final practice is an opportunity to both deepen your knowledge of these things and demonstrate what you can do.

On final practice trainees are usually expected to teach the whole class for most of each week for an extended period. You will have to produce weekly plans and daily or session plans. These may fit in with the school's medium-term plans, teachers' existing plans and the NLS objectives, and will relate to the Early Learning Goals or the National Curriculum programmes of study.

As with earlier practices careful preparation and discussion with the class teacher and school mentor are vital if you are to plan work that is appropriate to the children's needs and fits in with the way English is organised in school. Although you will have a much greater teaching load than on your previous practices, it is not unusual to begin the practice with only limited responsibility for planning and teaching, and then work up to your full complement of hours. This enables you to build up your own confidence and helps you to plan work that is well matched to the children.

Progression and differentiation

Your plans for final practice cover a much longer period than those you have previously produced. This means that in addition to listing learning objectives, making links to official curriculum documents and describing activities, they will need to indicate:

- how the children's learning will progress over the period

- how you will differentiate your activities in order to cater for the spread of abilities in the class

- how and when you will assess the children's learning.

Planning for progression ensures that children gradually extend their knowledge, understanding and skills over a period of time. It helps teachers to think about the different elements of knowledge and understanding that are involved in learning something new. Sequencing the elements from the most simple to the most difficult helps to provide positive and successful learning experiences for children. Being aware of the need for progression can help you to avoid planning work that covers what has already been explored and learned by the children.

When you are teaching you will usually have to address a learning objective through a series of staged activities that may take place over the course of a few weeks. Children need to encounter and practise new learning in a variety of ways. The following list shows how the objective 'represent story plots in a variety of ways' can be approached through a sequence of different and progressively more difficult activities.

- Read and discuss a story that has a linear plots.

- Identify the events in a known story.

- Represent the events on a time line.

- Encourage the children to act out the story in the imaginative play area.

- Give the children sequencing activities based on the story.

- Read a story that has a similar plot structure.

- Ask the children to draw and label a time line of the events.

- Ask the children to rewrite the story using the time line as a plan.

- With the children plan and write a similar story.

- Ask the children to write their own story using a time line plot.

- Read and discuss a story that has a circular plot.

- Represent the events on a story map.

- Read a story that has a similar plot structure.

- Ask the children to make a story map based on the story.

- Compare the two plot structures.

- Analyse some personal stories written by the class which have either a chronological or circular structure.

Differentiation means taking account of the different needs and abilities of all the children in the class and should result in an appropriate match between learner need and activities. You may expect all the children to undertake the same activity but expect different outcomes from different children. Alternatively, similar tasks may be presented in different ways with more or less support in the form of resources, adult help or preparation. Differentiation allows you to give particular attention to children with special educational needs, more able children and children for whom English is an additional language. In order to differentiate work, each of the following factors can be altered:

- the activity – different activities can lead to the same outcome

- the outcome – different children can produce different responses to the same task

- the input – the teacher can provide or arrange more or less preparation before the children begin the activity

- the support – adults and groupings of children can provide different degrees of support

- the resources – providing more, less or different resources can vary the difficulty level of tasks

- the criteria for success – this can be different for groups and individuals

- the intention – whether learning is to be explored, practised, consolidated or extended.

Medium-term plans

For English at Key Stage 1 and 2 many schools have adopted the medium-term planning sheet in the appendix of the *National Literacy Strategy Framework for Teaching* (DfEE, 1998c), or a variant of this, to record their medium-term planning. To complete this you need to identify the objectives from the Framework that you will work on for half a term and to decide whether these will best be learned through continuous work or a block of work. Continuous work is concerned with skills which need regular practice and attention throughout the school year. Developing fluent and legible handwriting might be an example of this. Blocked work is a discrete unit of work on a particular topic. For example, there might be a block of two weeks in Year 1 when children are introduced to writing non-chronological reports. The planner also asks teachers to identify the main texts that they will be using during the half-term and to ensure that these cover a range of genres. As tutors generally advise trainees to adopt the planning procedures used by the school they are working in, many of you will be working in this way. Some trainees may be asked to undertake additional planning and will be given advice about this (see Chapter 11). Figure 12.5 shows the start of a medium-term plan. The objectives are clearly stated and continuous work that will be worked on throughout the term has been identified.

Short-term plans

Short-term plans include weekly plans and daily session plans. For the former you will probably be using the NLS weekly planning sheet (Figure 12.6). This provides you with a clear overview of the week. It will help you to think about the balance of

Figure 12.5   Medium-term plan for literacy

National	Literacy	Strategy	Teacher
Medium-Term Planning Class	Half-Termly Planner Year Group(s) Year 2	Term 1 1st Half/2nd Half	Teacher
Phonics, Spelling and Vocabulary	**Grammar and Punctuation**	**Comprehension and Composition**	**Texts**
Continuous work	Continuous work	Continuous work	Range
6 to read on sight high frequency words likely to occur in graded texts matched to the abilities of reading groups	1 to use awareness of grammar to decipher new or unfamiliar words, e.g. to predict from the text; to read on, leave a gap and re-read 4 to re-read own writing for punctuation	1 to reinforce and apply word level skills through shared and guided reading 2 to use phonological, contextual, grammatical and graphic knowledge to work out, predict and check the meanings of unfamiliar words and to make sense of what they read 6 to discuss familiar story themes and link to own experiences	Stories with familiar settings Poems with familiar settings
Blocked work	Blocked work	Blocked work	Titles
Week 1 1 to secure identification, spelling and reading of long vowels digraphs in simple words from Y1 term 3 12 to begin using and practising the four basic handwriting joins – diagonal joins to letters without ascenders ai, ay, ea, ee	5 to revise knowledge about other uses of capitalisation, e.g. for names, headings, titles, emphasis, and begin to use in own writing	3 to be aware of the difference between spoken and written language 7 to learn, re-read and recite favourite poems, taking account of punctuation; to comment on aspects such as word combinations, sound patterns (such as rhymes, alliterative patterns) and forms of presentation 12 to use simple poetry structures and to substitute own ideas, write new lines	*Have You Just Seen Who's Moved in Next Door to Us?* Colin McNaughton *Peepo* A. & J. Ahlberg *Burglar Bill* A. Ahlberg & C. McNaughton *Mrs Lather's Laundry* A. Ahlberg & A. Amstutz

word-, sentence- and text-level work over the course of a week and where to best place any additional adults that work with you. In the example the numbers refer to the five groups in this Year 2 class. All of the groups do all the activities but groups receive more or less adult support and preparation according to their needs. The specific objectives that each activity is designed to address will be on the medium-term plan (see Figure 12.5) and should be included on your session plans (see Figures 12.1, 12.2 and 12.3).

You may need to write a daily plan for each part of the literacy hour and one for each group activity that you design. This may seem a great deal of work but session plans help you to be absolutely clear about how you intend to organise and teach the children. This should contribute to the success of your activities, in particular the group work. It is this part of the literacy hour that generally poses most problems for trainees and the session plans are one way of helping you to manage this section of the hour effectively.

Problems on teaching practice

Despite careful preparation and planning every trainee has days when everything appears to go wrong.

> The children found one activity too difficult, others completed a task too quickly, some did not understand what I had asked them to do, although I planned to spend time with one group one child demanded a great deal of attention and I had to leave the teaching group and deal with her disruptive behaviour. (Extract from a trainee file)

These problems do not just arise for trainees – experienced teachers can also encounter unexpected difficulties. If things go wrong do not despair. Your teacher and your tutor will understand and be sympathetic. However, they will want you to analyse what went wrong and begin to think about how you might avoid similar problems in the future.

- If the activity was too difficult could you provide more or different input, support or resources or do you need to simplify the activity to ensure that the children experience success?

- If the activity was completed too quickly was it too easy or just too short? Do you need to make the activity more challenging or have an additional activity for the children?

- If the children did not understand what was expected, could you spend more time on initial explanations, use plenary sessions to prepare some children or

Figure 12.6   Weekly plan for literacy

National	Literacy	Strategy	Teaching	Objectives			Equal opportunities – exploring difference
Weekly Plan Year 2 Term I							
Enlarged Text *Have You Just Seen Who's Moved in Next Door to Us?* Colin McNaughton	**Guided Reading** *Peepo* A. & J. Ahlberg *Burglar Bill* A. Ahlberg & C. McNaughton	*Mrs Lathers Laundry* A. Ahlberg & A. Amstutz *Have You Just Seen Who's Moved in Next Door to Us?* C. McNaughton		**Cross Curricular Support** Imaginative play – role play, small world toys	Art – portraits, houses, plans, maps Geography – maps	D&T – plan, design, build homes Story times – Happy Families	Equal opportunities – exploring difference
Whole class – shared reading and writing	Whole class – phonics, spelling, vocabulary and grammar	Guided Group Tasks (reading or writing)	Guided Group (reading writing)	Independent	Group	Tasks	Plenary
Shared reading of *Have You Just Seen Who's Moved in Next Door to Us?*	Read street sign 'High Class Tailor'. Shared writing of ai and ay words	Guided Group writing write a new verse based on a verse from the book for display T 5	Guided group reading *Peepo* 5 OA 4	ICT, listening station, catch up time for writing, display work 3	Draw a character, write a dialogue bubbles and character's name 2	Compile list of ai and ay words to share and display 1	Share new verses with the class 5
Shared writing dialogue bubbles and characters' names	Examine misheard phrases and make up new ones together	Write a new verse based on a verse from the book for display 1 T	Guided group reading *Peepo* 1 T 5	ICT, listening station, catch up time for writing, display work 4	Draw a character, write dialogue bubbles and character's name 3	Compile list of ai and ay words to share and display 2	Share character illustrations and writing with class 3

Shared reading of one verse and shared writing of a new verse	Examine text for question marks. Look at children's writing	Write a new verse based on a verse from the book for display 2 T	Guided group reading *Have You Just Seen …* 1 T	ICT, listening station, catch up time for writing, display work 5	Draw a character, write dialogue bubbles and character's name 4	Compile list of ai and ay words to share and display 3	Share ai and ay words with class 1,2,3
Shared reading of part of text. Discussion of text	Read street sign 'Song Bird Going Cheap' to introduce ea and ee	Write a new verse based on a verse from the book for display 3	Reading *Mrs Lather* supported by a tape 2	ICT, listening station, catch up time for writing, display work 1	Draw a character, write dialogue bubbles and character's name 5	Compile list of ea and ee words to share and display 4	Share ea and ee words with class 4
Shared reading of part of text. Discussion of text	Revise long vowel phonemes ai; ay, ea, ee	Guided group writing write a new verse based on a verse from the book on display T 4 OA	Guided group reading – *Burglar Bill* 3	ICT, listening station, catch up time for writing, display work 2	Draw a character, write dialogue bubbles and character's name 1	Compile list of ea and ee words to share and display 5	Discuss responses and the week's work based on *Have You Just Seen …* all

provide more adult support?

- If the success of the session was disrupted by poor behaviour you may need to focus on your management rather than your teaching for the next few days. Simple activities for all the children and an emphasis on appropriate behaviour might be what is needed (see Chapter 8).

Evaluating your preparation, planning and teaching should reveal the source of the difficulty and indicate what steps you need to take to rectify the situation. Discussions with your support teacher and your tutor should help you to plan for more successful times in the immediate days.

HOW YOU ARE ASSESSED

On your final teaching practice your teacher and your tutor will assess you using the standards issued by the DfES (DfES/TTA, 2002). You will be expected to have reached a satisfactory standard in knowledge and understanding of the primary English curriculum, your planning, your classroom teaching skills and your assessment of pupils' capabilities in English. Your daily work with the children and your teaching practice file should provide evidence of your ability to meet the standards in these areas.

Your own professional drive, your taught programme and your work in school, the support of your class teachers and your tutors will in most cases result in a successful outcome to your course and help you attain newly qualified teacher status.

INVOLVEMENT IN SCHOOL BEYOND TEACHING

During your time in school you may get opportunities to add to your understanding of English through attending staff meetings and professional development days, and these can be very beneficial. Other school-based opportunities include observing or discussing the national tests and tasks, becoming involved in a book week or extracurricular activities such as drama or book clubs. If possible talk to teachers, particularly the subject leader, about the teaching of English and ask if you can occasionally observe others.

In particular those of you who are English subject specialists should find out as much as possible about how English is taught and resourced in school. It might be helpful to ask teachers about current issues and their concerns about teaching English. These may be areas that you wish to investigate further. You might also want to find out more about the role of the subject leader.

LOOKING TO THE FUTURE

The end of a teacher training course is only the beginning of a teaching career. The introduction of an induction year in which newly qualified teachers have a reduced teaching load, receive support from a school mentor and attend courses for newly qualified teachers acknowledges that beginning teachers still have plenty to learn. While newly qualified teachers can bring fresh ideas and a great deal of enthusiasm to their first post, they lack the depth of knowledge and practical skills that result from experience.

The initial priority for most newly qualified teachers is to find efficient ways of managing the children in their class and organising their learning. At this stage their concerns are usually general rather than specific to one subject area. It is when the class is running fairly smoothly that teachers begin to think about their teaching of individual curriculum areas. For many newly qualified teachers one of the first subjects they wish to know more about is English. The emphasis in the primary school curriculum on literacy and language, parents' interest in how well children are progressing in reading, in particular, and in writing and the national tests at ages 5, 7 and 11 mean that most teachers want to make sure that they teach English well. In order to do this, talk to the English subject leader. You may also find that your school will support you as much as it can by making it possible for you to attend courses and through in-house staff development sessions.

SUMMARY

For most practitioners, learning to teach English well is a lifelong endeavour. Very few newly qualified teachers emerge from their training satisfied that they have nothing more to learn. If your course has enabled you to meet the DfES standards and has given you an enthusiasm for English and the will to develop your teaching further, you will be well on the way to becoming a successful teacher of English.

This chapter has described how trainees can get the best out of the different elements of their course and so develop into effective teachers of English. The key points covered in this chapter were:

- what to do in school during the early part of training
- getting the most out of school-based assignments
- preparing and planning for early periods of teaching
- teaching successfully towards the end of the course.

ISSUES FOR REFLECTION

- Consider the balance between speaking and listening and reading and writing in your teaching. Do you feel that you are helping children to learn about all aspects of English? Do you need to make any alterations to your teaching programme? Could you redress any imbalance through incorporating objectives for English into other areas of the curriculum?

- During your training you will have observed a number of teachers teaching English in different ways. Note down the most important things you learned from each teacher. Can you use any of these to enliven or vary your own teaching or to solve a problem that may have arisen on teaching practice?

- Are you keeping track of all the children's learning in English? Are you involving children in making assessments of their own progress in English? Try to incorporate assessment opportunities for you and the children into your weekly plans.

Further reading

Browne, A. (1999) *Teaching Writing at Key Stage 1 and Before*. Gloucester: Stanley Thornes. Specifically written for students, this book contains a number of examples and suggestions about how to plan for language and literacy, and includes examples of how to differentiate and plan for progression.

Browne, A. (2001) Developing Language and Literacy 3–8. London: Paul Chapman Publishing. This is a practical and comprehensive introduction to teaching and learning English for trainee teachers.

Evans, J. (ed.) (2001) *The Writing Classroom: Aspects of Writing and the Primary Curriculum 3–11*. London: David Fulton. This book is a collection of chapters on teaching writing in the primary school.

Wray, D., Medwell, J. and Poulson, L. (2002) *Teaching Literacy Effectively in the Primary School*. London: RoutledgeFalmer. This book describes and explains the characteristics of effective practice in teaching English.

Chapter 13

Teaching numeracy

Derek Haylock

What counts in teaching numeracy successfully? The format of primary mathematics teaching has changed considerably in recent years. Derek Haylock explains some of the reasons behind these changes and, using a range of practical examples, explores some of the recommended ways of teaching numeracy in the primary classroom.

INTRODUCTION

In this chapter I outline some of the background to the implementation of the National Numeracy Strategy (DfEE, 1999b) and its successor, the National Primary Strategy (DfES, 2003). I identify some of the key principles that underpin these initiatives in primary mathematics. To illustrate what this would look like in practice, there is an example of a numeracy lesson for a Year 3 class. I then provide a checklist of questions for evaluating how well you are teaching numeracy and conclude with some examples of my observations of trainee teachers doing this well.

THE NATIONAL NUMERACY STRATEGY

The implementation in 1999 of the National Numeracy Strategy (NNS) in England (DfEE, 1999b), supported by very substantial levels of funding from central government for the provision of materials and in-service training for teachers, has proved to be a far-reaching and influential curriculum initiative in primary schools. Alongside this development in England there were initiatives with similar emphases, arising from similar concerns, in primary schools in Wales and Scotland (Welsh Office, 1999; Scottish Office Education and Industry Department, 1997). For many primary school teachers these involved a radical change in their practice. Prior to the NNS, mathematics in British primary schools had become dominated by an approach that relied on children working individually through commercially produced mathematics schemes. The adherents of this approach would have argued that it allowed each child to work and progress at their own rate, according to their individual abilities. The reality was that pupils often made poor use of their time in mathematics lessons, sometimes spending long periods waiting for help from the teacher. They received very little actual direct teaching, and they worked their way through the mathematics scheme without really understanding much of what they were doing and often without being really challenged to engage with mathematical ideas (see findings of Ofsted, 1994).

Results from international studies, such as the Third International Mathematics and Science Study, prompted serious concern about the standards being achieved by British primary school children compared to those in countries with similar social and cultural backgrounds, particularly in the area of number and calculations (Keys et al., 1997a; MacNab, 2000). Inevitably, and justifiably, inferences were drawn about the relationship between our pupils' poor performance and the classroom teaching approaches prevalent in Britain that contrasted with those used in other, more successful countries (Keys et al., 1997b). Studies revealed such differences as: an overemphasis on – and too early introduction of – formal calculations in vertical layout and a corresponding neglect of teaching of mental calculations strategies; an overreliance on individualised work in mathematics, with a corresponding neglect of explanation by the teacher and discussion of mathematical processes and ideas with the whole class; and a rather careless use of calculators, discouraging pupils from developing their own mental methods for manipulating numbers (Bierhoff, 1996; Bierhoff and Prais, 1997).

The National Numeracy Strategy for primary schools was therefore launched, following encouraging trials in schools participating in the National Numeracy Project, with the following key principles:

- There should be a daily mathematics lesson, from 45 minutes for younger classes, up to one hour in later primary years: the so-called 'numeracy hour'.

- There should be a greater emphasis on developing specific mental calculation skills: this would involve at least a daily five- to ten-minute session of oral and mental number work, no teaching of formal vertical layout for calculations before Year 3 and no access to calculators before Year 3.

- There should be more emphasis on interactive whole class teaching: question-and-answer sessions, whole-class discussion, direct teaching of mathematical processes, feedback from individual and group work to the whole class.

● There should be a more controlled approach to differentiation according to ability: all the pupils engaged in mathematics around a common theme, with usually no more than three levels of work, in order to maximise opportunities for the teacher to interact with the pupils' learning.

Additionally, the NNS framework provided a clear and substantial set of objectives for mathematics, a shorter set of key objectives intended to be the main focus for assessment, and a suggested programme for each year group. The subsequent revision of the National Curriculum for mathematics (DfEE, 1999b) was undertaken with a view to ensuring that the NNS framework was consistent with statutory requirements for mathematics for primary schools. So, although the Strategy refers to 'numeracy' and the Curriculum refers to 'mathematics', in reality they are talking about the same thing. So in the current usage, in relation to the primary schools' curriculum, teachers tend to use the words as synonyms, although the use of the word 'numeracy' usually implies that the teacher is implementing the specific policies and approaches of the NNS framework.

In 2003 the DfES in England launched a new Primary National Strategy (DfES, 2003). This was in essence a response to concerns of primary schools that the rigid structure of the National Curriculum and the Numeracy and Literacy Strategies were resulting in a very narrow range of educational experiences for primary school pupils. The new policy embraced concepts such as enjoyment and creativity, and was designed to encourage a broader and more flexible view of how the curriculum might be delivered. As far as mathematics is concerned, the new strategy does not replace the Numeracy Strategy, but builds on it. In particular it opens up the possibility of some aspects of the mathematics curriculum being delivered in cross-curricular contexts. An obvious example would be the data-handling strand in the primary mathematics curriculum. None of this needs to be taught in discrete numeracy lessons, since there are plenty of opportunities in science, geography and history, for example, to develop these skills in meaningful and purposeful contexts. However, the nature of numeracy is such that most of this subject will continue to be taught in primary schools in distinct numeracy lessons.

COMPONENTS OF A NUMERACY LESSON

Typically, following the NNS guidance, a numeracy lesson would have three components: a short oral/mental starter, a main activity and a short plenary session at the end.

The oral/mental starter is used: (a) to rehearse number facts and skills, such as number bonds for addition, subtraction, multiplication and division, and counting forwards and backwards in ones, twos, tens, fives, threes, and so on; (b) to discuss how to derive unknown facts from known facts (for example, how to find 3×8 if you already know 3×4); and (c) to promote the learning of specific mental strategies for calculations (see QCA, 1999). This section of the lesson can sometimes focus on particular skills needed for the main activity that is to follow, but it is often just a discrete component. The inclusion of this oral/mental starter into the numeracy hour format is designed to guarantee that all pupils practise and develop their mental number skills every day.

The main part of the lesson would then normally start with some interactive direct teaching and discussion related to the learning objectives for the main activity. This would be followed by individual work, paired work or small-group activities. The main activity might involve consolidation and practice of written or practical skills, the application of already learnt skills to problem-solving or practical tasks, or more open-ended investigational work. The source for this might be the teacher's own material or commercially produced materials – but it is important that pupils are given direct teaching and that they engage in discussion with the teacher about the mathematics involved. Teaching skills such as explaining mathematical ideas and giving clear instructions for tasks are essential at this stage.

The main activity can sometimes be essentially the same for all pupils, particularly when the school uses ability-setting for mathematics across a number of classes. On other occasions the teacher may plan up to three different levels of activity, differentiated for groups within the class, but all around the same theme. The insistence on a common mathematical theme is to ensure that all the pupils can participate in some way in a whole class discussion with the teacher about their work.

The last 10 minutes or so of the lesson is used for a plenary, in which pupils share with the rest of the class what they have been doing and the teacher reinforces and summarises the key mathematical ideas from the lesson. The teacher may also explain homework to be done and how today's work will be followed up tomorrow. This part of the lesson also requires careful planning, to ensure that it is effective in consolidating pupils' learning and making this explicit to them. Good practice is to ensure that pupils know in advance what they will be expected to report to the plenary.

AN EXAMPLE OF A NUMERACY LESSON

Figure 13.1 is an example of a numeracy lesson for a Year 3 class. In this lesson some of the material for the oral/mental starter is actually a preparation for the main activity. For this class, with a wide range of ability in mathematics, the teacher has planned three levels of expectations in the work for the main activity; these are for

Figure 13.1 Numeracy lesson for a Year 3 class

Year 3 class, 29 pupils, mixed-ability
Monday 12 June 0935–1030
Time available: 55 minutes

Major objective
'Begin to find remainders after simple division' [NNS Y3 programme, page 51]

Relationship to other lessons
This is the first in a series of lessons this week focusing on remainders. Most pupils are confident with 2, 5 and 10 tables. They have previously met the idea and notation of division using both equal-sharing and inverse-of-multiplication structure, but without remainders. I shall be introducing the idea of a remainder in the main part of this lesson.

Mental/oral starter [10 minutes]
Pupils on carpet around overhead projector (OHP).
<u>Strategies/skills:</u> (a) Practice of counting in fives forwards and backwards; (b) turn a multiplication statement into the corresponding division statement.
<u>Content of session:</u> Pupils count forwards and backwards in fives while teacher points to numbers on clock face. Repeat several times, and finally stop while pointing at 6.
Put 5 × 6 = 30 on OHP with transparent tiles. Play *Turning the Tables* with this result: in this activity the teacher asks questions such as, 'What's 5 sixes?' 'What's 6 fives?' 'How much for 5 sweets costing 6p each?' 'How many 5s in 30?' 'How many 6s in 30?'... and so on. Finish with formal division statements and get pupils to arrange tiles on OHP to show '30 ÷ 5 = 6'. Stress the relationship between the × and ÷ results.

Main part of the lesson [35 minutes]
<u>Objective:</u> Using counters if needed, pupils will be able to work out a simple division of a number up to 40 by 2, 3, 5 or 10 in cases where there is a remainder, using grouping, and identify the remainder.
<u>Key language:</u> Division, divided by, left over, remainder.
<u>Introduction:</u> [15 minutes] Pupils still on carpet around OHP. Display key language, comment on 'division', 'divided by'. Revise grouping idea of division, using 15 ÷ 3 (how many 3s in 15?) and counters on OHP. Get pupil to demonstrate. Point to new words: 'left over' and 'remainder'; explain today's lesson is to learn about remainders in division. Get pupil to do 17 ÷ 3 on OHP. Discuss what's left over – call this the remainder. Repeat with 13 ÷ 2, 21 ÷ 5, 32 ÷ 10. Can pupils predict results and remainders? Show how to record results, such as 17 ÷ 3 = 5, remainder 2.
<u>Individual work:</u> [20 minutes] Pupils work on group tables on examples written on board. Counters on tables – encourage them to use these for set A. All groups to complete set A orally/practically in group discussion – lower group (5 pupils) only oral/practical work, no written recording. Other groups also do at least set B and top group aim also to do set C, recording answers as shown. Sets B and C to be done as individual work in silence. Encourage them to try first without using counters. Teacher to work mainly with lower group, leading discussion. Graded examples written on board in advance.

Set A:	12 ÷ 5,	9 ÷ 2,	16 ÷ 5,	22 ÷ 10,	17 ÷ 2
Set B:	24 ÷ 10,	24 ÷ 5,	25 ÷ 2,	19 ÷ 5,	33 ÷ 10
Set C:	41 ÷ 5,	49 ÷ 10,	33 ÷ 3,	21 ÷ 4,	47 ÷ 5

Plenary [10 minutes]
Reminder of key language and what we have been learning today. Give homework. Ask how many pupils in class. How many groups of 5? With what remainder? Ask pupil to write corresponding division result on the board (29 ÷ 5 = ...) If we dismissed pupils in groups of 5, how many would be left? Then do this, dismissing pupils for play-time in fives, discussing how many left at each stage and how many fives have gone.

Homework
Pupils to count up at home how many teaspoons in the house (ask parent first for permission and help) and to divide this number by the number of people living in the house. Write the calculation on a piece of paper and bring it in tomorrow.

Resources needed for the lesson
Clock; overhead projector; transparent numeral and operation tiles; cards with key language; counters and maths exercise books on tables; a teaspoon.

the lowest ability group of five pupils, the middle group of 18 pupils in total, and the top group of six pupils.

EFFECTIVE TEACHING OF NUMERACY

Here is a checklist of some characteristics of effective teaching of numeracy. It is written as a set of questions that trainee teachers can ask themselves from time to time in reviewing their mathematics teaching. This is then followed by some examples from observations of trainee teachers teaching mathematics related to a selection of these questions.

Planning

- Do I base my teaching of number on clearly focused objectives that are made explicit to the pupils?

- Do I plan opportunities to emphasise and clarify key mathematical concepts, principles, properties and relationships, and the associated language?

- Do I plan teaching to counteract common errors and misconceptions in number?

- Do I plan effectively for progression in number for all pupils, including the most able and the lowest attaining?

- Do I plan the oral/mental starter to promote learning of specific skills and strategies and not just to rehearse existing learning?

- Do I structure my teaching sessions to ensure that as many pupils as possible get substantial teacher-input and opportunity to talk about number?

- Do I plan pupils' contributions to the plenary and tell the pupils what these will be in advance?

- Do I ensure that pupils have regular and substantial opportunity to practise and consolidate numerical skills and processes, both written and mental?

- Do I aim to promote confidence with number through its integration into data-handling, problem-solving and investigative work?

- Do I incorporate calculators sensibly, efficiently and effectively into number work (Year 3 onwards) to promote understanding and confidence with number?

- Do I make good use of IT, textbooks and other resources for teaching number, in a way that is not scheme-driven?

Teaching

- Do I use whole-class sessions to explain and to question pupils about mathematical processes, concepts and relationships with confidence and clarity?

- Do I vary the level of questioning effectively to involve all pupils across the range of mathematical ability?

- Do I use small-group activities effectively for teacher input and to promote pupil-talk and interaction about mathematical properties, processes and relationships?

- Do I motivate pupils to be excited by mathematical processes, properties and patterns?

- Do I emphasise mathematical language, both vocabulary and key language structures?

- Do I help pupils to make connections between language, concrete experiences, symbols and pictures?

- Do I encourage and develop pupils' informal strategies for calculations regularly and frequently, making key mental strategies explicit?

- Do I teach pupils how to use images that support mental strategies for calculations, such as empty number-lines, hundred-squares?

- Do I teach written methods of calculating clearly with an emphasis on understanding the process, rather than simply learning a recipe?

- Do I exploit unplanned opportunities to discuss mathematical ideas and processes?

- Do I relate the pupils' mathematical work to the real world?

MAKING LEARNING OBJECTIVES EXPLICIT

In a numeracy lesson you will probably have one main learning objective for the oral/mental starter and another for the main activity. It is good practice to make these explicit to the pupils, using language they can understand. This helps pupils to focus on what it is that they are supposed to be learning and what they will have to demonstrate to you as the teacher that they can do at the end of the session.

Working with a Year 2 class, Claire has permanently up on the wall a colourful picture of a target with an arrow through the bull's-eye. She begins the oral and mental starter with some practice in counting backwards and forwards in 5s and then she pins onto the picture the target for the next bit of the session: 'Use 20 as a stepping stone for addition.' Reference is made to this objective as children are taught how to calculate 17 + 5 on a number-line by thinking of it as 17 + 3 + 2. Other examples follow. Ten minutes later she asks the children to tell her what they have been learning to do, hence reinforcing the objective. She then introduces the main activity by pinning up the target for this section of the lesson: 'Use a balance to decide which objects are lighter or heavier than a kilogram.' There follows a brief discussion of the target, ensuring the pupils understand the key words involved (balance, lighter than, heavier than, kilogram), before the teacher outlines the practical activities the groups will be doing. In the plenary at the end of the lesson, each group is asked to show one object and explain how they decided whether it was heavier or lighter than a kilogram. The teacher then asks the class to tell her what they have learned to do today and whether they have hit the target.

MAKING KEY LANGUAGE EXPLICIT

Pupils have to learn the specific vocabulary of mathematics. The National Numeracy Strategy puts a particularly strong emphasis on this and teachers are now provided with clear guidance about the key language to be developed in each year group in primary schools (see DfEE, 1999c). Pupils generally enjoy learning technical language, so trainee teachers need not be fearful of introducing terminology such as 'pictogram' in Year 1, or 'multiplication' in Year 2, or 'hemisphere' in Year 3, or 'quadrilateral' in Year 4, or 'divisor' in Year 5, or 'icosahedron' in Year 6 – provided, of course, that they themselves understand the words and use them accurately and appropriately!

It is important to note that there are many mathematical terms that are used in everyday language, often very loosely and sometimes with different meanings. For example, pupils will first associate the word 'volume' with a button on the TV remote control, not with the amount of three-dimensional space occupied by a solid object. 'Difference' can mean any kind of difference in everyday language and can be applied in mathematics to any kind of measurement comparison; but when we ask, 'What is the difference between 5 and 9?' we are focusing on a very specific mathematical process, that of subtraction. Similarly, 'similar' applied to shapes in mathematics has a much more precise meaning than it does in everyday language. A sugar cube need not actually be a cube. 'Just a minute' is rarely just a minute. The village square is rarely a square. And what can 'mean' mean, apart from a measure of central tendency in a set of numerical data? (See also Cockburn, 1999.)

It is very helpful for pupils if the key language used in a mathematics lesson is made overt and displayed clearly (for example, on flash cards). In the best lesson-plans the key language to be developed will have been identified in advance. If there are differences in the ways in which particular words are used in everyday life and in mathematics, then discuss these differences with the pupils – and challenge them to find other examples!

> Karen is teaching a Year 1 class. She displays the key language for the session, on individual flash-cards: 'taller, shorter, tallest, shortest'. She gets the class to read the words together. A group of three children is asked to stand up. The teacher, each time holding up the appropriate flash-card, asks questions requiring comparisons between their heights; such as, 'Who is taller, John or Sam?' For each answer, the class repeat together the correct statement; for example, 'Sam is taller than John.'

In addition to vocabulary, there are characteristic language patterns associated with statements about number relationships that should be made explicit and taught to pupils. These would include statements having such formats as: 'N is N more than N'; 'N is N less than N', 'N shared equally between N is N each'; 'N sets of N is N altogether'. These can be written out in this form, displayed, and then referred to in your teaching, to assist pupils in learning to connect the symbols of mathematics with the corresponding language patterns.

> Geetha is planning to teach her Year 6 class how to share out a sum of money in a given ratio; for example, to share £24 in the ratio 3:5. At the start of the session she puts on display and talks about the key vocabulary to be used: 'share, ratio, total'. She then displays the language pattern to be used, in this form: 'Share a N between A and B in the ratio N:N' and discusses with the class what this might mean.

You also have to be careful to use language in a way that supports mathematical understanding – and to avoid careless use of language that can actually mislead. For example, to talk about 'borrowing a ten' when doing a subtraction calculation by decomposition is misleading; to talk about 'exchanging a ten for ten ones' provides a better match between the language used and the mathematical process. Similarly, to ask the question, 'Is this a square or a rectangle?' carelessly obscures the fact that a square is a special kind of rectangle; more accurate would be, 'Is this a rectangle?' followed by 'Now, is this rectangle a square?' To say, 'Six take away negative three' when discussing '6 – (–3)' is totally baffling; but to ask, 'How much more than negative three is six', with the support of an appropriate number-line diagram, removes the mystery and promotes understanding.

SIGNALLING EXPECTATIONS FOR THE PLENARY

The plenary session in a numeracy hour can be one of the most stimulating components. It can also be used in a predictable and unimaginative way, with the teacher not having planned this part creatively; for example, simply asking the group to tell the class what they have been doing, or just working through one of the questions the pupils have been doing on the board. Here is a trainee teacher using the plenary well with a Year 4 class:

> John's objectives for the main activity are that pupils should know a half, a quarter, three-quarters and a tenth of a litre in millilitres, and be able to recognise whether the capacity of a container is about a litre, half a litre, a quarter of a litre, three-quarters of a litre, or a tenth of a litre. This involves mainly practical work with water, containers and measuring jars, with some recording on a prepared table. The set of containers given to each of the groups of pupils are all fairly easy to predict. During the practical work John takes to each group one additional container that is really very difficult to estimate: such as a tall thin tube, a squat circular container and a distorted vase. He tells them to measure its capacity in millilitres and that they will be asked in the plenary to challenge the other groups to estimate whether it is about a tenth, a quarter, a half, three-quarters or one litre. For the plenary session the teacher first ensures in good time that the groups clear up and dry their tables, with the containers arranged neatly in the centre. There is then a five-minute discussion about what the class have been learning, highlighting again the key language used and the facts they have been learning: half a litre = 500 ml, and so on. Each group is then asked to hold up their special container and to challenge the rest of the class to estimate its approximate capacity. There is some brief discussion about why a particular container might be misleading. The teacher then explains to the pupils, with a few recall questions, that in tomorrow's lesson they will be doing something very similar about kilograms and grams. Next he gives the pupils a task for homework: with a parent's permission, to try to find one item at home that is sold as a litre, one as half a litre, one as a quarter of a litre, one as three-quarters of a litre, and one as a tenth of a litre. If any of these are empty to wash them out and to bring them in to school tomorrow for a display.

DIFFERENTIATED QUESTIONING IN WHOLE-CLASS SESSIONS

Trainee teachers may recognise the value of interactive direct teaching of mathematics with a whole class but they often get concerned about how effective this can be as a teaching approach with a class in which there is a wide range of ability. The teaching skill to be developed here is differentiated questioning around one topic. This skill is particularly important in teaching mathematics, where the range of competencies is often most marked and the issue of differentiation is therefore most acute. Here's an example of this being done well:

> Rita, working with a Year 3 class, is leading a whole-class question-and-answer session about fractions. Her objectives for this part of the lesson are that pupils should develop their skills in calculating mentally a half of a given number and to connect this with their knowledge of doubles. With most of the children her questions focus on finding a half of a number up to 40, getting pupils to explain their thinking. For

example, a pupil calculates half of 28 by partitioning it into 20 and 8, to get $10 + 4 = 14$. She asks another, more able pupil, if they know what is half of 30, and how could they use this to find half of 28. The teacher then follows this by asking a less confident child what is double 14. The connection between the halving and doubling is discussed. Each question about halving then provides an opportunity for a less confident child to handle the corresponding question about doubling. At one point the teacher directs a question to one particularly able child asking her to find half of 128 – and to explain to the others how she did it. She then asks her least able pupil to put up all his fingers and then to put one hand behind his back. Her questioning leads this pupil to recognise that the 5 left on view is half of the 10. Very skilfully, the teacher is ensuring that all the pupils are involved and able to participate, using her knowledge of the children to match carefully some of her questions to the different levels of mathematical ability within her class.

USING ASSESSMENT INFORMATION IN PLANNING SUBSEQUENT LESSONS

The Numeracy Strategy framework is often implemented in schools in such a way that the class will spend a few days on a particular topic for the main teaching activity and then will be required to move on to a new topic. Trainee teachers, conscientiously making their ongoing assessments of pupils' learning through feedback from question-and-answer sessions and their marking of the pupils' written work, are then sometimes puzzled about what to do when this assessment information indicates that various pupils need further help in achieving the learning that had been intended. The NNS framework suggests that important topics will be revisited each term – but that will seem like a long time to wait for the pupils and no help for the trainee teacher who will probably not be there next term and who has to demonstrate now that their assessment is informing their planning. One approach is to try to pick up some of these problems in the oral/mental starters. Here's an example:

Having spent three days in which they developed their skills in ordering numbers up to 1,000 and rounding numbers to the nearest 10 or 100, a Year 3 class is then expected to move on to addition and subtraction calculations. Matthew, a trainee teacher, is disappointed that quite a number of the pupils have made numerous errors on a written task requiring the rounding of numbers to the nearest 100. He wants to find time to revisit this process, making better use of the number-line to enable pupils to understand it. So he builds some further teaching and discussion of this process into the oral/mental starter for Monday, Tuesday and Wednesday of the following week's numeracy lessons. By the end of these three days, the informal feedback from the question-and-answer sessions indicates that the pupils are now much more confident with the ideas involved.

RESPONDING TO UNPLANNED OPPORTUNITIES

One of the characteristics of a really good teacher of numeracy is the confidence to respond to opportunities that arise from pupils' ideas or contributions that you had not planned. Here's an example where a trainee teacher did not do this – and thereby disappointed his tutor!

> In an oral/mental session with a Year 4 class Andy is using questioning very effectively with the whole class to explore mentally questions such as '5 × N = 35'. He makes good use of the 'tell us how you did it' approach, drawing on the pupils' knowledge of the multiplication tables. Then one girl, Clare, gives the correct answer to '6 × N = 54' and explains how she did it: 'Well, if it was 10 sixes that would be 60, but 54 is 6 less than that, so it must be 9.' The trainee teacher is clearly impressed and rightly congratulates the pupil – but then just moves on to the next question in his lesson plan.

> A really confident mathematics teacher would seize this opportunity to explore this approach with the rest of the class. For example, asking: 'How could we use Clare's idea to find the missing number in 3 × N = 27? In 8 × N = 72? In 4 × N = 32?'

USING IMAGES THAT SUPPORT MENTAL STRATEGIES FOR CALCULATIONS

Research into the development of children's mental strategies for calculations (Beishuizen, 1999) has shown how the 'empty number-line' can provide pupils with an effective image to support their manipulation of numbers. An empty number-line is used to represent the relative positions of numbers, without concern for the actual scale. Teachers regularly using this approach in discussing calculations with pupils have found that many pupils by the end of Year 4 are able to handle confidently the addition and subtraction of numbers with up to three digits by non-standard, informal methods. This is especially effective with those calculations that conventionally cause so many problems when done by standard vertical layout methods, such as subtractions involving zeros in the first number. Here's an observation from a Year 4 class working with a confident trainee teacher:

> In her plenary session Kate draws an empty number-line on the board, writes '302 – 197' and asks one girl to come out to the front to demonstrate to the class how she worked this out. The girl marks 197 and 302 on the line and then uses 200 and 300 as stepping stones to find the difference (3 + 100 + 2 = 105), as shown in Figure 13.2. The teacher discusses the picture with the class, specifically emphasising the language 'stepping stones' and 'difference' to underline the method used. She then writes '402 – 197' on the board and asks which numbers could be used as stepping

Figure 13.2   **Using an empty number-line to calculate '302 – 197'**

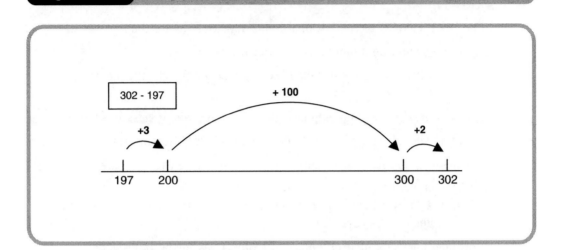

stones for this calculation. The children respond quickly and enthusiastically (using 200 and 400 as stepping stones, the answer is 3 + 200 + 2 = 205). Another number-line is drawn and another child demonstrates the calculation. The teacher follows this up with '502 – 197', '602 – 197', '702 – 197', which most of the children are now able to calculate mentally.

RELATING MATHEMATICS TO REAL LIFE SITUATIONS

A good teacher of mathematics will always seek to ensure that pupils connect what they do in school with their everyday experience and the real world outside the classroom. Mathematics is applied in almost every sphere of life and it is poor teaching if pupils rarely get to see the point of what they are learning in school.

Mike is a trainee teacher working with a Year 4 class on reading the time of day from an analogue clock, using a.m. and p.m. notation. The school's mathematics scheme has worksheets involving drawing hands on clock faces. Mike has decided not to use these because he thinks the activity is totally unreal. Instead he takes the classroom clock down from the wall and runs a question-and-answer session with the clock as a visual aid, using questions related to the events of the children's day, such as: what time is this? What will we be doing when the clock shows this time and we are at school? What will you be doing when the clock shows this time and you are not at school? Each pupil is then given a piece of paper with a time written on it in a.m./p.m. notation and told that if during the rest of the day they present the piece of paper to the teacher when the clock says that time he will give them a team point. Somehow or other all the pupils manage to succeed with this task!

SUMMARY

The key principles of the National Numeracy Strategy are that:

- there should be a daily mathematics lesson
- there should be a greater emphasis on developing specific mental calculation skills
- there should be more emphasis on interactive whole class teaching
- there should be a more controlled approach to differentiation.

The main components of a numeracy lesson following the structure of the NNS framework are:

- an oral starter focusing on development of number knowledge and mental strategies for calculations
- a main activity focused on specific objectives in the framework
- a plenary to consolidate and make explicit what has been learnt.

In this chapter a range of teaching skills necessary to do this effectively have been identified and some of them illustrated with examples of observations of trainee teachers teaching.

ISSUES FOR REFLECTION

- To support good practice in teaching numeracy what should you look for in a commercially produced mathematics scheme to be used within the numeracy hour in primary schools?

- In what ways might the NNS approaches conflict with parents' expectations about children's work in mathematics and how should a teacher or a school tackle this problem?

- Are the NNS proposed lesson structure and the NNS framework incompatible with the possibility of pupils undertaking extended problem-solving or investigational projects in mathematics?

- In what practical ways can primary school teachers address the issue of differentiation across the ability range in mathematics without compromising the principles of the Numeracy Strategy?

- Which aspects of the mathematics curriculum in primary schools could be taught or reinforced most effectively through purposeful activities in other areas of the curriculum?

Further reading

Harries, T. and Spooner, M. (2000) *Mental Mathematics for the Numeracy Hour*. London: David Fulton. This is a useful source of ideas for teaching mental mathematics in primary schools, with some good suggestions for resources that can be deployed effectively.

Haylock, D. (2006) *Mathematics Explained for Primary Teachers*. 3rd edition. London: Paul Chapman Publishing. In this book I aim to provide a comprehensive and accessible explanation of the mathematics that primary teachers need to understand, to underpin and to inform their teaching. Whatever mathematical topics you have to teach there's a chapter in here to help you sort out your own understanding first.

Haylock, D. and Cockburn, A. (2003) *Understanding Mathematics in the Lower Primary Years*, 2nd edition. London: Paul Chapman Publishing. This book gives teachers an understanding of the mathematical material taught to children aged 4–8 years. Numerous activities designed to promote understanding of mathematics are provided, covering number, calculations, measurement, shape and space, pattern in number, data-handling and mathematical reasoning.

QCA (1999) *The National Numeracy Strategy, Teaching Mental Calculation Strategies*. Sudbury: QCA. This booklet produced by the Qualifications and Curriculum Authority is designed to complement the NNS framework, providing more detailed guidance on what mental strategies should be taught in each year group and suggestions for how to teach them.

QCA (1999) *The National Numeracy Strategy, Teaching Written Calculations*. Sudbury: QCA. This booklet produced by the Qualifications and Curriculum Authority is also designed to complement the NNS framework, providing more detailed guidance on how, why and when to introduce pupils to various forms of written recording of calculations and formal written methods.

Thompson, I. (ed.) (1999) *Issues in Teaching Numeracy in Primary Schools*. Buckingham: Open University Press. This is a very useful collection of material providing the research and theoretical basis for many of the principles underpinning the National Numeracy Strategy.

Thompson, I. (ed.) (2003) *Enhancing Primary Mathematics Teaching*. Maidenhead: Open University Press. This book is a collection of articles that take as their starting point the fact that the National Numeracy Strategy and its successor, the National Primary Strategy, have had an enormous effect on the way in which mathematics is taught in primary schools. The book provides a useful balance between practical and theoretical considerations of how primary mathematics teaching can be most effective.

Chapter 14

Teaching science

Ann Oliver

How can you help develop children's thinking, creativity and confidence – the great challenge of science teaching? In this chapter, Ann Oliver demonstrates how the use of scientific enquiry can be a highly effective and inspirational way in which to engage children in science. We are treated to examples of trainees' actual work which illustrate good practice. The chapter shows that, by using such skills as observation, questioning and analysing, pupils and teachers can become intrigued, challenged and motivated to discover a subject which was often taught in rather sterile and meaningless ways in the past.

INTRODUCTION

They didn't tell me science was about everything! (Daniel, aged 10)

The purpose of this chapter is to encourage trainee teachers to consider how science can be taught well in the primary school and to give information which will help them achieve this goal. All primary teachers are expected to deliver the science curriculum, and to do this in an informed, positive and enthusiastic way demands confidence.

Some would argue that at primary level we are not training scientists but teaching science: that delivery of the science curriculum is all that is required. Others hold a well-established view that a main aim of school science is to promote enthusiasm for the subject and to enhance pupils' understanding of, and interest in, scientific issues. Trainee teachers face the difficult challenge of incorporating both agendas in order to be effective teachers of primary science. To do this, trainees need to develop certain types of knowledge which enable children to grasp ideas, question evidence and have a sound understanding of scientific concepts. These include:

- subject knowledge (their own personal understanding)
- teaching knowledge (their knowledge of ways to make science accessible for primary aged children).

Knowledge is necessary but so is enthusiasm. Inspirational teachers are able to display both. No wonder teaching science is considered a challenging and complex business with few easy answers. To claim that there is a definitive way to teach science is to misunderstand the nature of science teaching. A good starting point is to remember that scientists work in different ways, and have different outcomes often in collaboration with other scientists. Recognising both the precise and analytical part of science, as well as the tentative and exploratory aspect, will certainly inform teaching. If science education does not respect and represent this variety a distorted image of science and the work of scientists may be conveyed. To this end Ross (2000) urges us to consider how scientific theory has developed in the past. By exploring historical developments within science we can begin to form a more realistic view of how science works. This can easily be done at primary level through telling stories about scientists, comparing how famous scientists made discoveries and considering how theories change as new evidence is recognised.

Developing a sense of the subject: theory into practice

Not surprisingly many trainee teachers' principal perceptions of primary school science relate directly to their own experience of secondary school science. Unfortunately, trainees often have a clear memory of secondary school science being boring or difficult, presented as value-free and certainly not relating to everyday experience. Many cite the experience as a transmission model of teaching in which the trainee displayed little input or responsibility for learning. Selley (1999) points out that although secondary students often held mistaken ideas or misconceptions about science, the traditional strategy was for their teachers to ignore these ideas and try to present science in a way that could be memorised. If this is similar to your experience you may well identify with the notion that attitudes to science are often negative and not easily changed, perhaps going as far as considering it boring and dull.

TEACHING SCIENCE

Creating a positive learning environment

Perhaps most importantly, trainee teachers need to realise that children's interest in science is likely to be stimulated through practical application with time to reflect and share ideas. Lessons which finish in a rush, with little time to raise questions, discuss ideas or consolidate understanding, frustrate the learner and offer no incentive to pursue scientific thinking. If pupils are taught science so that they are encouraged to question their understanding it will seem natural for them to adapt their own ideas as further evidence is presented. Note-taking from the board, filling in prescribed worksheets and copying diagrams without practical application does little to involve the learner in doing science. An approach without creative practical application, or imaginative use of resources, does not promote the idea that science is fun, interesting or applicable. Good science teaching will involve, inspire and enthuse children to compare findings, raise questions, interrogate data and raise more questions to try and answer. It will not benefit the learner to see it as a finite activity. Scientific enquiry is often not a straightforward process and recognition that we expect to make mistakes and find data difficult to interpret is realistic to science practice. Such an approach is also more likely to promote enquiry among young children than a *right* answer expectation. Sometimes pupils worry about giving the teacher the *right* answer and, although this may be appropriate when carrying out calculations such as reading a temperature scale or measuring the length of a shadow, there are many instances when concern about the *right* answer can exert a tension which hinders learning.

Scientific understanding of both subject knowledge and process skills is more likely to be promoted by trying to work out reasons for a particular observation, considering alternatives and researching ideas. Encouraging pupils to explore their thinking at the appropriate level is a vital aspect of developing curiosity and confidence. Children and teachers need to be concerned with asking *why* and *how* things happen to promote scientific understanding. Time for creative reflection as well as rational thinking can usefully be incorporated into science teaching. This practice applies to teachers, trainee teachers and pupils. To illustrate this point imagine this scenario:

> Early on a warm, June morning a Year 5 class went into the school wildlife area to observe their animal traps (small containers filled with pieces of rotting fruit sunk into the soil under a hedgerow a few days earlier). To their delight many of the children discovered a variety of minibeasts in their traps, such as ants, beetles, snails, slugs, flies and worms. One boy seemed disappointed because there were no animals in his trap and in a quiet voice said, 'Mine hasn't worked'. If the teacher had replied saying, 'Never mind, have a look at somebody else's' or 'No, I can't see any either' or even 'I wonder why it hasn't worked?' his feeling of not having achieved the desired results would be reinforced and the opportunity to do science would be lost. His understanding of what science is about would also be limited or diminished. Fortunately this was not the case. The teacher asked him to look carefully to see if anything in his trap had changed. On closer inspection he discovered teeth marks, made

by a small rodent, clearly visible on one piece of apple. This generated much teacher-led discussion concerning teeth marks, types of teeth, the effect of the presence of a larger animal on smaller ones and the importance of interpreting clues to try to make sense of observations. The teacher was expertly concerning the pupils with both science subject knowledge and the process skills of science in a context of immense interest. After many questions and suggestions from the ever-growing group of children as to what creature had taken a bite from the apple the teacher made a suggestion. Perhaps the boy might like to take a small bite from a new piece of apple and compare the marks made by his teeth and that of the mystery animal. Then using a microscope and reference sources see if he could identify the animal. The boy began to do science. This led on to a discussion about forensic science and the possibility of identifying a robber by teeth marks left on an apple core at the scene of a crime.

This example highlights clearly how a teacher's knowledge, enthusiasm and understanding of science can guide thinking in a way which not only promotes enquiry and develops science skills but also gives pupils an insight into how interesting and rewarding science can be. As a result of the way the children were encouraged to develop a particular line of thinking, purpose as well as interest in science was recognised. Children began to relate scientific experience to practical application and saw science as something not only done in school. Responding to pupils' ideas and questions to sustain enthusiasm and develop understanding is fundamental to teaching science well. There is a feeling of how scientists work in an enquiry-based approach. Teachers who stimulate curiosity, not only of the exceptional but also of the ordinary, communicate an ongoing sense of wonder of our world.

Involving children by creating a positive learning environment and making learning meaningful

The following examples of PGCE trainees' work shows how learning can be a meaningful process involving children in practical, scientific explorations. Imaginative interpretation of the National Curriculum is evident in each case.

Len (PGCE 1999–2000): friction with Year 1

The children were carrying out a test to compare the effects of friction between two surfaces and the suitability of purpose of familiar materials within their experience. Friction as a force is often explored in school science. Examples of different footwear, often trainers on different surfaces to show the results of friction, are commonly used as a way of relating science to experience. Children can relate to slipping when wearing smooth-soled shoes playing football. But how many children relate the effects of friction to writing or eating or just being able to sit on a chair?

If many connections are made and many situations explored, then a fuller understanding of friction and the way in which the effects can be controlled will be understood. Helping children to make connections between scientific concepts and personal experience is one way of making learning meaningful. Len decided to set up a friction task in which children wrote a symbol on various surfaces with the purpose of comparing the results in discussion. This was followed by testing a variety of writing implements on the same surface and once again results were compared. The children were then asked to choose the paper and writing implement which they considered would produce the best result. (In this instance 'best' refers to the ease of writing and clarity of marks made.)

By exploring everyday materials in this way the science behind the task (friction is a force which opposes movement) can be explained so that children relate learning to experience, perhaps realising that friction can be useful and that we control it to suit our purposes. Children enjoy drawing using a variety of implements and surfaces but it is unlikely that they have analysed their preferences or considered reasons for suitability of one paper compared to another. What is important in developing science understanding is that children question observations and with guidance begin to make some sense of what they observed. In this way the teacher transformed a play activity into learning about the concept of friction. Using a microscope to compare the surfaces of materials tested will help even young children make connections between *bumpiness* and ease of writing. This wide variety of experience helps children make connections between friction as a force and everyday happenings.

Tom (PGCE 1999–2000): particle theory with Year 2

Although particle theory does not enter the curriculum until Key Stage 3, Tom wanted to introduce the idea to young children that things we can see are all made up of smaller parts. He thought this introduction could act as a foundation for understanding more difficult concepts in the future. He devised several tasks using art, ICT, Lego and photography in a cross-curricular approach to stimulate interest and develop understanding of this concept. Through a variety of experiences children were involved in:

- Describing a section of a computer image of a Seurat painting which had been enlarged so that the individual dots were visible, trying to identify the subject from the information available. A zoom facility reduced the image until it could be seen as a face.

- Using 'Dazzle' to produce their own dot pictures.

- Comparing five different designs of space vehicles built with an identical LEGO kit, using the same components to construct their individual designs.

- Looking at photographs of the school field from a distance describing what they saw as the photographs became progressively closer until individual blades of grass and particles of soil were visible.

Once again many situations are explored. In this case children were encouraged to make connections concerning particle theory and experience at a level appropriate to their understanding. Building young children's understanding of a complex and complicated aspect of science involves structuring interesting activities at a level suitable for the learner.

Teresa (PGCE 1999–2000): Earth and beyond with Year 5

As part of a lesson on Earth and beyond, Teresa wanted to convey to her pupils some understanding of the relative size of the Earth, Moon and Sun. She used a large orange ball of approximately 2 m diameter to represent the Sun, a peppercorn to represent the Earth and a sunflower seed to represent the Moon. This is not so unusual in itself but the way in which she structured the activity certainly made her audience aware of the vast difference in size between the three bodies. This is some-thing not often accomplished in the school setting, partly because school textbooks often represent a model of the solar system considering the ratio of size and distance involved in spreadsheet form. Such a mathematical representation only works for those able to construct a mental model of relationships from a page of figures. Many young children have not developed such skills and, although they can marvel at large numbers involved, the relationship between them is not recognised. Another model often used in primary school to represent the Sun, Earth and Moon includes a light source for the Sun, a ball for the Earth and a smaller ball for the Moon. This analogy also gives little impression of the vast size of the Sun or the enormous quan-tity of light energy emitted from it or the relative sizes of each body.

This is why Teresa rejected such ideas. She wanted her pupils to imagine how each body is viewed from various aspects, reinforcing the idea that the Earth is not the centre of the universe, by offering a different point of reference. The peppercorn (Earth) was placed on the playground, with the sunflower seed (Moon) close by, the orange ball (Sun) was placed 50 metres away, the group stood by the peppercorn (Earth) and looked at the ball (Sun), observations were made concerning the appar-ent size of the ball at a distance. The group then walked to the ball (Sun) and looked back at the peppercorn (Earth) which was not visible. With any analogy there are flaws: however, in comparison with this model never again will a light bulb and ball be seen as an equally good example of representing the Sun and the Earth.

Each of the above trainee teachers planned creatively to address difficult scientific concepts in a way which required pupil involvement. A firm scientific understanding of the particular aspect of science taught (subject knowledge) is evident by the way tasks were structured to allow children to explore a progression of ideas usefully. Academic theory was not transmitted before pupils were ready for it.

The practical nature of teaching in this way opens up to children the whole methodology of science. Not only subject knowledge but also teaching knowledge was used with the intention that learning science can fulfil formal requirements in an enjoyable way. It might be encouraging for future trainees to know that none of the three postgraduate students cited here have science degrees. Even so they all demonstrated a good understanding of primary practice in teaching science. Seeing through a child's eyes and not 'watering down' secondary science is an approach evident in each case.

In trying to help children make sense of science, Len, Tom and Teresa each:

- organised activities to develop science understanding at a level appropriate for the learner

- planned activities to address complex scientific ideas in a practical way

- presented complex scientific concepts in simple, visual forms

- selected a variety of resources and approaches to address learning intentions

- compared different viewpoints and approaches.

Imagine you have been asked to teach a science lesson to a class of primary aged children, just like Len, Tom and Teresa. Where do you start? To inform your own development as a teacher it would be helpful to begin with the following questions:

- What *subject knowledge* do I need to plan and teach this lesson?

- How can my *teaching knowledge* be used effectively to involve the learner?

- How might pupils' understanding be restructured as a result of their involvement?

- How can I encourage discussion, interact and intervene to promote enquiry?

- How can I promote observation and exploration ?

- How can I help children relate science to experience?

- How can I make science fun?

STRATEGIES FOR SUCCESS

Managing primary science

Science, in primary education, is a practical subject which needs to be well managed. Trainees can learn a great deal about management and delivery of the science curriculum by observing practising teachers. To get the most from observations it is advisable to concentrate not only on what the teacher does, but also on what the children do in response. Knowing what to look for in ascertaining successful science teaching is an important and difficult skill for a novice. Each teacher has a unique way of working and a different way of teaching science. Organisation of group work, the use of appropriate resources and management of practical activities are in constant flux. There is more to managing a science lesson than organising and providing the correct equipment. Resources need to be readily available and organised in a way for easy access. Children need to be organised into groups for collaborative activities and discussion. The teacher needs to circulate and monitor involvement and assess understanding. Understandably, trainees often concentrate on management and control issues because they perceive them to be crucial to the smooth running of a lesson. What is not so well understood by novice teachers is that the most effective form of control occurs when children are on task and motivation is sustained through involvement in learning. If children are absorbed in the planned tasks then managing science is less stressful. In successful sessions where pupils are totally motivated the teacher can join in or stand back and make informal assessments. Successful lessons are more likely if teachers:

- provide well-structured, interesting science lessons with clear learning intentions

- challenge scientific thinking in a non-threatening way

- involve children in learning relevant science skills and procedures through practical activity

- have a creative, imaginative and fun approach

- encourage a degree of independent enquiry

- focus on quality not quantity

- assess understanding and give progressive feedback to support development of ideas.

At this point it would be reasonable for trainees to be concerned about how this ideal might fit in with government requirements and the National Curriculum programme of study. The following two science lessons (lesson A and lesson B) both taught to a Year 6 class might help clarify such concerns. In lessons A and B the learning objectives are identical and relate to the same programme of study in the National Curriculum. Although the starting point is the same, the teachers' role and pupils' learning outcomes are very different. You can use the above bullet points as a checklist to focus on teaching and learning implications in both lessons.

Lesson A

The class watch a video about hovercrafts. The teacher gives a description of how a hovercraft works. The pupils copy a diagram from the board and the arrows which represent movement of air. They watch as the teacher blows up a balloon and watch as the balloon moves in a spiralling motion at random as the teacher releases the balloon. They are encouraged to explain the connections between the balloon's movement and how a hovercraft works. Some of the children log in to the website, *howitworks.com*, and print the information on a hovercraft. Other pupils use reference books to find information and a third group draw pictures of a hovercraft for a display. To finish the lesson children complete a cloze procedure worksheet on how a hovercraft works. At the end of the lesson all children have a drawing of a hovercraft and a cloze procedure worksheet to put in their science folder. Some have information from the website.

Lesson B

The teacher brainstorms pupils' ideas on hovercrafts to assess current levels of understanding, including asking them how they think a hovercraft moves. On a smooth surface the teacher demonstrates a simulation of the hovercraft's lift and movement with a polystyrene tile and balloon secured in a cork with a small hole in the centre. A few pupils demonstrate this simulation to the class using the same materials. In discussion the teacher ensures that pupils are made aware of key points: *what forces are causing the tile to lift slightly? The downthrust of air is matched by the upthrust from the floor. Air is a substance and takes up space. It exerts an upwards force on the tile and causes it to lift.* Pupils are then asked to think about what would make a difference to how a hovercraft moves. Suggested ideas include: *what would make a difference to how high a hovercraft lifts? How fast it moves? Which direction it travels in?* The children are organised into five mixed-ability groups. Pupils set up their own small-group investigations, making hovercrafts, making predictions and noting observations. Fair testing is emphasised. There are clear instructions that each group will report back to the rest of the class their findings. One group investigate whether the size of the balloon made a difference, another group consider the shape of the balloon, a third group look at different surfaces and the fourth group explore the size of the hole in the tile. In the pupil report-back session, explanation as well as description are encouraged. At the end of the lesson each child is given a copy of *How a Hovercraft Craftily Hovers*, and shown an OHP used to discuss how a real hovercraft actually moves.

In each case ask yourself:

- How was the learner involved in learning science?

- How was the teacher involved in teaching science?

- How was teaching successful?

- How was learning successful?

In Lesson A it is likely that only the brightest pupils would be able to pick up the clues from texts and guidance from the teacher and arrive at the intended learning outcomes. If teachers adopt the view that theory is so obvious, how easily interpretation of information and understanding of principles is left to chance.

In Lesson B, the planned teacher interaction, plus planned independent exploration, demand intellectual involvement from children. Inherent in such an approach is the notion that ideas will be challenged, discussed and reported. Analysis of observations, results of predictions and surprises at outcomes all serve to inform pupils about the science in the task. It is important to remember that such outcomes may not always be planned and children often see things differently from adults. An important role of the teacher is to use children's observations to maximise understanding and to structure situations in which children can test ideas. As de Boo (1999) recognises, if teachers work from children's innate and instinctive curiosity, then even young children can develop rigorous investigative skills and an enquiry-based approach can enhance children's learning while still giving them curricular entitlements.

WHY THINGS CAN GO WRONG

There are many reasons why trainees perceive lessons to *go wrong*. Often situations can be easily rectified or adjusted. It might be a need to organise resources more efficiently, or group pupils differently to encourage involvement or time lessons to maximise learning. Areas which can cause *things to go wrong* which are not so easily remedied by the novice, have been identified in discussion with PGCE trainees. These include:

- Where to start?

- How to explain?

- How to promote scientific enquiry?

- How to make sense of evidence collected?

Many trainee teachers have problems with *where to start* and *how to explain.* The impact of these two aspects of teaching science is far-reaching and needs consideration.

⬤ Where to start?

To start teaching science effectively teachers need to be aware of children's conceptions and understanding of a particular aspect of science for study. To do this it is necessary to find out *where children are at.* Finding out what children know allows you to plan an appropriate next step. If this effective next step does not happen then boredom, confusion and apathy can follow. The role of the teacher is crucial in providing conditions in which children feel confident to put forward their ideas. The following examples indicate how problems might arise if assumptions are made concerning pupils' prior knowledge and thinking before planning teaching.

Example 1

Imagine this. Before planning a series of lessons on Earth and beyond for a Year 5 class the trainee teacher asked children to write or draw what they knew about *space.* The pupils had no prior warning of this task. One boy in the class, Ian, wrote 'silver starry soot' and illustrated this with a drawing of tiny stars on a dark background. Another boy, Robert, wrote a whole side of accurate text (no reference books were available) finishing with 'you would be in a time continuum'.

From this example it can be seen that the same programme of study or style of teaching would not benefit both Ian and Robert equally. If the assumption is made that a series of lessons would be appropriate for the whole class then it is easy to see that *things could go wrong.*

But remember that although Robert could recall facts, this alone is not a true indication of understanding. Consequently, the teacher asked him to draw a model of the solar system and give an explanation of how day and night occurred. Both tasks were completed with understanding. However, his knowledge of why seasons occur was found to be less accurate. The teacher then decided this was his starting point. It is impossible to accommodate all pupils in this way, but some effort needs to be made to differentiate expectations according to prior knowledge and ability. For those with special needs it is crucial to structure tasks at a level appropriate for the child's development. This applies to the more able as well as the less able pupils.

Example 2

A Year 4 class were questioned in an informal way about their understanding of gravity, relationship and relative size of the planets, the movement of the Earth and

Figure 14.1   Year 4 child's theory about the Sun and planets

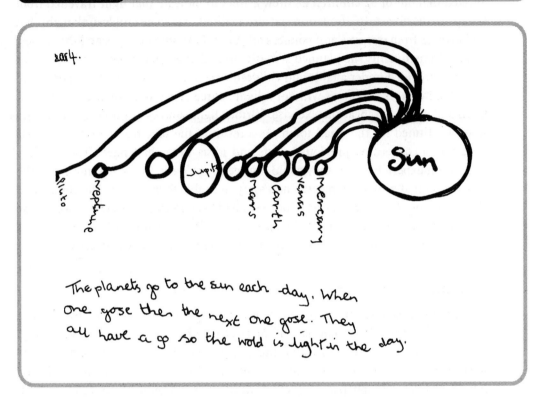

2004.

Pluto neptune Jupiter mars earth venus mercury Sun

The planets go to the sun each day. When one gose then the next one gose. They all have a go so the wold is light in the day.

why we experience day and night and the seasons. Discussion was encouraged. Owing to a skilled teacher and secure environment children became animated in putting forward their theories, including one which stated that 'each planet travelled from a starting position to the Sun and back in one day, the planets were in order with Mercury nearest to the Sun' (Figure 14.1). Many varied, individual naïve ideas and misconceptions emerge through discussion. Some ideas are so individual that teachers can be very surprised by them, as was the case in the above example. Without knowledge of children's naïve ideas teaching cannot be focused on individual needs.

Example 3

A trainee teacher was asked to teach a Year 5 class about *light*. The trainee not only referred to the National Curriculum and the Qualifications and Curriculum Authority documents on Key Stage 2 science but also, remembering a lecture on pupils' misconceptions in science, read the SPACE project research on children's misconceptions about light. Giving the class the diagram of a person looking at a candle used in the SPACE project, she asked pupils to put arrows on the line (indicating a beam of light) in the direction they thought the light was travelling. She was amazed that out of 32 children 28 drew arrows to indicate that light travelled from the eye to the object. In discussion she also realised that some children thought that 'light comes from our eyes and bounces off things back into our eyes and that is how we see'. Consequently she planned activities to challenge this misconception. A dark area was provided under a table and children were asked to draw simple shapes and then more complicated ones without a light source. They were then given a small torch and asked to repeat the exercise. Various light sources of differing intensities were substituted for the small torch. As a result of the practical activity questions were raised concerning previous beliefs and ideas were challenged. The children knew from experience that they could not see in the dark. Many had not made the connection that a light source was necessary to enable them to see. The connection that we see because light travels to our eyes had been misunderstood by most of the class. If the trainee had proceeded in planning a block of work without recognising this common misconception problems in understanding could easily arise.

Example 4

In considering how electrical current flows in circuits of different lengths, Eleanor, Year 2, put forward the notion that; 'if the electricity has a long way to travel it stops halfway round for a rest'. To Eleanor this is a perfectly logical explanation although science knowledge of electricity is not evident. The teacher faces the challenge of helping Eleanor develop understanding of electrical circuits by moving her thinking from a common-sense view to a scientific one. Explanation by itself will have little impact and could confuse a young child (as with Example 3). Eleanor needs to have experience of observing circuits of different lengths working and making her own circuits using different lengths of insulated wire to complete a circuit. This can be followed by a discussion or questioning session in which the teacher explains at an appropriate level, through analogy or simulation how electrical energy is transferred.

Example 5

As 3-year-old Evie observed a small ball of fluff move across the floor she asked, 'Why hasn't fluff got a face?' Many young children believe that if something moves it is alive; fire, clouds and clocks are well-recognised examples (Hollins and Whitby, 1998). Evie probably thought this too and thus went on to reason that things that are alive have a face. It is important to seek out the child's meaning rather than accept our own interpretation without question.

If starting points are not directly related to prior understanding then things can quickly *go wrong*. Restructuring children's understanding is no easy matter but what is important is to realise each child has a different starting point and some way of finding out key ideas is necessary before planning a series of lessons. Children's prior knowledge and experience including misconceptions and naïve ideas have a huge impact on how children take part in a lesson and accept or reject information offered. If you find yourself having an informal chat with a pupil, take the initiative and practise structuring your questions, comments and responses to elicit their ideas related to current science sessions. Ways of finding out children's ideas can be through unplanned or opportunist conversation.

Example 6

Year 2 play in the playground, it is a hot afternoon. Nick keeps returning to a shaded corner under a high hedge and then runs out to join the others. Eventually he stays near the hedge.

Teacher: Do you like this place?

Nick: I'm hot there (pointing to the others).

Teacher: If you stand here (moving a few steps out of the shade) what does it feel like?

Nick: Hot, it makes me hot.

Teacher: Why do you think it is hot out here?

Nick: 'Cos the sun makes me hot.

Teacher: But not near the hedge?

Nick: No 'cos the hedge stops it, look it can't get through, like a cave (makes a large, circular gesture).

Teacher: This morning I noticed it was sunny here, because, do you remember, we looked at a butterfly opening its wings in the sunshine resting on the hedge.

Nick: Yes.

Teacher: Why do you think it was sunny here this morning?

Nick: (Looks at the sky) because there are more clouds now, anyway it's always more sunny here in the morning.

Although the above conversation was not part of a lesson, the teacher seized the opportunity to assess Nick's understanding and challenge his ideas in an informal manner. Many teachers are expert at this skill and trainees will do well to emulate such practice.

Figure 14.2 Year 5 pupil's concept drawing

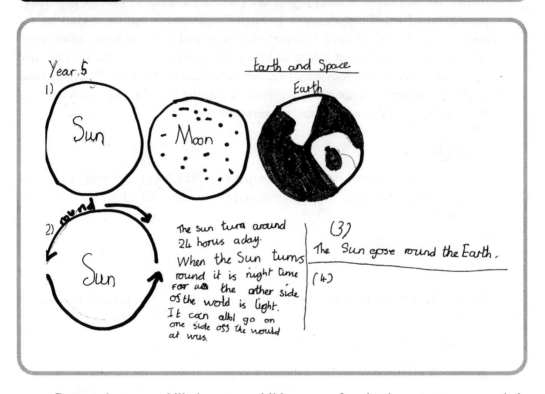

Because language skills in young children are often inadequate to express their beliefs and understanding, finding out is often best done through talk or drawing. Concept cartoons (Naylor and Keogh, 2000) are an excellent starting point. Children enjoy considering ideas such as 'a snowman will melt faster wearing a coat'. Discussion is stimulated and thinking is challenged in a fun way. You might like to devise your own concept cartoons when beginning a new block of work in science. This can be an entertaining exercise to do with a fellow teacher or even pupils. Another method of eliciting children's ideas is through *concept drawing*. Figure 14.2 was drawn by a Year 5 pupil before taking part in a series of lessons on Earth and beyond. Figure 14.3 was drawn by the same child after completing six weeks' work on this topic. Drawings are evidence of understanding but remember to talk about drawings with the children involved – their interpretation might surprise you.

Finding out *where children are at* can be achieved in many ways. Formal tests or planned assessment tasks are one way but do not necessarily offer insight into individual misconceptions. If time permits it is worthwhile doing your own reading and research into children's understanding of science concepts. To help with this aspect of teaching, suggested reading is included at the end of the chapter.

Figure 14.3   After 6 weeks' study

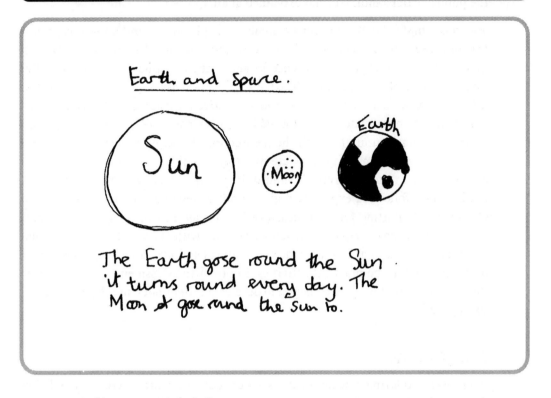

Earth and Space.

Sun   ·Moon   Earth

The Earth gose round the Sun.
it turns round every day. The
Moon dt gose rund the Sun to.

How to explain?

Good teacher explanations are vital to developing a child's understanding of science. At the primary phase of education complex science subject knowledge can confuse children especially if it is presented in a theoretical way. Science ideas are often too complicated or difficult to convey to young children. If explanations are not at the right level for developing understanding then things can easily *go wrong*.

Children build mental constructs and acquire knowledge in a variety of ways. To do this they need to have experience of not only practical exploration but also interaction with people in social and cultural contexts. Models, simulations and analogies can also be used effectively to build mental images of what is going on. Trainee teachers are adept at setting up practical activities in which children can explore and investigate materials, phenomena and ideas, such as: which is the best toothpaste? How to make a bulb work in a circuit. Making glue with things from the kitchen cupboard. Do all tomatoes float? Which colour is the safest to wear in the dark? Can plants grow without soil? Does warm water make better bubbles? Taught well such sessions can be both enjoyable and informative. However, problems can arise if messages about science subject content are not explained at a level appropriate to the pupils' understanding or not explained at all.

You might find it helpful to prepare some key explanations and questions prior to teaching a session. This not only helps focus thinking on *what you want children to learn*, but also raises your confidence in answering questions and understanding pupils' varying abilities. But don't panic – if children ask a question that you find difficult to answer, do not worry. It is good practice for teachers to be seen as questioners too. Congratulate pupils for asking questions. Trying to explain can be a productive joint venture for both the teacher and the pupil. In considering explanations it might be more appropriate to set up practical activities for children to explore ideas. Such activities should be designed to generate discussion. Explanations following exploration give pupils a concrete experience to relate to. Confidence in putting forward ideas can be increased in this way. Trainees have used the following examples on teaching practice with success. In each case there was clear evidence that pupils made observations and raised more questions after being involved in the practical activities. Informative assessment, often in conversation, showed that pupils had begun to develop a fuller understanding of scientific concepts involved.

Example 1: Year 6

Pupils were exploring how light travels. One group of children were given old, flexible vacuum-cleaner tubes and torches of different sizes. They were asked to shine a beam of light on a marked spot on a piece of black card by projecting the torch beam through the tube. The teacher made a maze for another group with rectangular bricks; in the centre was a toy princess. Using plastic, coated mirrors the pupils had the challenge of positioning the mirrors in the maze so that the princess could be seen from the entrance. To differentiate this activity a further challenge was to find the minimum number of mirrors needed to achieve this.

Example 2: Year 1

Imagine a warm afternoon, the science lesson is outside (wonderful). One activity exploring *forces* involves children experimenting, filling plastic syringes with water and seeing how they might control the stream of water. When the syringes had no water in them Naomi made the observation that 'there is nothing in it' (the syringe).The teacher took another syringe and held it near Naomi's hand, pushing the air out quickly, so that she could feel the movement of air.

Teacher: Did you feel anything?

Naomi: Yes, it tickled (*giggle*).

Teacher: Do you want a go? Do you want to try it on something else, like this balloon?

(Naomi experiments and soon realises that if there is no water in the syringe then she can feel the movement of air with a push and observe its effects.)

Teacher: What do you think is in the syringe?

Naomi: Air – you can feel it when you push.

This method of challenging thinking and explaining concepts involves the learner and is far more effective than merely explaining by telling. Through first-hand experience children are more likely to make sense of the science behind what they see. The skill of the teacher in helping pupils make such links cannot be underestimated.

Questions to ask yourself about explaining include:

- What are the key concepts I want children to learn?

- How can I explain these at a level which will enhance understanding and aid learning?

- What activities might I set up to explore concepts prior to explaining?

- Have I answered questions and given explanations at an appropriate level for pupils' understanding?

How to promote scientific enquiry?

Sometimes *things can go wrong* because trainees perceive their role as teaching science in a way which imparts information and facts. An initial concern is that as a teacher they should know all the answers. This view is counterproductive to doing science. Children benefit from seeing teachers joining in searching for explanations. Such a collaborative approach encourages pupils to make inferences and draw conclusions. Sharing an interest in making sense of data generated by explorations and investigations is influential in promoting a positive attitude to science enquiry.

Enquiry requires a questioning attitude. Children can find asking the required questions to initiate enquiry daunting and this can be a problem for the trainee teacher. One way to encourage pupils to raise questions is to use their innate curiosity. This is a powerful motivating force. Imagine the teacher has an old shoe box on his table, he carefully lifts the lid and peeps inside before gently replacing the box on the table. At least one child will want to know why or what is inside. Innate curiosity can be used effectively by teachers to motivate an interest in science in a variety of ways; for example:

- facial expression – a surprised or puzzled look, a big smile

- gestures – hand cupped to the ear, finger to the lip, open hands

- comments – 'I'm surprised they move so quickly', 'Show me how to mix this'

- questions – 'Do you think it will be stronger?', 'How are they different?'

- artefacts, collections of shells (diversity), buttons (classification), shoes (materials, suitability of purpose, friction)

- posters, books, magazines, photographs, websites, videos, audio tapes can all be used effectively to stimulate an interest and promote enquiry.

Raising questions and teaching children how to raise questions are essential teaching skills in promoting scientific enquiry. The above starting points can all help develop a questioning approach. Trainees who teach science successfully demonstrate an ability to involve children in answering, raising and considering questions of a scientific nature.

Making use of evidence collected

Many trainee teachers consider *interpreting evidence* as a most challenging aspect of Sc1 (science enquiry). Currently Sc1 has an assessment rating of 50 per cent at Key Stage 1 and 40 per cent at Key Stage 2. The high weighting on this aspect of science education indicates the importance placed on it by the government. Skills connected with the process of science, including observing, making predictions, measuring and recording, help build a bank of data. How very young children make sense of and use this information is an aspect of teaching that many trainees find difficult. Making evidence accessible for children to discuss is an important part of teaching science. The need for such evidence to be at a level appropriate to independent understanding is crucial if children are to make sense of *what they found out*. Representation of evidence, in the form of simple charts, pictograms, tables and graphs which do not confuse understanding, help pupils make connections essential to developing understanding.

For very young children this is often best done with pictorial additions. By allowing children to consider evidence at a level appropriate to their understanding connections will begin to be made between scientific data and scientific concepts. The following examples from PGCE trainees show successful recording methods to aid interpretation of data used with Key Stage 1.

Example 1: Year 1

A tennis ball was dropped onto different surfaces: sand, clay, grass, concrete and shingle. The question for children to explore was 'On which surface did the tennis ball bounce the highest?' So that pupils were able to interpret and discuss the data collected, the teacher made a chart. A drawing of a brick wall underneath which samples of the surfaces on which the ball was dropped was presented to the children. The ball was dropped from the same height, against a breeze block wall, onto the different surfaces. The children indicated the top of the bounce and counted the bricks. The Mr Man character, Mr Bounce, was used to represent the height of each bounce. On the concrete bounce he cleared six bricks, his hands were in the air and he was smiling. On the sand bounce he didn't even clear one brick and he looked glum (see Figure 14.4).

Figure 14.4   Mr. Bounce measures the bounce

Example 2: Year 4

In considering 'Why do some things float?' children were asked to predict which items from a selection of fruit and vegetables would float. More usually materials such as cork, polystyrene and metal or objects such as toy boats, stones and bottles are used to encourage children to explore the concepts of floating and sinking. By using fruit and vegetables there are more *surprises*. The teaching intention was to challenge misconceptions through considering evidence. To do this a simple pictorial representation was used so that children could independently make comparisons and connections between their predictions and observations. A drawing of a tank almost full of water was presented to each child and they drew where they thought a grape, banana, apple, tomato and potato would rest after being placed in the water. The children were encouraged to give reasons for their choices with the teacher acting as scribe for the group. Pupils' predictions were compared to a drawing of where the objects came to rest and once again children were asked why they thought some things floated while others sank (see Figure 14.5).

To be effective, evidence gathered and presented for consideration and analysis must focus on the science which has been done by making it comprehensible to others. The plenary session is crucial in helping pupils address this issue. By helping children make sense of their findings, purpose and rigour in science will be evident. There is little purpose in trying to find something out without considering the outcome. This is a message that teachers give if they say, 'Right it is time to stop now, put your books and equipment away, off you go to play', or 'Oh, we have run out of time we will talk about what we have done next time we do science'. This approach is not conducive to learning science. Ensure that your planning and time management allows for a plenary. A plenary needs to be planned to address the learning intentions and outcomes. Hopefully children will come up with their own ideas and questions too. If questions and comments are relevant to the enquiry this is a clear indication that pupils are thinking about science and becoming confident in communicating their ideas. The skill of the teacher is to use these conversations to enhance learning and understanding.

PREPARING FOR A SCHOOL PLACEMENT

An important part of your training will take place in schools. At the beginning of the course your focus will be on observation and teaching small groups. By your final teaching practices in two separate Key Stages you will be expected to teach whole-class science across the primary phase. To prepare for this you need to consider not only how to link theory to practice but also the nature and methods

Figure 14.5 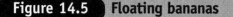 Floating bananas

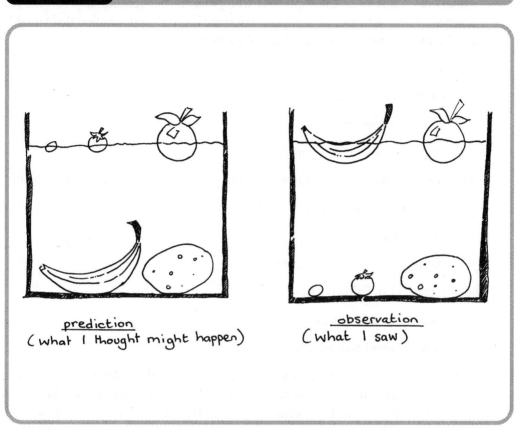

prediction
(what I thought might happen)

observation
(what I saw)

of working in your particular placement. The level of ability, age of the children and previous experience of the class in doing science are all key factors to consider. The National Curriculum for science is followed by almost all schools. How it is implemented, including the time allocated and the importance placed on enquiry, can vary considerably. Some teachers still find teaching investigative science a daunting prospect and some science co-ordinators in primary schools have no background in science. When visiting a school for the first time it would be useful to arrange times to talk to the science co-ordinator or class teacher about science in the school and observe as many different teachers teaching science as possible. In this way you can compare styles, reflect on examples and build up a bank of ideas. Talking to teachers and children about science education can offer useful insight for your professional development. As you progress through the course your questions will become more focused relating to reflection on your practice. To begin with they will be more general (see Chapter 17, 'Identifying areas of concern' section).

When you begin teaching you will be working alongside a teacher or teaching small groups of children. At this time you will probably be working closely with the teacher's plans. When you begin planning there is certain information that you will need from your placement school including their:

- science policy
- safety in science policy
- long-term science plans
- medium-term science plans.

From the class teacher to whom you are allocated you will need to find out about:

- timetable considerations
- resources available
- preferred methods of working
- records of individual assessments
- assessment procedures
- organisational and management issues.

For every new school placement you will have to gather this information and make yourself familiar with the content. On your final teaching practice you will have to demonstrate the ability to produce your own medium- and short-term plans (see Chapter 11) and teach in a way that demonstrates that you have achieved the standards to gain qualified teacher status.

GAINING QUALIFIED TEACHER STATUS (QTS)

The government has introduced a statutory curriculum for initial teacher training in science and this became a legal requirement in September 1999. Annex E of Department for Education and Employment Circular 4/98 (DfEE, 1998a) identifies the knowledge and skills that trainee teachers need to have to satisfy the science standards for gaining qualified teacher status.

As one of the core areas of the curriculum, science can provide particular challenges to teachers in gaining qualified teacher status. The beginner teacher needs to be concerned with developing skills, knowledge and attitudes which will enable them to teach science well. Understandably, the nature of science as a subject and personal attitudes towards science will shape individual teaching styles. However, the human endeavour involved in making sense of the world is what science is about – to help *all* children see the relevance of science in their lives whatever their culture or place in society, to encourage them to be inquisitive and challenge ideas but also keep an open mind, accepting that scientific understanding is at best only partial and provisional, are important goals.

In 2003 the Teacher Training Agency (TTA) introduced standards for the award of Qualified Teacher Status in *Qualifying to Teach: Professional Standards for Qualified Teacher Status and Requirements for Initial Teacher Training* (DfES/TTA, 2003; www.tta.gov.uk). Standard S2.1 states that those awarded QTS must demonstrate a secure knowledge and understanding of the subjects they are trained to teach.

GETTING THE MOST FROM YOUR COURSE

The teacher is the most important resource children have. Your enthusiasm, knowledge and ability to make science stimulating and accessible for *all* your pupils will shape their attitudes.

Subject knowledge

To teach with confidence you need to feel secure with science subject knowledge. To achieve this most teachers research areas of the curriculum prior to teaching a block of work – *invertebrates*, for example. Because of the broad nature of primary science it is unrealistic to expect trainee teachers to be expert in all aspects of science. Even trainees with science degrees feel that they are wobbly in certain areas. To support self-study there are some excellent texts written for teachers of primary science recommended at the end of the chapter as well as many websites which can easily be accessed through a search engine to answer questions and give information.

Teaching knowledge

Teaching knowledge comes with experience. It is about learning a way of doing science which enables pupils to develop their knowledge and understanding of science. The success of this venture will depend on how well you know your children and how well you inspire them to be enthusiastic about learning science. To be effective you need to consider a wide range of approaches, activities and resources. Children learn in different ways and different aspects of science present particular problems. Effective science teaching is a result of considering alternatives, trial and error, reflecting on practice and adapting to your audience. To be able to do this you need to observe many different teachers and children in science sessions, consider science in different cultures, not be afraid to have a go and try out ideas, and to recognise how children best learn science.

A final checklist for getting the most from your course includes:

- identifying personal goals for subject knowledge and teaching skills

- using self-study teaching materials and audits as appropriate

- collaborating with and supporting peers

- observing experienced teachers teaching science

- observing children doing science

- keeping reflective notes of your observations, development and progress

- research websites to answer science questions and find information

- thinking creatively about science, asking questions, having a go, joining in

- being enthusiastic and enjoying the subject.

SUMMARY

- The nature of science is precise and analytical as well as tentative and exploratory. To teach effectively both aspects need to be considered.

- Delivery of the science curriculum is strongly influenced by a teacher's experience and perception of science.

- Teachers influence learning by the choices they make.

- Pupils' interest in science is more likely to be stimulated through practical involvement by promoting science as part of experience.

- Children's individual ideas and understanding of scientific concepts might not always be what the teacher expects. Some knowledge of naïve ideas is needed to ascertain starting points and develop understanding.

- By helping pupils make sense of their findings purpose in science will be evident.

ISSUES FOR REFLECTION

- What do you see as the key features of effective science teaching? Do you think everyone would be of the same opinion? Why do you think teachers' opinions vary?

- To what extent is an approach which questions evidence confusing for young children?

- What kinds of activities are likely to involve children in the practical exploration or application of science? Can you give examples with genuine purpose?

- How might you use cultural diversity to stimulate discussion of scientific ideas?

Further reading

To help develop your skill in stimulating an interest in science and considering ways of promoting enquiry:

de Boo, M. (1999) *Enquiring Children, Challenging Teaching*. Buckingham: Open University Press. The author has obvious experience of the classroom, describing the development of children's enquiry skills and the teacher's role in a very readable way.

Harlen, W. (2000) *The Teaching of Science in Primary Schools*. 3rd edition. London: Paul Chapman Publishing. This is a comprehensive and informative book. Trainees might find the following chapters especially useful: Chapter 7 'Experiences that promote learning' and Chapter 8 'Teachers' and children's roles in learning'.

Hollins, M. and Whitby, W. (1998) *Progression in Primary Science*. London: David Fulton. The sections on children's understanding included in each chapter are especially helpful in gaining understanding of children's ideas.

Wenham, M. (2001) *200 Science Investigations for Young Trainees: Practical Activities for Science 5–11*. London: Paul Chapman Publishing. An excellent resource for trainee teachers seeking to broaden their knowledge of science activities appropriate for primary children. Many tried and tested practical ideas are included.

To support development of your subject knowledge:

BBC Bite Size GCSE revision website: www.bbc.co.uk/education/gcsebi./

Farrow, S. (1999) *The Really Useful Science Book: A Framework of Knowledge for Primary Teachers*. 2nd edition. London: Falmer Press.

Kennedy, J. (1997) *Primary Science: Knowledge and Understanding*. London: Routledge.

Nuffield Primary Science Teachers Guides (1995) London: Collins for the Nuffield Foundation.

Peacock, G.A. (1998) *Science for Primary Teachers: QTS Audit and Self-Study* Guide. London: Letts.

Wenham, M. (1995) *Understanding Primary Science: Ideas, Concepts and Explanations*. London: Paul Chapman Publishing.

To support using ICT in science:

Meadows, J. (2004) *Science and ICT in the Primary School: A Creative Approach to Big Ideas*. London: David Fulton.

Useful websites:

The Association of Science Education (ASE): www.ase.org.uk

To answer primary science questions:
www.wsu.edu/DrUniverse/

To initiate discussion and assess understanding:
www.conceptcartoons.com/index-flash.html

Making ICT meaningful

Rob Barnes

ICT is all around and seems to be the medium in which each one of us is destined to swim. Getting to grips with this in terms of your teaching may seem a major challenge. In this chapter Rob Barnes introduces both novices and experts to some of the wide range of opportunities ICT has to offer 3–11-year-olds in schools. He explains how it can complement and enhance traditional teaching and learning, but warns that its value can be lost without thoughtful implementation.

INTRODUCTION

It is a pretty safe bet that anyone who has become proficient at using a computer has also been frustrated, lost a file, maybe screamed at a microchip, or cursed a printer that decided not to print. Despite the advances in technology, computers still seem to take ages to do searches and other tasks. There is no evidence whatever to support the view that proficiency in using a computer equates with genius and incompetence equates with stupidity. Computers may be much more reliable than they were, but they sometimes display unfriendly warnings which are best ignored. It may be tempting to run at the sight of the first unfriendly message. Fortunately most educational software is inspiring rather than daunting, so there is every chance you will feel confident about using it with children once you have practised. You need a basic understanding of how to use a computer and a sophisticated understanding of what to do with the educational software.

WHAT IS ICT?

Naturally, trainees have varied backgrounds in using a computer. If you are unfamiliar with all the jargon words, you are not alone. They change from month to month within information and communications technology (ICT). In fact the word 'communication' was added to 'information' and 'technology' (IT) in the late 1990s. This was because we now use various devices, including hand-held mobile equipment to send messages and access information. It is not enough to limit ICT to computing or technology. At the beginning of the twenty-first century, few can deny that word-processing, access to the Internet through computers, and mobile hand-held equipment is well established. A mouse is no longer only something that eats cheese, and mobile equipment has become a fashion accessory and status symbol. Wireless technology means that the Internet can be accessed from almost anywhere, and the difference between a phone, camera and computer is blurred. The quality of colour displays increases with each new model and the speed increase shows no sign of slowing down.

You may not yourself want to be part of the revolution, but it is as pervasive as the electricity which makes it possible. If, by contrast, your computing experience has so far been highly specific, and gained on state-of-the-art equipment, educational computing may come as a culture shock. Imagine being in a classroom where you can take none of your previous high-level experience for granted. The software programs likely to attract children are not those you would find in a business office. Very young children, for example, are unable to read pages of text found on the Internet, so they need a different provision. If your starting point is a very basic one, remember that ICT is about children, education and how to use some of the most exciting software ever devised.

This chapter looks at ways to make information and communications technology meaningful for yourself and for the children you teach. I see this as a creative quest for all teachers, and not one where they dream of having the latest suite of networked computers and photo-standard printers that work first time, every time. I will concentrate mainly on the practical use of personal computers in the classroom using examples from surveys and word-processing. You will not find my favourite list of software mentioned here because everyone has their preferences and schools favour different things. Using a computer might sound an obvious starting point, but remember that ICT covers equipment such as remote controls used for TV and video recorders, game machines, supermarket bar-code readers, washing machines, timers, heating controls, alarm systems, cameras, phones and electronic displays. The more advanced electronic displays in large stores are 'flat' screens using full colour. You might know what they are for, but do your pupils? Even the destination display on the front of a bus may be electronically generated, and you may be sure that your pupils will know of many other examples. It is tempting to restrict ICT to computing, but young children will be surrounded by so much else that they need a wider understanding of how information devices are used.

FIRST ENCOUNTERS IN SCHOOL

Once a word-processor is loaded on a school computer it will seem familiar territory, but actually finding it on a strange computer can be very irritating. Imagine arriving home to find that someone suddenly changed the colour of your front door. On your teaching practices you are almost certain to find that school computers are set up slightly differently from those you have already used elsewhere. In most cases this different appearance is the result of security software and networking arrangements, usually decided by a local authority education department or the school itself. School security start-up software is annoying at first, but once you are through the quirky additional layer, then the skills you have will make more sense. Think of your first encounter with a new computer as one whose superficial wrapping needs removing so that you can begin to find your way into the parcel.

The trainee teachers who do best in their ICT are those who dream of interesting tasks and projects for children, not of acquiring a checklist of skills. You could describe your ICT computing skills as a formal list if that helps. This might include loading and saving files, using a word-processor, finding information from the Internet, sending electronic mail and creating a graph. How cold and impersonal this is as an indicator of real competence in ICT. There are far more important aspects, such as knowing how to incorporate word-processing with literacy, knowing which of the programs will run without needing much teaching from you, and being able to link ICT with science investigations and database surveys. How much more relevant ICT is when you can set tasks which inspire pupils to learn otherwise dull skills. This means developing a mind-set which looks for opportunities to use ICT whenever it is going to be worth using, rather than just because pupils will find it addictive.

A trend in many schools has been to have a dedicated ICT suite where there are enough computers for a whole class. This allows some step-by-step instruction and the advantage that pupils can discuss a common experience and practise skills together. An added luxury is to have this suite alongside laptops in every classroom and some hand-held devices. Lower primary, infant and nursery classes are less likely to have a room dedicated to computer use and with younger children the style of teaching does not so easily lend itself to whole-class instruction on computers. You will definitely need to find alternatives to demonstrating in front of a display screen. Whatever resources there are will have advantages and disadvantages in timetabling pupils' computer use. If there is only one computer per classroom, by the time individuals return to it, they have all but forgotten what they did last time. If computers are used only once a week in a dedicated room there are lost opportunities for making links with ongoing classroom tasks.

CLASSROOM TEACHING AND ICT

A question I am frequently asked by teachers is 'How can I use one computer with 29 children?' The question is not the right one to ask because it ignores the need to know what software can do. Some software will run itself (very little will actually) but most needs discussion and teaching. Sometimes pupils can take it in turns to enter data on a database. Taking turns to 'have a go' at using a computer game is not learning much about ICT. Some practical options for teaching computing are summarised:

Peer teaching Teach one pupil to use a program thoroughly and follow this by having that pupil teach another, and so on until pupils all learn to use the software.

Display Use examples of computer printouts and pictures to inspire future work and discussion away from the computer.

Pre-teaching Away from the computer, set up a survey or a task in mathematics which leads to computer use later on.

Templating Create a partly prepared page in a word-processor, spreadsheet or a database survey which children then change or complete.

Whole group Demonstrate a piece of software and its potential to a group or class, then have a rota for its use.

Record data Have children take turns to add data to, for example, a questionnaire, or plot a simple graph.

Targeting Target children already involved in an activity to extend it through ICT.

Proofread Set up 'peer proofreading' of text from each other's word-processed story. Emphasise improving, correcting and refining.

Self-run Load and run a program which needs no teaching as it already has 'on-screen' instructions which are easy to follow. Examples are 'talking stories' and adventure programs.

Use ILS Integrated learning software (ILS) is designed so that each individual enters their name and the software creates a record of what that child attempted. It uses this information to decide what the next task and level of difficulty is. Typically used in a maths program.

Problem-set Set a computing problem for a computer club, such as 'What LOGO commands find the treasure in map number three?' Award a small prize for winners timed against the clock.

Paper designs Get your class to design web pages on paper, complete with links, ready to turn into an Internet website. Make simple graphs using paper and pencil crayons as a prelude to using a graphing program.

Evaluate Have your class write their evaluation of a piece of software, such as an information CD-ROM.

Subject quiz Use a database such as 'Junior Viewpoint' to create a maths quiz which each pupil completes over a period of a week. The spreadsheet will instantly show you how they did.

ICT quiz Revise computing skills and ideas in a pencil and paper quiz. Set a quiz for which the only resources are computer printouts.

Some paired (peer) teaching and learning is often the only way to teach children to use software. One pupil is taught to use a specific package of software and teaches another, who teaches another, while the teacher devises further tasks which lend themselves to this. Peer teaching is not ideal, but it can be efficient and fuel discussion about computer use. Pupils are often the best people to pass on skills, provided that you insist that the pupil learner is in control. Avoid peer teaching where the 'expert' of the two grabs the mouse or keyboard and thinks this is how to teach. The learner needs to be helped by doing, not by watching. Peer-teaching can lead to peer-learning where two pupils already have some experience of using a piece of software. Even when they have, you will find it far better to put expert with novice, rather than two novices together. The more knowledgeable pupil can still help the less knowledgeable (though, again, watch that the expert does not try to take over).

Think what you want to achieve. If you are not trying to teach pupils to load and run their program from the very start, then load the software for them. Pupils arrive to find the computer up and running ready to use. If you want pupils to be able to load, run, save files, print out results and shut down a computer, you have a different agenda. Alternatively, your task for the session might be 'How can this design/writing be improved?', in which case you would be teaching children to refine their work in progress. Whatever the approach you use, you will need some simple means of recording pupils' progress and use of a computer. This needs to be a simple tick-list of completed tasks and can be based on the completion of two or three designs. You may wish to develop a pupil profile for ICT, and that is up to you, but consider the way you use your time. Some teachers would have a self-assessment sheet for pupils, covering a tick-list of skills such as 'I can load a program', 'I can save my file', 'I can print my results'.

CREATIVE TASKS

The rise and rise of home computing has already seen the day when some parents support pupil learning by using similar software to the school. Carefully organised teaching is still needed at school to make the best of the opportunities to become familiar with any software and attempt something worth doing. My approach would be to try to set such an intriguing and creative task, that pupils want to spend extra time at breaks and computer clubs, even time at home solving problems and creating solutions. A good teacher will set tasks that already have important skills built into them. By contrast, if you teach repetitive skills and use low-level, entertaining, but limited software then you will diminish pupils. The best tasks build on simple skills and then become complex as the need arises. If ICT is about information and communication, then what do you want your pupils to learn and communicate?

One way to invite creative ideas is to choose a simple flexible task that requires only a few words to be typed. This minimises the time spent laboriously typing lots of words on a computer keyboard. Choose a task that allows plenty of freedom to try out fonts, colours, graphic images and layout, but one which has variety of outcome. Pupils can, for example, use a word-processor to design a pop-up greetings card, an award certificate, menu, brochure or advertisement so that design and craft skills are included. Tasks like these can teach pupils to resize text, import images and photographs, think about design and purpose. Pupils can learn how to move text, shade it, edit text and add decorative borders. There are papercraft, folding and cutting skills needed to create pop-up cards. Advertisements can be linked with 'persuasive writing' in literacy sessions. Pupils may even be able to use a digital camera to take pictures for their cards and adverts. The need to move text, turn it to an angle, stretch it and make it fit specific spaces teaches technical skills like 'dragging' text by holding down a mouse button, but much more than this, it teaches pupils about the potential of a powerful piece of software. A real bonus is that pupils cannot go wrong as there are so many possible outcomes. They can make discoveries, share skills and do some of the work away from the computer.

Once children have a few skills, they will find ways of using them themselves to create things like small folding booklets, poems and decorated labels. Set a problem or give a prize for the most interesting use of word-processing. Let children design step-by-step instruction sheets for software. Acrostics, puzzles, joke books, captions and recipes are all a means to learning how to be inventive with a few words. Teachers frequently tell me they have little time for displaying work. If they wrote the captions they wanted on scrap paper and gave them to children to produce, teachers would involve pupils in creating their own displays. A teacher could, for example, set up a whole lesson where their children devised questions about a display of their work. The questions could then become the display captions. In literacy, for instance, pupils could try to find the most appropriate font for a display about the genre of writing, such as 'horror' or 'science-fiction'.

Compare this with an overdose of 'browsing software' just to see what happens. Children may discover the potential of software by accident, but it is more effective if you know its power in advance. I have yet to see children absorbed in 'browsing' software without instruction. They need a task or they can very soon become bored to the extent that the software loses popularity amongst its users. Browsing a database at random can quickly lose pupils' interest. What is the alternative?

The most interesting database tasks can be those linked with investigation, particularly in science. One I like to use is a 'Healthy Eating' survey because of the potential for disagreement and debate over environmental issues, health and organic versus processed produce. It can be intrinsically motivating (see Chapter 5). When children are not gathering data about food, they are writing, debating and discussing what it all means. 'Healthy Eating' is likely to produce memorable displays and captions including clip-art food as a visual aid. The data also lends itself to mathematical calculation and 'fair testing'. You can begin by letting pupils collect food packaging which has printed data of content. Away from the computer, they can debate what is meant by consumer information like fat, protein, carbohydrate, energy and so on, per 100 grams. This immediately raises the problem of how to divide content such as fat into healthy (necessary) fat and fat likely to be unhealthy. Some healthy diets, for example, ignore fats and concentrate on a low carbohydrate intake per day. Others will declare that animal fats are unhealthy and a good diet is one of reduced fats in milk and cooking.

Pupils can take this a stage further concentrating on what nutrients are in, for example, food containing fish oils, supplements, vitamins and products claiming to keep the immune system in peak condition. Additives, eating habits, food 'sell by' or 'best before' dates and processing of foods are part of the possible science of survey. Using ICT, children can learn to interrogate data and question what they find on the supermarket shelf. If you think this is a project that will take some time to complete you are right. Along the way, they learn to enter data to a database, search files, create graphs and answer questions as seemingly simple as 'Which chocolate bar has the greatest fat content?' and 'Does eating half the amount reduce your fat intake by 50 per cent?' Such a survey also teaches pupils about graphs. There may even be a creative prelude to all this, by using a very simple graphing program (one requiring few instructions) to teach pupils about graphs and what they mean. They can graph very simple surveys, like 'Different Sandwiches Taken on the School Trip', 'Favourite Chocolate Bars' or 'Time Taken to Arrive at School'. Your pupils could of course create graphs using squared paper, a ruler and coloured crayons, and they will do that too. Since most of the graphs they will see in later life will be printed using computer technology, it makes more sense to experience using graphing software if they can.

Information and communications technology has its own important vocabulary, one necessary to teach at the same time as the technical aspects of software. Children in Year 5 (9–10-year-olds) need to know database vocabulary as part of any survey they might do. There are specific words, such as 'field' and 'record'. There are search criteria, such as AND, NOT, less than, more than, equal to and their mathematical operators' $<$, $>$, $=$, used to query (interrogate) data.

The real teaching often takes place to find out what data and resulting graphs actually mean and how they can distort information. More sophisticated questions can be posed with older children, such as 'Why might a bar graph be better than a pie chart to show the height of pupils?', 'Why is a line graph of no use for showing the distribution of eye-colour in the class?', 'Why is a pie-chart useful for showing percentages?' These are some of the commonly asked questions, but if you are creative in your teaching, you will photocopy graphs and set pupils tasks with an open-ended question such as 'What can you tell me from looking at these different graphs?' That way, you can reveal errors in the interpretation of graphs, and build on this to construct a more complex survey.

As a teacher, your creativity is put to the test in two related questions:

- How can ICT make connections with subjects in the curriculum?

- How can subjects in the curriculum be linked to ICT?

Both these demand a creative outlook as you become predisposed to look for chances to use ICT. Like a tightly sprung jaw waiting to snap as an appetising morsel swims by, you learn to seize on the connections you make. Is there something, for example, you want to teach that could be adapted slightly to use ICT? Is there an ICT task that could be adapted so it includes science? Are you, for example, recording plant growth during various conditions? Whenever you plan your teaching, look for ways in which with the smallest of changes your lesson offers pupils a wider opportunity.

JUST A WORD-PROCESSOR?

The very keyboard attached to a computer can be a barrier to learning how to use a word-processor. What a pity it is if word-processing is used only to spruce up a hand-written draft of text. When children are not adept at using the conventional keyboard they struggle and take ages to do very simple sentences. For the creative teacher there are solutions, most of which involve the use of partly constructed sentences, word-banks and images which load into the text at the click of a button. If you are streetwise, you will begin to create word lists, 'writing frames' and partly constructed templates that give children a starting point. Software already exists to provide an extensive and flexible word or sentence resource (word-banks) so that children have minimal typing to do. There is nothing new in this, except it is on a computer instead of being a photocopied example. The advantage of a computer is that sentences can be added to, edited and honed, giving pupils adult skills in writing. If you provide a good third of the text as a framework, there is a good chance children will creatively fill in and adapt the remainder.

Many word-processors for children have a speech option built in. This is very useful because children can hear what they have written and create messages for one another, check the words they typed and have an overall sense of fun in their writing. Speaking and listening in the UK National Curriculum can be exciting and interesting if you also use talking software. Speech is probably rather mechanical in a talking word-processor, but the 'alien space-age' voice used seems to entertain children as well as inform them. In using the speech option, there are advantages to clicking rather than typing in when writing a poem or story. Pupils can create extended sentences and incorporate words that might otherwise not be used because they are difficult to spell. One obvious advantage is that pupils can be introduced to many descriptive words, phrases and images they might otherwise not use.

You can offset the drawback of learning to use a keyboard by setting such tasks as 'highlighting' words in a display of prepared text, then changing their colour. For example, pupils could identify verbs, nouns, suffixes and so on by learning to colour them differently on screen, printing out the results. While this might not seem the most creative of activities, it has the advantage of manipulating prepared text, teaching the skills of changing the font's colour and identifying parts of speech. It makes an otherwise laborious process more feasible in terms of time spent at the computer screen. If children are trying to learn about conjunctions or personal pronouns, a word-processed 'template' for them to correct or extend is ideal.

Sooner or later, of course, children need to use a keyboard, but the bonus of these click or press devices is that they can be used together with the keyboard. Think of them as stepping stones to keyboard use or additional resources. To summarise: if you want to sustain interest, buy software that excites pupils, talks back, is versatile, easy to use, has pictures and can use comically synthesised speech and sounds. Quirky effects, like shading fonts from one colour to another, arranging animated pictures and sending secretly coded messages, are not what I need myself, but these extras certainly keep children involved. They become adept at showing off what they have found out. You may yourself have written 15 pages of solid text using the same font, but this is not usually what children want to do. They respond better to a task which lets them find out what magic there is in an all singing and dancing 'show-off' piece of software. The magic lies partly in being able to review work in progress, a practice which needs to be encouraged so that they become used to evaluating what is happening. Reviewing is important because it is already an integral part of UK schools' programmes of study in the National Curriculum.

CHECKING THAT ICT IS WORTH USING

I have four criteria for making ICT meaningful:

- It is used to support a purposeful task.

- Pupils are better off for having used it.

- It is used because it does the job better than anything else.

- It opens up a wider range of possible questions and solutions for learning.

The last criterion is sometimes overlooked by those teachers who see computers merely as a means of organising and word-processing more efficiently than with paper and a pen. I cannot think of a computer program where no teaching would ever be involved, even if it is looking at results or discussing the experience. There are a few programs which teach children without you having to be close by. Some maths programs have step-by-step levels of difficulty, as do stories and quizzes. Computers are also very good at creating simulations of weather, including cloud patterns and rainfall. 'Adventure' simulations run themselves, often with tasks built into them to teach pupils to predict the effect of their actions. These are simulations rather like computer games which include timers, controls and animated pictures. They require logical thought and planning and encourage problem-solving. Simulations explore the realms of fantasy, reality and possibility without necessarily teaching computer skills. Most are 'point', 'click' and 'drag' actions using a mouse. However, what makes them worthwhile is that the best of them include problems and tasks related to maths, science and cognition. You may not yet know about the programming language called LOGO, but it finds its way into many simulations as pupils try to find their way out of mazes, castles and rainforests. In using a simulation which requires escape from a building, maze or an island, children can learn about points of the compass, coordinates, distances and instructions. Where a program requires very little teaching, a creative teacher will still find ways of turning the experience to advantage.

INFORMATION ON DEMAND

You can safely assume that if you have no information to seek, the Internet can be a very time-consuming and dull experience. The Internet or 'World Wide Web' is like a large dustbin full of millions of pages, some of which you might want to read. As a teacher you will often need to try out websites before letting your pupils loose to find information. There are plenty of sites specially designed for children and teachers. Of these, the obvious ones are The National Grid for Learning, BBC Education, and Channel 4 Learning. Several sites are also supported by teachers who send in lesson ideas, a rich harvest which changes frequently. Of one thing you may be certain: the Internet is already a very interactive place for children and likely to become even more so. Most schools are on broadband, which means that they are permanently connected to the Internet and can use interactive programs that move the user from page to page. The BBC has well-established education pages of animations, puzzles and learning games. Remember, however, that teaching through the Internet assumes reasonably fast download times for information. CD-ROMs, such as a child's encyclopaedia, may sometimes offer a better solution for the search for information. CD-ROM (Compact Disc Read-Only Memory) works as quickly as the computer will allow, rather than relying on contact with an Internet Service Provider and a long wait.

You will obviously need some purpose in mind before searching the contents of the Internet. For example, if pupils are already studying the history of the Vikings, it is worth having at least eight questions to ask before even starting to look on a website. Much Internet information is written with no particular age range in mind, so a clear focus of questions is more efficient when searching. Otherwise, pupils will return with enough printouts of pages to fill a dustbin of their own and not know where to start classifying any of it. Yes, of course pupils may enjoy touring a 'virtual museum', but ask yourself what they actually learn from doing this. They need to extend or develop their learning for the virtual tour to have been worthwhile. 'What can you find?' is a naïve question, flexible though it is as a starting point. Even using a CD-ROM such as 'The Human Body', you will need a question like 'How does the human eye work?' instead of indulging a complete head to toe browse.

USING ICT PURPOSEFULLY

There is a downside to any technology if it displaces rather than enhances perfectly good ways to teach and learn. The Internet is fascinating and dull almost by turns. I want to give an electronic warning here, especially if you want to teach pupils that there is more to life than can be found on an electronic display screen. It may be *highly desirable* to use mobile devices, including mobile videophones, laptop computers and text-messagers. In a few cases it is essential for businesses and communications to run effectively. It may be *highly desirable* to video-conference and feel in contact at the push of a button or press of a key. Fully addicted to technology, *highly desirable* can seem essential when in education it is actually nothing of the kind. 'Would like to have' slides imperceptibly into the collective psyche as a 'must have' when the latest innovations become the focus of fashionable advertising. As far as your pupils are concerned, there is still a world out there where they can hear birdsong, see crops grow, smell the scent of flowers and there not be an electric switch to be found. It is easy to misunderstand what the technology really offers. Cynics might say 'very little', but that is to misunderstand what information devices do very well. Information and communications technology is a tool for learning and can do certain things like searching through data very quickly. Other things it does all too slowly, like sending information down telephone lines that were never designed for the purpose.

The future of ICT probably lies in the further development of the small pocket communicator videophone or hand-held device. These already provide email, text-messaging, photographs, telephone and Internet access with a video colour display. They promise ever faster access to the Internet, though not everyone wants devices reduced in size. There is a price to pay in reducing the size of a QWERTY keyboard to phone-button size. Videophones already have a huge advantage which is that they are actually digital cameras and can save images as well as transmit them. Technology changes rapidly with the latest commercial innovation, social hype, and desire to promote electronic commerce driving it forwards. There will certainly be developments of yet smarter 'smart card' banking and shopping where a small plastic card, used with a hand-held device, has numerous functions.

What becomes socially acceptable continually finds new norms and each innovation brings its disadvantages as well as bonuses. In education, technology can displace other things and its use in schools needs careful thought if it is not to take over. The latest WAP devices and computers can be addictive, creating their own momentum just as more sophisticated photocopiers did.

EVALUATING AND ASSESSING

The ICT National Curriculum covers ICT skills in their own right as well as ways to use ICT within subjects like literacy and numeracy. In any evaluation of learning through using ICT there are obvious technical skills, such as file-saving. Less obvious are skills such as 'predicting' and 'relating cause and effect' to the activity. I still do not believe that drawing up a list of 'can do' ICT skills can be isolated from purposeful and creative tasks. One school I know of has a policy of awarding certificates for the development of a number of basic skills, mouse-dragging and file-saving included. A more meaningful way to tick off these skills is to examine the tasks you devise and see for yourself what basic computing skills children need to complete them. If the task has been completed, you may be sure that a number of skills have not only been covered, but used in context. Computers do certain tasks very well indeed, such as sorting, searching for information quickly, programming, presenting, counting and calculating. There are plenty of opportunities to devise real-life tasks which cover these attributes. There are also social spin-offs if children have learnt to work collaboratively on a memorable problem-solving activity. They may even manage to make connections with other areas of the curriculum and understand better how computers help.

Finally, there is nothing so effective in computer learning as planning for consolidation and revision of ICT skills. You can achieve this by planning a similar task that uses previously acquired skills and understanding. It is, in itself, a form of evaluation (sometimes a skills memory-test) because it throws into focus the need to look again at procedures, mouse clicks and key-presses. A helpful way to consolidate children's learning is to build in the need to use more than one piece of software within a topic or project. Obvious examples are to use a word-processor to describe findings after using a data-handling program, or to include a graph whenever data are generated in science lessons. Not much Internet information is already in the form needed for a project. Children may have to change the way it is presented, which is something of a bonus. They consequently learn about editing and structuring a report, and this is an information-handling skill in itself. There are web pages offering mathematical calculations, catalogues of books, music and statistics about life in other countries of the world. These are meaningless in themselves unless they are woven into a richer task than that of using a printer to churn out Internet data. Evaluation of your own practice is going to include some appraisal of whether pupils have enough opportunities to prepare work before they use a computer and plenty of time to follow it up afterwards. The exchange of ideas after using a computer may be just as meaningful as what happened when pressing a key or clicking a mouse.

SUMMARY

- Think of your first encounter with a new computer as one whose superficial wrapping needs removing so that you can begin.

- Children's learning is much more than their being at the cutting edge of the latest computer software.

- Just as important as computing skill is an understanding of what computers can do.

- Away from the computer, the real teaching takes place, such as finding out what graphs actually mean.

- Children need software that excites them and is versatile.

- I have yet to see children absorbed in 'browsing' software without instruction.

- Plan for consolidation and revision of ICT skills within a task.

ISSUES FOR REFLECTION

- Think about your level of ICT expertise and your attitude towards the subject. What implications do you think this knowledge might have for your classroom practice?

- Note when teachers use ICT. Does it always enhance pupil learning in the sessions you observed? How would you know? Might there be other ways to teach the same topic? Do you think that they would be more or less effective? Why?

- Observe children working on the computer on their own and with others. What are the benefits and downsides of these ways of working?

- Ask yourself 'How can I organise ICT so children take responsibility for remembering what to do?'

Further reading

Bennett, R. (1997) *Teaching IT: Teaching at Key Stage 1*. London: Nash Pollock. A general purpose overview of teaching this age range.

Cook, D. and Finlayson, H. (1999) *Interactive Children, Communicative Teaching.* Buckingham: Open University Press. Full of references to the importance of play and ICT with young children. Gives case study cameo pictures of what children do.

McFarlane, A. (1998) *Information Technology and Authentic Learning.* London: Routledge. A look at learning through using computers. Edited by the author, this is a compilation from various writers.

Scrimshaw, P. (ed.) (1993) *Language, Classrooms and Computers.* London: Routledge. Focuses on the use of language and ICT.

Sharp, S., Potter, J., Allen, J. and Loveless, A. (2002) *Primary ICT: Knowledge Understanding and Practice.* 2nd edition. Exeter: Learning Matters.

Straker, A. and Govier, G. (1996) *Children Using Computers.* 2nd edition. London: Nash Pollock. This second edition is still one of the most approachable all-round sensible coverages of the subject.

Chapter 16

Working with other adults

Gillian Preece and Graham Handscomb

Partnership contributions are transforming learning. Increasingly primary teachers are working as part of a team with other adults in their classrooms. Whether they are teaching assistants or parents, your work with them can bring great benefits to children's learning. In this chapter Gillian Preece and Graham Handscomb consider some of the many ways teams can work together successfully, and give guidance as to how you can best manage to achieve this.

INTRODUCTION

It is very likely that all teachers will now find that they work alongside other adults in primary classrooms. Whether the other adult is a parent or a qualified employee with years of experience, their support can prove invaluable. When you start your first teaching practice, it is important to develop an awareness of how you can operate effectively with other adults, rather than just muddle through. The answer lies in preparation, planning and building confidence in a team-based approach. This means making sure that you, the other adults and the children are confident in working with a variety of people. It is also important to think and carefully plan how you work with other adults in the classroom for another fundamental reason. New evidence is demonstrating that teaching assistants working within the classroom are not just an extra pair of hands but have a very real contribution to make to the learning and progress of children (Watkinson, 2003). Teaching assistants are increasingly receiving training and Her Majesty's Inspectors have reported that 'the support for teaching and learning given by trained specialist teaching assistants is helping to give children in school improved learning experiences and to raise standards' (Ofsted, 1997, p. 7).

The working situation in the classroom is a dynamic one with the potential for considerable interaction between professional colleagues all with their own job descriptions and individual roles. As a trainee teacher, if you are offered the opportunity to work with other adults then it is something that you should welcome, even though it may be challenging at first. The experience you gain will be invaluable in preparing you for your future role as a teacher. Having the opportunity to work with adults in the classroom, and in the wider school, can bring great benefits. This has been recognised as a major feature of Workforce Reform and Re-Modelling which aims to reduce teachers' workloads, release them from 'bureaucratic' tasks, and free them up to concentrate on teaching.

This chapter looks at how you can have successful experiences working with other adults on your teaching practices in schools. It considers ways in which you may work alongside them and how to prepare yourself for this experience. It also looks at some of the issues surrounding working with parents.

JOB TITLES

The adults who work in Nursery and Reception classes may have a variety of job titles, depending on the school in which you are working. Job titles include: teacher assistants, classroom assistants, non-teaching assistants, learning support assistants, bi-lingual assistants and educational assistants. Perhaps the most commonly used term is teaching assistant (TA). Anne Watkinson (2004) has reflected at length on the range of contributions that TAs can make within the classroom. This includes: supporting pupils directly; supporting teaching processes within the classroom; supporting teaching processes in non-pupil contact time; supporting teachers directly; and supporting school processes. Examples of the sort of tasks that TAs might do in each of these different categories are given in Box 16.1

Some have had recognised training and hold a formal qualification; for example, the NNEB (National Nursery Examination Board) Diploma or the BTEC Nursery Nurse qualification. NNEB and BTEC nursery nurses will have completed two-year training courses, normally at a college of further education. These courses provide a practical training in all aspects of care and education of children from birth to 7 years of age. Other adults employed in the classroom may come without formal qualifications but frequently will have spent many years working with children in a variety of capacities.

BOX 16.1

The range of tasks that might be undertaken by teaching assistants (adapted from Watkinson, 2004)

Supporting pupils directly	Individual support for those with special educational need (SEN)
	Counselling and giving guidance
	Providing emotional support
	Providing social learning support
	Acting as a learning mentor
	Supervising pupils on accelerated learning programmes
Supporting teaching processes within the classroom	Using specialist phase skills (for example, working with foundation stage pupils)
	Giving Literacy and Numeracy support
	Asking leading questions to promote development of thinking and critical learning skills
	Explaining things clearly
	Conducting circle time
	Keeping reading records
	Supporting across a range of subjects in the primary curriculum
	Assisting in or taking ICT classes
Supporting teaching processes in non-pupil contact time	Lesson planning
	Taking part in post-lesson analysis and coaching sessions
	Maintaining displays
	Accessing curriculum and subject knowledge needed for planning

	Using technical ICT knowledge to support teacher planning
Supporting teachers directly	Sharing the recording, reporting and reflection on the findings of SEN assessments
	Carrying out observations of children's learning to help diagnose problems
	Possibly covering of lessons when teachers are absent – within carefully worked out and agreed school procedures
Supporting school processes	Assisting in annual reviews for SEN pupils
	Contributing to the development of school behaviour management techniques and assisting the teacher in their implementation
	Running extracurricular activities
	Attending and participating in parents' evenings
	Helping to organise school educational visits, and accompanying school visits as an additional adult

However, it is not always possible to tell from the job titles given which people have had a formal training and which have not. With the introduction of the National Literacy Strategy, in particular, there has been a recognition of the need for groups of children to work independently of the teacher. In many cases, throughout both Key Stages 1 and 2, schools have recruited extra adults to support such independent activities.

Depending on the setting of the class or school, there is also a variety of other people with whom teachers work. They do not usually form part of the basic, or core, team, but are used in other ways. For example, if there is a pupil with special educational needs in the class then extra support might be provided for that child. Extra adult support for children with special needs may also include speech therapists or educational psychologists. In many schools where a high percentage of the children have English as a second language support may be provided for those children in their first language. This type of support can be permanently attached to the school but there are many situations where, if there are only one or two children requiring support in a particular language, peripatetic support may be available.

PARENTS/CARERS

Many schools have positive policies for welcoming and encouraging parents/carers into schools. Often teachers may find themselves working alongside parents/carers of the children in their class. These adult helpers can provide information for teachers that would not be available if the relationship between the home and school was poor. Parents/carers have been the chief educators of their children before they enter school and it is important that teachers listen to, and respect, what they have to say about their own children. It is also vital for schools to set up strong links with the home so that parents/carers can build up a good understanding of the best ways that they can support their child's learning once they have started school.

PREPARATION FOR TEACHING PRACTICE

It is likely that, prior to your teaching practice, there will be several opportunities for you to visit the class with which you will be working. It is crucial to find out as much information as you can on such visits. Some of the things you need to find out are mentioned in Chapter 4 on observation. However, it is also important to ask the class teacher about the adults who will be working with your class during your teaching practice. The questions you need to ask include:

- What are the names of the adults?

- When will they be coming in?

- What are their duties?

- Is there a schedule for the organisation of their work?

- Do they usually work with the same pupil or group of pupils?

- Do they plan and prepare their own work or is that the teacher's responsibility?

● Where in the school do they work?

● What opportunities will you have to work and plan jointly with them?

Each adult employed by the school will have a job description. In some schools considerable detail is put into these job descriptions and there is a high expectation that staff will carry out the duties described. You must be sure, therefore, that if you are asking someone to do something then it is indeed their responsibility and it is appropriate for them to do it. Moreover, it might be that, as well as providing classroom support, some teaching assistants have additional duties such as first aid, or supervising children at lunch time. If this is the case, it is possible that they will have to leave the classroom earlier than might otherwise be expected, or arrive a few minutes after the beginning of a session. Staff who join sessions late or leave sessions early will obviously have an impact on how you plan the use of their time. For example, how do you plan for those children who are waiting for the nursery nurse to arrive? What do you do with a group of children when their support leaves 15 minutes before the end of the session? This of course links to the need to be aiming to provide 'personalised learning' for the pupils in your charge. This involves giving thought to how you design your teaching and curriculum experiences around the needs and learning skills of individual pupils.

SPECIAL NEEDS

A teaching assistant may be assigned to provide special needs support for an individual child for whom extra resources have been provided, possibly through a statement or as part of an IEP (Individual Education Plan) procedure. (IEPs and statements are phrases that refer to the documentation process by which a child with special needs is recognised.) Other adults are employed to provide support throughout the whole class. If this is the case, the trainee teacher will need to determine how the teacher usually organises this.

In terms of responsibility for planning, in some cases (for example, a speech therapist) the extra adult will come to the class with a planned set of activities which they feel will help a particular child. In contrast, a nursery nurse providing general support will not normally be expected to plan and prepare activities for the children.

In some cases it might be that the adult supporting your class withdraws particular children and works with them away from the classroom for some or all of their time. If this is the case you need to know where and when this usually happens.

COMMUNICATING

In the early stages of your relationship with a class you should explicitly recognise that the teaching assistants have something that you do not yet have – a thorough understanding of the individuals in the class. They may well have been at the school for many years. Additionally, they will probably have a good knowledge of and relationship with other members of staff. They will certainly know the routines of the day and what should be happening at particular times. It may now often be the case that teaching assistants will have acquired considerable expertise and some will have gained qualifications such as National Vocational Qualifications (NVQs). Parents, of course, have prior knowledge of their own children. They will know why their child is upset at the start of the day, for example.

It is vital to set up a positive relationship with the people with whom you will be working. Bilingual assistants, for example, will often be able to communicate with some of the children in your class in a way that you cannot and their particular skills should be recognised and valued.

Trying to strike the balance between appearing bossy and domineering and completely subservient and overawed can be difficult. It is not always possible to judge the best way of working simply by observing how the teacher is with teaching assistants, as their relationship may be based on several years of working together. However, it might be useful to find out how the teacher lets the classroom assistants know what they will be doing. Does the teacher pass on the activities on a daily or weekly basis? Does this happen at planning meetings or does the teacher speak to the teaching assistant on an individual basis? Are the teacher's instructions passed on verbally or is there a file or notebook where the instructions are recorded? It is a good idea to ask the different individuals with whom you will be working how they would prefer this to be done. Some might like things to be written down in a notebook; others might prefer to have a discussion at planning meetings where they can make their own notes.

CLARITY

When you are discussing with your adult assistants what you would like them to do for a particular activity, remember to be clear about your expectations. For example, giving an instruction, 'I want this group to do some creative writing using the key vocabulary we have been working on this week' might elicit a number of responses, not all which you intend. So, if you have particular expectations as to how the work should be presented, if you expect any illustrations or if you want the pupils to be working within a particular theme, then you will need to ensure that more detailed instructions are given.

There will be times when you will feel you have been sufficiently explicit and yet the work that you see at the end of the session is not as expected. Before you take a colleague to task over this, however, look at the work and try to see if you understand why the task has been completed in the way that it has. If you are unable to see how your instructions could have been interpreted in such a way, it is not usually helpful to say in a forthright manner, 'This wasn't at all what I wanted. What I told you to do was ... '. Try to be a little more circumspect and tactful. For example, you could say, 'This is interesting. I hadn't thought of doing it this way. What was it that gave you the idea?' By listening to the response you will begin to gain a better understanding of how your colleague interprets what they are being asked to do.

When these and other tensions arise it is important to take time to reflect on your relationship with the teaching assistant or adult helper. Is it a true partnership, designed to plan and carry out high-quality teaching and learning experiences for children? If not, how can you ensure that each person has an important part to play in creating the right environment for learning and teaching in the classroom?

PARENTS

Parents have always been involved in their child's education. They are the child's first educators and the attitude they have to the school will, to some extent, affect how well their child gets on. In the past, schools have not always recognised the need to actively include parents in the education process but have involved parents in a more distant or formal way. These methods of involvement still exist and they include:

- pre-admission meetings
- home visits
- parents' evenings
- school reports
- fund-raising events
- celebration concerts or assemblies.

However, it is important that parents are more actively involved in the life of the school and the education of their children. Schools are now encouraged to work in partnership with parents and to recognise the contribution they can make in helping their child to achieve in school. Research has indicated that schools that form closer links with parents can build effectively on the experiences gained by children before they start school (Tizard and Hughes, 1984). The importance of strengthening the partnership between parents and schools has been recognised by the Qualifications and Curriculum Authority (QCA) who have stated: 'Parents are children's first and most enduring educators. When parents and practitioners work together in early years settings the results have a positive impact on the child's development and learning. Therefore each setting should seek to develop an effective partnership with parents' (1999c, p. 17). This partnership has been described by Suffolk County Council (1999), in their evaluation of the curriculum for the Foundation Stage, as a three-way partnership with each member of the partnership having their own 'needs'. The document outlines the needs of teachers, children and parents in this partnership:

- Teachers need: time to meet with and be available for parents and other carers, such as pre-school leaders and health visitors; time to reflect regularly on how well their policies and activities to involve parents are working.

- Children need: to feel their parents are happy and comfortable about their new learning environment; to feel that home and school are in harmony and that their parents understand and support the aims of the school; to feel that the teacher is interested in their values and knows the relevant details of their family.

- Parents need: time for talking with staff; to feel welcome at school, especially in their child's own class; to feel their child is happy and every effort is being made to help them to enjoy their time at school; to be reminded that they are valued and that they are their child's first educators; to be informed about the school's aims; to feel comfortable about staying, playing and learning with their child when possible. (Section 6, p. 3)

Many parents have welcomed the opportunity to become more closely involved with their child's school and work alongside teachers on a regular basis. This involvement may be organised so that parent volunteers are on a rota. Or parents may attend sessions in a less organised way, coming in when they have the time available.

Strong links are particularly important when a child is first starting school. It is important for parents to become aware of how the school approaches the teaching of various areas of the curriculum. This can then enable parents to support their child at home in a way that is consistent with the school policies. In *Early Learning, Ensuring Quality Provision for Children Under 5* Norfolk County Council (1997) suggest that: 'Educators need to be willing and able to explain to parents how the experiences offered to the children contribute to their learning and to describe how their children are progressing' (para. 12.1). As a trainee on teaching practice you will be expected to work alongside parents, so you need to understand why the school has particular school policies. You should be able to explain to parents both *how* you would like them to help out and *why* you are doing a particular activity. In the true spirit of partnership it is also useful to welcome information on their children, together with any suggestions and new ideas from parents. Before you start your teaching practice there are a number of ways that you can be well prepared for working with parents. Try to find out:

- Do any parents come in to the class?

- If so, which ones?

- Do they come in at a regular time or do they come occasionally when they are able?

- What do they normally do when they come in?

- Do they work with their child only, or are they happy to work with a small group of children?

- Do they usually do a similar activity each time they come in, or have they been happy doing a variety of activities?

Some parents will feel most confident providing support on a creative activity. Others have a particular skill that would be useful to encourage in the classroom. It is useful to know if the parent is confident using the computer, for example. In a particular class we quickly discovered that one child's parents were both professional artists: the mother came in regularly and worked with groups of children on watercolour painting. You may, of course, find that a parent with particular skills may feel inhibited about using them. Certainly use your tact, discretion and powers of persuasion if you feel it is important, but remember, ultimately, a caring adult helper is better than one who feels press-ganged.

It is possible that the parent is coming in to provide encouragement to their child because the child is finding it difficult to settle. In this case, they may wish to work just with their child. However, an underconfident child may not always benefit from their parent/carer working alongside them. Just having them there in the classroom can be enough of an encouragement. Better still, however, is to arrange for such parents to contribute by coming into the classroom with the understanding that they are there to support the learning and teaching in the class as a whole and thus be deployed to support and address the needs of children wherever that occurs.

PARENTS AS PARTNERS

Working with parents is so important. It is helpful to see them as being able to offer potentially a range of things to the school and your classroom. They have, of course, a particular knowledge and expertise regarding their own children and they have a range of experience and skills that they can bring to bear from their various backgrounds and places of work. Above all they have a stake in your school, and it is sensible for you to recognise and to be taking advantage of this. This links with the increasing view that we will be more effective in helping children to develop and learn if teachers work in collaboration with a range of others beyond the school, and this very much includes parents (see Chapter 2). They have a real contribution to make to the learning and progress of children in your school.

However, many parents may be reluctant to participate. For some, their view of school may very well be coloured by their own bad experiences when they were children at school. Walking through the school gate may make them feel vulnerable and inadequate. Many schools are doing something about this. You may want to check out what arrangements are made to help make parents feel at ease. Does the school have a family learning programme? Are parent open days arranged so that parents can experience directly the sort of learning activities that take place within the school? All these things will help create the welcoming atmosphere to encourage parents to come into the school and participate within the classroom.

As with teaching assistants, it is important to make sure that all the requests you make of parents to help in the classroom are clearly stated. If a parent does not carry out an activity in the way you were expecting, try to think about what they have done and what might have been the reason for the confusion.

If you are asking a parent to work on an activity that requires a lot of resources, make sure that you have prepared in advance everything that the parent will need for the activity. Plan where the parent will be working. Is the space appropriate for the activity? For example, will children be painting or gluing and sticking near a carpet area? If the space is inappropriate, you might either need to rethink the activity or to find a different area for the group to work in.

You might like the parent to carry out an activity on a one-to-one basis with children. A good example of this is when parents are asked to hear individual children read. It is important that you understand how this activity is approached at the school. You should also make sure that the parent is fully aware of what they should be doing. For example, how does the school introduce new words, or how does the teacher help the child when they are stuck on a word? Guidance about teaching reading would normally be available in an existing school policy document – possibly in both the Parental Involvement policy and the English policy – so the trainee teacher needs to be aware of such guidance and must ensure that the parental help is consistent with it.

Some activities might require the parent to work away from the classroom. Check with your class teacher in advance that this is acceptable. Some schools have separate areas for cookery or design technology, for example, where parents might work with a few children on practical assignments. However, there might well be implications for the school should a child have an accident while being supervised by a parent. Many schools will have school policies that deal with these issues.

Some schools will have a booklet explaining to parents the different ways that they might become involved in their child's education. This will cover many of the areas already outlined in the chapter. It may also include a copy of the school's Health and Safety policy. Reading such a booklet will give you a better understanding of how parents work in your teaching practice school and the boundaries that might exist in terms of the activities with which they should become involved.

SUMMARY

- Teachers are increasingly working alongside other adults in the classroom.
- There are many benefits of working with other adults.
- Some adult helpers will be colleagues who provide support for individuals or groups of children.
- Others may have an expertise in an area that teachers do not have.
- Teaching assistants may have a range of expertise and qualifications.
- An important part of being an effective teacher is careful management and deployment of other adults within the classroom.
- Working with other adults is a partnership, involving joint planning outside the classroom and team work within it.

- It can be very helpful to encourage and welcome parents into the class-room.

- Opportunities for the sharing of ideas with other adults are important.

- Parents are essential partners in the school's core business of teaching and learning.

- A shared sense of purpose can be developed between teacher, children and parents which can encourage ways in which parents can support their children's learning at home.

- Giving parents informal opportunities to talk can also help teachers gain a better understanding of the children in their class.

- Trainee teachers should develop their own skills in managing and communicating with all the adults in the classroom

ISSUES FOR REFLECTION

- Think of an activity that you might discuss with and ask a teaching assistant to carry out. Draft a set of guidance for that planned activity. Give this guidance to friends on your course and ask them to explain to you what they think you have asked them to do.

- Plan a whole lesson for a class and think through the ways in which the teaching and classroom organisation tasks might be shared between yourself and a teaching assistant.

- During your observations in school you will probably have seen teachers working with classroom assistants and/or parents. Note the different activities you have seen the assistants and parents doing. What are the similarities and differences between the activities carried out by classroom assistants as opposed to parents?

- By what means can schools make parents feel valued and welcome?

Further reading

Drury, R., Miller, L. and Campbell, R. (eds) (2000) *Looking at Early Years Education and Care*. London: David Fulton. This book contains contributions from different authors who discuss the many issues challenging the early years practitioner. One easy-to-read chapter on involving parents details the author's experiences and some of the issues arising from them.

Fox, F. (1998) *A Handbook for Learning Support Assistants, Teachers and Assistants Working Together*. London: David Fulton. This is a practical handbook containing useful information for learning support assistants and teachers. Arising from work with children with special educational needs, the book highlights ways for teachers and assistants to work effectively together.

Lally, M. (1991) *The Nursery Teacher in Action*. London: Paul Chapman Publishing. The chapter, 'Leading the nursery team', is particularly helpful and demonstrates the benefits and difficulties facing adults working together.

Norfolk County Council (1997) *Early Learning, Ensuring Quality Provision for Children Under 5*. Norwich: Norfolk Educational Press. A comprehensive document that has one section on working with and involving parents in school life. It includes checklists and pro formas for practising teachers.

Watkinson, A. (2003) *Managing Teaching Assistants: A Guide for Headteachers, Managers and Teachers*. London: RoutledgeFalmer. This is a useful practical guide to the role of teaching assistants and how they can be effectively managed and deployed.

Watkinson, A. (2004) To teach or not to teach? *Managing Schools Today*, 13(3), January/February. This short article comprehensively explores the contribution that teaching assistants can make to teaching and learning.

The tutor's visit

Ann Oliver

Will you regard the tutor's visit with a sense of alarm and feel that you are on trial? This need not be the case as Ann Oliver explains in this chapter. Being observed and assessed is an inevitable part of training, but much can be gained from the experience if it involves genuine professional dialogue and recognition of teaching as a process of lifelong learning.

The purpose of this chapter is to discuss the implications of a tutor's observation of trainees' teaching. (Anecdotes used to illustrate points are based on personal experience, although names have been changed.)

OBSERVING TEACHING

Teaching is an observable performance with two main elements: a behavioural component and a cognitive component (Kitson and Merry, 1997). The behavioural component is a set of observable actions. The cognitive component is a combination of perceptions, interpretations and decisions. Tutors gain first-hand evidence to support and assess trainees' competence through observing them teach and talking to them about their teaching. This provides evidence of practical skills and understanding allowing tutors to form crucial judgements on trainees' teaching ability.

THE TUTOR'S PERSPECTIVE

Qualifying to Teach: Professional Standards for Qualified Teacher Status and Requirements for Initial Teacher Training (TTA, 2003), Ofsted expectations, course competence guidelines, Career Entry and Development Profiles are all part of competence-based training. Trainees and assessors are bound by this documentation and a tutor will almost invariably assess a trainee's teaching competence against the criteria of standards in *Qualifying to Teach*.

However, a tutor will have their own way of gathering evidence to support assessments of teaching progress, development and ability. This is useful for the trainee to know. Tutors gain evidence of the trainee's teaching ability by observing them teach, reading their file, observing pupils, looking at the classroom and discussing progress and concerns with the trainee and the teacher. Although evidence is gained in this way, because of the nature of teaching, there is no set sequence or order in which judgements are made. The trainee might not be aware of what the tutor's particular focus is or that it changes as a result of observations made.

Tutors are used to the classroom and realise that even the best plans can go awry. They recognise the arbitrary nature of their visits and make allowances for this. No decisions about failing trainees are made on one observation, by one tutor. A tutor's visit is part of an ongoing catalogue of visits. Assessment of a trainee teacher's progress and ability involves the trainee, tutors and teachers. What is important is that trainees have realistic expectations, recognise success and failure and learn from them. In adult-based training routes like the Graduate Teachers' programme, and School Centred Initial Teacher Training (SCITT), this visit is likely to be carried out by an LEA adviser or a participating school headteacher.

Understandably some trainees find the whole process of being observed when teaching a nerve-wracking experience. Hopefully, by being made aware of what a tutor is looking for, insights will be offered which will help allay such fears.

THE TRAINEE'S PERSPECTIVE

Teaching practice can be a lonely time if experiences are not shared. It is quite common for trainees to feel isolated and think other trainees are having an easier time. A tutor observing several trainees has a very different perspective. All trainees at some time experience problems. How these situations are handled and how trainees respond to them is all part of learning to teach.

> Jamie was teaching a maths lesson to a Year 6 class. It was towards the end of his second teaching practice. His tutor sat at the back of the room taking notes as part of a formal assessment of Jamie's teaching. The children, a top maths group, were collecting and collating information about individual shoe sizes. The lesson progressed well with pupils working collaboratively in small groups. Questions were posed to develop their understanding of mode, mean and median were at an appro-

priate level to help develop understanding. In the plenary Jamie asked questions about frequencies of shoe sizes. He wrote these on the board. He then started to explain about the mean, but after only a few words said nothing. The silence only lasted for seconds but was obvious to the tutor. With a big smile Jamie turned to the class. Holding out the chalk and in a bright voice, he said to a girl at the front, 'Rachel would you like to explain to everyone how we find the mean shoe size in this class?' At first Rachel looked shy but was very pleased with herself when she finished and was praised by Jamie. He then carried on with the lesson in a confident way. In discussion with the tutor after the lesson Jamie said that he *froze* and couldn't remember what he wanted to say, so he asked Rachel, one of the brightest pupils, to explain. When she had finished he felt composed enough to carry on. The children did not realise his dilemma and Rachel's involvement was seen as a planned part of the lesson.

Jamie was nervous about being assessed, which is understandable, but his quick thinking worked and even enhanced his teaching. This was recognised by both Jamie and his tutor. To retain a sense of humour and have realistic expectations can sometimes be difficult. But if we learn by consequences then mistakes could be seen as a vital part of the process of learning.

HOW TO BE PREPARED FOR A TUTOR'S VISIT

First, it is important to think through the lesson to be observed, making notes if necessary. Think about management, organisational and teaching strategies which address learning objectives and involve children in a meaningful way. Ask yourself: 'What will I be doing? What will the children be doing? How will the children be doing what they are doing? Why will the children be doing what they are doing? How can I tell if they are progressing and learning?' Secondly, think about contingency plans. What will you do if things do not go to plan, for individuals or the class? What strategies will you use to keep children on task? How will you deal with disruptions? It is impossible to cover all eventualities, but if contingencies are made this can add to your confidence even if you do not follow them through.

The following suggestions offer a checklist for trainees:

If possible make sure

- the children know there will be a visitor
- the teacher and the tutor are introduced
- the classroom is well presented

- there is somewhere for the tutor to sit.

If relevant, discuss with school staff

- your plans

- their role

- organisational problems

- resources, space, time

- pupils' needs

- how the visit may affect other staff.

Ensure that

- your teaching file is well ordered, up to date and available

- there is a copy of your lesson plan for the tutor

- the tutor is aware of any special circumstances, for example, pupils with special needs

- the tutor has a clear understanding of your intentions

- any displays are well presented

- children's work is marked.

Identify for discussion

- aspects of your teaching which are successful

- areas of concern

- questions you want to ask

- difficult situations or problems.

Remember a tutor will not see everything. Make sure you sell yourself and point out aspects of your teaching that you are pleased with or feel enthusiastic about. This might, for example, involve asking children to show their work, talking about a display or relating a particular incident in which you recognised a leap of understanding – yours or the pupils.

USING TUTOR'S VISITS EFFECTIVELY

Early visits

On early visits the tutor's agenda will be concerned with how the trainee is beginning to teach. Not surprisingly being observed can be a daunting experience even for the most capable individual. When trainees start teaching few are used to the noise, activity and constant involvement needed to make sense of everything that is happening in the classroom. There is a lot to take in. The significance of the teacher's actions, the interplay or intervention needed to encourage learning, as well as dealing with disruptive children, means it is difficult for the trainee to know where to start. Tutors are aware of this concern about *where to begin*. The need to identify specific targets crucial to trainees' development is a major aspect of the tutor's role. To decide which aspects have the biggest knock-on effect to teaching effectively involves the ability to recognise individual needs and progress.

Many trainees prefer points to be written down by their tutor or to make their own notes as the tutor is talking. Guidelines concerning teaching strengths and areas for development typically form the basis of feedback. The class teacher, trainee support teacher and other teachers in the school have day-to-day contact with the trainee, which the tutor does not have. Tutors only gain snapshot evidence of the trainee's experience on teaching practice but they have the breadth of experience of working with a range of trainees. Therefore it is important that everyone works as a team and talks about the trainee's progress together. This should be seen as an essential part of a tutor's visit.

Building on success

To build on success, but also analyse the reasons for that success, is an ideal way to begin. In discussion tutors might ask trainees, 'What have you enjoyed? What do you think went well? Were you pleased with anything that happened?' Followed by the important *why* questions which are intended to help trainees reflect on how their actions, decisions and choices affect children's learning, 'Why did you decide to do that? Why do you think the pupils were so fascinated? Why do you think that went so well?' As discussed throughout this book, it is useful for trainees to recognise their successes and reflect on them to inform their future practice.

> Louise was teaching a group of Year 2 children science/English. They went on a nature walk and collected things which they brought back to the classroom includ-

ing leaves, acorns, blackberries and an old sock. The children were interested in the sock because moss and grass were growing on it and they couldn't pull it apart. Two of them got carried away doing this and Louise took the sock away. The discussion which followed was designed to allow the children to develop language skills, raise questions and put forward ideas. Louise asked them about the blackberries (Had they eaten them?) and the leaves (Had they seen them before? Which trees did they come from?). Almost immediately there were some problems with children not listening to each other or her. They did not appear interested and some started to be silly. Louise then began to draw pictures on a flip chart and encouraged the children to take part by adding to the pictures or doing their own, afterwards explaining to the group what they had drawn. One boy added roots to the grass and a discussion followed about what it was like under the ground. All the children drew a picture of roots under the ground. One in particular was detailed with twists, overlapping each other across tiny worms and insects spaced about. Louise then asked them if roots needed the ground to grow. The lesson finished with the promise that they would plant some seeds, beans and cress, and watch them grow. Louise asked them to think about what they would like to grow their seeds on, suggesting sand, carpet and toilet paper. The children became animated and the boy who had drawn the complicated root drawing asked if he could grow his in a glass jar. He wanted to see all the roots growing (he had done this at home). Another boy wanted to grow them on his sock. A girl wanted to try mud. When the children left they were still talking about what the roots might look like. The next day the girl brought in some seeds.

In discussion with the tutor Louise cited the second part of the lesson as a success. She felt very pleased with the outcome, but was concerned that she had not followed her plan. She was not happy with the way the children responded to her questions about the blackberries. She said she began to panic as she could see they were not interested and was worried about losing control. The drawing activity was not part of her plan, but she decided to introduce this to involve the children in a different way and hopefully regain their interest. She was surprised it worked so well and felt that from then on the questions, ideas and interest generated were very rewarding for both her and the children. She enjoyed this part of the lesson and was looking forward to the next time she would work with this group. She realised that the initial discussion had not progressed well because she was more concerned with trying to follow her plans rather than responding to the children's interest. In planning she had covered the science and English content. She had not considered how the children might react. By restructuring her questions and involving them in a way which encouraged them to develop their own lines of enquiry she achieved her objectives, 'to develop language skills, raise questions and put forward ideas'.

Identifying areas of concern

On a tutor's early visits it can be difficult to identify areas of concern on which to focus. Quite often trainees lack the skills for recognising significant problems or they feel nervous about telling tutors about their perceived weaknesses. Relationships between the tutor, trainee and teacher are new. The tutor has little experience of working with a particular trainee and is learning how best to support them.

Appreciating that relatively simple adjustments can make a major difference to teaching is often a surprise to the trainee.

> Ian had organised his Year 6 children into groups for a history lesson. In each group there were five or six pupils. Handouts about siege weapons were on each table, as were pencils (rollers), bricks (heavy objects) and Newton meters. Instructions were on another handout. The lesson was not successful, several children did very little and some did nothing. Ian became increasingly stressed and ended up shouting at children for not taking part. The lesson was not completed in the planned time. Understandably this was a distressing experience which Ian had no wish to repeat.

The tutor suggested two main changes: a demonstration before the children embarked on the activity and smaller groups to ensure that individual involvement could be monitored. The tutor also asked Ian to think about what he said as he moved about the room and to try to focus his comments on the task rather than behaviour. To the experienced teacher such adjustments will seem obvious but to the novice this is often not the case. A crucial aspect of the tutor's role is to provide an environment conducive to discussion in which successes and difficulties are examined openly. To gain understanding and develop reflective skills, trainees need to be able to raise concerns and ask questions. The tutor's visit is an ideal time to do this. Until trainees see the relevance of advice related to their own experience it is difficult for them to learn. A two-way dialogue in which tutors and trainees communicate openly is ideal. A skilful tutor can do much to enable this to happen. Often, however, a trainee can help the process significantly. Consider the implications of the following hypothetical conversations:

Example 1

Tutor: How did you feel the lesson went?

Trainee: OK, the children all did what I wanted them to do.

Tutor: Were you pleased with how the more able children participated?

Trainee: Yes, I think they found it interesting.

Tutor: What about Craig and Jenny? They finished quite a while before any of the others.

Trainee: Yes they always do. They did it very well. I was pleased with their poem.

Tutor: They sat quietly and waited.

Trainee: (looks at the tutor)

Tutor: I saw you go over to them after a few minutes. What comments did you make?

Trainee: I told them it was good and that they had done well and that I liked the way the poem made me feel.

Tutor: How did they feel about their work?

Trainee: I'm not sure, I think they were pleased.

Tutor: You then asked them to read.

Trainee: Yes, for the last 10 minutes.

Tutor: Next time they finish early what might you do?

In the above conversation the tutor led the dialogue to ascertain the trainee's awareness of how to offer learning opportunities for early finishers. Although the tutor's questions were answered, very little about the trainee's intentions was discovered. In this case it would be easy for the tutor to assume that the trainee had not considered the need to respond to early finishers or differentiate expectations of brighter pupils.

Example 2

Tutor: How did you feel the lesson went?

Trainee: OK, the children all did what I wanted them to do.

Tutor: Were you pleased with how the more able children participated?

Trainee: I think they found it interesting. I was concerned that they finished so quickly. I felt that Craig and Jenny had done what I asked very quickly but I was pleased with their poem.

Tutor: They sat quietly and waited.

Trainee: I realised that they had finished but I was talking to another group and it took me a while to get to them.

Tutor: Perhaps you could indicate to them that you knew they had finished and tell them you would be over in a minute. Perhaps think of a short task associated with their work which they could do until you were ready.

Trainee: Yes, but I still feel nervous about talking across the class when you are in the room, so I didn't.

Tutor: We can discuss ways in which you can practise this. For example, talk to a child on the next table then increase the range. Is it a problem for you when I am not here?

Trainee: Not when I am on my own with the class, but when a teacher is in here it is.

Tutor: I saw you go over to them after a few minutes. What comments did you make?

Trainee: I told them it was good and that they had done well and that I liked the way it made me feel.

Tutor: How did they feel about their work?

Trainee: I'm not sure, I think they were pleased. I would have liked more time to discuss it with them. They had used adjectives well but adverbs were not so well used. I could have asked them to pick out the verbs in their poem and try to think of a few adverbs to describe each one.

Tutor: You then asked them to read.

Trainee: Yes, for the last 10 minutes. I don't think I thought it through. It surprised me that they finished so early. Next time I will have an extension task ready or try to give them a task as a result of what they have done. The paired poem ideas works well for some children, but there are some pairs which do not work so well. I need to talk to you about this.

In this conversation the trainee responded in a more open way. The tutor was able to ascertain her reasons for lack of action, awareness of missed opportunities and future intentions. The trainee, herself, identified concerns and suggested ways forward. Consequently, the tutor could offer advice which related to the trainee's identified needs.

OBSERVING TRAINEES TEACH

Typically, trainees will be told the criteria on which they are being assessed: at the present time these are given in *Qualifying to Teach* (TTA, 2003). Trainees also tend to know that the tutor will be observing, and collecting evidence of, their planning, teaching, assessments, reflections and aspects of their professional development.

What they probably do not know is how a tutor goes about collecting evidence. It might be helpful if they did. In the following section one tutor's perspective is offered. The tutor's agenda is based on final teaching practice visits, when all aspects of trainee's teaching are assessed.

During final teaching practice assessment is rigorous, involving the tutor in gaining evidence of how trainee teachers:

● help pupils learn and develop

● deliver the curriculum

● develop their teaching style

● develop relationships with pupils and staff.

To gain evidence the tutor considers questions such as:

● What do I need to ask the class teacher?

● How do I need to respond to what the class teacher says?

● What would it be best for me to do when I am in the classroom observing a trainee teaching?

● How can I best give advice?

● What will be the most effective way to support the trainee?

● How useful is the advice I give?

● How can I encourage the trainee to become more independent?

● How can I make the trainee feel able to talk openly?

● Is there evidence of development in the trainee's learning as a result of my actions?

● Has the trainee become more reflective?

● Is there improvement in areas of identified weakness?

● How can I now best support the trainee?

THE TUTOR'S AGENDA

Although there is not always a definite sequence to actions, the tutor has a set agenda. On entering the classroom, if the children are present, the tutor scans the room gauging pupil involvement, eye contact and facial expression. (In the early stages of teaching trainees are surprised by this and often expect the tutor to concentrate on them.) The tutor *is* observing the trainee but trying to do this in a way that is not obvious, by looking at the trainee's notes or reading a child's book. If possible the tutor smiles at the trainee to try to put them at ease and briefly asks, 'How is it going?' or tries to make a quick, positive comment, 'This display looks interesting' or 'I hear you had a very good PE lesson yesterday'. The tutor asks to look at the trainee's folder and indicates what he or she will be doing. 'I will read your file, watch you teach, talk to the children and look at their work. Afterwards I will talk to you and your teacher about the lesson and your teaching. Please try to ignore me. I'm looking forward to your session.'

In making conscious decisions about what to say on entering the room the tutor's intention is to inform and relax the trainee. The tutor wants the trainee to be able to teach without wondering or worrying about what the tutor is going to do. If trainees want to introduce the tutor to the class they could say, 'This is Mrs X. She has come to watch us work today. She might talk to you about what you are doing, but don't worry as she used to be a teacher and likes talking to children about their work.'

To be able to observe and analyse trainees teaching as thoroughly as possible it helps if the tutor can move about and talk to members of the class. This obviously has to be done in a sensitive manner and is not always appropriate. Nevertheless it offers good insight into children's involvement and learning as well as the trainee's teaching.

GAINING EVIDENCE

At first the list of standards in *Qualifying to Teach* (TTA, 2003) will seem very long, especially to a trainee on first teaching practice. Trainees might find it helpful to use the list to inform their teaching, aid planning, analyse their own practice, focus reflections and support discussions with teachers and tutors.

A tutor will gain evidence of the trainee's ability to address the standards in a variety of ways, including the following methods.

Written evidence

In the trainee's teaching file, the tutor looks for:

- session plans with clear, purposeful learning objectives, relevant to the National Curriculum and pupils' ability, allowing for progression and continuity, planned assessment opportunities and safety considerations

- tasks and activities, differentiated to involve children in addressing learning objectives in an interesting, creative and appropriate way, offering a degree of independence

- planned use of a range of appropriate resources to enhance learning

- lessons which accommodate all pupils including SEN and EAL (English as an Additional Language)

- planned expectations of learning support assistant (LSA) support

- reflections and evaluations which focus on learning and individual needs and which are used to inform future teaching

- assessments of pupils' progress and achievement.

Teaching evidence

Observing a trainee teach, the tutor looks for an enthusiasm for teaching, a clear ability to put children at ease and engage them in learning and a good understanding of the subject. Evidence will be found of the way a trainee teacher manages, organises and communicates learning. A tutor will look for the following.

Good communication and interpersonal skills which sustain interest and involvement including:

- effective and varied use of voice and non-verbal communication

- clear explanations and demonstrations

- well-focused questions at an appropriate level

- clear communication with other adults

- interventions which enhance learning

- discourse rather than superficial conversation.

Skilful management and organisational strategies to ensure pupils focus on learning, including:

- organisation and preparation to ensure the smooth running of the session

- effective management of individuals, groups and the class

- appropriate differentiation for groups and individuals

- encouragement of peer support and collaborative skills

- organisation of a variety of appropriate resources
- effective use of adult support
- effective strategies for maintaining discipline and control.

An ability to productively engage children in an enthusiasm for learning by:

- providing an atmosphere conducive to learning
- demonstrating good subject knowledge
- a creative interpretation of the curriculum
- clear and realistic aims
- high expectations
- a sound understanding of individual pupils and their needs
- purposeful monitoring and record-keeping to inform assessment
- opportunities which encourage independence
- a flexible approach in response to children's needs
- skilful handling of misconceptions
- supportive, targeted feedback.

Pupil evidence

Observing pupils, the tutor looks for:

- how children work and respond
- a willingness and enthusiasm to participate
- good study skills, involvement in the task
- co-operation and collaboration
- evidence of productive learning
- the enjoyment factor
- the quality of pupils' contributions
- a positive learning ethos.

Classroom evidence

Observing the classroom the tutor looks for:

- well-presented displays of pupils' work

- interactive areas connected with aspects of study

- well-organised resources

- areas for independent exploration

- quiet corners

- a visually stimulating environment

- an environment which encourages involvement

- a sense of order.

DISCUSSIONS FOLLOWING A TUTOR'S VISIT

In discussion following a teaching observation, the tutor and trainee may discuss any of the above observable components of teaching. The cognitive aspect of the trainee's teaching will also form an important part of any discussion and feedback. By talking to trainees about their perceptions, interpretations and decisions the tutor will gain valuable insights into the trainee's beliefs, values and ideas, their style and development. The tutor will base feedback not only on the trainee's teaching performance but also on their:

- understanding of pupils and their needs

- reflections on pupils' learning

- awareness of the relationship between aims and practice

- ability to analyse implications of performance

- reasons for choices and decisions

- consideration of alternatives

- ability to assess success and consider ways forward.

Verbal feedback: what to expect

The tutor will make comments and ask questions about particular observations across the range of standards in *Qualifying to Teach*. Such conversations are not usually documented but are useful to the trainee.

For example:

It was really good to see the children sprawled across the floor doing their history drawings of the Egyptians on such a big scale. It would have been restrictive just using the desk top. They really had a chance to explore ideas on a grand scale. Don't you think it was impressive how well they co-operated with each other and how they knew exactly which part to work on? We were able to talk about your teaching without being interrupted. Not many trainees would have had the confidence to let children work like that. I really enjoyed watching them. How did you decide to organise the groups? Who decided who did what? What are your plans for the finished pictures?

In this case feedback refers to the fact that children worked collaboratively and that the trainee's control of the class was good. The tutor was able to find out about the trainee's choices in group design and task allocation. From a brief discussion a great deal of information was gleaned about the trainee's teaching ability. This type of evidence is crucial in building a picture of progress but is not always so evident in detail in formal written feedback. Interactive dialogue, involving the trainee and the tutor, is to be encouraged and is a good time for both parties to raise any points or concerns they wish to discuss.

Written feedback: what to expect

Most trainees, understandably, place a great deal of importance on written feedback. Often after a session they find it difficult to take everything in, especially in the early stages of teaching. They find productive comments relating to building confidence, improving practice and considering alternatives useful to analyse their teaching and guide their learning. The tutor should be aware of the need to make suggestions, channel thinking and give a clear framework in which trainees can develop ideas and experiment. Reflection on practice can be developed in this way. Helpful comments will:

- praise performance, building on the positive, recognising strengths and commenting on them

- focus on one or two areas which are weak or need developing, suggesting alternatives and discussing possibilities to improve practice

- encourage conversation so that trainees have the opportunity to analyse their teaching, ask questions and consider their development

- explain what is required and clearly state what the trainee is expected to do in a problematic or failing situation

- empathise with a particular set of circumstances, including class size, previous experience and inherent difficulties

- focus on individual pupils and their development

- provide targets for the trainee to work towards.

Giving reasons for comments made and offering alternative suggestions increases the value of the tutor's feedback because it offers the trainee a way forward. Inviting comment from the trainee in a way that would aid reflection on practice might include asking them about:

- particular choices made interpreting the curriculum

- where they got their ideas from and ascertaining if more than one source was used. What degree of autonomy did they have?

- talking to the trainee about pupils to gauge understanding of individual needs, relationships, expectations and development. Asking about changes they would like to make and why.

CONCLUSION

I can hear you say, 'What a complex and complicated process ... I'll never do all that ... Do teachers really do all these things? ... It's so demanding, challenging, difficult!' This is all true. It takes time to teach well. There is always more to learn. There are no easy answers. What works with one group might not work so well with another. Learning to teach can be viewed as an ongoing process which is both rewarding and frustrating. It is not a smooth passage and often there are no easy answers. Remember: a tutor's visit is not only about assessing progress but is also about *supporting development*.

CAREER ENTRY AND DEVELOPMENT PROFILE

Towards the end of your final teaching practice you will be expected to fill in a document called a Career Entry and Development Profile (CEDP).This will involve identifying your particular teaching strengths and areas for professional development. Choices made as to which criterion to select will be as a result of discussions with mentors in school and university tutors but will be your responsibility. Once you decide which targets identify your professional development needs you will enter them into your Career Entry Development Profile at transition point 1. Your CEDP will act as a focus for your professional development at the beginning of your teaching career and should be taken with you on your first teaching post.

SUMMARY

- In making observational visits the role of the tutor is to support the trainee's progress and assess their competence against the standards in *Qualifying to Teach*.

- To gain evidence on which to base judgements the tutor observes the trainee teach and talks to them about their teaching.

- Ideally an open dialogue in collaboration with teachers and the trainee offers the tutor insight into the trainee's development.

- Trainee competence is assessed using stated criteria although a tutor will have their own methods of gaining evidence.

- Typically assessment of trainee progress involves identifying areas of strength and areas for development. Identifying specific targets and offering advice is crucial for individual development.

- To alleviate the stress factor trainees are advised to prepare thoroughly for a tutor's visit.

ISSUES FOR REFLECTION

- To what extent might your contribution to any dialogue be helpful in recognising your concerns? Can you think of questions you might ask to help identify problems?

- A positive approach to feedback is generally advised, but does this enable tutors to give a frank account of a trainee's progress?

- In what ways might tutors help trainees to become aware of alternatives without 'telling them what to do'?

- To what extent might a trainee's own understanding or reflection influence a tutor's judgement of their development in a positive/negative way?

Further reading

Clegg, D. and Billington, S. (1994) *The Effective Primary Classroom*. London: David Fulton. The section on pages 26–35 'What we know about effective classrooms' provides some insight into reflective practice.

Hayes, D. (2004) *Foundations in Primary Teaching*. London, David Fulton. The child, learning and teaching are explored in a personal way, providing a comprehensive introduction to all aspects of teaching.

Hayes, L., Nikolic, V. and Cabaj, H. (2000) *Am I Teaching Well?* Exeter: Learning Matters. Self-assessment strategies to encourage reflective practice feature highly in this book. Its emphasis on self-reflection and self-evaluation will be particularly valuable to trainee teachers.

Kitson, N. and Merry, R. (1997) *Teaching in the Primary School.* London: Routledge. This book is a coherent introduction to teaching written by experts in primary education. There are several relevant chapters extremely useful to trainees with a clear focus on learning relationships.

Proctor, A., Entwistle, M., Judge, B. and McKenzie-Murdoch, S. (1995) *Learning to Teach in the Primary Classroom.* London: Routledge. This is a very comprehensive book which includes several highly relevant chapters by experienced teachers to support trainee teachers in the school-based element of their course.

Chapter 18

Your first teaching post

Anne Cockburn and Graham Handscomb

You have successfully trained, and are now set for the delights of securing your first teaching post! In this chapter Anne Cockburn and Graham Handscomb discuss some of the best ways to look for your first teaching post; how to prepare your application to show yourself in the best possible light; the interview process and the next steps. Throughout they stress the importance of thorough preparation and recognising the need to make career decisions about which you feel comfortable.

INTRODUCTION

In this chapter we describe the main considerations you should take into account when applying for jobs and briefly discuss the induction period. People are often surprised by how demanding and time-consuming the whole process can be. Do not be caught short: read on so that you do not have a last minute major panic on your hands.

When it seems as if you have only just begun your pre-service training people will start asking you about jobs:

- Where are you planning to work?

- Which pools have you applied to?

- What have you written in your personal statement?

Some counties start looking for newly qualified teachers very early on. Indeed, it is not uncommon for some applications for 'the pool' to be in before the end of January. Other counties are much more laissez-faire and many of their jobs do not come up until May, June or even July. Both extremes can be hard for the people concerned. It is not easy, for example, to complete an application form demonstrating your confidence and experience when you feel that there is so much to learn and you still break into a sweat when you have to plan, and teach, several class sessions in a day. Nor is it easy to stand back and watch all your colleagues land jobs when you are desperately waiting for a post in your area and coping with the demands of your final assessments. Knowing that applying for jobs is invariably stressful generally helps but rarely makes it any easier. Fortunately, however, there is a strategy which can lighten the burden – namely, thorough preparation.

WHERE AND WHEN TO START LOOKING

If you are at a college or university it is likely that they can advise you on where and when to start looking for your first post, but here are some pointers which might prove helpful.

It is important to recognise that job hunting may well take considerable time and attention. During your training you are unlikely to have much time and attention to spare. It is important, therefore, if at all possible, to plan times when you can devote yourself to the task. It may be, for example, that you will have time over the Christmas holidays to update your curriculum vitae and outline your personal statement. Or you might have some time available between assignments. We would suggest that you begin the drafting process sooner rather than later as it will give you time to reflect on what you have written and improve your application as a result.

Pre-service teachers tend to find out about jobs in one of five ways:

- the *Times Educational Supplement*
- weekly education supplements in newspapers such as the *Guardian* and the *Independent*
- lists issued by local education authorities (obtained by telephoning specific authorities)
- the university or college
- word of mouth (for example, it might be your teaching practice school).

Think carefully about when you are going to start applying for jobs. Factors to consider are the urgency in obtaining a post, your personality, the popularity of the area where you wish to apply, your relevant experience and your other commitments. For example, if you are an anxious person who requires a job as soon as possible, then you may wish to start applying sooner rather than later. If that is the case remember that it is unlikely that you will be able to write much about your course or your teaching experience on your application form. In contrast, you may wish to wait until you are fairly confident that you are going to complete your training successfully and then turn your attention to looking for jobs. There you run the risk of having fewer jobs to apply for but having more relevant information to include on your application form.

CHOOSING YOUR AREA

Rather than applying for every job advertised, in the first instance it is a good idea to sit down and consider where you really want to teach. Discuss possibilities with family and friends. If you are footloose and fancy-free it is often easier as you are likely to have great scope to move to a new area. Nevertheless it is important to remember that moving to a new area would not only involve starting a new job, but also entail moving house, finding your way around, making new friends and so on. In other words you would have a lot on your plate. On the other hand, if you moved early on in the summer, just after your training had finished, you would have a chance to get settled, coupled with the excitement of meeting new people and beginning a new career.

Planning where to apply can also include decisions as to whether you want to apply to a 'pool' and/or opt for individually advertised jobs. In essence – although there are regional variations – if you decide on going for a 'pool', you complete a general application form. In most areas, if it meets with success you will then be invited for an interview.

Again there are likely to be regional variations but, basically, two or three people will interview you (usually including a headteacher and a representative from the local education authority). Depending on your performance they will grade you – A to D, for example. This information will then be made available to schools in the area. The higher your grade the more likely you are to be offered 'a look round' a school and, with luck, a job. Typically, a formal interview at the school is unlikely in these cases.

In other areas where there are such general applications your form will simply be made available to any headteachers who wish to consult it in their search for new staff. If your application appeals to them you will then be asked to an interview for their specific school.

You may decide to apply to both a 'pool' and individual jobs or focus on one or the other. Individual posts tend to start being advertised from late February (when there are very few) onwards. If you have not seen anything suitable by April/early May do not worry as there tends to be a flurry of jobs in early June. These arise as half-term – typically the last week in May – tends to be the last date teachers can hand in their notice. Not only are there a reasonable number of posts therefore but most of the applicants will be people in your position or people returning to teaching after a break.

Two cautionary comments before focusing on applications: it is important to have a fairly clear idea about where you wish to teach at this stage. If you are too vague you will waste a lot of time, energy and money. If you are too specific you will dramatically reduce your chances of finding a job: while it might be very convenient to teach just around the corner, the job – if there is one – may not be advertised for ages. You may not get it and there may then be very few other jobs available. Added to which, many would argue that you should only stay in your first job for two to three years and then move on (see below). It is also important to remember that not only moving house but also moving to a new area can be highly stressful. Making new friends, finding your way around and so on takes time and energy: both may be in short supply when you take on a new job.

APPLICATIONS

It is well worth putting considerable time and thought into your applications: if your efforts are not of a sufficient standard you will fail to pass even the first test. Again there are variations but you will almost certainly have to provide one, some or all of the following:

- an application form

- a personal statement

- a curriculum vitae

- an accompanying, covering letter.

Opinions vary as to whether these documents should be typed or handwritten. Stephens and Crawley (1994) are definite that they should all be word-processed if possible or, failing that, written impeccably in black ink. We have heard some headteachers argue, however, that it is useful to see someone's handwriting as it reveals something of the writer. The choice is yours but, for the time being at least, it is likely that you will have to complete at least part of an application form by hand. We suggest you do so as neatly as possible using black ink to make for easy photocopying. (Some of you reading this, and what follows, may think that we are obsessed with neatness but we can assure you, first impressions matter: why lose the chance of a really good job when an extra couple of minutes of care and attention could make all the difference?) However you decide to produce your application, do make sure to check it thoroughly for spelling mistakes, grammatical errors and style. You will find it helpful to consider the information that you have to supply and the space you have been given in which to do so. For instance, think about the grades you obtained in schools and higher education: have you been given too much or too little space for them? It can pay off to plan out how you fit this information into the space available, rather than find you run out of room and have to squeeze in the remainder untidily.

The early sections in application forms are generally straightforward requests for biographical information. You will be asked for details of examinations taken. Try to be as detailed and accurate as possible: the fact that ten years ago you took a GCSE in music or art may make all the difference to whether or not you are asked for an interview.

PERSONAL STATEMENT

Later sections of the application tend to be more tricky. You may be asked specific questions about your views on various issues and/or you may be asked for 'a personal statement' – with little, or no, guidance provided. These are often seen as the most challenging part of the application procedure. They do, however, provide you with an opportunity to demonstrate what you have to offer in terms of personal qualities, philosophies and outlook.

When drafting responses to such requests it is important to keep the following in mind:

- As people who do the shortlisting of applicants, it is a fairly boring task sifting through application forms: make yours stand out by presenting it in a lively and interesting style.

- You are not only unique but – however, tired and lacking in confidence you are – you have a range of strengths you can offer a school. Think back to all your achievements and interests, remembering, apart from anything else, that you would not have been offered a place to train as a teacher if you did not have the potential to be successful.

- Be honest. While it might be tempting to imply that you are an expert at this, that and the next thing, don't do it as you might find yourself (with your Grade 1 piano certificate) playing in front of an entire school at assembly. More appropriately, you might say that you have an interest in 'x' or 'y' that you would be keen to develop if the opportunity arose. In addition, avoid volunteering for numerous extracurricular activities even if you would like to take some on. You might be landed with more than you bargained for and, without beating about the bush, your first job is likely to require all your time and energy without extra demands being put upon you.

- You may be applying for several jobs in different counties but remember to include some specific statements about the particular school or region to which each application is destined. It is important for both you and the those involved in the selection process, after all, to be sure that you are appropriate for the post or area in question. You might, for example, comment on the support provided for newly qualified teachers or the opportunities in information communications technology.

- Be concise but not list-like. It would be inappropriate to provide your life history and, indeed, even if selectors were interested they would not have time to read it. On the other hand, a list of achievements, attitudes and aspirations would be very dry and lack substance. Rather than 'I think play is very important', for example, try something along the lines of, 'Having worked in three contrasting Reception classes, read some of the relevant literature and attended lectures on the subject, I am developing a view that play can have a very effective role in children's learning. For example, one day, I observed … ' (that is, give a brief account of a child, or children, learning through play).

- Think very carefully about how you present your personal and professional philosophies. Again there is a need to be as honest as possible without shooting yourself in the foot in the process. For example, if you have strong views about how particular subjects should be taught (for example, through a play-based approach) and you are not prepared to teach in any other way then you should say so. You should, however, recognise that, by doing so, you may well be significantly narrowing your choice of jobs. It is not necessarily that the interviewing panel would disagree with your philosophy but more that they might be hesitant in employing someone who appeared to have rigidly held views.

Sometimes personal statements are included as part of the application form and sometimes they are not. If they are not it is usually a good idea to include them in your covering letter.

As part of your application you will almost certainly be invited to say something about your personal interests and hobbies. Again, be honest, but try to give the impression that you are a 'rounded' person (McBride, 1994). Selection panels want to be reassured that you are a lively and interesting person who has a range of interests and friends but that you are also someone who enjoys their own company and who is not always dependent on other people for their rest and relaxation.

CURRICULUM VITAE AND LETTER OF APPLICATION

An opportunity to present details of your examination results and other notable achievements is also very likely to be included in the application form, but if it is not or if you deem it insufficient, you may wish to provide a copy of your curriculum vitae. The style of such documents can vary but, to be successful, they need to be word-processed and presented in a professional manner. Two examples are given in Figures 18.1 and 18.2.

Crafted with care, the curriculum vitae can be a very effective way in which to present the main details of your background and experience, and some of the key messages you wish to convey. A concise and well-organised CV can help short-listing panels to take in quickly who you are and what you might bring to the post. However, for some applications you may be instructed not to supply a curriculum vitae. This is because some schools prefer the information about applicants to be presented in a common format structured by the application form. They consider it easier to look at and compare details about all applicants if they are in a similar format. In these cases it is advisable not to be tempted to enclose your curriculum vitae anyway. This may duplicate information you put in the application form and frustrate the selection panel when considering your application.

Within the body of the application form it is likely that you will be asked to write a letter of application. Sometimes this incorporates the personal statement. There is often a blank page towards the end of the form for this letter of application, and you may also be instructed to provide a separate page if needed. It is important that you write enough but avoid writing at too great a length. If you are given full details about the post, school or local education authority in the application information sent to you, then it is useful to gear what you have to say about yourself and your outlook to this information. Remember that the selection panel is likely to be dealing with a number of applications. So your job is to make its task as easy as possible by presenting the main details about yourself and your approach to the post in a clear accessible way. Don't worry about leaving some fine details out. Again remember that there will be opportunity to discover more about you through the interview process. The goal of the application is to say enough at this stage to interest the selection panel and to secure an interview, where you will then be able to say more. Finally, make sure you address the basics of neatness and accuracy. Do not use lined paper, and do not make spelling or grammatical errors. If you are unsure, find a book on the subject, such as those listed at the end of the chapter.

As part of your application form or your curriculum vitae, typically, you will be asked to include the names and addresses of two referees. Specific details as to whom you should approach (for example, your personal tutor) may be included but it is usual to use someone involved in your pre-service training (for example, the head of one of your SCITT or GTP schools or a PGCE tutor), and a tutor who worked with you on your first degree. Sometimes it may be appropriate to include one of the headteachers from a teaching practice school. Whoever you select be sure to ask them *before* you send in your application and thank them after the event. Apart from the obvious courtesy, it is important to remember that you may need to call upon such people again in the future.

When sending the application off it is useful to attach a covering letter. This can be very brief and almost a courteous formality along the lines of 'I enclose my application for the post of ... Thank you for your consideration'. Nevertheless, be sure that it is neat and professionally laid out.

Some very important last points to remember are, before you post your application, be sure to:

- Ask two or three constructively critical friends to read it to check for spelling mistakes, lies and grammatical errors. They will also be able to tell you if you are under- or over-selling yourself.

- Take a copy so that you can refresh your memory if you are asked for an interview.

INTERVIEWS

Preparation

As with the applications, it is important to prepare as thoroughly as you can for interviews.

If you do not know the school you have applied to, it is a good idea to visit it before-

Figure 18.1   Curriculum vitae (example 1)

CURRICULUM VITAE

[SAM HOPE]

Home Address: 6, Low Road   **Term Address:** 7, High Road
              Sunny Town   Spring Town
              Devon   Somerset
              WX3 4TY   UN2 8YT
Telephone number: 0123 456 7890   **Telephone number:** 0198 765 4321
Date of birth: 10/9/77   **Sex:**   female

EDUCATION

1990–1996	The Best Comprehensive School, Sunny Town, Devon
1994	GCSE: English (A), Mathematics (A), Biology (A), French (A), History (A), Music (B), Art (B)
1996	'A' level: English (B), French (B), History (B)
1996–1999	South West University BA Honours Degree in English (class 2.i). Subsidiary: European History
1998	Grade 8 piano
1999–2000	Primary PGCE gained through Brightly School Centred Initial Teacher Training (SCITT) Consortium. Awarding Body: Western University

WORK EXPERIENCE

Summer 1997	I helped run a play scheme for sixty 5–13-year-olds in Sunny Town
Summer 1998	I was an assistant co-ordinator of the above play scheme
Summer 1999	I worked in a home for 5–12-year-olds with special needs

For the past year I have acted as a voluntary classroom assistant in a local primary school on a weekly basis. I have worked with children across the age range helping, in particular, with music, art and drama.

INTERESTS

Music: I am a very keen musician who, from the age of 8, has always been a member of some musical group. I have grade 8 in piano but I can also play the trumpet and the oboe.
Travel: I love travelling and every year I try to make a point of visiting a new country. This year I had a particularly exciting trip to Outer Mongolia.
Reading: I read a wide range of fiction and non-fiction books having been shown from a very early age how books can broaden one's horizons.
Voluntary work: worked on Environment renewal project run by Newstart Borough Council

REFEREES
Mrs H. Friendly (Headteacher)   Mrs J. Kind (Personal Tutor)
Mount Pleasant School   The School of Education
Happy Valley   The Western University
South Town   Spring Town
Cornwall   Somerset

Figure 18.2   Curriculum vitae (example 2)

PERSONAL DETAILS

Name: Oosha Zaehner   **Date of birth:** 2/9/70   **Sex:** female
Address: 3 Rose Street   **Marital status:** married
        Northern Town
        Cumbria   **e-mail:** o.zaehner@homespace.com.uk
        CH3 4JG   **fax:** 0126 678 8954
Telephone: 0126 678 8933

EDUCATION

1982 – 1988	The Grammar School, Northern Town GCE 'O' levels: English, mathematics, physics, chemistry (all grade A) geography, art and Russian (all grade C) GCE 'A' levels: Physics (A), chemistry (B), mathematics (B)
1988 – 1991	University of the North East BSc psychology (class 2.i) with minors in mathematics and sociology Dissertation: 'The value of play in the early years of schooling'
1999 – 2000	University of the North East – PGCE in primary education with a specialism in mathematics

WORK EXPERIENCE

1991 – 1997	Care Assistant in St Michael's Home for the Elderly
1997 – 1999	Classroom assistant at the Little School, Northern Town

SKILLS

Clean driving licence, experience with Word for Windows, fluent Russian

INTERESTS

Sailing: we have the use of a small sail boat which we take out whenever the opportunity arises.
Camping: we have travelled all over Europe enjoying the variety of cultures and scenery.
Deep sea diving: I hope to take some diving qualifications during the summer 2000.
Voluntary work: helped as a playgroup assistant with Christ Church Play group

REFEREES

The Dean	Professor G. Clever
School of Education	Department of Psychology
University of the North East	University of the North East
Northern Town	Northern Town
Cumbria	Cumbria

hand to ensure that you know where it is: you do not want to be wandering round the streets on the day of the interview trying to find it.

Sometimes it is possible to look round a school prior to the interview day. Seize the opportunity if you can but, on the one hand, try to avoid missing any important sessions or teaching opportunities and, on the other hand, try to visit when the school is in action! You can learn a tremendous amount about a place by the way staff and pupils greet you. Is the school somewhere you would like to work or do the people in it make you feel uncomfortable and unwelcome?

If you are in the midst of, for example, teaching practice when you are invited for interview it is often possible to visit a school when the children have gone home. When visiting be relaxed and yourself, but also be aware that, whilst this is not a formal part of the interview process, you will nevertheless be 'on show' and so be conscious of the impression you are making. Make the most of the opportunity to find out more about the school and think through any questions that you might want to ask beforehand. Don't overdo the questioning, so that you appear 'pushy' but just show interest in the school and the post on offer.

Phone the headteacher beforehand and check whether a visit is feasible and arrange a mutually convenient time. Generally schools will be very pleased to be approached, and welcome the fact that applicants are showing such an engaged interest. If your request is denied, do not be dismayed as it may be that so many people wish to visit that it is not possible to accommodate them.

Prior to your interview it is important that you prepare yourself as well as you can. Remind yourself what you have written in your application, but also think about the questions you might be asked. Remember that the interviewers will have your application to hand and may want to explore aspects of the information that you supplied. Ask colleagues what questions they have been asked and think how you might have answered them. Some fairly standard questions include:

- 'Why do you want to teach?'

- 'What do you think makes a good teacher?'

- 'What makes you want to work with children?'

- 'Can you describe the range of experience you have had in the classroom?'

- 'What are your views on the role of play in the curriculum?'

Practise your replies out loud to encourage your fluency. You will not be able to prepare for all the questions you will be asked (see below) but if you have thought through some of your answers you will present a more relaxed and confident view of yourself on the day.

Having practised answering questions you would also be wise to consider whether you have any questions. Remember, interviews are a two-way process: you need to be sure that you want the job on offer (see below) just as much as the interview panel need to ensure that you are the best person for the job. Typical questions you might prepare are: 'If I were to be offered the post, what provision will there be for me as a newly qualified teacher?' or 'I have grade 8 piano; might there be any possibility to join in, or start, an after-school music club if I were successful today?'

Some schools ask candidates to do a short presentation on the day of the interview. Others ask interviewees to take a class for a story or some similar activity. Again, thorough preparation is of the essence. As far as possible practise what has been asked of you beforehand. Make your life as easy as possible by, for example, preparing index cards with key words or phrases on them in case you 'dry up' on the day. If asked to teach a class prepare this as thoroughly as you would during you initial teaching training and see if you can ask a tutor or a colleague to look at what you have prepared beforehand.

Finally, several days before the interview, think about what you are going to wear for the great day. This may sound trivial but first impressions are crucial. Many years ago I had a student who, on the first day of her teaching practice, went into school wearing white shoes. Unfortunately they were not dazzlingly clean and, from then on, every time I visited the school the headteacher not only commented on those shoes but gave the impression that such a lack of cleanliness was the mark of a weak teacher.

When surveying your wardrobe for the appropriate outfit select something that is smart but not overpowering. As a female I would always opt for a skirt or a dress rather than a top designer suit. (The fact that I do not have one of the latter is not the point: I simply would not wish to intimidate the interviewers.) Men, we think, should opt for a jacket and tie. A suit is a possibility but we certainly do not think it is worth buying one just for the occasion. Eggert (1992) advises that you should dress to suit yourself, be traditional rather than avant-garde and that, 'darker colours are more powerful than lighter colours' (p. 35).Whatever you decide upon, ensure that it is comfortable, crease-resistant and unlikely to show any stains. (There is a certain law which states you will spill something on your outfit a few minutes prior to your interview!) In summary, it is important that you appear smart, as this conveys the message that you value the interview opportunity and are treating it seriously and with the appropriate respect. Given this, it is also important that what you choose to wear feels natural and helps you feel comfortable and at ease with yourself.

The day of the interview

Allow plenty of time for your journey and arrive at the school in plenty of time. We would suggest 10–15 minutes early. Any earlier and you have too long to panic. Any later and you may begin panicking about whether you will make it there on time. If you find that you are running late owing to unforeseen circumstances, telephone the school to explain and give an approximate arrival time.

On arrival at the school, unless you have been told otherwise, make your way to the secretary's office. Several possibilities might happen at this point – a tour of the school, a coffee, the interview – but, be warned, as soon as you come into contact with anyone at the school you are likely to come under scrutiny! It is not uncommon, for example, for interviewees to be shown round the school by a member of staff and your guide's opinion canvassed afterwards.

When it is your turn to be interviewed, again remember that first impressions are crucial. Over 40 years ago Springbelt (1958) suggested that interviewers often make up their mind about a person's suitability within the first few minutes of the interview. We understand this point of view but, even if this is the case, professional interviewers will make sure that they spend the rest of the interview thoroughly testing such initial judgement rather than assuming that it was correct in the first instance. We have found that despite such initial impressions we quite frequently change our minds, so do not worry if you do not appear quite as you might like – a good interviewer should be able to see well beyond appearances.

Enter the room with a smile on your face and try to give the impression that you are delighted to be there. Sit back – but do not lounge – and try to relax. If you are physically relaxed you are more likely to be mentally relaxed. If you are too laid back you are likely to come over as arrogant and unaware.

The number of interviewers is difficult to predict but, usually, there will be between two and four. One of these is likely to be a headteacher and, depending on whether it is a pool or specific job interview, the others might be a school governor, a teacher or a member of the local education authority. Typically they will start with simple factual questions or questions they imagine you will have prepared, such as:

- 'What made you apply for a job at our school?'

Answer as honestly and fluently as you can, having listened carefully to what you have been asked. People will expect you to be nervous so take your time and do not worry if you stumble over the odd word or two. It is important to include everyone in your answer. In other words, rather than stare fixedly at the person who asked the question, look at the other interviewers too as you answer the question. If you do not understand a question say so! This is not always easy but, We can assure you, it is better than providing a totally inappropriate and incoherent response.

A common failing of interviewees is that they are either too verbose in their responses or monosyllabic. Remember that your interviewers are trying to find out about you so, rather than one-word answers, they need some clues as to who you are. They do not, however, require your life history. Talking too much or too little is often a sign of nerves but it can also indicate a lack of awareness of your audience: not a good characteristic in a potential teacher. So, in your answers try to give a clear response to the main issue in the question and, if possible, a brief example to illustrate your point. In other words, address the heart of the question, and say enough to interest and intrigue, leaving the panel to ask any supplementary questions if they want more from you on this issue.

During the course of the interview you may well be asked questions you had not anticipated. Try not to panic! It is quite in order for you to take a couple of minutes' thinking time. Interviewers will often pose questions that they know you could not have prepared to see how quickly you can think when on the spot. They will not expect a perfect answer but evidence that you are intelligent, practical and thoughtful, and not someone who will blurt out the first thing that comes into your head when put under pressure.

Some interviewers are highly experienced and will use techniques designed to show you at your best. If, for example, you have given rather a short answer they will provide you with a prompt which will encourage you to say more. Other interviewers are not so adept and you may find yourself being asked what you consider to be rather facile questions. Keep cool and try to respond in a mature and intelligent manner. You may think the interviewer concerned is ignorant – or even bigoted – but it does not do to share your thoughts with the panel, especially if you want the job. Even if you later decide that the job is not the one for you, remember that word can get around, and that it is as well to keep your negative thoughts to yourself.

Towards the end of the interview you will almost certainly be asked if you have any questions. It gives the impression that you are thoughtful and well prepared if you have one or two queries. Any more and the interviewers will be watching the clock. If it has not already been discussed, you would be wise to ask about induction arrangements (see below). Eggert (1992) warns, however, that you would be unwise to, 'break out of the role of interviewee and interview the interviewer by asking for … opinions or suggestions' (p. 73).

If you have no questions you would be wise to say something along the lines of: 'I found your brochure/introduction so informative that I don't have anything to ask, thank you.'

Arnold et al. (1998) warn that some interviewers are overly influenced by the 'recency effect'. In other words, they have a tendency to give too much weight to the last thing a candidate said or did. Accordingly, be sure to smile and thank the interviewers before leaving the room.

AFTER THE INTERVIEW

It is likely you will hear whether you have been successful on the day or within a day or two of the interview. Before you receive the letter or the telephone call decide whether *you* want the job, regardless of whether you are offered it. It is important that you think you would be happy in the post but try not to be too fussy. In many schools it is common practice to ask applicants to wait and then to give them the outcome of the interview on the day. Opinions vary on this, but many people feel it is bad form to go through the whole interview process and then turn down the post, particularly if the school has given a lot of opportunity to visit, tour and get to know the school. Indeed, in some interviews one of the questions might be, 'Having had an opportunity to view the school are you still interested in the post?' So, if at all possible, it is better to do your thinking about whether you would accept the post beforehand. You can reject one, or possibly two, jobs after interview but you are tempting fate – and creating a bad image – if you decline any more.

If you do want the job and are offered it – congratulations!

If you are unsuccessful try to view the experience constructively. It is common practice for one of the interview panel to offer feedback and you should heed the advice given. If such an offer is not forthcoming, it is perfectly in order for you to ask for a debriefing.

Should you find that you have been rejected after two or three interviews, have a chat to your tutor or headteacher, or visit your local careers centre. It may be that, unluckily, there is someone better qualified than you for the jobs you have applied for, or it may be that you are making some simple mistakes which can be easily rectified. Remember, you were successful in gaining a place to train as a teacher, so you must be pretty good!

If you have not succeeded in finding a post by the end of the year put your name down on the supply list and/or volunteer at your local school. If you make yourself known, respected and liked it should not be long before you land your first job.

INDUCTION

At the time of writing all students undertaking teacher training successfully in England have to complete literacy, numeracy and ICT tests prepared by the Teacher Training Agency by the end of their first year of teaching. In addition, in order to continue in the profession, newly qualified teachers must pass a period of induction. This was introduced as part of the Teaching and Higher Education Act 1998 and 'should combine support, monitoring and assessment of your performance as a new teacher' (DfEE, 2001, p. 1).

The induction period is usually one academic year but may be completed pro rata if you decide to work part-time. For example, if you take on a 50 per cent post, your induction will take two years. Should you opt for supply work, you may only count periods of one term or more in a school and only if the headteacher agrees at the start of your employment. There is currently no time limit for starting your induction (unless you have completed the equivalent of four terms' supply) but you would be wise to complete it as soon as possible after your training to make the most of the expertise you have acquired.

Most of the schools you are likely to apply to should be able to offer you an appropriate induction programme. If you are planning to work in the independent sector, however, you should check whether this is the case and ensure that they teach the National Curriculum and follow the Primary Strategy. You should also be cautious if you are considering a school under special measures as particular conditions apply.

In all schools your headteacher will be formally responsible for your induction programme and will either act as your induction tutor or delegate this to a senior member of staff. Provision should be tailored to meet your needs. It should be based on the strengths and weaknesses identified in your Career Entry and Development Profile (see Chapter 17) which, very early on in your post, you and your mentor will convert into an action plan designed to help you consolidate and develop your teaching skills.

As a newly qualified teacher you will be given a lighter timetable than more experienced colleagues (that is, 90 per cent in a full-time post) and 'The remaining hours must be protected and used for professional development' (Clark, 2000, p. 30). During your induction period you should be observed and have a number of formal review meetings. You should also be given the opportunity to see more experienced colleagues teach. Towards the end of your programme your headteacher should tell you whether or not you will be recommended for successful completion. In essence this means whether you can meet the standards laid out in *Qualifying to Teach* (TTA, 2003; see also Chapter 17). Good practice in support for newly qualified teachers entails colleagues being given ongoing mentoring and coaching, clear arrangements for monitoring and evaluation, and regular feedback on performance and encouragement. The local education authority has a responsibility to monitor and ensure that schools are providing the appropriate quality of support, development and management of its NQTs. Although it is unlikely, if you feel that you are not being treated appropriately then your should contact the named LEA officer about your concerns. In the unlikely event that you should be unlucky enough to fail you may appeal to the Secretary of State or the General Teaching Council for England. More positively, however, the Department for Education and Employment 'expect the vast majority of newly qualified teachers to complete their induction period successfully' (DfEE, 2001, p. 2).

Good luck!

SUMMARY

- Applying for jobs is demanding and stressful: take it one step at a time.
- Think carefully about where you wish to apply.
- It is worth spending time and effort on your applications.
- Make the most of any opportunity to visit and tour the school.
- Prepare thoroughly for interviews and remember to reread your application.
- During interview aim to keep calm and focused, and show interest.
- Remember it is in the interviewers' interest that you show yourself at your best, and they will want to help you do this.
- Where possible do your thinking about whether you want the job beforehand.
- Try to be constructive and learn from your rejections.
- Remember that you do not have to accept a job if it is offered to you.

ISSUES FOR REFLECTION

- Think about your strengths and weaknesses and be prepared to discuss both!
- What sort of school would you really like to work in? Large? Small? Rural?
- Decide what you would want to gain from the opportunity to visit the school before interview.
- Can you articulate your professional philosophy? What, for example, do you think are the most important aims of primary education? What should be the role of parents in their child's education?

Further reading

There are numerous books on job applications and interviewing but here are two you might like to look at:

Eggert, M. (1992) *The Perfect Interview*. London: Century.

McBride, P. (1994) *CVs and Applications*. Cambridge: Hobsons.
  We also like Alan Jones' book listed below as it has a section entitled 'Ten hazards to overcome' which covers issues such as being too young or too old and 'job hopping'. Rebecca Corfield's book also appealed as it is very upbeat and includes a section on 'How to provide proof that you are the right candidate'.

Jones, A. (1996) *How to Write a Winning CV*. 2nd edition. London: Century.

Corfield, R. (1999) *Successful Interview Skills*. 2nd edition. London: Kogan Page.

Finally, we suggest you read the regular guidance column and articles for teacher trainees and newly qualified teachers in the *Times Educational Supplement*, and commend the following as very practical guides to your first year in teaching:

Hayes, D. (2000) *The Handbook for Newly Qualified Teachers*. London: David Fulton.

Holmes, E. (2003) *The Newly Qualified Teacher's Handbook*. London: Kogan Page.

References

Alexander, R. (1992) *Policy and Practice in Primary Education*. London and New York: Routledge.

Alexander, R. (2004) Still no pedagogy? Principle, pragmatism and compliance in primary education. *Cambridge Journal of Education*, 34(1), pp. 7–33, March.

Alexander, R., Rose, J. and Woodhead, C. (1992) *Curriculum Organisation and Classroom Practice in Primary Schools: A Discussion Paper*. London: Department of Education and Science.

Armstrong, M. (1980) *Closely Observed Children: The Diary of a Primary Classroom*. London: Writers and Readers in association with Chameleon.

Arnold, J., Cooper, C.L. and Robertson, I.T. (1998) *Work Psychology*. 3rd edition. London: Pitman.

Assessment Reform Group (1999) *Assessment for Learning: Beyond the Black Box*. Cambridge: University of Cambridge School of Education.

Assessment Reform Group (2002) *Assessment for Learning, 10 Principles: Research-Based Principles to Guide Classroom Practice*. Cambridge: Assessment Reform Group (downloadable from www.assessment-reform-group.org.uk).

Beishuizen, M. (1999) The empty number-line as a new model. In I. Thompson (ed.), *Issues in Teaching Numeracy in Primary Schools*. Buckingham: Open University Press.

Bennett, S. N. (1976) *Teaching Styles and Pupil Progress*. London: Open Books.

Bennett, S.N., Desforges, C.W., Cockburn, A.D. and Wilkinson, B. (1984) *The

Quality of Pupil Learning Experiences. London: Lawrence Erlbaum Associates.

Bierhof, H. (1996) *Laying the Foundations of Numeracy: A Comparison of Primary Textbooks in Britain, Germany and Switzerland*. London: National Institute of Economic and Social Research.

Bierhof, H. and Prais, S.J. (1997) *From School to Productive Work: Britain and Switzerland Compared*. Cambridge: Cambridge University Press.

Black, P. (2003) *Assessment for Learning – Putting it into Practice*. Maidenhead: Open University Press.

Black, P. and Wiliam, D. (1998) *Inside the Black Box: Raising Standards through Classroom Assessment*. London: King's College (reissued 2004 by NFER Nelson).

Bloom, B.S. (ed.) (1964) *The Taxonomy of Educational Objectives, Vol 1: Cognitive Domain* and *Vol 2: Affective Domain*. London: Longman.

Board of Education (1931) *Primary Education* (the Hadow Report on Primary Education). London: HMSO.

CACT (Schools Council/Open University) (1980) *Curriculum in Action: An Approach to Evaluation*, Book 1. *An Approach to Evaluation*, p. 11. Buckingham: Open University Press.

Central Advisory Council for Education (England) (CEAC) (1967) *Children and their Primary Schools* (Plowden Report). London: HMSO.

Clark, S. (2000) No way back, *Times Educational Supplement*, 16 June.

Clarke, P. (2000) *Learning School, Learning Systems*. London: Cassell.

Cockburn, A.D. (1986) An empirical study of classroom processes in infant mathematics education. Unpublished doctoral dissertation, University of East Anglia.

Cockburn, A.D. (1999) *Teaching Mathematics with Insight*. London: Falmer Press.

Cole, P. and Chan, L. (1994) *Teaching Principles and Practice*. 2nd edition. New York: Prentice Hall.

Cordingley, P., Bell, M. and Temperley, J. (2005) Mentoring and coaching for learning, *Professional Development Today*, 8(2), pp. 15–19, Spring.

de Boo, M. (1999) *Enquiring Children, Challenging Teaching*. Buckingham: Open University Press.

Department for Education and Employment (DfEE) (1998a) *Teaching: High Status, High Standards, Circular 4/98*. London: Department for Education and Employment.

Department for Education and Employment (DfEE) (1998b) *Target Setting in School, Circular 11/98*. London: Department for Education and Employment.

Department for Education and Employment (DfEE) (1998c) *National Literacy Strategy Framework for Teaching*. London: Department for Education and Employment.

Department for Education and Employment (DfEE) (1999a) *The National Literacy Strategy Training Modules: 1 Teaching and Learning Strategies*. London: Department for Education and Employment.

Department for Education and Employment (DfEE) (1999b) *The National Numeracy Strategy, Framework for Teaching Mathematics from Reception to Year 6*. Sudbury: Department for Education and Employment.

Department for Education and Employment (DfEE) (1999c) *Mathematical Vocabulary*. Sudbury: Department for Education and Employment (originally produced by BEAM Education for the National Numeracy Project).

Department for Education and Employment (DfEE) (1999d) *All Our Futures: Creativity, Culture and Education*. London: Department for Education and Employment.

Department for Education and Employment (DfEE) (2000) *The Code of Practice on School/LEA Relations*. London: Department for Education and Employment.

Department for Education and Employment (DfEE) (2001) http://www.dfee.gov.uk/iateach/contents.htm

Department for Education and Employment/Qualifications and Curriculum Authority (DfEE/QCA) (1999a) *The National Curriculum: Handbook for Primary Teachers in England*. London: Department for Education and Employment/Qualifications and Curriculum Authority.

Department for Education and Employment/Qualifications and Curriculum Authority (DfEE/QCA) (1999b) *The National Curriculum for England*. London: Department for Education and Employment/Qualifications and Curriculum Authority.

Department for Education and Employment/Qualifications and Curriculum Authority (DfEE/QCA) (1999c) *The National Curriculum for England: Mathematics*. London: Department for Education and Employment/Qualifications and Curriculum Authority.

Department for Education and Employment/Qualifications and Curriculum Authority (DfEE/QCA) (2000) *Curriculum Guidance for the Foundation Stage*.

London: Qualifications and Curriculum Authority.

Department for Education and Skills (DfES) (2001) *Learning and Teaching: A Strategy for Professional Development*. London: HMSO.

Department for Education and Skills (DfES) (2003), *Excellence and Enjoyment: A Strategy for Primary Schools*. London: Department for Education and Skills.

Department for Education and Skills (DfES) (2004) *Every Child Matters*. London: HMSO.

Department for Education and Skills/Teacher Training Agency (DfES/TTA) (2002) *Qualifying to Teach: Professional Standards for Qualified Teacher Status and Requirements for Initial Teacher Training*. London: Teacher Training Agency.

Department of Education and Science (DES) (1988) *National Curriculum Task Group on Assessment and Testing: A Report*. London: HMSO.

Desforges, C.W. and Cockburn, A.D. (1987) *Understanding the Mathematics Teacher*. Lewes: Falmer Press.

Doddington, C. and Flutter, J. with Bearne, E. and Demetriou, H. (2001) *Sustaining Pupil's Progress at Year 3*. Cambridge: University of Cambridge, Faculty of Education.

Doyle, W. (1979) Making managerial decisions in the classroom. In D.L. Duke (ed.), *Classroom Management*. Chicago: University of Chicago Press.

Drummond, M.J. (1996) Teachers asking questions: approaches to evaluation, *Education 3–13*, p. 10, October.

Dyson, A. (2001) *Building Research Capacity*. National Educational Research Forum Sub-group report. NERF.

Edwards, D. and Mercer, N. (1987) *Common Knowledge*. London: Methuen.

Eggert, M. (1992) *The Perfect Interview*. London: Century.

Essex County Council (2002) *Educational Enquiry and Research in Essex*. Forum for Learning and Research Enquiry (FLARE), Chelmsford: Essex County Council.

Essex County Council (2003) *Early Career Continuing Professional Development*. FLARE. Chelmsford: Essex County Council.

Fielding, M. (2004) 'New wave' student voice and the renewal of civic society, *London Review of Education*, 2(3), pp. 197–217, November.

Fish, D. (1995a) *Quality Mentoring for Student Teachers: A Principled Approach to Practice*. London: David Fulton.

Fish, D. (1995b) *Quality Learning for Student Teachers: University Tutors' Educational Practices*. London: David Fulton.

Fisher, R. (1995) *Teaching Children to Think*. Cheltenham: Stanley Thornes.

Fisher, R. (1998) *Teaching Thinking: Philosophical Enquiry in the Classroom*. London: Cassell.

Fulwiler, T. (1987) *The Journal Book*. Portsmouth, NH: Boynton/Cook.

Gagné, R.M. (1976) *The Conditions of Learning*. 3rd edition. New York: Holt, Rinehart and Winston.

Galton, M. (1995) Do you really want to cope with thirty lively children and become an effective primary teacher? In J. Moyles (ed.), *Beginning Teaching, Beginning Learning*. Buckingham: Open University Press.

Galton, M., Simon, B. and Croll, P. (1980) *Inside the Primary Classroom*. London: Routledge.

General Teaching Council (GTC) (2003) *Teachers' Professional Development Framework*. General Teaching Council, http//www.gtce.org.uk/TPLF.

Great Britain Consultative Committee on the Primary School (1931) *Report of the Consultative Committee on the Primary School*. London: HMSO.

Handscomb, G. (1995) Sense of purpose, *Education*, p. 12, 21 April.

Handscomb, G. (2002) It's cool to collaborate, *Professional Development Today*, 5(2), pp. 3–6, Spring.

Handscomb, G. (2002/03) Learning and developing together, *Professional Development Today*, 6(1), Winter.

Handscomb, G. (2004) Collaboration and enquiry: sharing practice. In P. Earley and S. Bubb (eds), *Leading and Managing Continuing Professional Development*. London: Sage.

Handscomb, G. and MacBeath, J. (2003) *The Research Engaged School*. Chelmsford: Forum for Learning and Research Enquiry (FLARE), Essex County Council.

Hargreaves, D. (1998) *Creative Professionalism: The Role of Teachers in the Knowledge Society*. DEMOS Arguments Series 22.

Hargreaves, D. (2003) *Working Laterally: How to Make Innovation an Education Epidemic*. Publication in partnership with DEMOS and NCSL. London: Department for Education and Skills. Also available via download on www.standards.dfes.gov.uk/innovation-unit or www.demos.co.uk/workinglaterally.

Harris, A. (2002) *School Improvement: What's in it for Schools?* London: RoutledgeFalmer.

Hart, S. (2004) *Learning without Limits*. Maidenhead: Open University Press.

Hawkins, D. (1974) *The Informed Vision: Essays on Learning and Human Nature*. New York: Agathon Press.

Haylock, D. and Cockburn, A. (2003) *Understanding Mathematics in the Lower Primary Years*. 2nd edition. London: Paul Chapman Publishing.

Headington, R. (2000) *Monitoring, Assessment, Recording, Reporting and Accountability: Meeting the Standards*. London: David Fulton.

Heywood, J. (1982) *Pitfalls and Planning in Student Teaching*. London: Kogan Page.

Hollins, M. and Whitby, V. (1998) *Progression in Primary Science: A Guide to the Nature and Practice of Science in Key Stages 1 and 2*. London: David Fulton.

Holly, M.L. (1984) *Keeping a Personal-Professional Journal*. Victoria: Deakin University Press.

Hopkins, D. (2002) Presentation at the launch of the Networked Learning Communities Initiative. National College for School Leadership.

Hurst, V. and Joseph, J. (1998) *Supporting Early Learning: the Way Forward*. Buckingham: Open University Press.

Hutchin, V. (1999) *Right from the Start, Effective Planning and Assessment in the Early Years*. London: Hodder and Stoughton.

Keys, W., Harris, S. and Fernan, C. (1997a) *Third International Mathematics and Science Study, Second National Report, Part 1: Achievement in Mathematics and Science at Age 9 in England*. London: NFER.

Keys, W., Harris, S. and Fernan, C. (1997b) *Third International Mathematics and Science Study, Second National Report, Part 2: Patterns of Mathematics and Science Teaching in Upper Primary Schools in England and Eight Other Countries*. London: NFER.

Kitson, N. and Merry, R. (1997) *Teaching in the Primary School*. London: Routledge.

Kyriacou, C. (1998) *Essential Teaching Skills*. 2nd edition. Cheltenham: Stanley Thornes.

Macharia, S.N. and Wario, L.H. (1989) *Teaching Practice in Primary Schools*. London: Macmillan.

MacBeath, J. and Stoll, L. (2001) A profile of change. In J. Macbeath and P.

Mortimore (eds), *Improving School Effectiveness*. Buckingham: Open University Press.

MacNab, D.S. (2000) Forces for change in mathematics education: the case of TIMSS, *Education Policy Analysis Archive*, 8(15). http://epaa.asu.edu/epaa/v8n15.html.

Marshall, H.H. (1988) Work or learning: implications of classroom metaphors, *Educational Researcher*, 17, pp. 9–16.

Mason, J. (2002) *The Discipline of Noticing*. London: RoutledgeFalmer.

McBride, P. (1994) *CVs and Applications*. Cambridge: Hobsons.

McIntyre, D. (2001) The expert teacher. M.Ed. presentation, Essex LEA/University of Cambridge.

Mortimore, P., Sammons, P., Stoll, L., Lewis, D. and Ecob, R. (1988) *School Matters: The Junior Years*. London: Open Books.

Naylor, S. and Keogh, B. (2000) *Concept Cartoons in Science Education*. Sandbach: Millgate House.

Norfolk County Council (1997) *Early Learning, Ensuring Quality Provision for Children Under 5*. Norwich: Norfolk Educational Press.

Office for Standards in Education (Ofsted) (1993) *First Class: the Standards and Quality of Education in Reception Classes*. London: HMSO.

Office for Standards in Education (Ofsted) (1994) *Science and Mathematics in Schools: A Review*. London: HMSO.

Office for Standards in Education (Ofsted) (1997) *Training Specialist Teacher Assistants: A Guide to Good Practice*. London: HMSO.

Pedder, D. (2005) Consulting pupils. Presentation at FLARE Conference, 27 May.

Pedder, D. and McIntyre, D. (2004) The impact of pupil consultation in classroom practice. In M. Arnot, D. McIntyre and D. Reay, *Consulting in the Classroom: Developing Dialogue about Teaching and Learning*. Cambridge: Pearson.

Petty, G. (2004) *Teaching Today: A Practical Guide*. 3rd edition. Cheltenham: Stanley Thornes.

Qualifications and Curriculum Authority (QCA) (1999) *The National Numeracy Strategy, Teaching Mental Calculation Strategies*. Sudbury: Qualifications and Curriculum Authority.

Qualifications and Curriculum Authority/Department for Education and

Employment (QCA/DfEE) (2000a) *Key Stage 2, Assessment and Reporting Arrangements*. London: Qualifications and Curriculum Authority/ Department for Education and Employment.

Qualifications and Curriculum Authority/Department for Education and Employment (QCA/DfEE) (2000b) *Key Stage 1, Assessment and Reporting Arrangements*. London: Qualifications and Curriculum Authority/ Department for Education and Employment.

Quinn, V. (1997) *Critical Thinking in Young Minds*. London: David Fulton.

Reynolds, D. (2003) So near but yet so far, *Times Educational Supplement*, 20 June.

Richards, C. (1999) *Primary Education – at a Hinge of History*. London: Falmer Press.

Robinson, K. (2005) What is education for? *Times Educational Supplement*, January.

Ross, K. (2000) Constructing a scientific understanding of our environment. In M. Littledyke, K. Ross and L. Larkin (eds), *Science Knowledge and the Environment: A Guide for Students and Teachers in Primary Education*. London: David Fulton.

Rudduck, J. and Flutter, J. (2004) *How to Improve Your School: Giving Pupils a Voice*. London: Continuum.

Schon, D.A. (1991) *The Reflective Practitioner: How Professionals Think in Action*. Aldershot: Avebury.

School Curriculum and Assessment Authority (SCAA) (1995) *Planning the Curriculum in Key Stages One and Two*. London: School Curriculum and Assessment Authority.

School Curriculum and Assessment Authority (SCAA) (1997) *Teacher Assessment in Key Stage 2*. London: SCAA.

Scottish Office Education and Industry Department (SOEID) (1997) *Improving Mathematics Education 5–14*. Edinburgh: SOEID.

Selley, N. (1999) *The Art of Constructivist Teaching in the Primary School: A Guide for Students and Teachers*. London: David Fulton.

Springbelt, B.M. (1958) Factors affecting the final decision in the employment interview, *Canadian Journal of Psychology*, 12, pp. 13–22.

Stenhouse, L. (1971) The Humanities Curriculum Project. In R. Hooper (ed.), *The Curriculum: Context, Department of Education and Science and Development*. Edinburgh: Oliver and Boyd in association with the Open University Press.

Stenhouse, L. (1981) Action Research and teacher's responsibility for the educational process. In J. Rudduck and D. Hopkins (eds), (1995), *Research as a Basis for Teaching, Readings from the Work of Lawrence Stenhouse*. London: Falmer Press.

Stephens, P. and Crawley, T. (1994) *Becoming an Effective Teacher*. London: Stanley Thornes.

Stevenson, A. (1989) *Bitter Flame: A Life of Sylvia Plath*. Boston, MA: Houghton Mifflin.

Suffolk County Council Education (1999) *The Next Step, Planning and Evaluating the Foundation Curriculum in Early Years Settings*. Ipswich: Suffolk County Council.

Task Group on Curriculum and Assessment (TGAT) (1987) *National Curriculum: Task Group on Curriculum and Assessment*. London: Department of Education and Science and the Welsh Office.

Teacher Training Agency (TTA) (2003) *Qualifying to Teach: Handbook of Guidance*. London: Teacher Training Agency.

Tizard, B. and Hughes, M. (1984) *Young Children Learning: Talking and Thinking at Home and at School*. London: Fontana.

Waring, M. (1999) Plan and prepare to be an effective teacher. In G. Nicholls (ed.), *Learning to Teach*. London: Kogan Page.

Watkinson, A. (2003) *Managing Teaching Assistants: A Guide for Headteachers, Managers and Teachers*. London: RoutledgeFalmer.

Watkinson A (2004) To teach or not to teach? *Managing Schools Today*, 13(3), pp. 17–21, January/February.

Welsh Office (1999) *Raising Standards of Numeracy in Primary Schools: A Framework for Action in Wales*.Welsh Office/OHMCI (Wales).

Woods, D. (2000) *The Promotion and Dissemination of Good Practice*. London: The Education Network.

Wragg, E.C. (1997) *An Introduction to Classroom Observation*. London: Routledge.

Wragg, E.C. and Brown, G. (1993) *Explaining*. London: Routledge.

Index

Added to a page number 'f' denotes a figure.